Love's Shadow

Love's Shadow

Stories by Women

Edited by
Amber Coverdale Sumrall

The Crossing Press
Freedom, CA 95019

Library of Congress Cataloging-in-Publication Data

Love's shadow ; stories by women / edited by Amber Coverdale Sumrall.
    p. cm.
  ISBN 0-89594-584-3. -- ISBN 0-89594-583-5 (pbk.)
  1. American Literature--Women authors. 2. American
literature--20th century. 3. Women--United States--Fiction.
I. Sumrall, Amber Coverdale.
PS508.W7L65 1993
810.8'0354--dc20

                                    93-8984
                                    CIP

For Bruce Doneux

Contents

——— The Suburbs of Eden ———

——— War of Hearts ———

—— Survival in the Wilderness ——

Preface

Love is an act of faith. Each encounter with love provides us with an opportunity to remake the past. Love is a process, not a destination. Unfortunately, we are not educated in love's realities; rather, we're romanced by its fantasies. The distinctions blur. If, as the saying goes, love is blind, then it must be for the purpose of concealing love's shadow side. Terrible things are done in the name of love. It evokes extraordinary feelings and creates havoc with our lives, similar to a state of temporary insanity. We know how it feels when love goes or when love goes wrong. For some of us it is the most intensely painful experience of our lifetime. All of us bear scars.

Jody Aliesan, one of the contributors to *Love's Shadow*, writes, "The dark side is primal, compulsive, demonic, insane and very human—we want to hide the humiliation of it, but witnessing its power makes for more human compassion."

As I was completing my previous collection, *Lovers*, a wonderful and tragic love affair was also coming to an end for me. I went looking for a collection of writings by women that spoke specifically to the shadow side of love, some context in which to validate my experience. I didn't find such a book. Compiling this anthology seemed a perfect way to exorcise love's demons. It provided an opportunity to explore a topic that intrigues and compels many of us. It was only by walking in love's shadow, learning to find my way in the darkness, and even to embrace that darkness, that I was able to move into the light again.

Love's Shadow gives voice to the complexities of relationship—the secrets, the disappointments, the betrayals, the fantasies, the losses, the obsessions and the violence. The stories and poems range from humorous to horrific, illuminating areas we often would prefer not to acknowledge.

As I began to assemble *Love's Shadow*, piecing the stories and poems together—a process similar to working a jigsaw puzzle—I discovered the hyacinths. I'd forgotten about the bulbs in their colored glass jars in the darkness of the pantry closet. I'd put them there in autumn, to root. Two bulbs had refused to take root, one had long white tendrils floating in water but no emerging stalk, another had sent up spindly green shoots. The remaining three had produced beautiful and fragrant blooms in the darkness. So it is with love.

I want to thank the contributors to *Love's Shadow* for their bittersweet words. To Elaine Goldman Gill, John Gill, and the enthusiastic staff of The Crossing Press, I am deeply appreciative.

—*Amber Coverdale Sumrall*
Santa Cruz, California, 1993

Love In Extremis

I'm not frightened of the darkness outside.
It's the darkness inside houses I don't like.
—Shelagh Delaney

Not everyone's life is what they make it.
Some people's life is what other people make it.
—Alice Walker

Love in Extremis

by Enid Harlow

N atalie, two months shy of three years of age, keeps up a loud, voluble stream of communication at the luncheon table. She knows so many words. Lovely, musical words. She knows the names of all the Sesame Street characters and the names of all the different foods spread across the table in little blue bowls and on flat white plates. Sometimes she puts these words together and makes up stories about them: "Oscar the Grouch likes olives"; or, "Elephants and tigers jump out of the sky and eat strawberries." She watches her father's face to see if her stories please him. If they don't seem to, she will try other words or will repeat the same ones more forcibly until her father notices. There are so many words going around inside her. Spinning colors on a pinwheel. Each with a different sound. Some stay inside and spin. Other burst forth like stars, like music. Her music, her special stars to make her father happy.

"We love it here," her father says to Shelley Hamilton, his luncheon guest with the short golden curls. "It's such beautiful country." He brings the word "beautiful" up from deep in his throat, lets it linger on his tongue awhile, as if it gave him particular pleasure, before releasing it.

"Beautiful," Natalie says, trying to make the sound lingering and deep the way her father does. "Beautiful country," she says, trying to do what he does with his lips and tongue when he says the word.

"My, she's cute," says Shelley Hamilton.

"Just carrying on," her father replies. Then he throws back his head and laughs.

"Ha, ha, ha, ha," Natalie laughs, trying to make the sounds quick and short like her father's. "Ha, ha, ha, ha." To reproduce them exactly, giving his own joy back to him. "Carrying on, carrying on, just carrying on." The words jump like jelly beans inside her.

"Hush, dear," her mother says.

Natalie kneels in her chair and turns toward her father. Placing her palms back to back, she stretches out her arms. Lacing her stubby fingers together, she revolves her wrists, bringing her hands back in toward herself. Then she threads one elbow through the crook of her other arm, and attempts to shove her head through the hole without releasing her hands.

"Oh, look what she's doing!" cries Shelley Hamilton. "She's twisted like a pretzel!"

"Leaving the city was the best move we ever made," her father continues. "I'm seeing nature in a whole new way."

Natalie's head is too big for the hole. Her fingers come loose as she forces it through. Quickly, she clasps them together again around the back of her neck.

"Don't, dear," her mother says. "You'll strangle yourself."

"Strangle yourself. Strangle yourself." Natalie opens her mouth and unfurls her tongue. With her contorted arms wrapped around her neck, her head hanging loose and crooked, her tongue dangling, she is turned inside out for her father.

"I don't miss the city at all," he says. "Not at all."

Natalie undoes the tangle she has made of herself and sits down in her chair. She takes a small sip of milk and holds it in her mouth without swallowing. Then she leans over and brings her mouth down to the tabletop next to her father's place. Using the gentle pressure of her tongue, she forces the milk out through her teeth. There, before her father, she lays a pool of the purest elixir, milky white manna, precious drops of nature's secret powers.

"That's disgusting!" her father cries and slams his napkin down upon the milk.

But Natalie has another offering. Not of musical words, or heavenly moisture, but of pure, unadulterated sound. A seamless tone that stretches from basso profundo to mezzo soprano and is richly adorned with runs and trills and shining embellishments at the top. A siren wail that flies higher than airplanes, runs deeper than submarines and glows green in the dark. A wail, now piercing and shrill, now thin and airy, the most delicate piece of lace to graze across her father's lips and steal his breath away.

Slowly she releases her siren, draping it with care and constraint in elegant loops around the heads and shoulders of her parents, then in fast figure eights through the golden maze of Shelley Hamilton's quivering curls.

"The woods are lovely up here this time of year," her father says. "They're so deep and lush." His voice rises like a thick black fog. Natalie's siren leaps to pierce the fog. "I'm out in them at seven every morning. There are more trails than you can imagine." Her siren plunges through the underbrush, darts down a trail, turns and darts down another.

"Hush, Natalie," her mother says. "We can't hear daddy."

"One of these days I'm going in with an ax and machete," her father says. "Blaze a trail for myself straight through to the center."

"You might find yourself in so deep you can't get out," her mother remarks.

The siren wail would get him out. Its strong green light, twisting and turning like muscle through the forest, would force apart vines, uplift bushes and trees to come to his rescue.

"Then I'll make my home in the woods." Her father turns and smiles at Shelley Hamilton. "I'll live with the deer and the fox and drink from the creek and eat berries off the trees."

"Fox O! Fox O!" The nursery rhyme pops into Natalie's mind. The words are so lovely she cannot get enough of them. "Fox O! Fox O! A visit from Mr. Fox O!"

"That'll do, Natalie."

"I'll stay in the woods so long," her father says, "by the time I come out everything will have grown back up around me."

Natalie takes up her siren wail again, releasing it decibel by decibel on the inexhaustible power of her breath. Free as liquid, it flies from her throat, spiraling forth into a solid stream of sound. It follows the trail her father blazes through the woods and calls to the rabbits and the bear, the deer and the fox and everything growing up wild behind him to come and keep him company when he has lost his way in the dark.

"Quiet, dear," her mother says.

Triumphantly, Natalie's siren winds its way out of the woods and loops back across the luncheon table. Making beautiful, daring passes in the air, it skims the top of Shelley Hamilton's golden head, bounces off the high peaks of her father's wavy hair. Now it dives into their mouths, turns and exits through their eyes, then divides into fours and shoots back in through their ears. What a lovely sound, what lovely, musical words. It's music inside her that she makes for her father, the life inside she offers to him.

"I go to the woods to find some peace," her father says. "You can see why." He looks at Shelley Hamilton and throws back his head and laughs.

Natalie loves her father's laugh. She scoops it up like a pile of leaves in the follow of her siren, then tosses it—round, full, joyful—as she sometimes does the leaves when he is lying on the lawn, back into his face.

"Stop that carrying on!"

The sharpness of her father's voice turns her own on edge. Whittling her wail to a fine surgical point, she makes a clean incision in her father's chest and neatly plucks out his heart.

His hand flies up from the table and clamps down hard on her wrist. Her flesh seized, the siren is instantly silenced. Her father's fingers squeeze her arm so tightly everything backs up from them. Voice, blood, pulse and breath are pushed back up her arm to her shoulder. From there they are shoved into the base of her throat and come bubbling like hot oil out her eyes.

"Geoffrey, let her go."

But her father doesn't loosen his grip. Instead, now that she has turned off her siren and he sees he has her full attention, he looks right back at her through the blur in her eyes and gives her arm another savage squeeze.

"You're hurting her," her mother says.

"All that showing off," her father replies.

Natalie takes a deep breath and exhales it in a dazzling scream. Her mouth opens wide. Strong, beautiful buzzing hornets and wasps fly out of it. Shining asteroids and flaming comets burst into the atmosphere. Excited little bees swarm over her father's face, covering it with kisses. Fiery fragments of a distant galaxy dance before his eyes. He turns his head away and blocks his ears.

"Silence!" he cries.

Instantly, the hornets and wasps and bees are recalled. The asteroids and comets are sucked back down into the black hole of her mouth. The universe goes mute. Her jaws clamp shut, her eyes squeeze tight. No movement, no life travels in or out of her.

"Breathe," orders her mother.

Natalie's cheeks turn scarlet, her ears clog up, her eyes bulge. The music inside her stifled, she gives her father what he wants. The silence is absolute.

"Natalie! Breathe!"

Her father pushes back his chair, stands at Shelley Hamilton's side. "Let's go for a walk," he says.

Gasping at air, Natalie fills her lungs. She leaps from her chair and bounds out the door.

"Sweetheart, your shoes!"

The graveled path is a bed of nails beneath her bare feet, the stone walk fire. Her mother tackles her from behind, wrestles her down onto a neighbor's lawn, forces her feet into socks, into sneakers.

She must fly like sparks to catch up. Her father has rounded the corner, gained the path at the foot of the hill. She can see the peaks made by the dark waves of his hair already bobbing up the hill.

"Careful! You'll fall!"

She is glad for the sneakers now. They give her traction over the dry land. Twigs snap beneath her feet as she runs. Tiny yellow flowers pop into view and disappear at the sides of the path. Prickly weeds brush against her shins.

"Geoffrey, wait for her! Wait up!"

Her mother's voice is weak behind her, sapped by wind and distance. Natalie is faster, stronger, lighter than her mother. Her feet move fleet as dreams over the forest path. They could run straight up the trunks of trees, scurry across their branches like squirrels. They could drop down upon her father from above, landing like birds in the soft nest of his hair.

The sun races through the leaves, in and out of shadow, slightly ahead, as if showing the way. As the brush thickens overhead, the sun for a moment is obliterated and Natalie trips on the dark root of a tree that has broken through the dry earth. She tumbles and sprawls in the dirt, scraping her knee and elbow. Picking herself up, she licks at the blood where the skin has broken, but doesn't cry.

The fall has put her so far behind she can no longer see her father. His great tall back and bobbing head, marking the path for her, are lost to view. She runs fast, calling to him with her mind to make him hear. The words she calls are alive in her brain, quivering with energy, jumping from her mind to his.

"Natalie? Natty, sweetheart? Where are you?"

It is her mother's voice, small and weak behind. So weak Natalie can hardly hear it. It is her father she wants, not her mother. She would grow wings on her back and fly into his heart. She would sharpen her teeth like the ridges of a saw and open his ribcage to make him take her in.

But she can't see him. Only the rising trunks of trees and hanging interlocking vines pass before her line of vision. She feels the sunshine warm on her legs as she runs, wrapping around her calves like bandages to make them strong. A moment later, a ceiling of leaves closes in and her legs go cold. She can't see her feet or the path beneath them. The prickly weeds and yellow flowers are covered by darkness. All the life of the forest is in an instant blotted out. The sun itself has disappeared. She herself will disappear next, sucked feet first down into the dark. If she doesn't hurry, she will never see her father again. Bears will eat him. Or wolves. The blackness will swallow him whole. She must run faster than she has ever run in her life to save her father.

Her heart is slamming hard from side to side in her chest. It hurts to run. But she must keep running, even if her heart should explode. Something dashes across her path. A rabbit. Or a big brown squirrel. Running blind, Natalie veers out of its way and brushes hard against a tree. A searing pain rips through her hip and shoulder. She doesn't care if they are broken. She would take her limbs in her hands and twist them until they snapped for her father. She would arrange her fractured bones into a pile, place her ruptured heart on top and set it afire to make him see.

As she swerves into a wild bush, a tendril rips across her face. She can feel the flesh tear below her left eye. Nothing matters but saving her father.

Suddenly the sun breaks through again. Natalie feels it on her back, beating against her, urging her on. The sun is her ally. It heats her blood and coils tight inside her feet, turning them to springs that lift high off the ground and come down hard upon it without ever getting tired. Over and over, lifting high, coming down hard, springs of pure, gleaming, tireless steel cut into the path.

Then abruptly they stop. Her knees lock, her heels dig into the dirt. The path has opened onto a clearing and Natalie's feet, as if hitting up against an invisible barrier, stop just short of it. She stands back out of sight in the shelter of the trees, trembling in fear and outrage.

The sun, too, is aghast, but not afraid. It sends its full, blinding light down upon the clearing. Paled by its terrible power, Shelley Hamilton's short golden curls turn white. They wiggle on the air like worms.

Natalie stands still in the shadows as an insect under siege. Her father and Shelley Hamilton are pressed close against one another, like vines that have grown together. Natalie's throat dries up, her tongue sticks to the root of her mouth.

Shelley Hamilton lifts her face. One side of it catches the dappled pattern of the sun shining through the leaves. A blotched stain, like an ugly birthmark, spreads out on her cheek. Natalie's father lowers his head and presses his lips to Shelley Hamilton's, and Natalie goes dizzy with confusion.

But as her father slowly removes his lips from Shelley Hamilton's, the confusion is dispelled. In an instant of perfect collusion, just as if he had jumped into her own mind and told her, Natalie understands exactly what her father wants her to do. She waits until he and Shelley Hamilton have broken apart. Then, when they are standing, just two separate people in a clearing, she releases her siren wail.

She sends her wild, energetic music, filed razor-sharp and gleaming like glass in the sun, straight to the stain on Shelley Hamilton's cheek. Wailing for the deer and the bear and the fox to come and bear witness to her act, she cuts into the flesh around the ugly mark. Excising the stain, she lifts it free and carries it, impaled on the sharpened point of her siren wail, as she knows her father wants her to, from the surface of Shelley Hamilton's face down into the depths of her own soul.

"Look at her eye!" Shelley Hamilton cries. "She's bleeding!"

Buried within her, her father's secret will entomb her heart.

"Oh, it's nothing," her father says. "Come here, Natalie."

Her siren wail hits a final note of transcendent glory as her heart is covered over by bramble and moss.

"And stop that noise!"

They would have to carve it out of her with knives. They would have to hack for years through the underbrush of her strangled heart, and still they would never know. Her father is safe.

He lifts her up, dead weight, into his arms. "She's not hurt. Just carrying on."

Evidence

by Sallie Bingham

Even now when it's all over, I sometimes see my friend Kirsten when I'm
falling asleep. She's holding her arms over her head like one of those
cheap dolls with unarticulated limbs. Her arms are parallel, the hands
like mittens. Her doll head won't tilt and so she stares straight ahead. I know
she is looking at my father.

Kirsten died when she was five, or at least she disappeared, taken off the
sidewalk in front of her family's house in the compound. Since her body was
never found, I used to think she was still somewhere, using a different name,
living a different life from the one we'd shared as part of the Big Family at Los
Alamos. She might still be playing jacks or pulling her short white socks up out
of the backs of her patent leather shoes or skipping rope to one of the rhymes
we all knew—Plain Jane, Come Again, or Over the Seas to Scotland.

Newspapers at the time of her disappearance in 1946 tried to make a
connection between her father's secret work and her kidnapping, but the facts
didn't jibe. Nobody at Los Alamos was talking and after a while the reporters
gave up trying. Harry McNeil, Kirsten's father, went on working in the Big
Building and her mother, Jane, went on running the compound library, and
their other children grew up and left home during the fifties, just like the rest
of us.

Her disappearance was never solved; there were no suspects, no motives,
no ransom notes, and gradually we stopped talking about her and Kirsten, five-
year-old Kirsten McNeil, my best friend, disappeared.

The first time I dreamed about her, I was living on the other side of the
country, working as an editor in a publishing house in New York and
commuting to a suburb fifty minutes north of the city. I was married again and

my husband, Ted, was beginning to have his difficulties with Clare, and she with him; she had just turned thirteen. But we were still living in the glow, no, in the thick hot haze, of having met and fallen in love "like that"—it sounds like a magic trick—when we were both too old and presumably too wise for such nonsense, and so problems with Clare seemed like the inevitable result of taking an important step—marrying—without really knowing why, other than that you simply have to do it.

I was waking up earlier and earlier—five o'clock, then four—and it was winter, and very dark. I'd wake up as though someone had shouted in my ear, sit up, wrap myself in my shawl, and try to see it again—the flash of Kirsten's face and her raised arms against what looked like old car upholstery. Ted would stir and ask what was wrong, or I might eventually turn on the light, but no matter how I tried, the image of Kirsten remained in my head, stuck in one position like a slide jammed in a projector.

I didn't want to see her. I didn't want to remember anything about 1946. There was nothing for me there; it was ashes.

Sometimes I'd be able to lie down again and drift off to sleep for a little while before the alarm, lying close to Ted and grateful for his warmth. Later when I was getting ready for work, I'd remember the days when I was dressing Clare for day care, brushing her hair or buttoning the back of her dress. That brought Kirsten back, too. We always helped each other. The adults in the compound were kept busy running things, the commissary and the laundry and the library and the school as well as the physics lab, and so the children, the girls especially, learned to help each other with buttons and shoelaces and more complicated problems.

When I told Ted about the dream, he suggested trying to forget it; he was always protective of my state of mind. Besides, he'd never known Kirsten or even seen a snapshot of her, and so to him she seemed irrelevant, especially compared with the problems he was having with Clare.

That evening he had another blowup with Clare—he slapped her for calling him a name—and I knew I couldn't put Kirsten off any longer.

I set aside a Saturday afternoon when Ted was planning to play tennis and Clare was certain to be asleep; she slept all day on the weekend to prepare herself, she said, for the rigors of high school. I made a fire in our living room fireplace and brewed a pot of tea and brought out all my old photograph albums. My mother used to keep them religiously, with dates and names.

It was one of those winter afternoons when the sum comes and goes; the glass table under the albums flashed when the sun came out. Then the clouds would gather and the whole room would go dim. That flashing and dimming light fell across the snapshots from my childhood, mounted in a green Leatherette album.

I hadn't looked at the albums for a long time; they came to me a while back, after my mother died. I hadn't asked for them, but she specified in her will that I was to have them. I didn't understand why, at the time.

The snapshots were perfectly ordinary, small black-and-white snatches of birthday parties and Christmas trees, with the glaring reflection of the flashbulb caught in a window; some of them were of people's turned backs or awkward gestures, late at parties when the camera got picked up more or less by chance. My mother didn't throw any snapshots out. She was a meticulous woman who kept my outgrown clothes boxed and labeled in her attic: "Alice. Summer. 1946."

Snapshots from that summer were in a second album, one with a red cover. I saw the back of Kirsten's head at a picnic. The back of her neck had a long narrow dent. It was one of Kirsten's unusual, attractive features, like her eyes. Adults said her eyes were hazel; they were greenish brown, flecked with gold.

She turned up in several more snapshots, playing with me in the sandbox outside of Community Hall or walking in a group of children and adults to the dining room or wearing a hat and carrying a tiny purse to church.

Los Alamos was a homogeneous community—we were all there for one purpose, and even the children who didn't know what the purpose was knew that. Our movements outside the base were restricted, and we were always aware of the high fence with the barbed wire on top that enclosed us "for our own safety," we'd been told, although what actually threatened us in the miles of mountain around the compound I never knew. We used to joke that the fence kept the coyotes out and kept us in.

We tended to do everything together, Kirsten and I, and after a while I noticed in the snapshots that we even looked alike, although that was partly the style of the period. In that church snapshot, for instance, Kirsten and I are wearing identical short flared coats, although I believe mine was navy and hers was cherry red. Her legs look conspicuously long between the edge of her short coat and the tops of her white socks. My father commented on that, I remember.

Yes: Paul—Paul Chambers, my father, Dr. Chambers—the well-known physicist, as Ted called him, noticed how long Kirsten's legs were, for a five-year-old, and said something funny about it. I don't remember exactly what: "Those legs will really take her places, later on," something innocuous like that. I noticed only because Paul never said anything about my friends; I don't think he saw them. He was a somber man who didn't crack jokes; "Long as from here to next week"—was that it? Trying to remember, I smelled engine oil and sun on macadam and something else I couldn't for a long time identify: the smell of old car upholstery. "You shouldn't have made me give her a ride," Paul—my father—said.

That sentence went round and round. I couldn't make sense of it, couldn't fit it in. I looked through the rest of the snapshots while the sun went in and out and finally down. "You shouldn't have made me give her a ride." But when had I ever made Paul do anything?

Finally I put the albums back on their shelf. Actually there were only a few snapshots of Kirsten; most of them were of me and my brother, or my mother in shorts and a halter on a rare occasion when Paul had the camera. Then I went into the kitchen to make more tea. While I was filling the pot with water, I saw Kirsten again, with her arms raised, and I saw Paul coming towards her with something in his hand.

My view was cut off at the corner so I couldn't see what he was carrying. It was as though the person taking the snapshot had her finger partly across the lens.

I poured a cup of tea and sat down to try to understand. Ordinarily my memories are like other people's—bits and pieces, a few sequences. I can still see the cabin where Ted and I spent a couple of nights ten years ago—I can even make out the wormholes in the logs; and I remember the color of the meat he was slicing, that last day; but I can't describe the inside of my office in New York. Memory, as they say, is selective, which is why I've never depended on it.

Now my memory was starting to unroll in all directions. Things were spilling out, flashy little images, like the plastic pigmy elephant and the doll's-house binoculars we found in those crepe-paper balls they gave out at birthday parties. We'd unwind the crepe paper, round and round, and now and then the ribbon would turn a different color, or something little but unusual would drop out, something I'd try to hold on to but that often got lost. In the end we'd get to the core of the ball and a balloon and a paper hat.

In the memory ball I found the silver belt buckle Paul wore in those days, and Kirsten's plaid skirt, flat as a paper doll's under the edge of her bright red flared woolen coat.

That dress had a rickrack collar, I remembered, and a sash that tied in the back, and her mother didn't want her to wear it any more because the skirt was so short. Kirsten was growing.

So she was wearing her good red coat when it happened, and it was Sunday.

When Ted came back from his game, I told him about the things I'd seen, and he said, "You can't do anything about this now."

"Kirsten was five years old," I said.

"Your father's a respected scientist," Ted reminded me.

"Maybe there's a connection," I said, and he laughed. Ted valued my past.

Clare came down then, yawning, in a shirt, and asked what I was planning to cook for supper. I told her I wasn't planning to cook anything, and she said one of her favorite words and Ted shouted at her. She laughed at him and before I could say a word, he was chasing her up the stairs.

I started up the stairs and then I knew I didn't have time to stop him and I grabbed the fire extinguisher we keep next to the stove and began to spray white foam over the banisters and the stair treads, and Ted heard the sound of the sprayer and came down.

When he saw what I was doing, he lifted his hand as though he was going to snatch the fire extinguisher, but I said, "No," and he stood there watching me until the foam ran out. Then we had—or I had—one hell of a mess to clean up.

A few hours later, Ted came back to check on my progress; he'd taken Clare to get pizza. I was just about done, and the stairs had never looked so clean. I turned on all the lights in the halls, upstairs and down, to show them off. Then I asked Ted, "Don't you understand what I mean? The buckle on Paul's belt was undone."

Ted said, "You're going too far, Alice," and I think I knew then it was the beginning of the end, although in between we did try some things.

The things I remember don't illustrate trying; for example, our last real conversation, before silence took over. Ted was in the kitchen slicing steak for stir-fry—he was a fine cook—and I was leaning in the doorway telling him about something I'd read in the paper, the latest statistics on rape. He looked at me and said something I can't remember, but I saw his eyes, I saw how far he was from what I was saying. Then I looked at his hands, nice hands, holding the knife against the grain of the slab of beef. That's what I remember.

Three years later, my father stood in a courtroom in Santa Fe and listened to the verdict. Paul is an old man now, stooped and fragile-looking, and no one in court except me remembered how tall and solid he'd been as a young man, a young physicist, a young husband and father. He'd put on one of his old business suits, and I recognized the big knot he always made in his ties.

That was the thirteenth day of the trial, and there was a packed, dazed feeling in the courtroom; one of the jurors was yawning. Even a murder trial goes flat at the end.

Later on a reporter got to Paul and asked him a few more questions. One of them was why he'd stopped to pick up Kirsten on the sidewalk in front of her house, that Sunday more than forty years ago. "My daughter made me do it," Paul said, and he looked straight at me.

I wonder how many people believed that, and I also wonder why I care. After all, Kirsten is dead, and even the dream of her with her hands over her head doesn't come anymore. But there's a spark of color in the darkness at 4 A.M. when I wake up, missing Ted's warmth—a bit of red rickrack, the edge of a girl's collar. I can see it now.

Ballet (1943)

by Linda Smukler

S ylvia remembered that they had been around forever, living together up on the eleventh floor. Sylvia lived on the second floor, just above her father's bar. Elva, the older one ("that baby of a girl is gonna leave me someday for a younger woman"), baked brownies for her. Elva would tweak her cheek in the hallway near the elevator while Sandy stood there shaking her head, saying, "Always wanted kids, didn't you? C'mon now, Elva, let's go." In the hall Sandy wore a dress. It looked like a costume on her. Up in their apartment, she wore pants, and that's how Sylvia thought of her: Sandy, the one in the pants.

Elva told Sylvia to come up anytime and she often did, even though she had to be sneaky about it. Her mother didn't like her going up there. "You stay away from those girls," she would say. But Sylvia loved food and Elva's brownies only next to ballet dancers.

Up there, Sandy and Elva lived like they were married. Elva would show Sylvia pictures of her mother in Texas, while Sandy, feet up on the sofa, listened to the radio in the living room. Sylvia's mother never let her put her feet on the sofa. Elva would ask Sylvia about school and listen to her talk about the ballet. Elva was a better person to talk to than anybody. She never stopped her, never interrupted, never had something else to do.

The pink slippers are on the table. They're brand new and Elva's given them to her. She can't stop looking at them.

"Look, Elva," Sylvia says. "Look, can't you see? I'm up there, up on a stage. My chest is thin and my skirt goes out from me like a pink cloud. Look, my arms are up, stretched so high I can touch the ceiling. No, the sky. Look Elva, there's green behind me painted with deer and swans. My legs are long and thin and my feet are stretched up, up. I'm not touching the floor anymore. Oh Elva, thank you, thank you."

Elva comes around the table and hugs her and says, "Have another brownie." Sylvia's already had two, but she takes another and puts it in her mouth. Her skirt is too tight now, but she doesn't care. Elva makes better brownies than her mother. "I'm gonna be a ballet dancer," Sylvia says. "I'll put on these shoes and they'll make me like air and I'll fly."

They hear someone walking down the hall. "It sounds like my baby's finally made it home," Elva says. Something heavy falls on the floor outside the door. "Damn, damn," they hear. Then there's another loud bang.

Elva gets up and goes to the door. She opens it and says, "Having trouble, honey?" Sandy slams the door open, hitting Elva in the arm. Elva's face gets hard.

"Sandy, you been downstairs with Max again?" Max is a girl too. Sylvia's seen her here before, drinking beer and listening to the radio with Sandy and Elva.

"I ain't been nowhere," Sandy yells. "So look who's here." She walks over to the table and stares into Sylvia's eyes. "It's Elva's kid. Elva's lousy kid. Always wanted a kid, Elva, huh, huh?" Sandy crushes Sylvia's ballet slippers under her elbows. Suddenly Sandy whirls around and strides across the kitchen to Elva who's still at the door and still looks mad. Sandy grabs Elva's rear end with her hand.

"Not in front of the child," Elva yells. Sandy doesn't listen. Laughing, she drags Elva across the kitchen to Sylvia. She sits down in a chair, pulls Elva backwards onto her lap and holds her arms pinned behind. Sylvia can see Sandy's slicked-back hair and leering smile above Elva's shoulders.

"You ever seen a woman before?" Sandy asks Sylvia.

"You leave Elva alone," Sylvia screams and gets up. She starts to hit Sandy with her fists but Sandy laughs and pushes her away hard. Sylvia hits her head against the wall.

"I asked you," Sandy says, "you ever seen a woman before?" Sylvia can't answer. Her head hurts and she's crying.

Elva's screaming, "You bitch! Let me go—This child—!" Sandy won't let her finish. She holds Elva's arms with one of her hands and rips open her blouse with the other. Elva's got on a brassiere underneath. It's so white that it hurts Sylvia's eyes. Sandy pushes Elva forward and unsnaps the bra. It falls around her shoulders. Sandy jerks Elva back up so she faces Sylvia again.

"There," Sandy says, cupping Elva's breast for the girl to see. "Pretty, ain't it?" Sandy pinches the nipple red.

Elva is pale. She says, "Sandy, stop, please stop."

"Come here, kid," Sandy demands. Sylvia doesn't move. "See it?" Sandy asks as she pinches the nipple harder. "See what happens? Yours'll stand up too one of these days. Want to try? No?" Sandy pulls Elva's skirt up her legs. She spreads Elva's legs over her lap. Elva doesn't move now. Her underwear is white like Sylvia's. Sandy grabs in between Elva's legs and pulls away the underwear. It's brown and hairy. Elva's making another noise.

Elva! Sylvia wants to scream.

"You'll be that way too." Sandy's voice rushes across the room. "Just wait." She pushes Elva on the floor. "C'mon, Elva. Let's show her some more." Sandy sits down on Elva.

Elva moans and yells to Sylvia: "Take your slippers and get out!" She sounds both desperate and mean. Sylvia crawls to the door. She stands up and reaches the knob. She will have to go past them to get the slippers. "Get out!" Elva screams again. Sylvia's eyes go wide and black as she backs out of the door, leaving her slippers behind.

Red Onion Salad

by Joan McMillan

The red onions at the market
were always a bargain, their skins
fragile as rice paper
dipped into burgundy wine,
the best ones chosen by my mother, her touch
reading every flaw on a surface:
smears across a mirror's hard shine,
the gray puddle-shape of bruises
anywhere on her children's bodies.

This is not the story of how a mother's love
was concealed like the rosaries
of ebony and plain glass, blue and yellow crystal
locked at the bottom of her jewelry box
next to rhinestone earrings in a sunburst pattern.

No prayer kept her safe from my father,
his voice slapping like hands
which might contract to fists,
then bring gifts the next day:
white stars of gardenias with their dense perfume,
a slim envelope of new money.

This is a story of the mother
who cut tomatoes into fat wedges, cucumbers and onions
into parchment rounds to soak in vinegar and clear oil
for a daughter who was thin as the slat of light
piercing the kitchen blinds,

a mother who silently
dropped ivory satin wedding shoes
and a purple felt banner from Immaculate Heart College
in a Goodwill bin,

relinquishing each treasure piece by piece
until little preceded her years of marriage
except girlhood photographs
and her recipe for a red onion salad
that I could taste on my lips
hours later, a pungence
blade-sharp as the moment before tears.

Breaking the Lethal Circle

by Paola D'Ellesio

Although I didn't realize it at the time, for me the destructive, generational, abusive cycle that was our family heritage began to rupture that day I phoned my mother. Phoning her is itself a noteworthy event, given the nature of our relationship and the way we communicate. In the past twelve years we've talked on the phone less than a dozen times, and I've initiated most of the calls. Via the conduit of my father, my mother has let it be known that it's my duty to call her. After all, she's the mother and I'm the daughter.

My mother is a guidance counselor, working one-to-one with elementary school kids who have emotional problems. During this phone conversation, my mother shared a recent professional triumph of which she was extremely proud. In an exuberant voice she told me about Joseph, an engaging, gentle child of eight, unable to express himself in anything louder than a whisper because he's scared to speak up. Joseph is a battered child: physically battered at home and verbally battered at school. Acting as his advocate, my mother took action against his parents and intervened with his teacher and the school's principal.

As I listened to a voice that makes my hair stand on end, my throat swelled, preventing me from swallowing. I had to hang up because I was overcome by the irony of this situation. At one time I too was barely audible. Like Joseph, I was battered and abused. The perpetrator was my mother.

She was twenty-two when I was born; by today's standards, a child herself. Then, two years later, my brother was born. I used to believe my brother and I were at fault when she lost her patience and lashed out. I thought we deserved the beatings, that if we hadn't behaved so badly, Mom wouldn't have beaten us with her fists, or whatever household object was close at hand. When, as an adult, I found the courage to step back into the terror of my childhood, I discovered that we weren't bad kids. I realized my mother's rages had been unpredictable and, for the most part, unprovoked by anything we'd done. My brother and I were just regular kids. It was my mother who was "irregular."

From the onset, she couldn't cope with motherhood. She was burdened by a fury against unnamed, therefore overpowering, forces. She had been an emotionally deprived child and she seemed compelled to pass that on.

My brother and I were beaten every day. He bore the brunt of her anger because he was unable or unwilling to give in to her show of force. When she smacked me, I cried, and she'd stop hurting me when she felt my humiliation was complete. My brother was different—tougher, maybe, or more stubborn. When she'd pummel him, he'd laugh in her face or he'd sing a nursery rhyme over and over. His seeming indifference to the pain fueled her fury. She'd hit him harder. And the stronger her punch, the more raucously he'd laugh.

I'm thirty-seven years old and I have had recurring nightmares, haunting flashbacks I can't exorcise where I am forced to relive the horrors of the past. In these memory-dreams my mother picks me up and flings me against the wall. My head smacks the edge of the bookshelf and the impact sends books cascading to the floor. Aiming for whatever part of my face she can reach, my mother uses a book as a battering ram. Instinctively, my arms fly up to protect my eyes but they're ineffective. My brother and I plead with her to stop and she relents for a moment. Then she redirects the attack onto my brother.

I watch as she yanks him by his ears and wrestles his pliable body to the floor. This hefty twenty-nine-year-old sits on her small son's chest, pinning his arms to the floor with her fat knees. She curses him, clawing the hair above his forehead. Using the thick strands as a lever, she bangs his head against the floor in an insanely syncopated rhythm. First I hear the profanity, then, unmistakable and frightening, the dull thud of my brother's head against those wooden parquet tiles she's so proud of. Apparently unfazed, he chants, "Mary had a little lamb," as if to ward off the evil befalling him and to invoke the protection of the patron saint of five-year-olds.

I'm frantic. Terrified she'll kill him, I jump on her back and try to pull her off, but it's futile. With a swat of her arm she dislodges me. I pitch books to no avail. She stops bashing his head only in her own time, when my brother's silence speaks to something in her that might be greater than her anger.

It was clear to me we needed protection. I went to my dad first, but he didn't believe me. My mother reminded him that I was a storyteller, though she needn't have interfered because my father rarely paid attention to me, unless I disturbed his peace and quiet or my mother reported that I'd been bad. Then he'd mete out extremely humiliating and entirely inappropriate punishments. It did no good to beg for leniency. This was the man who made me wear a too large, traffic-paint-yellow rubber raincoat and clunky, over-the-shoe, knee-high galoshes, for four consecutive sunny days, to and from school—just because he'd "caught" me carrying my rain boots instead of wearing them. He escorted me to class all four days, not only to make sure I kept this ugly gear on, but also to remind my teacher that, because I was being punished, I had to wear this outlandish garb during lunch recess and free play too.

In reality, I had little hope that he'd help us. I was invisible to him, not because of my age, but because of my gender. My father has always been king of the male chauvinists. Because he has no use for women except when we serve his needs, I was discounted and disregarded. My mother fared no batter. He treated her with condescension and disrespect. Though he never hit me, I was terrified of him and I'd mutter "mean old man" under my breath to his receding back.

Next, I told my maternal grandmother. I was seven years old and didn't have the savvy to realize my grandmother couldn't give credence to my reports; her acknowledgment could have wider implications. How could she accept the fact that her daughter did terrible things to her grandchildren? It might mean she too had been a bad mom.

My teacher was another dead end. She scolded me, insisting that if only I watched where I was going and paid more attention to what I was doing, I wouldn't bang into things and bruise myself. She kept saying what a lovely person my mother was. "So sweet. So nice."

She was right. My mother was nice—to our teachers, the neighbors, and, occasionally, even to our friends. But she was rarely nice to us.

I have heard that if a dog births pups when her instincts for mothering are immature or nonexistent, the dog may simply abandon her litter. Maybe my brother and I would have been better off if my mother had deserted us, or acknowledged she didn't love us or couldn't care for us. Her truth might have saved us. But my mother couldn't face these feelings. Instead she seduced us with, "I love you. Who else is going to love you the way I do?" Tucked in bed each night in my lightless room, I prayed that no one ever would.

The beatings ended abruptly when I was twelve or thirteen. We three were in the kitchen. My mother was chopping vegetables, my brother and I were eating at the counter, he in the seat closest to her, I next to him. Suddenly, brandishing the knife, she lunged at him. My brother ducked under the counter and ran out of the kitchen through the door farthest from where she stood. He took refuge in his room, slamming the door behind him. She flung it open with such violence that the brass doorknob punched through the hollow closet door directly behind. I was close on her heels, tearing at her shirttail in a vain attempt to thwart her. Using the small pool table which stood in the middle of the room as a partial cover, my brother scooted around and crouched low. Awkwardly, my mother came after him.

In what seemed like slow motion, my brother stood up and reached for the wooden cue stick. At first, like a warm-up batter, he rested the pool cue against his shoulder for one brief moment before he touched the blue-chalk-stained tip to her breastbone.

"Put the knife down."

My mother didn't move. She seemed mesmerized.

"Put that knife down."

Something in my brother's voice scared her. It scared me too. Gingerly, she placed the knife on the green felt table.

"If you ever touch us again I'll kill you. I'm going to break both of your arms and then I'm going to stab you. Don't come near us again."

Afterward, I stayed out of my mother's way as much as possible until I left her house for good. I had no idea where my salvation lay but I did know that to survive I had to flee. Books and school became my haven. Men too. At seventeen, I married the man I fell in love with. The two of us became family. It was all the family I wanted.

From the time I became sexually active until well into my late twenties, I was extraordinarily vigilant about birth control. Just one method wouldn't do. I used two and sometimes three different devices at a time because I was terrified of passing on my genes and my heritage. Just before my thirtieth birthday, my husband, the voice of sanity on this issue, suggested I examine the pain of my childhood in order to free myself from this fear.

It made sense. But I continued to sidestep the question of motherhood until my body, with an agenda of its own, flooded me with the desire for a child. Still, I shied away because I was afraid I, too, would be an abusive mother. I tried sedating myself with work, with food, and then with alcohol. But ultimately, my past demanded attention.

I know so few of the details of my mother's history. Because both her parents worked outside the home, my mother was cared for by her great-aunt, a woman she loved and who loved her dearly. Her father, absent more often than not, was the family disciplinarian although he didn't believe in hitting kids. When she'd exceed the limits her folks set for her, her father would deliver excruciatingly lengthy lectures that my mother found agonizing. She said she'd have preferred a beating. My mother doesn't talk about her mom a lot, but I too know the sting of my grandmother's sarcasm.

For as long as I've known her, my mother's been in a state of siege—an enraged woman unable to admit to the volcanic anger churning beneath the thin veneer of her sociability. Her frenzied emotions endangered us but the real devastation was caused by the denial of her feelings.

I have other siblings. None of us escaped unscathed. My brother had his first epileptic seizure at nineteen. Might his epilepsy be related to the beatings about his head? None of us knows. None of us talks about it.

My own recovery has been painful. My separation from my mother did little good because, unconsciously, I'd assimilated her bitter legacy and her corrosive attitude about the world. Unconsciously, I'd internalized her spirit. My mother could wound with her fists or her words but I could perpetuate her self-denial, her masochism, her martyrdom. She was, after all, my first role model. From her I learned that a woman was a second-class citizen, slightly more valuable than the family dog because my mother, at least, earned her keep by tending to everyone else's needs. I saw that a woman's feelings and ideas didn't matter. My mother kept hers to herself because no one cared enough to ask what she thought. I watched my mother cower in the face of my father's aggression and learned that a woman never spoke up for herself; she wouldn't presume to challenge a man. My father was the head of the household, the breadwinner, and as such, he knew best. She taught me that a woman didn't dare harbor hopes or dreams for herself. What would be the point, since the best my mother could do would be to accept whatever place the men in her life, my grandfather and father in turn, allowed her? Above all, a woman was selfless; the needs of others always came first. Like a girl scout, my mother was prepared, ready and willing to cater to everyone else no matter what the cost, no matter how great a toll it took on her physical, emotional or financial well-being. From her, I learned women were powerless and doomed to a life sentence of drudgery, dependence and depression. My mother was a good teacher and I an attentive student.

Day in and day out, I mutilated myself, biting my nails to the quick and yanking strands of hair from my sore scalp. Always anxious and afraid I'd do or say the wrong thing, I wouldn't speak spontaneously. Instead, I'd silently rehearse whatever it was I wanted to say, but by the time I finished practicing, the conversation had already passed the point at which my contribution would have been appropriate. So I remained mute. The rare times I spoke, I prefaced my words with a schoolgirl ritual: I'd raise my hand, then ask permission to speak, and when it was granted, I'd whisper. When introduced to someone new, I'd duck my head and stare at the laces of my shoes. I'd extend my arm in a blind handshake. It embarrasses me now to admit that I behaved like this until I was almost twenty-seven years old.

Because I felt helpless in the face of larger issues, I sought relief in such meaningless things as sorting my shoes by color and style and lining them up in rigid rows on the closet floor. Alphabetizing the books on my shelves made me feel better, composed; it gave a false, but needed, sense of self-mastery. I was compulsive. I'd reorganize immaculate desk drawers and rewash and refold clean towels. As if in a one-woman crusade against city grime, I'd scrub my apartment with a vengeance born of misplaced anxiety.

And I expected more from myself than I did from anyone else. While I'd forgive my friends their mistakes, I couldn't absolve myself. Essentially, I demanded the impossible—perfection—which doomed me to failure. There was never a time when I was good enough, smart enough, talented enough, funny enough, attractive enough or competent enough. I was deeply distressed. Clinically depressed. And though the healthiest part of my psyche knew I was troubled, I didn't seek help until suicidal thoughts became a constant preoccupation.

What prompted me finally to phone a psychiatrist friend for a referral is what I now refer to as my "walking nervous breakdown." On my way to work one morning, a good samaritan stopped to ask if I needed help. Puzzled, I asked why.

"You seem upset. You're crying," he answered. And when I touched my face, wet and tear-stained, I was shaken. I knew then I was in desperate need of professional help because I was thoroughly out of touch with my feelings. When I confided in a trusted colleague, he wasn't at all surprised. In fact, he said that during the two years we'd worked together he'd never seen me smile. Because I'd pictured myself as a happy-go-lucky person I was shocked. Obviously, something was "off."

Therapy was a time-consuming and difficult process. It required courage and lots of money. Often, I lacked both. I made a few false starts. The first doctor was a Freudian who insisted I free-associate while lying on the couch. Uncomfortable with this method, I pushed for face-to-face "talk" therapy. Still, I toughed it out three times a week for almost nine months, until the following unpleasantness convinced me that neither this method nor this doctor was right for me. During one fifty-minute "hour," I was interrupted by an electronic beep. The noise prompted me to ask if my sessions were being taped. The psychiatrist responded, "Well, what do you think?" Unable to get a simple yes or no, I finally walked out.

Next, I saw a woman who was extremely empathetic and helpful. Unfortunately, we worked together for only a month before she referred me to someone else who had more time available than she. I felt betrayed and had difficulty trusting the new therapist. When he asked about my childhood I told him it had been idyllic. That's how I remembered it then. After more than a year of therapy he suggested hypnosis. With hypnosis, I recovered pieces of my past that I had long since buried.

After this, I worked with a woman trained in transactional analysis, then a therapist who helped me act out my anger and despair physically, in a protected environment. All told, I spent close to six years in therapy. At the time, I was frustrated by the little progress I was making, but, looking back, I believe it saved my life. The high level of anxiety I'd always lived with (and which I therefore didn't realize was destructive) disappeared. As did my suicidal thoughts.

This phone call to my mother left me debilitated. Regressing to that once familiar childhood behavior, I was speechless. I couldn't ask for details about Joseph, nor could I ask about my memories. At a loss, I hung up and wandered aimlessly around the apartment, talking to myself. Angry and bewildered, I tried to make sense of our conversation. Who is this woman to whom I'm still tied? What motivated her to defend a child in her care when she'd been unable to tend to her own with compassion? And, most importantly, how could I put closure on the past? Temporarily incapacitated, I paced, repeating my personal mantra, "calm is the key." This worked. And with the advent of self-control, I sat down and wrote my mother a letter.

Dear Mom,

You often suggest we meet so that we can catch up and stay in touch. But when we're together I'm disappointed and uncomfortable. Disappointed because we're unable to have an authentic conversation and uncomfortable because I sense that you want something from me.

I was taken aback by our last conversation, about Joseph. Timid Joseph, who's afraid to speak up because his father beats him and his teacher calls him names. I was staggered by the irony because I was just like him. Unbidden, childhood memories plague me still.

I can't begin to understand your behavior. What drove you to act as you did?

I know that, like every other woman, you had no preparation for motherhood. On-the-job training meant following your instincts and relying on the models others provided. It must have been difficult having us so close in age when you were a young newlywed. Everyday chores must have been a nightmare when we lived in that second-floor walk-up. How did you manage the stairs with the two of us and a stroller? I don't remember a baby-sitter. And I know Dad wasn't home to help. Did anyone relieve you? I can imagine how hard it was with an active toddler and a chronically ill newborn.

Isn't it absurd there's no training for parenthood? Unlike driving a car, no license is required. We spend years in school getting degrees, preparing for our future, but parenting isn't part of that. How bizarre!

Standing up for Joseph shows how much you've grown. Your brave deed gave me a chance to reexamine my idea of who you are. It made me think about your personal struggle. What made you decide to protect Joseph? How did his welfare become your priority? I'm glad you helped him.

Unlike Joseph, I'm an adult now and don't need protection. What you couldn't give me then, you can't give me now. I have to leave the past behind. It'll free me to envision my future and seize its possibilities.

Do my prospects include a genuine relationship with you? I don't know if it's possible to forge a new way to be together.

Today, I'm thinking about the sweaters Grandma knitted, particularly, the blue turtleneck she made when I was a teenager. The pattern gave her trouble and more than halfway through, she abandoned the written directions altogether to follow the promptings of her imagination. When she finished, the sweater didn't fit. Unhappy with the way it'd turned out, Grandma unraveled the wool. Holding my hands upright and parallel, I mimicked the function of a spindle as she rewound the blue yarn around them. First, she smoothed the once-used yarn, then tied it tightly into a ball. She began all over again.

Using her example, I want to reweave the threads of my past into the tapestry, the work-in-progress, that is my life.

This is one of the many letters I've written to my mother over the years. I've mailed none of them. But this time there was a difference. Instead, I decided to meet with her to talk about the past.

The evening was difficult for both of us. I felt guilty because she was at a distinct disadvantage. After all, she didn't know the evening's agenda. I tried to be gentle; still, I wounded her. And her tears unsettled me.

First, she denied my account and my memories, accusing me of having an overactive imagination. She suggested I talk to my brother to learn the truth about what really happened. I agreed he'd be a reliable source.

It was from my youngest sister and not my brother that I learned that my mother, visibly upset, appeared on my brother's doorstep, unannounced, a week after our meeting. He said only that his childhood happened long ago and he thought it best left forgotten.

A month after our dinner, I phoned. During our chat, my mother touched on our meeting only once and very briefly, saying she'd consider sending me a letter. Now, many months later, I've received no letter and she's never mentioned our talk again. Our relationship remains unchanged.

But something had changed—by finally confronting my mother with the truth, I had made a breakthrough within myself. I no longer felt like a frightened, abused child but like an empowered woman with the inner resources and resolve to break our deadly circle.

Passed from one generation to the next, this circling had seemed to be my legacy. Now, for my own sake and for the sake of the children I may have someday, I decided it must end. And so I have stopped it; because I am determined that my children's birthright will not be one of fear and abuse but one of love. And acceptance. And laughter.

Writing in the Dark

by Sandra Dorr

I was a child born from my father's mouth. Straight, black-haired, high-cheekboned, he was guessed Indian or French, secretly nervous in the feet. Coming out of the shadow of the garage, climbing down from the wood rafters that hung over his car, in his dark, protected area, the small wooden building next to my mother's house, I heard him in his feet, hurrying with a humid, half-soft step—the pull forward to work, to work, hitting now the pavement, the grass—he must be going after the hose, which is where I am, crouched next to the cool garage door, holding my legs. I'm ready to pee, the sting bursting into my hips but I don't want to move, his steps coming closer and the pain inside, the quickness of his steps.

When I turn eighteen, sitting in my new, cotton T-shirt dress in the living room, waiting for my first man-love to appear, I want to wait in the dark, feeling again the smooth hair of my legs. I am the dark, waiting under the shadow of something become shadow. I know that this separation between light and the cool, powdery dark makes me press my legs together, creates excitement. The boy's soft, jaunty voice at the door makes me jump. The lover ten years later puts his hand on my forehead and I feel in his large, moist palm the potential to kill me.

Father appears. Fast steps while I crouch, why does he come so fast, his feet going beyond him, something pushing him from out there in the world, away from the warm oil-smelling cement floor, and this frightens me so I make myself into a little ball holding water. He doesn't see me; his heavy brown pants brush by. Shout of the boys down the alley, stones flying from the next garage as I stagger up from behind the door, and follow my father in. I prefer him to the boys, they're no good. "Dad?"

He whips around in the dark as if I'd struck him. "Aren't you going to build me a tree house?"

He hesitates, a fumbling figure with gawky arms trapped in this moment, and I hold my breath to see if he's going to be angry or just sad. He nervously rubs his chin, his other hand fingering the nozzle of the slick hose, and I am sorry for having asked, but I want him, in the dark, he must see me. "Waal," he says, "maybe when I get some of this work done. Here," he shoves the neck of the hose into my hand, "go put this out back. Tomatoes need watering."

"I have to go to the bathroom," I say, hopping on one foot into the sunlight. I feel everything, the hopelessness of having asked, the death in the dark garage, the outside world with grass and bushes where I can sneak out and pee, calling me back.

But next week, after the saw has screamed and there has been a terrible pounding of wood and thwacking of paint, something appears in the garage, for all of us, though I am the only one who would have asked: a chug, something like a country race car made of flat boards over wheels, a little house where you put your knees, and a rope that pulled from left to right as it flew down the alley hill. "Well, it's something new to fight over," he said to us, but I knew he was proud from the way he ran his hand over the boards, painted the same color as all his inventions, a muddy blue-white turquoise. The hardware store had given away gallons of it, free, and that paint became the color of my father, slapped over the bicycle we shared, the chug, the wagon, the fertilizer-spreader, the soap-shredder, the paint-dryer, and finally the garage itself.

The sky is opening now. When I think of my father, I see two, three frail blue tulips in the sky, flowers floating with soft brown tips, shrunken veins, and the watery stems split open. Sometime in my twenties, when I live in New York and refuse to see any of my family, preferring, instead, the company of a large commune, I dream of him floating out over the green banks of the creek that flowed near our home, giving me the land. The water came from a large man-made lake called Lake Hiawatha, which was surrounded by a golf course. There were three pine trees at the mouth of the creek; in one of them we had jammed boards, and sat, on clear days, on the warm bumpy planks in the top clumps of pine, imagining the lake was the rough velvet ocean and we were watching the ships coming in from Europe to Indian land. We ignored the golfers in plaid caps. My father had never played golf. He didn't know any Indian stories. It doesn't seem possible that he even knew of the three trees that stood for us like friendly spirits at the edge of the lake—the huge inviting mystery on which we skated until our feet were blue, the water that turned from ice to soft, silty, grey-green waves that swept me under, more than once, and buried Cathy Oner-sword when she walked into the drop-off.

He had never asked where we played, the origins of the violets and lake-smelling fuzzy cattails collected in jars of water that sat on the square kitchen table. He did not walk down to Lake Hiawatha, as my mother did, when she was turning over questions in her mind. Is it this time she will leave us, I wondered in my pajamas, watching her go down the street into the dusky, fading dark. "No," he said from the couch, "she's gone for a walk." I couldn't believe him until she returned, usually with something from the drugstore. Neither of them could construe a walk, in itself, as a pleasurable event.

How was it that he stood in the dream, showing me the curves of the creek, the slopes of the silent golf course, land and water that lived through him as though he had been there all the time, and wanted to give it to me? While my mother screamed, gripping the cliff over the waves, fighting the drop? I cannot remember a single caress from my father, a glass of water in the night, one physical, exploded image of love. He hurried in and out of the bathroom, as we all did, bent, clutching our towels, strange-eyed creatures afraid of mirrors. When he emerged from the bath, gaunt and steaming, I saw him from the door of my bedroom as a savior, an odd man who hung from the cross like Christ, with a white cloth wrapped around his sucked-in abdomen.

He comes down the steps into the basement, carrying a bucket and two sparkling, freshly shot pheasants. My brothers are ice-fishing up north, and it is I, standing next to the wringer with an armload of newspaper, who is going to help strip the bodies for dinner. From upstairs floats the smell of potatoes my mother is cooking, that we will eat with the gravy. Back in the kitchen, we will be in her house, breathing her air. Here we are surrounded by dust and machines in the dark.

I lay paper over the speckled cement floor next to the drain. My father rolls up his sleeves under the yellow light of the bulb hanging from the ceiling. He has been hunting all day, I know, because I have checked the long wooden box in his closet and found it empty. And once I have even gone with him into the forest, where the squirrels nicked and scrinched and danced in the high trees, and I ate cold apple pie from a sack and tried to feel proud when the sky exploded and the birds screamed. It is the same numbness I feel now, when he cuts off the blue-green tails, and I ask for a feather.

"Yah," he says. "Hold the pail."

His big hands slice the knife into the dull brown girl pheasant, and he pulls out runny eggs.

"Pregnant," he says.

"Uh-huh."

The bird's head falls next. The red pouring into the bucket is brilliant, redder than spaghetti sauce, covering our hands and the newspapers, shining in a mosaic of glittering feathers and organs. When I visit the marbled Medici coffins in Florence, my first year in Europe, I remember the intense splattered image of those birds in the basement, and the warm, sweet smell of fresh blood. I remember—as I wander the famous statues and sculptures—the softness and limpness of the pheasant feathers, and the passion and revulsion I felt for my father at that moment. We yank mounds of feathers from the greyish skins, feeling the weight and heat of our hands, and I am happy and sick to be there with him.

It was his mother who opened her arms to us, a tiny, frail woman who, my mother suggested, had some kind of mental illness. Retarded. My mother said this and curled her mouth every time Clara's name came up.

In the last years of her life Clara lived with us and with my uncle Stu's family, more often with them, because they only had two children, a nothing of a family next to our clan of six. Their children were fat, and their father drank more than ours did. I had seen him on Christmas on his back in their kitchen, his mouth red, crying and dribbling on the floor.

Clara was the happiest adult we knew. She sang "deetle-lee, deetle-eet, eet, leetle-deet" and spun around in our living room, dancing to the new hi-fi we had all gotten for Christmas, the dark, lacquered magic machine, with lime-green station dials that went up and down. We came home from skating to find her whirling in the late afternoon sunlight, giggling like a tiny fairy in a long dress, the wisps of her white hair flying around like sparkling cotton candy on her pink head. I had read the entire wall of Fairy Tales at the Roosevelt Public Library, and Clara was to me the German story incarnate of the woodpecker: the little old woman in a black-and-white dress with a red apron who gave away smaller and smaller bits of food to the birds, until she flew away herself.

Clara fed us, too. She loved Easter, and made us Easter baskets year-round, weaving pink and green crepe paper into frills that stood up like stiff colored lace around the edges of the flimsy wood, filled with blue-red, violet and yellow candies, because Clara adored color. I rarely saw my father with her, because he worked a split shift until ten o'clock at night, and Clara usually dropped off to sleep in the den right after dinner, lopsided, whistling through her nose and clicking her gums. At Sunday dinners, she swung her legs under the table, tapping a pit-tit-pit-tit on the wooden legs, and calling my father "Paulie," which made us giggle and look at each other. Maybe my mother saw her as a child, helpless, demanding, another one she did not want. Stronger, most likely, was her fear of Clara being in our blood, to turn us into children forever.

Was it in the brain, what made her recede into the world of color and sound? In Duelm, my father's hometown, buried in central Minnesota, there was only a long white bar and a tall church, one gas pump and a graveyard. I learned later, during a week-long attempt to trace the family genealogy, tape-recording my relatives' singsong voices, that Clara's first husband had left her a widow in that desolate farm country. She had at the time three young children: my father, my uncle Stu, and my aunt Viola, whom I remember as tall, with startled eyes, chokers and lots of makeup, who died in a rooming house from drinking—"*the liver,*" adults murmured, passing around plates of sloppy joes in Duelm after her funeral.

Clara went to work for a farmer with two children who had lost his young wife. It was a situation in which Clara was generally imagined, in the voices of my relatives, to be powerless and probably sinful. We don't have any pictures of her. Eventually Clara married him and had three more children by this strange grandfather, whose name I don't recall. What little history remains is the following: he had migrated to Minnesota in search of better land, he would not listen to advice, his crops failed, he liked to play the electric pinball machine in the Duelm bar, he died young (this said with some satisfaction), and he would only call Clara by the name of Eileen, his first wife. "Terrible," my mother said, picking sweet corn out from between her teeth with a matchbook cover. "Your father had a terrible childhood. We both did."

And yet we felt in Clara's frail, worked hands, her feet tapping at the dinner table while she ate bread with both hands and grinned at us, a cherishing of our existence, a complicity that transformed mashed potatoes into castles, green peas into jewels. When my father came home from the hospital, quieter than he ever was—quiet even in his feet—and took a long time to hang his spring jacket on the closet doorknob, not wanting to turn around and face me sitting on the couch, or my mother standing in the hallway with her hands wrapped around her elbows, waiting, supper interrupted, I knew Clara was gone, and that he was trying to swallow, to keep inside love, love that had been real, not phantom, but innocent, unmotivated, that had remained through the years of her namelessness and her disappearance into herself, like a voice drowned in a well. To have spoken to him right then, to show the pity that we felt, would have brought on huge, unassailable waves of grief that I knew were forbidden in our house. If they started the waves would never stop, and if they continued he would be on the floor like Stu, and our mother's house, and all of us, would be lost.

When it's spring, and green and pink leap out at me from Easter cards, I dream of Clara. I want to buy a flowery, silly card and send it to her. I know that it was Clara's warm, unbashful hands that saved my father, and it is Clara that I sought in him, knowing she was there. Parents broke off inside you like cookies, said my older sister, Jean.

When I turned twenty-one Jean and I went down to the Hi-Lo Bar on Hennepin Avenue, where my father was said to have proposed to my mother, although he actually never mentioned anything about this. It was my mother's story we wanted to relive. The inside had red velvet walls, tired regulars, and the distant, achy feeling of a bar whose heyday had been World War II. There is a picture of my mother in the family album sitting atop a rock in Colorado wearing her WAC uniform, next to the photograph of my father smiling in his narrow beige army hat. They both look handsome, poised and secure: my mother's brown hair tumbles over her shoulders, she is not hiding her "bad" teeth by holding her mouth shut, my father seems genuinely relaxed, his eyes almost sleepy, seductive.

They must have studied each other over the saucer-sized tables of the Hi-Lo. Both farm kids, they had grown up within ten miles of Duelm, and suddenly they were wearing brown uniforms and sipping highballs in a dim city bar, my father about to leave for the Pacific.

"Paul," my mother said, "aren't you going to take off your hat?"

He took it in his hands and twisted it. "You have to promise," he said.

She did. And all the years he was lost in the war she travelled around like a man in her WAC outfit, hungry for pleasure, free at five o'clock in Denver or Seattle or San Francisco. She tried head-splitting cocktails that came with fruit and umbrellas, she fast-danced on slick floors with soldiers who called her "doll" and "sweetheart," and she went wild over roller coasters and trolley cars. When her tour was over she saved everything—her brown dress and jacket, a trunkful of matchbooks, clippings and tall menus she'd taken from restaurants.

We played war with my father's duffel bag, canteen, and the metal plate he ate out of during his three years in the jungles of Japan. It always affected her. She watched us from the front steps, and when she began pacing the porch, her head slunk into her turtleneck, I snuck around the back to find her dialing the phone, and whispering, "Have you got the car? I've got to get out of here." She was talking to Elena Iglesrood, her divorced Swedish friend who had blond hair stiff as egg whites and a Ford named "Lime Pie," a pretty, light green convertible with a black top. "Yah," my mother said, excited, "just a couple minutes. I'll get the baby down." I knew she wanted to leave us, to go back to those days when candles melted in dark restaurants, and soldiers smiled at her on the street.

Sometimes Elena drove up right away, waving her pink fingernails out the window of Lime Pie. But for inexplicable reasons she often betrayed my mother, and didn't come over. Then my mother's lips trembled with humiliation. She chased us up the stairs, carrying diapers and toys and shoes, and sobbing, "You kids are driving me to my grave."

"We love you, Mom, yes we do!" we chorused, but she turned off the light and slammed the door. We took off our clothes, ashamed of our bodies.

She had married my father almost immediately after the war. He sat in the VA hospital overlooking the Mississippi for a long time, afraid to leave his room. There's a large waterfall nearby, where Hiawatha Creek flows over an enormous break in rock and thunders down to the river, and on nice afternoons veterans come out and walk around. But I guess he wasn't able to do that.

My mother picked him up and drove him home with papers in her purse marked "Nervous Disability." He looked gaunt and wild to her, his black hair jumping out from his forehead, and something gone behind his eyes. His hands lay aimlessly on his legs. He finally reached over to the radio as if it were a foreign object and turned it up until she jumped. "Sorry!" he said, and laughed in a strained voice.

Then he told her he couldn't hear right from the shelling. Then he touched her hand on the steering wheel, as if to make sure she was really there.

My mother tells us these stories in a half-silken voice as we peel potatoes in the kitchen, and when she lingers over the details of how poor and helpless they were and no jobs could he get and the shabby duplexes they rented, I think we grew out of their shadows, that they had all of us to defy the blankness of those years.

"Ma!" Jean screams. "Ma!" We're awake in our beds, a hot summer morning. My father is hitting the walls. My mother throws herself down by the bureau and yells, "Paul, Paul" as though they're on a rocking ship, and we put pillows over our heads and wait.

Then he gets up, holding onto the banister as he steps down the wood stairs, his tall head wavering like the fish on Saturday morning cartoons. "Your father is still dreaming about the war," my mother says, in a tone of injury and helplessness that closes the subject. We all sit at the table drinking juice, the green sun shooting in under the blinds, and I hear him, stumbling for the security of the garage.

"Stay inside." My mother catches me by the arm.

That afternoon (or is it the next day? Time's stopped in the house), I am rolling soft bandages in the amusement room of the basement. Blankets stretch over my head between the arms of two chairs and the bar, a stiff upright triangle my father had built to stand behind when company came. When we had moved into the house our parents had held parties in the amusement room, plugging in the electric fireplace that glowed like a red mouth against the walls of knotty pine, dancing on the hard tiled floor. But we had all played with the fireplace too often, and knocked over the bottles in the bar, and drawn crayon faces over the pine knots, until my mother said, "Give up. Let the kids have it."

Now I recklessly pour old liquor into little cups for the soldiers and dilute it with water, because they'll be thirsty when they come in, wounded and suffering. A knock sounds.

"Please enter." I arrange the bed, prepare shots.

As if I had called him, or dreamed him there, my father slides back the door and stands confused in his slippers and thin pants and sweatshirt, hugging a stack of magazines. He drops them in the corner of the room, and looks at the stack for a long time, as though the covers are talking back. Then he turns his head like a turtle, and spots me.

"Whaddya lookin at?" in a hoarse voice.

"Nothin."

I make myself into a tiny speck, one that does not move, does not feel, does not ask for anything. He takes two heavy steps toward the tent. His lips are as red as Uncle Stu's. His body smells like a bum's. In a minute he'll start crying or hitting.

"Dad," I whisper, "do you want to see my hospital?"

"Get outa there."

I crawl out from under the blankets. His black eyebrows bear down on me. Then his hand shoots out and grabs my shoulder.

"Stand up straight, soldier."

Sometimes he says this at breakfast. So I laugh a little and stand up.

"At ease, soldier!" His face explodes and he drops into a chair, laughing in queer gulps, hee-heeing until water drains from his red eyes. Now he's only going to cry . . . but his thumb presses into the bone of my shoulder, and he brings his hot, wet breath close to mine.

"You kids don't know nothin."

The grisly knots on the wall are grinning. He crouches down, and I shut my eyes. Something cold clicks against my head.

"They made animals out of us," he whispers.

If I stay very, very still. If I am only a speck.

And he holds me by the neck and whispers crazy things, about how he had to carry all his stuff up the hill and he didn't know what was on the other side, there was metal whining in the air and planes like flies in the sky, men screaming and holding onto trees.

"You don't understand," he cries. "Don't you get it?" But I can't speak.

"Aaaah," he sobs, and lays his rough cheek on my forehead. Tears fall on my braids, he grips my body and everything comes down on me, his weight, the crashing bottle; I open my eyes and scream as we fall through the tent onto the hard floor.

Warm blood trickles out of my nose.

All this is memory: words that dissolve as soon as they are written, and go back to their hiding places. That time with my father I absorbed like a wrapped white dream, something stillborn that returned to me only when I slept, years later, curled around a man who had become both lover and friend. I do know that my mother had some inkling of what had happened in the amusement room, because she went to Elena's the next morning and got Lime Pie, and put us all in the back seat. My father sat in the front, quiet, his face puffy, and my mother hooked her fist onto the steering wheel and headed for Duelm. She had on her pink checkered blouse and smooth navy heels, and as we sailed along, surrounded by windows and Kleenex and Lifesavers and books, she said, "Watch this," and pulled over, pressing the magic button that opened the black top to the sky. We laughed and clapped and chattered, and my father smiled and laid his arm along the warm upholstery.

We went up the old state highway, and my father began pointing out the toy-sized farmhouses on the horizon, and rows of cottonwoods and elms planted as windbreaks. He was becoming a farm boy with every inch of the hot, dusty fields we passed. Something relaxed in him, he rolled up his sleeves above his elbows, and he made short familiar jokes about Polish farmers, which my mother countered with cracks about German stock, and they laughed in ways that I, a girl of ten hanging over the back seat, hadn't seen before. Eventually he took over the wheel, and my mother powdered her nose in the mirror, tipped her throat and wrists with cologne, and became silent, almost dreamy, the way she was around her sisters.

We knew we were near Duelm when my father turned onto a rough road. It took us back past old farmhouses and blown-down barns, and we passed through these places like ghosts. He pulled into the gas station and said to my mother, "Get Lucky Strikes. They've always got Luckies," as if we lived there, as if everything had stopped in the two white buildings, and we were surrounded by what once was.

Then Lime Pie floated up a hill thick with apple trees and chokecherry bushes, and my father said to my mother how the orchard needed trimming, and she remarked that it was a miracle those trees hadn't fallen down. Through the branches I saw a tall white house with windows on either side, like ears, and a porch that knelt to the ground. Goats bleated in the driveway.

Women came running out of the house, followed by strange uncles and Indian Joe. He was a huge, brown-skinned, handsome man said to have Chippewa blood, although no one really knew, because no one in the cautious, hesitant family way had ever actually asked, but we called him Indian Joe. He had married Aetha, my father's half sister, a tiny woman with short curly hair who was hugging my mother. The rest were too many for me to remember. Joe ran his palm along the green fins and leaned all the way down to Jean and me. "This your car, girls?"

The children came out from behind the sagging barn, holding their caps, suspicious. "There's your cousins," Aetha said. "Go on and play, now! Go on!"

And we had all afternoon to explore the barn and the fields, and to stick our hands in the cows' mouths. It was glaringly hot. Whitey, our cousin nicknamed for her hair that bleached out like a light bulb every summer, snuck us into the tall, dry, rustling wheat. We crouched down and secretly watched the giant thresher crash around us, excited by the machine that could crush our bones like sticks.

My heart was full of pride and rage at my father, who had not spoken to me directly since he had staggered up from the hospital tent. He rode by on the wagon, his arms pumping up the big bales, not noticing us, not even caring if we were to die. The baler whirred up and down.

"Stay here!" Whitey said. But I jumped up and ran blindly through the wheat, the machine beating louder and louder behind me, like a huge, crippled cicada, the pain curling inside, and I screamed, "Dad! Dad!"

It stopped. The men leapt off and shouted after all of us scattering through the field. My feet kept going, up the side of a hill into the orchard, up towards the twirling windmill, when my foot caught and I fell on a cement cistern.

It was a slow walk to the farmhouse, the skin hanging from my knees, and this time my mother did not scold me, but searched for Mercurochrome and bandages, and held a dipper full of cold water to my mouth. The other kids came in for drinks.

"Lucky she didn't break her leg," Aetha said. "I've told Joe to fill in that cistern a thousand times." All the aunts murmured about the cuts and burns and bruises of their children, until Joe appeared at the door. He looked like a madman, his face dark red from the heat, and his hair slivered with straw.

"Keep the kids in," he said. Whitey wouldn't speak to me.

But that evening, after we have eaten a roast, and potatoes and fresh lettuce and sweet corn, all the families spread out on the porch, with the smallest children huddled in laps. I watch the smoke from my uncles' pipes and my father's cigarettes float out the front yard, to the approaching dusk. In the distance we hear the low hum of threshers.

"Just don't know when to pack it in," Joe says to nobody in particular. "Crazy farmers."

The doves are singing "cooh-ah, cooh, cooh, cooh," and in the pink light my father seems very handsome, his skin tanned dark and smooth as an olive. He and my mother are relaxing in plastic armchairs, and something stirs in me when he picks up the felled head of a geranium from the porch. I realize that Clara must be somewhere near, maybe sprinkling and petting the wild snapdragons in the back.

Whitey nudges me. "Let's play 'Starlight, Moonlight.'"

"I don't know." I want to stand behind my father, my fingers in my mouth.

My mother hears us. "We have to go pretty soon, pumpkin."

"Just one game?" Whitey pleads.

"I think it's pajama time," Aetha says, passing around a glass dish of candies.

My father turns around, as if he has felt the hunger of my gaze. He swallows, and jerks his knee. "Go on," he says, low. "Go play a game." He suddenly drops the petals into my hand, his eyes burning deep into my face.

Standing in the soft air, so close that I can smell the skin inside his shirt, I feel the darkness break and scatter around me, and sigh, as though it has given up. Flowers bloom in my father's eyes. They tell me that the darkness will come back, to be desired and fought and broken a thousand times, until what I hold in my hand is enough.

Veterans

by Molly Fisk

Our fathers padded down separate halls
in different years, to find us. She shifts
in her chair when I say I couldn't help it:
that's what bodies are made for. I didn't
want to, but I came. I was four, then eight,
twelve—I didn't know how to stop him.

We are reminiscing in her backyard
like army buddies from boot camp shipped
to different fronts of the same long war.
We didn't come home in trash bags—

we are here, under the fruit trees, nominally
whole—no wheelchairs, no bourbon bottles
under the bed; we carry scars invisible
to the untrained eye.

Our eyes are honed like lasers, they're the eyes
of hunted animals gleaming in the dark,
ciphering through choked air
across a kitchen table, measuring
the danger in every quiet sound.

For her it wasn't arousing, she waited
for him to be done. Once her body took off
on its own, responding—she wrestled herself
to a standstill, right at the edge of the world.

I got addicted to the feeling, made myself
come every day of my childhood. She says
her boyfriend taught her, at eighteen,
on the phone. We laugh at that—
with a pillow? On the phone?

Her dog barks. We come back
to what we live with now. I've given up—
at thirty-six I sleep alone, ignore
the breasts he fondled, the hips
I had to watch him lift in his broad hands.
My body shudders close to men,
holding down the scream.

She has gone the other way. Her coming
is a kind of armor—she's piling up sensation
the way I gather distance, still trying to build
a rampart against those indelible nights
we carry in our shuttered hearts like glass.

Runners

by Thea Caplan
(for Maria)

The day before Sherry did it, she told me she was going to run away. To Toronto, Yonge Street, boys with mohawk heads, razors in their ears. Boys with skinny hips, drugs up their nose, and Doberman pinschers. She bought me a grape Popsicle and we sat on the steps of Luke's Variety.

"I've had it," Sherry said. "I gotta get out of here. It's too weird at home." She wiped some juice off my chin, licked her finger, then stood.

"How come you're always so quiet?" Sherry asked.

A little boy in a Superman T-shirt threw himself flat onto the sidewalk and screamed at his mother, "Bubble gum. I want bubble gum."

I looked up at Sherry. She'd stand there forever, hands on her hips, waiting for an answer. *Say something,* I told myself, and the words jumped out of my mouth and even as I was saying them I knew I had made a mistake. "I heard you and Dad giggling. I heard ice cubes."

Sherry crumpled up the Popsicle wrapper, glaring at me from the corner of her eye.

For a while we just sat on the steps of Luke's Variety, biting our lips and watching the clouds bump into each other and drift away.

Sherry grabbed a large shopping bag and pulled out long black leather boots, trays of lipsticks, eye shadow, powders, hair mousse, mascara wands. Black nail polish with glitter in it. Perfume even. Lime green triangle earrings for me.

"Catch this micro mini," she said.

The leather was warm and smooth, just a few faint creases in the middle. The skirt was short, like a napkin.

"It's nice," I said.

"An open-air bikini, that's what the boys call it."

"Where'd you get all this stuff?"

"It was easy," she said, "real easy."

I remembered Sherry teaching me to figure skate, how she straightened my velvet skirt, spread nail polish on a hole in my stockings. "That'll stop the run," she had said. "Smile, no one will notice."

Sherry lifted my chin with a finger. "Like me to do you up?"

She rouged my cheeks, into my hairline. Layered navy mascara on my eyelashes. Brushed my eyebrows. Dabbed perfume on my neck, undid my ponytail. She looked me over. She threw the eyebrow brush and the rouge, the works, into the shopping bag.

"You're too young for this. You don't have the bones."

Two years ago, just after Sherry's twelfth birthday, I found a bottle of Smirnoff, half full, in her closet. The next day it was empty, stuffed in a boot. I remember Dad was away on an insurance convention in Windsor because he brought Mom plastic place mats that said "Windsor, Ontario" in red letters. I don't know if Dad left the vodka for Sherry, or if she snuck it from the cabinet in the living room.

Once Mom got so mad at Sherry falling asleep at dinner she asked Sherry if she wanted to eat it, or wear it. Dumb Sherry, staring into the yellow tablecloth, head in her hands. Mom asked her again, in a real loud voice. Sherry still didn't answer. She kept staring at the tablecloth, lips parted. Mom stood up, wiped her forehead, and dumped the steak, the carrots, and the gravy on Sherry's head. We all sat there. Then Dad slid out of his chair and put his arms around Sherry, rocking her. He's never done that to me. Sherry woke up, dazed, and started picking carrots off her blouse and steak from her hair. The steak bone fell into her lap. Dad glared at Mom and I waited for him to slap her, but he didn't. Dad carried Sherry upstairs into the bathroom and it was him that washed her hair and wrapped her in the beach towel.

After the steak thing, Sherry and Dad would whisper for hours in her bedroom. I'd hear ice clicking. She'd giggle when he burped. Once when I stood in the hall I heard this moaning coming from Sherry's room. I crept back to my room and shut the door.

Before Mom got back from her shift in the mornings, I'd see Dad leave Sherry's room. In the hall between Sherry's room and mine, he smoked a cigarette until he breathed normal. He carried the white turtle ashtray, carefully flicking the ashes in it, not getting any on the carpet.

Sometimes when Mom pinned up the hem on my skirts and said I had pretty legs, I'd think about telling her. One time I said, "Mom, when you're ou—"

"Turn around. Let's see if that's right," Mom said, slapping my elbow. Green eyes on the hem, she shook her head. "Look what I did. The left side is an inch higher." She pointed to my left knee. "See how much is showing?"

"Mom."

"Stop fiddling, you'll look cockeyed."

Mom often sat in the window seat with the cat. They'd gaze into the street, not touching, the cat purring. Dad would tease Mom, "On guard duty again?" With the sun coming in, Mom and the cat glistened. Her red hair sparkled, she looked like a princess. One day Dad said, "Anna, you look gorgeous," and he cupped her chin in his hands and rubbed his face in her hair. When Mom looked up she stared over Dad's shoulder, her eyes wide, bright. It made me think of the deer on the highway coming back from our trip to Grandma's. It looked like the fender was on top of its neck, but suddenly the deer turned and ran off into the woods, and for a long time I saw two shimmering circles, the eyes sparkling like ice in the dark.

Before Sherry ran away, I asked her if she thought Dad loved Mom.

"He says he loves us all."

I didn't say anything.

"Does Mom love Dad?" I asked Sherry.

"How the hell would I know. Why don't you ask the cat?"

Mom crouched at my feet and pulled at my hem. I pressed my fingers hard into my thighs, fighting the shakes. Mom stared through my waist, my shoulders, my nose. I hate when her eyes get like that. It's like when someone slaps you and nobody blinks or breathes. They're waiting to see what you'll do. You wait and watch each other. Then Mom let down the hem, pins in her mouth, and told me to get changed.

Dad says Sherry's a pinball whore. He won't let her come home. "Not a foot in our door," he yelled into the phone, long distance. On my twelfth birthday, Sherry snuck back. I was doing homework when I heard two bangs on my window. I ran down the stairs and raced out the back door, making sure it didn't slam, even though no one was home. I found Sherry in the narrow pathway between the houses, dancing, plugged into a Walkman, and chewing gum. She had green hair with purple streaks, wore mirrored sunglasses and had a safety pin in one ear. She had on these high black boots and had a black-green bruise near her right eye. I hardly recognized her.

Sherry took off the sunglasses and handed me a bag stuffed with bubble gum, stickers, and melted chocolate bars. I unwrapped a Hershey bar and it ran onto my shorts.

"How are you?" I asked, excited.

"I'm doin' great."

"Oh." I tried not to look at her eye.

"I'm sorry about the chocolate bars." Sherry's mouth curved down; for a moment she looked old, older than Mom.

"It's OK. I like them mushy."

Sherry swirled her finger in the chocolate. "How ya doing?" she asked, pulling my ponytail. Sherry was fourteen, two years older than me, but sometimes she treated me like a little kid.

"I made the track team. Nobody thought I'd do it, except Mrs. Burton, she's my gym teacher. 'Pretend your legs are windmills,' she said. 'Pump. Focus.' I get a beat in my head, find a pace. It's me against the clock. I came in second, knocked out Gail Kelly. Dad lost a fiver, but he laughed. 'Who knew the kid had it in her?' he told Mom. But he paid up, and Mom gave me the five bucks."

When I pace myself, I think of my clock, hear its ticking in my head. It's round and white, I like its soft tick-tick. Grandma gave it to me for my birthday. I time my legs to its beat, sometimes two strides for every tick, it depends. You have to have eyes in the back of your head, know who's where, what they can do. Get on the inside track, set your own rhythm. "Guard your reserve," Mrs. Burton says. "Rush that finish line."

"How's it going?" Sherry asked again, fluffing up her bangs.

"Dad bought me my running shoes. Nikes. The ones I wanted, with the ankle support and blue trim." I slumped against the house.

"Look at me," she ordered. "Hold still."

With her chocolaty fingers Sherry drew lines on my forehead, my nose, on my cheeks. The chocolate felt warm. I licked some off. It was sweet, creamy.

"Like when we were little," I said. "I loved when you finger painted my face."

Sherry stood back a bit, eyed me like a skirt she might buy. "I dunno," she said. "Look how it's caking."

It was. The chocolate hardened, pinching my skin.

Then Sherry said something in a soft voice that startled me. "Why don't you come with me? Toronto is where it's at."

I wondered if Sherry's feet were hot in her boots. It was warm and sticky, even though it was May.

"I'd get you black net stockings, like these. Stay-ups." She stretched out a leg, rubbed a hand down her thigh. "I'm getting my own apartment. I'm sick of having roommates hanging around."

"When?"

She licked some chocolate off her finger. "When I get it together. In the summer. July for sure."

"Could I come visit you?"

"Come with me," Sherry said. She had stopped chewing her gum. "You could stay up as late as you wanted." She touched my wrist with a fingertip. "You could read in bed, no lights out. Come with me."

I bent down, untied my shoelace, then tied it so tight it hurt. I hunched over so she couldn't see my face. I could feel Sherry bending over me, warm breath on my ear. "You could go to the track whenever you wanted. Toronto is full of running tracks. You could train for long distance. You'd like that, wouldn't you?"

I twisted off the elastic around my ponytail and made a new one, on top of my head. The kind Mom says looks like a palm tree sticking up.

Thea Caplan · 41

"We could pack you up a tote bag and be outta here in ten minutes." Sherry's gum cracked.

I'm only twelve, I almost said, but then I remembered Sherry was just a year older when she'd taken off. For a long time Sherry was quiet. I got nervous that she'd start up again about Toronto. It was five-thirty and I worried someone would come home.

Sherry whispered, "I could come back for you. Meet me at the track, Wednesday. You could be all packed. No one would know."

It was like I was running and going to hit the wall and Sherry was behind it and I couldn't touch her or see her.

Sherry yanked off a leather boot. Standing on one foot she massaged her swollen toes. Purple fingernails looked good against her light chocolate hands. She spat onto her fingers, making muddy swirls. Her hands came up to my face. When she leaned over a sweet and sour smell circled my face.

"You don't drink vodka anymore," I said, surprised.

"I don't have to," she said. "I drink what I like."

Sherry stared into my eyes and wouldn't stop, and I thought of when she'd sit and stare into the yellow tablecloth, and the time Dad hugged her and wrapped her up in a beach towel.

"Just think," she said, "nobody tells me what to do."

"Sherry," I said, "I can't go with you."

"Listen—" Sherry took one look at my eyes and snapped, "Forget it."

One time, I don't know why, Sherry phoned me. It was after school, she knew Mom and Dad wouldn't be home. I could hear her sucking little breaths of air. The train whizzed by tooting its horn and then it got quiet again. I almost told her about Dad. But she would've just told me to bum a ride, she's got some great apartment, she'd fix me up.

Dad has a friend who calls his sailboat "Silent Woman." And that's what Dad calls me, "my silent woman."

I sit on my hands to hide the shakes. In school, when I stand to answer a question I hold onto my desk. It's the vodka, it gives me the jitters and burns my stomach. I'm so tired I forget to eat, it drives Mom crazy. I know I could do much better at track. I'm a fast runner, got Mom's long legs. I stick to the sprints, but it's long distance I want to do. I can see myself running the five-kilometre, my ponytail bobbing on my T-shirt. Then I'd go for the ten-K. Mrs. Burton told me I have the perfect shape for running. "You're lean and you've got the strength. I wish you had more drive, though. You could be a great runner." She's always saying that. Once I almost told her. I waited for her after gym, but she was showing Gail Kelly something and when she came out of the locker room the bell was already ringing for the next period. No way I was going to hang around. Being late means detentions,—getting up early. Besides, I'd better not get any bright ideas, as my dad says.

"C'mere, you need this," is what Dad says.

"You love your Dad, don't you?"

I'm not like Sherry. I never think it's funny when Dad burps in my face. I hate the way vodka burns my throat and makes me gag. The room spins; I lose my balance, I bang into doors.

Muffled noises, Mom's crying again. She must have her face stuffed in the pillow. Two thuds; that'll be Dad throwing Mom's high heels against the wall. I throw my quilt over my head, snuggle into a ball. I've forgotten; I pull my arms out from under the covers and set my alarm for 7:15. Tick tick tick . . . I'm thinking it's pretty funny the way my clock keeps on doing the same thing when a voice in their bedroom yells, "Get out!"

I hope they keep arguing.

I pull the covers tight over my head, become a big lump in the bed. I'm remembering Sherry's visit. She put her hands on my shoulders and shook me, hard. "Get the hell out. Forget the old fart."

Forget the old fart?

"Split!" she yelled, as if I was deaf.

"Will you forget him?" I asked.

She stopped shaking me, stared into my face. "I'll get my own place. There'll be room for you."

"Will you forget him, Sherry?"

She blinked twice, her eyes full up with water. "Maybe *you* can," she said.

There's his footsteps on the wood floors, and I hope he's gone to brush his teeth, though I know he never brushes his teeth after a fight with Mom. Sometimes he takes a quick piss. It's quiet now, except for the ticking of my clock. I take a long breath, and after five clicks, I let it out, slow. My breathing is quiet and smooth.

Softly my door opens and in walks Dad, his hair wet, no glasses.

I see light sparkling off a bottle. I'm in big trouble—it's almost empty, he's juiced. *Click* goes the bottle against Dad's belt buckle. It's Smirnoff vodka, it always is. A good clean vodka, my father says, but what he means is it won't smell on his breath, or mine. It bites my throat, I'll never get used to it. Dad says a person gets used to anything. "You're almost twelve, you're not a baby anymore," is what he says. He rubs the lip of the bottle against my teeth. Once, I held five swigs, and he didn't even realize. "Atta girl," he kept saying, thinking I was getting loaded. Sometimes he's so dumb. Or maybe he's thinking about his crummy boss, or something, so it looks like he's dumb, but he's not, really.

Dad gently shuts my door with his foot, flicks on my closet light. He stands there looking down at me, squinting, the collar on his yellow shirt half up. It seems so loud, my clock ticking. I stare at the glass door handle, try to slow down my heartbeat to match the clock. I close my eyes and focus on the black space inside my head. But it isn't black. Bits of yellow jump around, and the clock's ticking is so slow I'll never match it. There's nothing I can do about my heart, my runaway heart, so I breathe in deep and take one breath for every four clicks of the clock. I can always change the pace.

Dad's so close to me I could touch his pants leg. He's tapping his foot on the floor like when he's in line at the supermarket. He bends over and yanks at something. "Jesus, that thing's annoying," he says.

I hear a plop on the floor.

Dad stands over me, he hardly blinks. His nose is shiny, but it's his eyes—they're so white, like little globes. I don't see any brown there. This pounding in my head, I'm so full up my ears are going to burst, and a rock, it's stuck in my throat. There's so much grey. And it's so quiet. Where's my clock? I turn my head. I make out its white shape. It's still on the dresser, not a sound coming out of it. I open my mouth, gulp air. I point to the clock, sucking noises are coming out of me.

"That ticking drives me crazy."

I shake my head, no, no. PLUG IT IN, I want to yell, PLUG MY CLOCK IN! But I can't say anything. Nothing. Spit bubbles out my mouth and I know he sees it.

Dad runs his fingers through his hair and says, "You can plug it in—later." He sits down, throws back his head, tilts the bottle. His neck is long and white. "I'll get us some more," he says, and smiles a slow smile. He likes to take his time. I scrunch the sheets in my fists.

Dad tosses the vodka bottle high, way over my head, just misses the ceiling. His arm's straight up, fingers curled a little. The bottle's spinning, but he catches it.

"How's my silent woman?" Dad says, twisting off the cap.

I stare at the fine red hair on his knuckles and he watches me.

I close my eyes, letting in a little bit of light. I'm thinking about a million Sundays ago when Mom, Dad, and Sherry and me were at the Exhibition. Candy floss, bingo, the Flyer. Being thrown around crazy in the little cart, the buckle digging into my stomach, Mom yelling, "Hold on!" Me, half hanging out, screaming silly, Dad yanking my arm, laughing too.

I like going on the rides on my own. Who wants a mother, father, and spacy older sister tagging after you? The best part is after the ride stops. When it's quiet and no one moves, and no one wants to believe it's over.

Not me. I'm ready to go. Why wait for an attendant? I could undo the safety buckle myself, jump out. But that Sunday I sat snug as a bug in my seat in the Whizbang and thought about the best part. The three of them standing at the exit ramp, waiting. Cotton candy covered Sherry's face, and Dad was smoking a cigarette. Mom was fiddling with her hair, then waved at me, hurry up! her hand said.

The three of them standing there waiting for me, that's the best part. And walking down the ramp toward them! No, *that* was the best. I walked slowly, slower than I needed to, leaning on the railing. They just waited, like all the other families. I loved watching them do that.

"You OK?" Sherry asked, sticking cotton candy into my face.

"How'd it go?" Dad asked. He looked at his watch.

My mother smiled.

I wanted to go on another ride, by myself again. The one where you stand up in a cage and get thrown around, upside down. "That one!" I yelled, pointing to a ride about a hundred metres away. My dad reached into his pocket. He had the ride tickets in his hand.

"This kid's a riot," he said. "She doesn't stop."

"Do you want anything to eat?" I couldn't believe my mother was asking that again. I had two hours in the midway and I wasn't wasting any of it stuffing my face. Sherry rolled her eyes at Mom so that she saw. I grabbed the tickets from Dad's hand and ran to the line-up for my ride.

The hard tips of Dad's moustache on my neck, up my nose. The weight of him on me. I'll never breathe cool air again, move my legs.

"You're so different from Sherry. You're so quiet, into yourself." He laughs. "That sister of yours has one hell of a mouth."

I can smell the lemon on my father's shirt. Mom uses Fab.

"But I like you too," he says, then kisses my eyebrow.

"No vodka," I say.

He looks at the bottle on my night table. "It's empty, remember? I polished it off myself, sorry."

"No vodka," I say.

He gives me a funny look trying to convince me he thinks I'm off my rocker, lost it somewhere.

"It'll put hair on your chest," he says.

"No vodka!" I say loudly, surprising myself.

"Shh! Shh!" His eyes dart to the door. "OK, relax. No vodka." His finger traces my lips. "What an uptight kid you are."

His belly is soft and helpless on my hard stomach. The weight of him on me is hardly a thing, and that is very strange because he's almost six feet. I think of him as a cloud over me. I think of the day, the day before Sherry ran away, when we sat on the steps of Luke's Variety and the clouds watched and then drifted away and Sherry made me up, eyebrows and all, and told me I was too young, I didn't have the bones.

I see Gail Kelly four paces ahead of me. *Your legs are windmills*, I tell myself, and crank it up. The wind's cool on my ears. I pass Gail Kelly, cut her off, slide onto the inside track. This time I'm fast and I'm first. I hold on, find a pace that'll work, guard my reserve. My chest rises and falls against the sheets. Slow and rhythmically I'm breathing, in time with the clock ticking in my head.

Taking Care of Calvin

by Melanie Bishop

C alvin Houston is the only Black person in my U.S. history class. It's an honors class; he's smart. All fall he sat way across the room from me, first seat, last row on the left. After Christmas vacation Mr. Babbin moved people around, for his own reasons, he said, and Calvin ended up right in front of me. Him in the first seat, me in the second, first row on the right by the door. It was where I'd been sitting all year, but Calvin was a change of scenery. I looked at the back of his head that first day, got a picture of it in my mind. Hair, spiraly black. Neck, dark caramel, smooth.

By the second day of this, Calvin was turning around in his seat to bother me, whenever Babbin wasn't looking, which was a lot. First he took my pen and when I tried to get it back he sat on it. I ignored this and got out another one. Then he reached his foot back and landed his heel right on my toes. I gave him a glare. At least ten times, this was a favorite, he turned a bunch of pages in my book so I'd lose my place. Not that I cared a goddamn about U.S. history, or what I was supposedly reading. But it annoyed me to have to keep finding Chapter nineteen, which was what we were on. All we ever do in that class is read the chapter, outline the chapter, take a quiz on the chapter. It would be boring even if it was sex education.

Calvin turns around to face me now.

"WHAT?" I say. It is the first time I've spoken to him.

"What do you mean, what?" he says. He makes these big Negro eyes at me.

"What do you WANT?" I say.

"Now there's a question," he says and laughs. "There's a real question— what do I want?"

He acts like some lunatic, making no sense, laughing way too loud. *I* want *him* to leave me alone.

46

After a solid week of this, I conclude that Calvin thinks he has to be extra funny and smart, being the only Black in that class, this being New Orleans in 1972. He has something to prove. He tries too hard. Makes jokes that no one appreciates and then laughs at them loud and deep, all by himself. People just look at each other, me included.

"Why don't you keep it down, Calvin?" I say one day. He's irritating me.

"Oh?" he says. "And could you please inform me just why I should be quiet for *you*? Please," he says. "Enlighten me. I'm waiting. Please."

"You're weird," I say, shaking my head.

"Calvin and Andrea," Babbin says. "If you two insist on talking, I'll move you to different corners of the room."

"He's bothering me," I say.

"I would be more than happy to move," Calvin says. He gathers all his stuff into one arm and stands up. "Just tell me where I should sit," he says. He's all hyper, starts moving from foot to foot, his eyes bugging out.

"Take your seat, son," Babbin says. "Both of you get busy."

I wasn't doing a thing," I say.

"That is precisely my point," Babbin says. "You are supposed to be outlining the chapter."

History has to be the worst class I have, worse even than Spanish or Algebra II. English and drama are the only things I like, and P.E. as long as we aren't playing softball. I can't catch a fly ball to save my life and they always sail my way. It's better not to even go for it if you know that you won't catch it. Save yourself the embarrassment. I don't trust the path of a ball; it can end up in your face. But history isn't even scary, just plain boring. At least with Calvin things get stirred up, even if he does annoy me to no end, always acting like an eighth grader instead of eleventh.

The only half-decent thing about U.S. history is each time we start a new chapter Babbin makes us read it aloud in class. I love reading out loud. I know how to pronounce almost any word, even if I've never seen it before; it's a gift I have. I read loud, pause when I'm supposed to, and just flow on through when I'm not. It's a lot like drama; I plan to be an actress one day. Because I am so good at this, Babbin lets me read for a longer time than anyone else. He knows the next person in line might stumble all over the place, take all hour to read a paragraph, even if this is an honors class. Just because you're smart does not mean you can read aloud. I know a lot of smart people who can't. Babbin likes to call on me and let me finish up the bulk of it. I could read aloud forever, even if it is history. I like the sound of my own voice.

One day after I've read three full pages of Chapter twenty-one, Babbin says: "Thank you, Andrea. You read exceptionally well." A comment like that can make my day. It makes me feel all hot, good, but I try not to let this show.

Calvin turns around a few minutes later as the weasel behind me is butchering the text up good, absolutely destroying the rhythm I set up.

"My, my," Calvin whispers. "If we haven't made ourselves an *impress-*

ion . . ." He makes those same oversized eyes, almost spooky, and leans way too close to my face.

"What do you mean, *we?*" I say.

"Well, well, you *are* touchy," he says. "Just forget I ever said a word." He turns back to face the front, and I feel sorry, but I don't let that show either. The rest of class, I'm stuck looking at the back of his head, nowhere near as interesting as the other side, those bulging eyes, whiter and blacker than anything I've seen.

"Andrea!" Calvin calls from behind me as we walk out of class. He says it like it's a command. I stop and turn to face him, my long hair following in an arc. All around us kids are moving from class to class, lockers opening and closing, people yelling to each other, at each other. I'm holding my books in front of my chest like some shield. "What?" I say. Calvin looks to my left, to my right, anywhere but at me. "You do read well," he says finally, and then puts both eyes on me. "And furthermore," he says, his forehead getting all wrinkled and serious, "you look awfully sweet in that blue dress."

My boyfriend up till a week before Christmas was Randy; we'd been together since the tenth grade. He got real weird on me, started reading all these books like Henry David Thoreau, and decided he should drop out of school. Well, as wrong a move as I thought this was, it was his business, not mine. Until he started telling *me* to drop out with him. Now maybe I've done some stupid things before, but I am not that stupid. Everyone knows that dropping out of high school means one big dead end. They drill that into you since about the first grade, for Chrissakes. Night after night he kept me up real late, out in his car in front of my house. He wouldn't let the subject drop.

"Just give me one good reason," he'd say. For staying in school, he meant. I'd tell him because you're supposed to. I'd say because you might want to go to college, you never know. Bullshit! he would say. Those are society's reasons, not your reasons. What are your reasons, he'd say. Sometimes I'd admit I just didn't know, hoping he'd give up and let me go in and go to bed. He'd shake his head at me like I was some kind of fool. You are so deceived, he said once.

For the longest time he was the best thing in my life, the only person I could depend on. Then he got all philosophical and we never saw eye to eye after that. We broke up. I wanted to find someone else fast; it was that or stay home at night and home was not always a good place to be.

Calvin would never drop out of high school. He's vice-president of the National Honor Society, and even though that's probably so much bullshit, too, according to Randy, it's nice to see people believe in something.

It was Friday that Calvin told me I looked sweet in my dress, and by the next week, Monday, we both know things are different. It's not what we say, but just the way we say normal, everyday things.

"And how was your weekend?" Calvin says.

"Okay," I say. "Yours?"

"I was very busy," he says. "I'm in a play downtown and we started dress rehearsals. I'm tired."

"What play?" I say.

"*Annie Get Your Gun*," he says.

"Oh," I say. I don't know this play but I don't let on.

Babbin comes in and shuts the door and Calvin turns to face front and we don't say anything else that day.

On Tuesday I ask him about the play, where it is, how he got the part and all that. Like I said, I want to be an actress. While we're talking, before Babbin starts class, Calvin says that his girlfriend who lives across the river is also in this play. He says this like it's nothing and before I figure out what question to ask him next, I have to read aloud, Chapter twenty-two. I can barely concentrate.

On Wednesday he is absent. It makes me crazy, U.S. history class without Calvin. The clock, of course, won't move. Fifty-five minutes is no short amount of time when you are not having fun. We're up to the outlining part. Thirty minutes into it, I have to get out. I ask to go to the bathroom. Babbin knows enough to let girls go when they say they have to. I walk as fast as I can to the hall outside of the cafeteria where the pay phones are. I look up his name, Houston—there are several; I only have one nickel. I pick the Houston on Lee Street, since that's in the Black section over by the TG&Y. A lucky guess. He says hello.

"Calvin," I say.

"Andrea," he says.

I say, "How did you know?"

"I know that voice," he says. "You should be in class right now, girl. You're going to get yourself in trouble."

"Are you sick?"

"Yes I am. I've run myself down and now I've got me a sore throat."

"When is opening night?" I say.

"Saturday."

"Will you be well by then?"

"I have to be," he says. "How did you get my number?"

"The phone book," I say. "I better go. Babbin thinks I'm in the bathroom."

"Well, it was very nice of you to call, Andrea."

"Get better," I say.

Calvin comes back to school on Friday. All he says is "Hello, Andrea," but after class he gives me a free pass to see *Annie Get Your Gun* at the Sunday matinee.

The pass is good for two people, so my mom goes with me; she loves plays. I like it when we do stuff together and get out of the house. Sundays can be bad days to hang around there. My father doesn't like how much time she spends at church and it usually starts things off wrong.

Calvin has a real big part. There must be seventy-five kids in the cast and I feel jealous of every single one. I point Calvin out to my mom, while he's singing and dancing, and I can tell she is starting to wonder just who he is to me. Now how do you know this boy? she says. He's in my history class, I tell her.

"He's adorable," she says. My mom has always thought Negroes were cute. At the A&P store she hands out pennies to the colored kids who wait by the gum machines. Little girls, with their hair in a bunch of skinny braids and colored barrettes. She gives all of Daddy's old clothes to Dorothy, our maid, for her husband. His name is Parker and my mother thinks he's adorable too. Especially once when he picked Dorothy up and he was dressed up in one of my dad's old business suits. "Isn't he just precious?" she said.

After the curtain call, Calvin takes me backstage, he says to meet his friends, but the first person he introduces me to is the girlfriend he mentioned before. She smiles at me, she's beautiful, her name is Julie, she's white; he has never mentioned this.

Now everything is different. I can't pretend.

"How come you never told me she was white?" I ask him in class. I write this on a sheet of scrap paper and pass it forward.

"What difference does it make?" he writes back. "You got something against white people?" I don't know what to say, so I don't write anything back. I don't know what difference it makes.

At the end of class I pass him a rectangle of paper with my number on it. "Call me tonight," I say.

He does and we talk till my sister makes me get off the phone. "You've been on over an hour," she says. The next night I call him, kind of late, I'm already in bed. There's a phone by my bed and my sister is out. We talk for two hours. I ask him everything I can think of about Julie. I tell him about Randy. He tells me Julie's parents don't allow her to see him; they sneak time together, after rehearsals. My parents aren't prejudiced, I say.

Another night, we get on the phone at ten and stay on till way past everyone else in each of our houses has fallen asleep. We have to speak in whispers. We talk about *everything*. He tells me Julie is a virgin; I tell him I am not. I tell him about the night me and Randy first did it, how I cried so much after because I wanted the virginity back. How it wasn't what I thought it would be, what I wanted. How irreversible it was. Sex isn't all it's cracked up to be, I say. He tells me the first time he did it, he was only twelve years old, that his teenage baby-sitter initiated him and his brother. He thinks it is pretty much what it's cracked up to be. We talk on through the night, all our secrets. For a while I fall into sleep and when I wake up he's still there; he says he listened to me breathing. He says he is thinking of me and can't stop. That I am turning him on, something fierce. I say what about Julie? He says we'll cross that bridge at the time. I figure he must love her a lot, it's dangerous, their love.

I want that for myself.

When we both fall asleep the phones drop from our ears and when I wake up in the morning, he isn't on the other end. He tells me later at school that he only hung up when he heard his mother's alarm go off at quarter till six.

"Are you tired?" he says and I nod. "Poor Andrea," he says.

That night, it is a Thursday, I borrow my mother's new car.

"I'm going to visit Calvin," I say.

"Oh, that cute Negro boy," she says.

"We're studying for a big test," I say. She doesn't blink.

"Going out with a spade, are you?" my dad says.

"We're not going out," I say, "we just have a big test."

"I see," he says, but he lifts his eyebrows like he doesn't see, like I will probably hear more about this later. I don't even care.

I drive to Lee Street, find his number and knock.

In the front seat of the car, we sit. We listen to the top-forty station. He tells me that he likes Al Green; I don't know who this is, but I don't say so. We find out we both have the same favorite song—"Killing Me Softly," Roberta Flack. When it comes on, I turn it way up. Calvin? I say. Yes? When are you going to kiss me? I say. His eyelids get lower and he looks like he thought I'd never ask. And then we are tangled up in each other, not even minding that the shifter is in the way. It is no different than kissing a white boy. It is every bit as nice.

The third time I go to Calvin's, my parents are up when I get home. My mother is falling asleep on the couch; my father is drunk in front of the TV, the volume high.

"There she is!" he says, like it's some big deal. I don't say anything. I was not expecting them to be up at eleven. My lips feel all chapped and full, like all the blood has been sucked into them. "How's the new boyfriend?" he says, again like a big deal. I go into the kitchen and get some water. "You know," he says, his words all liquidy, "your mother likes colored men too. They're supposed to have big penises. That's what she likes."

"Oh, stop," my mother says.

"Niggers have big dicks," he says. "It's a fact."

I go into my room and shut the door. He is drunk for sure because otherwise he would never call them niggers.

"Isn't it true, Andrea?" he says, loud enough to reach me in my room. I don't answer.

"Leave her alone," my mom says.

"You women are all looking for the same damn thing," he says, "a good fuck."

I'm hoping my mom will keep quiet. I don't want a fight.

"Andrea's going out with a spade!" he says, and repeats this till it is a song. My mother is telling him to stop. I cover both ears with my pillow, and sing

"Killing Me Softly," softly to myself.

Every chance I get, when the car is free, I go. I call Calvin first and he watches out the front window till I drive up, then comes out to the car. We still haven't gone too far but we've made up nicknames for the parts of us that want to. Inside his pants is Herman. In mine, Henrietta. We say that someday they may want to meet each other, face-to-face.

Whenever our song comes on we sing together, loud, we know all the words. Calvin's brother sneaks up and peeks in the window. "Gregory!" Calvin says. "Get your black ass in the house." This makes me laugh, makes me like Calvin more.

Calvin starts to act troubled one night. I ask is something wrong. It's Herman, he says. He wants you very much. What about Julie? I say. Andrea, he says, trust me, Julie has never met him. Just touch him for me, he says, and I do, through his pants. Just kiss him once, please Andrea, he says.

I have done this before with Randy. Not one of my favorite things to do, but I know how. Calvin unzips his pants and takes it out. I cover his lap with my face, tasting him, trying not to hurt him with my teeth.

While doing this, I remember a time when I was four years old, at the A&P store. On either side of the one Coke machine was a tall water fountain. I was by myself, my mother in another aisle, and I hoisted myself up for a drink, feet dangling. Suddenly I was pulled off by a fat lady. She put me down and shook her finger at me. That fountain's for niggers, she said. That other one's for white people. She lifted me up to the correct fountain, where I expected something different, but the water tasted the same.

Herman is liking this. Calvin too. He is moaning and saying yes, and before I know it, it is bitter and warm in my mouth.

I spit this into a Kleenex from a box on the dash. I drop it out the window in the ditch. Calvin cannot stop thanking me. Herman loves you so much, he says. What about you, I say. Of course I love you, Andrea. It is all I need to hear.

The next time I go over to Calvin's house it is the same. Afterwards I ask Calvin to put his arm around me. Tell me something about the inside of your house, I say. I've only seen it from outside. What do you want to know? he says. Anything. The curtains in the living room are lavender lace, he says.

And the next time I go over it is the same again, and the next, and the next. He hands me the Kleenex, I spit and drop it out the window. You make Herman so happy, he says. Calvin starts to depend on this. I am liking it less and less. In history we have stopped talking to each other; we are trying not to let anyone at school find out.

It is harder to keep it secret from my family when I'm taking the car several nights a week.

"When are you going to bring this guy over?" my sister says.

"I don't know," I say. I am thinking that probably never.

The next time Calvin unzips his pants I say no. He says: Please, Andrea. It is the only thing that relaxes me, the only way I get rid of my tension, he says. Please, Andrea, make him happy. I am starting to hate Herman. I am tired of the taste of Calvin's tension.

Afterwards I lean against his shoulder and ask him to tell me something. Like what, he says. Like a dream you have, I say.

"A dream at night?"

"No, like something you want to come true."

"Well," he says. "I want to get a scholarship at Baylor."

I don't know where Baylor is, but I know it's a school.

"To study what?" I say.

Calvin says, "Theater." He knows this makes me like him more, knows I want to be an actress.

One day in class, Babbin moves Calvin to the far back corner, left side of the room, without saying why.

"What did I do?" Calvin says.

"Just do as you're told," Babbin says. I sneak a look at Calvin later and smile.

Babbin asks to see me after class. "Andrea," he says, when the room is empty. "There's a rumor that you're hanging around with Calvin outside of class."

"We're just friends," I say.

"That's not what's being said," Babbin says, "and I don't think your parents would like the news." I'm thinking he doesn't know the first thing about my parents, that they are too busy with their own problems to ever care about what I'm doing.

"I'm just warning you," Babbin says. "I would hate to have to call them."

"My parents like Black people," I say.

"So do we all, Andrea," he says, "but that doesn't mean we associate with them outside of school."

Calvin is waiting for me down the hall. I only tell him that Babbin wanted to know what we were up to. That is absolutely none of his business, Calvin says, and I agree.

I don't go to Calvin's that night or the next or the next. I am worried about what people are saying, and how they found out. Calvin calls, begs me to come, but I say something about the car, and he lets it drop, but not for long.

Thursday night I go. I want to ask some questions about Julie. There's a new play that they are both in. I want to know how much she knows about me, and which one of us is his girlfriend, I want to know.

"Andrea," he says, "Julie is a very special friend. But I only see her when we're in a play together."

"How is she different from me?" I say.

"She doesn't take care of me the way you do."

"Do you kiss her?" I say.

"Andrea," he says.

"Well do you?"

"No," he says.

He tells me to turn on the radio. It's bad for the battery, I say. Since when, he wants to know.

"I've been missing you, Andrea," he says.

"You mean Herman has."

"Both of us," Calvin says, and he makes those eyes that plead.

"I have to get the car back," I say. "I can't keep using it so much."

Right then I see headlights coming from behind. The car stops; there isn't room to pass. Lee Street is unpaved and narrow. I'm not parked close enough to the ditch. Pull into the driveway, Calvin says. Why don't I just go now, I say. He repeats it: Pull into the drive. The car behind us honks.

I've never pulled into his driveway before. I'm too far to the right, too close to the fence, but it will do. I have to go now, Calvin, I say.

Just kiss him once, Calvin says.

I know there is no such thing as kissing Herman once.

I have to go, I say.

Andrea, please, I have been so tense. It's the only thing that makes me feel better.

I ask him where he gets all this tension from.

School. The play. Just being Black, he says, is a tension I will never understand.

Please, Andrea, he says.

After I do it, Calvin gets out of the car, and stands on the driveway while I back out. I'm too far to the right and going in reverse is always confusing. Trees in the rearview, ditch on either side of the road. I pull up again, then back, and the front right wheel is in the ditch. The bumper catches on the chain-link fence, makes a horrible noise.

I jump out. Calvin is still there. I'm in trouble if anything happens to this new car. It only hurt the fence, Calvin says, and he shows me where. I can't do this, I say, you do it. The car is now attached to the fence and it looks like it will take some maneuvering. Calvin gets in; I stand behind to make sure he stops before the trees.

I look at the bumper and the paint job and it seems like everything's okay. Thank God, I say. I get in; Calvin goes inside.

Driving slowly towards General Meyer Boulevard, I'm aware of the potholes, the way the car rocks in and out of them. Lee Street doesn't have any streetlights and I notice this for the first time too.

A big guy stands in the middle of the road, his hand is up, telling me to stop.

Two boys walk up on the driver's side and knock on the window. I roll it down about two inches.

"How you doin?" one says.

"Fine," I say.

"I'll say you're fine," the other one says. They both laugh. The one in front jumps up to sit on the hood. I don't want to show how scared I am, but they are bigger and older and blacker than Calvin and two of the car doors are unlocked. I lock them; they laugh. The window is still open a crack.

What are you scared of, we're not going to hurt you, we just want to have some fun.

I have to go home, I say.

This sure is a pretty car, one says. The guy sitting on the hood has his back against the windshield, like he plans to stay awhile.

How bout we have some fun?

I don't say anything.

How bout you do for us what you been doin for Calvin? I roll up the window fast and they laugh. One starts knocking on the window so hard I think it will break in my face. I look straight ahead. I start to step on the gas and the guy on the car jumps down, slaps both hands down on the hood, standing there so I can't go. They circle the car, slapping it in places. It occurs to me to lean on the horn, maybe Calvin will hear, maybe someone. This scares them, makes them mad, it is loud and constant. One picks up a big branch and brings it down hard on the back of the car. The guy in front moves to the side and says, "Get outa here, fuckin' white bitch."

I drive away while he's saying: "And don't come back."

I cry on the way home, I shake, I want things to be normal, but I don't know what that is. In the morning I will have to show the dent to my parents. Maybe they will put a stop to this.

Kala: Saturday Night at the Pahala Theater

by Lois-Ann Yamanaka

Mugs wen' buy the tickets for us 'cause he grad already.
I was shitting 'cause the theater lady,
she own the store where us buy slush afterschool
and she know I only seventh grade 'cause her daughter
our classmate, Nancy. NNNAaannccy. The one—
the one told us she had policeman in the sixth grade.
Policeman. Fuzz, brah, fuzz. Yeah, you neva know?
The theater lady is her *madda*.

She look at me *long* time when she rip my ticket in half.
Then she give me one real long piece toilet paper
for wipe the soot from the sugar mill off my seat.
Last time you and me went, she gave us small piece,
rememba? And when I went home, I wen' catch lickens
from my uncle 'cause my pants was all black.

Mugs walk first then Jimmy boy push my back part
for follow him. He walk behind me. All the Filipino
men sit in the last row. I smell the tobacco
they spit on the floor. They laugh when I walk past
and say some words in Filipino. I know they talking
about me. Jimmy boy push me again.

56

Of course neva have cartoons. You stupid or what?
You neva seen one X-rated movie before? Me too.
Okay. No tell nobody, okay?
Had five cheerleaders 'cause the movie
was *Cheerleaders Growing Up.* They all was haole
and they was on one picnic table like the one
we get at school. They was all telling their stories.

Had one, her was call to the office
'cause she was one bad girl smoking cigarettes
in the bathroom. The fat, bolohead principal, he make her
all sced. He say he going tell her fadda.
So the cheerleader, she all nuts, right? He say
he fix everything for her. But he tell her
she no can tell nobody.

Then the teacher, he a man, he come in
the office. He wearing a suit with one tie.
The principal, he sweating already so he wipe his glasses.
The teacher, he a real worm. He tie the cheerleader
to a chair. He tell her, *Don't be scared,*
and he gag her mouth.

Then the principal, he take off her shirt
and she crying. Her eyes all black underneath
from her eyeliner. Then he take off her bra and the teacher
suck her. For *real.* I *saw* um. *Don't cry,* he say
or we're going to have to tell your father what you did,
the principal say.

Jimmy boy hand go on my leg and he look at me long time.
I no look at him. *I like do that to you,* he tell.
Mugs, he laugh and make his eyebrows go up and down
at Jimmy boy. *Me and Mugs, maybe.*
Come my house with us in the back by the shed,
he say. *I going do that to you.*

I try to get up for buy popcorn or use the bathroom
or something. But Jimmy boy grab my wrist
and hold me down to the seat. *You sit right here,*
he tell. *So you can learn.* I shut my eyes.
Had four more cheerleaders.

Rites

by Terry Wolverton

She used to like to take me to the graveyard, half-daring me to be afraid, but of course, I would never resist her, my dark-eyed Valkyrie, two years older than me. She was seventeen and I thought she owned the whole world, owned it and cast it aside, finding it beneath her standards.

Her name was Leah, and she lived on her own, no mother or father, apparently for years. Her body thin and angular, sharply jutting bones, planes you could cut yourself on. Maybe that's why she wasn't afraid of anything.

She used to pick me up at school, waiting on the street astride her black motorcycle just before sixth period. I had a class sixth period—History—but I wouldn't keep her waiting; I'd pass through those doors, leaving history behind, and settle myself on the seat in back of her, not daring to look left or right, not wanting to read the faces of my peers.

She didn't have any peers, didn't care what anyone thought. She used to like to take me to the graveyard; we'd sail past those iron gates like two dark birds mating in flight, plunge deep along the path beside the silent gravestones.

After the first time, she always made me pick the site. I'd walk among the monuments while she leaned against the bike, watching. She never said anything, no matter what I chose, but I was always nervous, wanting to please her, wanting to make the right choice.

Myron Springer 1917–1974

Alicia Corland Dyson, Beloved Mother, b. 1912 d. 1968

Bradley Miller 1952–1959

Once I found a spot I'd sit down on the grassy rise of earth, nestling into a cushion of fresh flowers or a rustle of dried leaves. She'd strut over then and stand above me. I'd stare up at the sharp white corners of her collarbone, visible in the open triangle of her shirt. "Take off your clothes," she'd tell me, neither gently nor meanly, and she'd watch, carefully but without hunger, as I discarded my sweater, my plaid skirt, my loafers and knee socks. "Everything," she'd instruct me further, until I reluctantly yielded my bra and panties.

Then she'd have me stretch myself prone on top of the grave. I'd lie in the grass, feeling the wind over me, the earth beneath, and deeper still, the spirit in its house below the ground. I wondered what it thought, if it could think at all. I never saw what we did as desecration or sacrilege; she was the object of my worship then, and if she asked, it was mine to do.

Sometimes she would stretch out full beside me, and run her hands over every part of me until I gasped. Sometimes she would work me with her teeth, sharp, voracious. Sometimes she would not touch me at all, only talk to me about what she would do if she were to touch me, while I moaned and begged for her. One time she turned me over on my stomach and lay her whole body atop mine, thumping my ass with the stiff denim of her crotch. "Come on baby, fuck the corpse," her breath hissed in my ear, and I felt the taut embrace of bone.

At night, at home, alone in the white bathtub, far from the murmurs of my parents and the television downstairs in the living room, I used to love to search my body for the signs she left, the dark bruises on my hip, scratches on my thigh, teeth marks just above my breast. Neck-deep in the steaming water, I'd remember the mound of the grave beneath me, her dark mystery spread above, the cloying scent of lilies overpowering me still.

Edge

by Ronder Thomas Young

M r. Cordovan talked, from one bell to the next, sure and shimmering, with dancing fingers. He did not write with chalk.

Mr. Cordovan never returned our papers; we took them from his desk on our way out the door. "Nice work," he said to me. "You think like a man."

I smiled into third period.

"World too much for you?" He found me crouched in the supply room.

I claimed the close spaces. Closets and corners. "Not nearly enough," I said.

He smiled a new smile, smug and surprised at the same time, with the left side of his mouth up, the right side down. I gave him my hand. He gave me sanctuary. Everyone was at the pep rally, so the halls were empty. We did it on his desk. "You are a most logical female," Mr. Cordovan told me.

One night, when he let me out of his car at the bus stop two corners from my house, he said, "You're too beautiful to be so accommodating." He laughed, sure and shimmering.

In the summer Mr. Cordovan died by hanging, leaving me, no matter how hard I tried, more skeptical than sad.

I went far north for college. I tunneled with Nickie, he moved back through me, and it may have been love. Winters were long enough for reinvention. Springs were explosive and distinct. He strayed. He panicked. He wrapped his arms around my legs. He cried. He promised. I looked down on his voluptuous curly hair and touched it, surprised, as always, by its softness.

I dropped down to him. "It's okay," I said. "I forgive you." Nickie's eyes, more than sorry, scared, pushed away jealousy and hurt and anger, but an uglier thought whispered in my ear. "I really have you now."

And I did. And at the same time, I had a reason to leave when I was ready. If it was love, it was not enough.

Mr. Cordovan was a wonderful teacher. "How best to achieve power?" He folded his arms. "To seize it?" He paused a beat; the class looked around for a cue. "Or to have it given to you?" He raked his hair back off his forehead and sat down with a book. I don't remember what it was, but I do remember that it was a serious and important title.

We waited.

He would not look up for the next fifty minutes. He did say, "One thousand words. By tomorrow. Get started." This was inappropriate procedure for the high school classroom, but Mr. Cordovan taught electives, not requirements, and we were all there because he impressed the hell out of us. He could get away with it.

"Seize it," I wrote, "but make them think they gave it to you." It was all drivel after that, but it was enough for Mr. Cordovan. "You think like a man," he said.

Now I see that, no, it was a woman's thought. A compromise. A this, but on the other hand, that statement. It was the language, the bluntness, the directness, that confused him. It was the yes, but state of mind that allowed me to live. Mr. Cordovan died by hanging when he was twenty-seven years old. Too soon.

I remember his long fingers unzipping his pants. He watched them, then looked up at me, sitting, amazed and ready, on his teacher's desk. "On school grounds," he said. "You really have me now."

I called Harriet my best friend in high school. I told her about how I wet the bed when I was nine years old, on a sleep-over, and how I elaborately corrected my mistake. I told her my knees were too fat and my toes too long and that I liked her hair better than mine. I did not tell her about Mr. Cordovan, because I didn't understand what I was doing well enough to phrase it, because I was embarrassed by the secret sounds I made and odd instructions I followed.

I was only delaying my confession. I wanted Harriet for my best friend, but then Mr. Cordovan died by hanging, and I was trapped, on the other side.

When I was twelve I was hit by some vague adolescent guilt, some nagging seasonal depression. "A fine idea," my father said, the first Christmas Eve he drove me to the Searchlight Mission to serve meals. The next year he was less certain. "I suppose you feel," he asked, "a commitment?" The third year I went on Thanksgiving Day as well; that annoyed him. A week before Christmas a man died in a knife fight at the mission, and my father didn't want me to go at all. "You need to get this out of your system," he said. Still, he and his friends raised their glasses to me. "My daughter," he announced, "the angel of mercy."

Harriet went with me once. "They smell. They don't smile," she said. "How do you do it?"

"It's a habit," I said.

"It's a high, isn't it?" Mr. Cordovan said, when I told him. "The spit of the depraved, right in your face."

Mr. Cordovan knew.

Harriet said if she were patient, like me, she'd still be with Jeff. I studied Harriet and Jeff. The screaming on the phone. The slamming of car doors. Perhaps, I thought, noise meant love, but in the end it was as ugly as it sounded.

I couldn't tell Harriet about on the desk, in the car, crushed against the wall, in the last stall of the boy's toilet on the second floor, because she would have expected me to save Mr. Cordovan.

Good. Logical. Patient and serene. "You're an angel," Nickie said, pushing my head down. "A wonderful girl," my father's friends murmured, lifting their eggnog. Words, shimmering and sure, over and over, rose up and around me.

"Your hair shines," Nickie said, "like a halo." "Your skin," Harriet said, "is so clear and white, I bet it would glow in the dark."

The third year I was in college I went home for Christmas and stayed too late in Harriet's basement apartment, drinking wine and dreaming, to drive home. I slept with my feet on her coffee-table box, back pressed into the sofa end, arms open, all night. The next morning I drank tea while Harriet heated her mother's Christmas dinner leftovers on the stove. "I woke up early," she said. "I was still tired, you know, but awake." Harriet had slumped in a corduroy armchair. "And I watched you." She looked down and pressed her finger into a piece of quiche. Warm enough, she decided, and pushed it over to me. She sat down. "And for just this moment, I felt—" She raked back her hair; I saw Mr. Cordovan. "I was in love with you."

I chewed. I wondered exactly what mix of cheeses her mother used.

"It passed, you understand. I just thought I should tell you. It was so distinctly weird."

I looked around the little apartment with my cheeks still full, consciously, to lighten the moment. "You need better lighting in this place," I said. And I patted her hand across the table. Once, and quickly, but I did it.

Harriet told others I was one of her all-time favorite people because I was so serene, because I transcended her raving. Or, I asked, am I so distant? So alien? Of another place?

"Don't you think," Harriet would ask people, "that her skin glows in the dark?"

Ten years from the spring of Mr. Cordovan I ride from the city on a Friday afternoon, swaddled in a big scarf, pushed far into the corner of Ben's convertible.

I know Ben from work. Perhaps it's too soon to be here, but he has set me up and arranged me. He has passed my desk and played me well with the words and smiles and dark, self-effacing charm. Perhaps I've grown impatient and taken my place too soon, but still, it is my place.

Long fingers of one hand move up and down, with the radio music, on the steering wheel. Another hand lingers on my shoulder, in my hair, moving down. "Angel hair," he says.

The knife is small. I have used it twice to clean plastic from the necks of wine bottles. I stick his lavender shirt and resistant flesh, low, right above the waist. He swats instinctively, as if at an insect. The red plastic handle dangles in his pinpoint cotton. There's not much blood.

"Jesus Christ!" Ben's certain face surprises me. Slow to the curb, reach over to open and push me out.

Sidewalk strangers rush me. I look up to send the spit of the depraved right into their faces, but they tilt their heads, they reach their hands toward me. They know, they can see, what has happened. Ben is out of his car, his certainty reduced to confusion.

Mr. Cordovan pulled the buttons on my white shirt, one by one, back through their holes. "Over the edge," he said, moving the long fingers up, then down the two sides of my face, his skewed smile shimmering. "And, yet, not nearly far enough."

Betrayal

by Rebecca Baggett

I'm not sure what to say to you. The truth, you told me. But the truth is that my life with Richard was an unmitigated hell. And no one will believe that. Everyone thought he was such a nice guy. And so did I, before I married him.

He used to tell me how stupid I was, too dumb to be guiding anyone, what would the board of education think if they knew I couldn't even remember to record a check or to buy the right kind of razor blades. If I left a cup out or a book on the sofa, he'd go on for hours about how filthy the house was, how it looked like a pigsty, what a slut I was, a sloven, how he'd never have married me if he'd known.

He was too clever to use physical abuse—at least, not the kind that leaves marks. But sex with him was a kind of abuse: he never did anything to get me ready for him, just pushed into me and—raped me. Rape is what it was. And every night, every night in the week. Sometimes twice.

Bobby was so clean. That was the first thing that attracted me to him. I liked the way his hair always looked just washed, and his shirts were so bright and fresh. And even when he rode his board to school and came in sweating, it was a good, clean scent.

He isn't quite as tall as I am. I keep telling him he'll grow; he hasn't finished growing yet, but I don't really think he'll be tall. I don't mind. I'm not very big myself, and I like it that he doesn't tower over me, that his hands are the same size as mine. That's the other thing I liked. His hands. His clever, clever hands. Brushing against my fingers when he came to my office, resting for a minute against mine.

There wasn't much blood. Dian said there wouldn't be, if I did it right. She was worried, see, because they just put these Oriental rugs in the dining room, and she thought if he ran that way I might have to do it in there. But he didn't run.

It was funny, the way his face changed when I brought out the gun. Up till then, he was impatient, like he thought I was selling candy bars or raffle tickets door-to-door, money for the band or something. And I could see he didn't want to be rude, but he didn't want to buy nothing, either.

So he opened the screen door a little bit, kind of leaning out from behind the main door, and I pulled the gun from under my jacket and said, "Open it." For a second, I thought he might slam it instead, but he did it, he opened the door. His mouth was hanging half-open, and he kept looking all around the carport, but there wasn't nothing to see. Denny was out front with our skateboards, sitting on the curb. I'd been planning to have him come up to the door with me, in case we had trouble with Rich, but he was looking so chickenshit that I decided no. One look at his face, and Rich would've known something was up for sure.

I could hear the dog, breathing in the dining room. Every time I'd been over, it was sleeping in there, right by the window, where the sun made the rug warm. I hoped it would stay asleep. Dian was nuts about that dog; she didn't want it scared.

The reason Rich hadn't opened the door all the way was he wasn't wearing pants, just blue boxer shorts under a white dress shirt. Probably he'd thought it was Dian at the door, forgetting her keys or something.

"What do you want?" he was saying. "Money? You don't have to hurt me. There's money in—"

I told him to shut up. I was scared he'd wake the dog. I made him kneel down on the linoleum, and I put the gun against the back of his head. My hand was shaking a little bit, but I was behind him, so he wouldn't see. Some of it was nerves, but some was excitement, too. I hadn't known it would be exciting. I had a hard-on, and I was having trouble breathing.

"I don't—" he said, but I nudged the muzzle against his ear, and then he shut up. I told him to close his eyes. I didn't want her finding him with his eyes wide open.

"Oh, Jesus," he said. There was this soft, splashing sound. I looked down, and there was a puddle spreading on the floor, around his knees.

I wanted to stretch it out a little, but Dian told me to do it quick and get out.

"Don't," he said. He was breathing in little gasps, like he'd been running. "Don't—"

And I shot him.

First thing I did was take his wallet. There was fifty dollars in it; I took that and left the plastic. Then I took out my handkerchief and wiped the wallet off and dropped it beside him. I wiped the door handles and the edges of the door, where I might have touched. The dog hadn't even woke up, because of the silencer, I guess, or maybe it was just deaf. That was a relief—I'd been afraid I'd have to kill it, too, and then Dian would be pissed off but good.

I went to the counter and started turning things over, with my handkerchief around my fingers, one canister after another, until I got to the one with the wad of twenty-dollar bills in it. I didn't look at Rich again. I put the money in my pocket and closed the door behind me.

Denny was sitting on the curb. He looked up, but he didn't say anything, just handed me my board. We took off, fast, but not so fast we'd look suspicious. Just a couple of kids, hurrying to be home in time for supper.

We stopped a couple of blocks from Denny's house. I felt inside my pocket for the roll and peeled off five twenties. He started to say no, but then he held out his hand. I laid the bills in it, and he asked if I wanted to come on to his house. I said not now. My dick was still throbbing inside my pants, and I wanted to get to school, to Dian.

It was after six when I got there. Even the janitors were gone. She was in her office, with papers all over her desk, like she was writing up a report. When I tapped on the door frame, she jumped a mile.

She locked the door. Her face was white. When I told her how it went, she started laughing, this breathy laugh that sounded like Rich's breathing, at the end. Then she started touching me. By this time, I had the biggest boner of my life. I pushed her up against the desk and pulled down her panties and fucked her like crazy, her half-sitting on the desk, with her legs wrapped around my waist. It was just like *Fatal Attraction*—you know, the part in the kitchen?

I was wishing we had her camcorder. I'd've liked to have a tape of us, but she'd never let me do it. And then I started thinking I'd've liked to have a camcorder running when I shot Rich. You do something big like that, you ought to have some way to remember it. Thinking about it gave me another hard-on, so we did it again. Dian was bending over the desk, messing up all those stacks of papers, and I was rubbing her and talked dirty. She really likes it when I talk dirty to her.

He liked pretending we were making movies. Or that we were the actors and actresses. Glenn Close and Michael Douglas. John Malkovich and Michelle Pfeiffer. William Hurt and Kathleen—no. Not that one. No.

And he let me tell him what I liked. If something felt good, or if it didn't. He liked seeing me excited. And he liked to talk to me. I never really listened, so I don't know what he said. Now I wish I had. Maybe I'd have known then, what he was planning to do.

It was really dumb of me to tell Denny. I was thinking that it might be harder than it was, that I might need help. And that it would look more natural, if anyone remembered, two kids riding skateboards down the street. But Rich didn't give me no trouble, and it turns out none of the neighbors was even home when I did it. So it was really dumb. I see that now.

Dian was upset when I told her. That was two days after the funeral. I came by her house in the middle of the afternoon. Her folks had already flown home to Illinois, and Rich's had gone back to New York, so she was alone. She didn't want to let me in at first. She said the neighbors might wonder. But I started telling her about Denny, and then she told me to come in. I looked once, quick, at the kitchen floor. I don't know what I expected to see. There wasn't even a mark.

She sat in the corner of the sofa, and I told her. Her eyelids got all pink, like she was about to cry. I sat down beside her and put my hand on her leg. She said no, it wasn't safe. The curtains were closed, and everything looked dim and wavy, like we were under water. I promised her Denny'd keep his mouth shut. I promised her nothing would happen. I told her I'd been crazy, thinking about her. She took my hand and put it between her legs. She wasn't wearing any panties, so I knew she'd been hoping I'd come over, hoping this would happen.

I got down on the floor and pushed her dress up and licked her there until she thrashed around and pulled my hair and whimpered. Then I made her get down on all fours, and we did it like that. Right on her living room rug.

I looked toward this table beside the sofa, and there was Rich, staring straight at us from a silver picture frame. He looked just like I remembered— very straight and a little stupid and a whole lot surprised to see me fucking his widow on his Oriental rug. I looked right into those stupid, surprised eyes, grinning, and I came.

I told him after the funeral that we'd have to stop. That if anyone found out, we'd be suspected for sure. And then he told me he did it.

I couldn't believe it. I'd felt so safe. At night, I'd walk from room to room, touching everything—the china, the books, the furniture, the rugs, even the *walls*—and I'd think how nothing bad could ever happen to me again.

I let Jin sleep on the bed with me, from the first night on. He was Richard's dog before we were married, but he always loved me best. Since Richard was— since Richard died, Jin shies away from that spot in the kitchen. I have to feed him in the laundry room.

I couldn't believe it. Bobby. And his friend. Denny Moore. I knew him from school—a reedy boy with thin shoulders and nervous eyes. I'd seen how he looked at me. I couldn't believe Bobby had told him.

She said it wasn't safe anymore. Especially with Denny knowing. She said maybe we could start again in a year or two. After I graduate. What a laugh! She tried to look sad, but I could tell she wasn't really.

I started yelling at her. I said what'd she think I did it for? So we could be together. So we could be together whenever we wanted, like she'd promised me.

I said she wanted somebody else, was what it was really, wanted some old man with a real job and money to burn, who could take her to fancy restaurants and buy her things.

She started to cry. She put her head on my chest and said she didn't feel safe, she was afraid of Denny knowing, afraid he'd tell.

I told her Denny wasn't going to tell anybody. I told her she could count on me.

She was still crying, but all pressed up against me, with her mouth moving on my throat. And in a minute, she unzipped my pants and put her hand inside.

I was horrified when I heard he'd tried to kill that boy. I can't reconcile what's been happening with the Bobby I know—that sweet, gentle, loving boy I knew. Or thought I knew. I suppose we can never know anyone, really. The Bobby I loved would never have lied about me. Never.

I feel so terribly betrayed.

You know what this is like, don't you? This is like that movie, with William Hurt and Kathleen Turner, the one where she makes him think she loves him, and the whole time she's planning to lay the rap on him. That's what I keep thinking of.

It's not that I want her hurt. But it isn't fair, you know? For me to take it all. It isn't fair.

I keep thinking about that movie. And the way Dian held on to me, that afternoon on the sofa, all soft under me, and her mouth moving against my ear. Usually, like I said, I did the talking, but that day it was her, and she kept saying, "You won't let me down, will you, Bobby? You won't betray me. I won't let you betray me."

And I guess this is what she meant.

To Give Our Bodies Away

by Amber Coverdale Sumrall
(for R. H.)

There was no moon and its absence
brought stars closer: fiery arrows
shooting through darkness, the night
we parked on the bluffs near Malibu,
as we had so many nights that summer
to escape the heat that lay
like an Indian blanket over the valley.
We talked of our lovers, of how we wanted
this friendship to be enough.
Hungry for what might change us
we passed the pipe, listened
to the high wail of coyotes in the foothills.
Below us black waves sucked the cliffs
spraying white foam into air.
When I took you in my arms
grief loosened its knot in your chest.
For the first time you spoke
of your Apache mother: her drinking,
her rage, the pain that slashed
her life to shreds.

I held you tighter than I'd ever held anyone,
your long feathered hair damp with tears,
your silver cross pressing into my breast
leaving its mark.
Outside, wind rocked the car and howled
like some desert animal dying.
A month later I would walk away
from you in Emergency and the image of your blood
forced into places it did not belong.
It is your sorrow I remember after all these years:
how you curled into it, a long embrace
you could not pull away from.

Momma Don't Know Love

by Vicky Phillips

I

Momma on the front porch, talking at me. Her lips flying like bird wings. Momma talk and talk and talk. Momma got words for me this morning. Momma like a preacher with her words. So I stick my fingers in my ears and wiggle them about. My head sound like the river running, and I listen to the river, not Momma, because Momma don't know love.

Momma says love is like her Jesus, flung like a chicken across that old cross. Momma says love means you'd die just to show you're serious about whoever it is you're loving or trying to be loved by.

Momma says. Momma says. Momma says.

Momma got no teeth. Words fly in Momma's mouth like crazy blackbirds. But Momma don't know love. I know love. It ain't nothing like she says. And it don't come from no dead man either.

II

When I first saw Love I dropped to my knees and went after Him. I crawled through the brush on my knees, like Momma trying to get one of Old Man Weddle's chickens to come rest its neck on her chopping block. I went after Love, and we wrestled around in the bushes for a long time before I let Him know who I was and that I meant to have Him. Then I made Him swell up in his pants, and I took Him up between my legs, and sweet Jesus that was good love.

71

III

Momma says that ain't love. She says my kind of love is what happens in the body, and she ain't got no decent name to call it. She says I better stop my kind of love before I end up with a reputation and no love at all, not even for myself. Momma says my kind of love will pass like water if I just pray.

Momma squeezes my head and throws me on her mattress. Momma says pray. Momma slaps the back of my head and knocks loose some words for Jesus. Momma says pray.

When Momma slaps me down I pray for her.

Pray. Pray. Pray.

Momma goes to the grocery. I climb on her mattress and spread my legs and give that tin Jesus what hangs on the wall a real good look at my kind of love.

Momma says close your legs and run over to the church and pray. But I can't keep my legs together long enough to get to the church and speak with her Jesus. And her Jesus, he's like everybody nowadays. He don't make no house calls. No sir-ree. No house calls for my momma's gentleman Jesus.

IV

Dark, like Momma's mouth when she opens it to scream about my kind of love. I roll like dust through the house, out the door. I go out looking for my kind of love.

Love, He's got lots of names. But I don't ask His earth name no more. I just smile at Him and say, "Come on baby, and do what needs to be done."

And He don't say yes, or no, or use words at all. He just flops out a pair of hands and walks my body like I'm his private road to somewhere. He does like I say, because all He wants is His piece of my kind of love.

Come Sunday He'll go on over to the church and get a piece of what that dead gentleman has to offer, but right before, and right after, and sometimes right along with that Jesus love, He is thinking about my kind of love.

My love got nipples and wide swinging hips. My love can be touched and had, right here, right now, in the slippery cold, red clay of Talmage County, Tennessee. My love is something He can get at with His hands. And my love don't have no pretty words to make it stink.

V

Momma and me in the kitchen. Windows all black. Still night. Momma gives me a thick white cup of breakfast coffee. Momma says if Daddy was alive he'd tie me up and beat my kind of love right out of me. I say Momma don't know me. She don't know Daddy. And she don't know love.

Momma smacks my face with her hot cup. Makes me squawk like a chicken got the hot eye. Momma plucks the hair from my neck. Pokes my eyes with wiry white fingers. Jumps on my back and drums my head with her hands. Momma says she'll make me a retard if I don't get on my knees and pray to her Jesus.

Momma says, Say you're sorry. Say you're sorry.

VI

Just me, rolling on the old bed. Bed sounds funny . . . like some animal about to cry. I'm thinking about my daddy and his kind of love. Daddy is gone—to hell, some say . . . to heaven, Momma says—but I remember my daddy. My daddy was a lot like Betty Gossymeyer's daddy down the Sand Creek Lane. Our daddies liked our kind of love.

Momma says Daddy never wanted such love. Momma beats her head and says such love never has happened in Talmage County. Momma at my door kicking it crazy. Momma says no, no, no.

I say Momma better go to her room. Better get that tin Jesus above her bed to tell her the love it's seen. Because Momma don't know love.

VII

I come bursting in, my teeth all caked with man juice. My hair all wild from a night of rolling joy. I been with Him. I laugh and laugh so Momma will wake up and hear how much I been enjoying my kind of love.

Momma's lips fly like blackbirds. Momma winds up her arms. Chases me around the furniture.

Momma says these men just having a good time at my expense, just having a good time before going home and acting proper with their own little Mary Janes. Momma says she ain't got no decent name to call my kind of love. Momma says I'm Jezebel and Delilah and Sheba.

These women got pretty names. Names like water pushing the mill wheel around. Names like bugs gone crazy in the long grass. I say I like the sound. I say, call me Jezzie, Momma.

VIII

Just me, like a bug spun to its back on Momma's front porch. Momma inside, washing dinner dishes. Faucet screeches when Momma slap it on. Momma washing the dishes, banging pans, singing to the ceiling about her kind of love.

My belly swelling like white cake in Momma's oven. Belly like the big head of a bald man. Belly smooth, and cold, and white. Belly like the winter moon.

Momma says this baby bad. This baby grow up and be ugly like all my sins. I say this baby is my kind of love. This baby what her Jesus give me to love. This love come sliding out from my own insides. My kind of love come out with hot blood. My kind of love come out stinking with life. Till this baby come, I'm just waiting to be in the life. Till this baby come, I got nothing but my own flesh and what Momma says to make me know love.

And Momma, she knows her gentleman Jesus, but she don't know love.

Getting Out

by Louise A. Blum

My mother hits the brakes and pulls over. The side of the road is wide, gravel; the fields loom around us like a wasteland, no one in sight. "Get out," she says.

I am seven years old. The field is like hell, the Hades that my father talks about when he quotes the Old Testament. I look at her. Her eyes glitter at me, Nazi German blue. "Get out," she says again.

The gravel from the shoulder whips into my face when she speeds off, flung from the tires. I watch her fade away. Around me the field hums, caught in its solace. The sun beats down against my head. I think that I could grow to like it, this sanctuary that has been forced on me.

An hour later she comes back. I am still there, eating grass. "Get in," she says, and I comply.

We drive in silence for a while, the fields ticking by.

"Well," she says. "Have you learned your lesson?"

I look out the window. The telephone poles flash by. Here and there a bird nests on the wires. Grasshoppers sing as the sun grills down, frying them where they sit, vigorously sawing. I imagine myself running alongside the car, effortlessly, full of breath, tireless, while the sun buoys me up like an inner tube. Beside me, my mother keeps her eyes on the road. Have I learned my lesson? Yes.

I glance over at her. Her profile in the sunlight is sharp, full of edges that sparkle in the light. Her hands are loose on the wheel. She has it together. She keeps the car on the road with a touch of her fingertips. "Pull over," I say. "Let me back out."

She keeps driving, eyes on the road, but her knuckles are white. I've rattled her. I sit back in my seat, eyes on the fields that flash past my window, satisfaction a small round presence in my stomach.

My lover touches my hair, my brow, runs her finger across my lips, lightly, barely making contact, a shadow of a touch. I reach up and touch her hair, pull her face to mine. I slip my tongue into her mouth and taste her saliva. Her body against mine is a celebration, a treasure, a sifting of smells and sounds and feels. I push my hips against her and roll her over, press her head to the pillow with my mouth against hers, hear her moan. I run my fingers down her throat, across her breasts, lightly touch the nipples that swell beneath my fingertips, plunge them down into the hair that flows between her legs, part her lips and slip my fingers into her, rock against her gently, while her fingers on my shoulders grip so hard they leave a bruise.

My mother runs a comb through my hair, parting the snarls like jungle brush. She sighs, shakes her head. "So many wisps," she says. She pulls my hair back from my forehead with the teeth of the comb, examines my face in the mirror. My face is small and round and dark, small caverns dent my cheeks, the hair around my forehead is dark and wild, unruly. My mother sighs, her lips pursing together in the mirror above my head like a too tight stitch. "If I were you," she says, in her voice a deep and tragic resignation, "I'd have electrolysis done when I get older."

I am still seven years old. It's taking a long time, this growing up, and somewhere outside the window that field stretches like an unrolled ball of yarn, waiting for me, stretching on in gentle curves forever.

Ruth rolls toward me in the bed, spoons against me from behind, reaches around and holds me to her. She is shorter than I am, her breasts are larger; they spill across the sheets like fruit in a market stall. Her hips swell from her, the mound of hair rises from between her legs like an exclamation point. I can feel it against me now; I push against her, roll toward her. Her body in the bed next to mine is a soft warm rush of liquid, golden in the morning sunlight that spills across the sheets. When I touch her, I feel a power in my hands that nearly frightens me. She is mine. All mine.

My mother tells me I will never have a boyfriend. "You'll be just like me," she says, rubbing my back in the bed. "It's better to have small breasts," she says. "Really."

I do not ask why, lie with my face in the pillow and concentrate on breathing evenly, in and out like the bellows that my father sometimes pumps the fire with. Her hand rubs my back in smooth, even circles, stops when she gets distracted and rests on my body like an anvil, growing heavier as the seconds go by.

"You're so thin," she says. I can hear that distraction in her voice, like she's about to float up and bump against the ceiling. "Men don't like their women thin."

I breathe as slowly as possible, in and out, in and out, try to slow it, take breaths only when they're absolutely necessary. I pretend they cost money. Protect them, save them, dole them out only on occasion. Perhaps she'll think I'm dead, draw the sheet slowly up across my face, leave the room, leave me in peace. I open my eyes and stare straight ahead, into the darkness of the room, like the bodies I have seen on television, facing their eternity.

But she has recommenced with the rubbing. There is no escape. This is our together time, hers and mine. Necessary time, like a jail sentence. Someday I'll get out, break loose and float off into the sky like a helium balloon, fall over an ocean and choke a duck.

Her hand pauses, her fingers scrape against my skin. I tense despite myself, my tiresome attempts at even breathing. "Your skin has little balls on it," she says, shaking them from her fingers in distaste. "I don't know what's wrong with you."

I lie in the darkness after she has left, close my eyes and think about my field in the distance, peppered with dandelions, circled by hawks, here and there the trunk of a tree, thick and firm and wider than my arms when I embrace it; my fingers do not meet.

Ruth and I go for drives in the countryside on summer nights. We roll the windows down on my dark blue truck with the pink triangle on the back, let our hair blow in the wind, feel the scent from the flowering trees on our lips, turn the radio up loud, blast the landscape with Melissa Etheridge, the Indigo Girls, Michelle Shocked and k. d. lang and her unabashed country. I have a big, big love. I reach across the bench seat for her hand, squeeze it between my fingers. My mother is so far off now it is like she doesn't even exist. God be praised for small escapes.

I drop my foot against the accelerator like stamping out a roach and gun the truck down the country roads as if it were a chariot. It is early evening; the fields around us are full of fledgling corn, the sun is dropping through the sky, leaving a swath of light as golden as the fields that stretch on either side. I look at Ruth, her long hair whipping back from her face like a scarf. She is singing to the radio, moving her body in time to the music. Her shoulders are bare, touched only by the setting sun. Her breasts are barely contained by her tank top. She looks back at me. Her eyes are dark as stones.

"Hey," I say, seeing her eyes, burning in the dying light. "Do you want to fuck?"

We pull over so fast we nearly take out a row of corn, fall onto the ground together in the middle of somebody's field, fucking like dogs in the dust that still rises from the road, rises and spreads and forms a cloud around us, shielding us from view as the sun dips down into the fields and the sky grows darker all around us.

My mother tells me I'll never have a boyfriend, but when I see Johnny Martin across the playground at the beginning of third grade I know that he's the one. I don't even say anything to him, just start running, picking up speed all the way across the rock-hard pavement so that when I get to him I leap and grab his body somewhere around his waist. My momentum carries us both into the chain-link fence that holds us in; we roll against it and its clang brings the other kids running. They surround us as I straddle him, holding him tight between my thighs and pressing my mouth to his, ignoring the blood that is spurting from the scrapes on my elbows, just holding him to the ground and kissing him the way I've always seen them do on TV. The kids around us chant and cheer, but I ignore them, just go on kissing Johnny. He kisses back.

Ruth and I have lived together for nearly a year now; we've been lovers for nearly two. She bought me a drink in the local bar one night about six months after I'd arrived in town; her eyes caught mine in the darkness, her hair so long I can wrap it around my hand and use it to anchor her head while I kiss her till our lips are swollen and sore, that sweet pain you can never get enough of. I picked this town off the map, drove my truck in and slung my pack on the floor of a rented room over a dentist's office on Main Street. It had a bed, a chest of drawers. It was enough.

I got a job helping a vet during the week, helping fix cars on Saturdays. Ruth works in the library; she cards books and shelves them with her hair wrapped round her head like a turban. She wears full skirts, low-cut blouses, doesn't shave her legs. Her skin is dark and even. Her brows meet and she has a mouth that could suck me dry. When we moved in together, we found a house with a front porch. We scraped all the paint off and painted it yellow, planted tulip bulbs and roses around it. Ruth paints when she's not at work, uses one of the rooms as a studio, tacks big slabs of paper on the walls and covers them with paint. She uses huge strokes, vibrant colors. When she paints, a thin line shows up between her eyes and she catches her lip between her teeth. The muscles on her upper arm flex. She moves like a dancer, covering her canvas. I envy her her grace. Sometimes she paints me, takes off my clothes and spreads me out across the floor and bends me the way she wants me, makes me stay there without moving while she locks me to the canvas. When she shows me I am stunned—but it isn't me. This body she has created bears no resemblance to the one I see in the mirror when I undress at night, dress again in the morning. She is an artist; they do not replicate the world as it is. They have an edge that way. They have something on the rest of us.

When I am in junior high, I tell my mother I want to be a doctor. They make us dissect frogs in seventh grade. Sherry's frog is pregnant; black eggs spill like caviar across the wax paper they have spread across the table. Sherry has to leave the room. I feel sick, but I cannot take my eyes away. The teacher lets me stay after school to dissect the leftover frogs. I line their organs up, use their eyes to magnify a line of print. It feels like coming together, like things are making sense. The scalpel in my hand feels like it belongs there. I tell my mother with a sense of confidence, a sense of wonder. "I want to be a doctor," I say. "I know that I can do it. I know that it is what I want to do."

She is kneading bread on the kitchen counter; she has flour on her arms, across her face. She is concentrating, fold, push, turn, fold, push, turn. Her hair is pulled back from her face. Her upper arms are loose, flap away from the bone that stands out all over her like rock beneath the skin. She doesn't look at me, just keeps on kneading. Her concentration is endless, blocks me out. "I always thought you'd make a good secretary," she says, flouring her dough, pinning it to the counter with the heels of her hands. "With your grades," she says.

I choose auto mechanics instead. I like the cars; I like to lift their hoods and peer into their engines, touch my fingers to their grease, feel it like acid on my tongue when I lick my lips by accident, listen to their hum, diagnose their illnesses.

I go out with Johnny Martin all the way through high school. We wear leather jackets and smoke cigarettes under the pine trees out behind the vocational school, smoke joints in his room at night under the black light, surrounded by Dead posters. He has long black hair and half-shut eyes. When he touches me, his fingers flow like lines of poetry. I think I have made him this way. I think he is lucky I chose him, kicked his legs out from under him on a cement pad one afternoon in elementary school, straddled him and taught him how to love me while the wind whipped around us like a flag.

Ruth drags her easel into the bedroom, takes me by the hand where I sit reading on the couch. "Come with me," she says. She spreads me out across the bed, bends my knees and pulls my arms above my head, pulls back my head so that my throat is exposed. Her long hair brushes my stomach; I can feel myself growing wet. I catch her hand, direct it to my cunt. "Fuck me," I tell her. "Make love to me. Don't ever let me go."

She touches my cunt with her fingers, slips her middle finger deep inside me till I moan, close my eyes, till I feel she has touched the root of me, felt through to my core, till I can no longer contain myself, and my pelvis has become a machine, pulsing, pulsing, pulsing, till my rhythm has taken me over and I no longer know who I am, what makes me up. Ruth takes off her scarf, loops it around my wrists and knots it over the bedpost, drags her easel closer, paints with one hand while with the other she strokes my clitoris, goes so deep inside I nearly knock her over with my hips. The sun streaks into the room, floods us with light, fills us with a torment that is better than life, better than all that I know.

I stay with Johnny Martin all through high school; senior year he breaks up with me for a while, starts seeing someone else, a slender girl with a long neck and a doe's eyes and light brown hair that falls down her back like a tapestry. She's a junkie, wears leather miniskirts, a choke collar, but her eyes are full of fear, her face is open like a breaking dawn, like her name. Her lips are raw from the pull of her teeth. When I look at her I feel something stir inside my gut. I do not have a name for it. I go over to her house one night when I know that Johnny is out with his buddies, racing their motorbikes in some dark part of town. It's a guy thing; he never took me either, though he has me tune his car up, after. Dawn takes me up to her room; we sit on the bed and share a bowl, listen to the Moody Blues with the door shut and her parents downstairs with the television on, Archie Bunker's voice like a whining rasp through the floor, and she doesn't protest when I touch her face, doesn't say a word when I pull her toward me across the bed, touch her slender thighs with my fingers, push her skirt up toward her waist.

She's the best thing that ever happened to me. She is light and dark and every color in between. She is like a rainbow between my hands; her face when I make her come is like the face of an angel, lifted in transport, poised in prayer. She stretches her hands to the sides of the bed, arches her back and hangs on. Her tongue touches the side of her mouth and she closes her eyes with velvet lashes on her cheek. We do not have to talk. Her need is naked, enormous. It hangs between us, fills the air. It is all I have to know of her.

We spend hours together; she's always stoned, but she's pliable. Johnny's pissed, but so it goes. It's the parents that make the real scene. We keep it a secret for a while, make muffled love with the door closed and the radio on, but one night I have my head between her legs, probing her cunt with my tongue, in and out and in and out, and Dawn is lying on her back with her legs spread wide and when I look up at her she has her arm between her teeth, to keep herself quiet. This only makes me more excited; I run my tongue along her clitoris, plunge three fingers deep inside her. I come with her hand nowhere near me, I come in a long and shuddering rush that makes me gasp, makes the room revolve around me while with my fingers I work her orgasm like an engine valve and none of it seems real, we're not even on the planet anymore. Nothing seems to matter, and it seems to be in slow motion that she bites down too hard on her arm and nearly breaks the skin, jerks it away from her mouth and screams as if her soul were leaving her body, screams a series of screams that spill out of her like heartbeats and reverberate against the walls, fill the room, overflow and echo down the stairs, swelling through the house, bursting its seams, and we can hear the running footsteps coming toward us but we cannot stop, my fingers have taken on a life of their own, I keep pumping, pumping, pumping, and Dawn is gasping, moaning, her body moving like the beat of a song. It's out of our control; her left arm sweeps across her nightstand and knocks off everything on it, her clock, her birth control pills, her books, her junk, all crashing to the floor as she seizes for the bedpost and squeezes it until it seems that it will break, the teeth marks stark in her flesh like a brand, while with one smooth movement her father flings open the door and I bury my head in her cunt, hoping I will disappear, hoping it will take me in, suck me deep inside where I really want to go, swallow me forever.

"Jesus Christ," her father says. Dawn opens her eyes, sees him frozen in the doorway like an ice sculpture and kicks me in the teeth without even thinking about it, pushing herself to a sitting position. "Get out of here," her father says to me. I back away from the bed, checking to see if my jaw is still intact, wait for Dawn to say something, but she only brings her knees up to her chest and hides her face in her hands, covers herself with her hair, silver from the half-light coming in from the hall.

"Listen," I say, but her father cuts me off, orders me out of the house.

"Get out," he says. "You pervert." I make myself as tall as I can as I go past him out the door, summon all my body to me, but he does not look at me. His eyes are on his daughter, sobbing into her hands as if her heart will break. She doesn't look at me either; no one says another word. I walk down the stairs with this silence like blue light all around me; the house seems to be filling with it, slowly, freezing out the breath, obscuring everything from view. I open the front door and let myself out, walk down the driveway to my truck and open the door with fingers that shake, still wet with her come, that can barely fit themselves around the key that will get me out of here, get me away. It feels like there's a gun on my back. I don't breathe again until I'm on the road.

My mother is hanging up the phone when I walk into the kitchen. A fresh loaf of bread lies cooling on a wire rack on the counter, there's a warm breeze coming in from the window above the sink. The curtains ripple, twist slowly in the wind. She turns to face me, her hand still on the receiver; her breathing is hard and fast. Her look is deadly, her eyes hold me at knifepoint. "You," she says, spitting it out like bad milk. "You disgust me."

I walk to the counter, make myself breathe evenly, take up the bread knife and cut myself a piece of bread with hands still shaking, don't look at her as I take the butter from the refrigerator door. "Incidentally," I say, smoothing butter on the bread I hold in the palm of my hand. "You're right. I'll never have a boyfriend." I take a bite, force myself to chew with even bites. It's like trying to eat a matchbook, but I keep chewing anyway; when I swallow it feels like my tonsils are standing there with folded arms like bouncers, protecting my esophagus. I wear my nonchalance like butter; I am greased with it. "At least, not now," I say. I make myself look at her; she is standing perfectly still by the phone, her face is tight as a wire. It looks as if her cheeks will break. I look straight at her, straight at the eyes as blue as frozen water. "No man will ever be enough again."

My mother slaps my face but I slap her back, leave the imprint of my hand on the flour. It feels like God. It feels bigger than I am. It feels like everything I live for, everything I am inside.

She throws me out of the house and I throw my bag in the truck I bought from Johnny's dad. "Don't come back," she says.

"Don't worry," I say, "I'm out of here." I turn the key in the ignition; the engine fires like the answer to a prayer, the gearshift in my hand feels like salvation. I pull out of her driveway so fast I burn rubber turning onto the road. I drive first to Dawn's house but her parents don't let me in. It pisses me off, but she doesn't exactly come running out to greet me. I stand in the yard and yell up to her window, but the blinds are drawn and the curtains are still. I think they might have killed her in there, but just before I leave I glance back in the rearview mirror. Her window is open, just a little; she is watching me go. I touch the horn, wave out the window, leave her in her bedroom, where I imagine she is shooting up. We all do what we have to.

I go to Johnny's and we drive out to the river, sit there and smoke some hash his brother brought back from Vietnam. It is like cutting a swath through a jungle, the hawks overhead are like dynamite being dropped through the sky. We lean back on the bank and touch hands in the grass. All around us the trees are waving like regretful generals and the sound of the river is a rush in the darkness. We take a map from my glove compartment, close our eyes and touch down with a finger. He brushes the hair back out of my eyes, kisses my mouth. He gives me the rest of the hash and all the money he has.

I make good choices.

I squeeze his hand before I leave, fill up the bowl and lay the pipe on the seat beside me, take off slow down the road with the radio on low. I don't look back at him. I keep my eyes on the road; there's a field in the distance. I know I'll get to it.

My mother doesn't have my address. My mother doesn't know where I am. I drive through the night and then the day and then the next night, and I know when I drive into that town flushed full with the rising sun that this is it, flat, narrow streets and clapboard houses with wide front porches, kids with bikes on the sidewalks, dogs on runs in back yards, antique stores and one bar and a corner diner. I am so far away from my mother she is like a distant sunset. I can see her, waving her arms futilely as the earth sucks her down into its depths, her head visible for just a moment in a last gasp of dying breath before it disappears into the ground, the soil closing over her, burying her alive, on her own terms. I barrel into that town like a viceroy, empty of baggage except my one duffle bag bouncing around in the back of the truck. My hair is loose around my shoulders, my arms are brown from the sun, my hands on the wheel are tight and thin and strong. My jeans are frayed at the knees, tight at the ass. I am hell on wheels. I am a comet that shows up once every sixty years and you'd better fucking be watching, or you'll miss it all as it goes past.

Ruth and I are the talk of the town. We kiss on the front porch, hold hands on the street. We meet in the bar after work, sit at a table in the corner and drink shots of Jack Daniels with chasers of beer. We like our work—it has little to do with us, with who we are. She shelves books, I hold down kittens for shots, sweep up dog hair, ride out to the farms with the vet silent at the wheel beside me. Our knees touch beneath the table, our fingers touch where they rest around our glasses. The bar is dark; a few guys shoot pool. No one bothers us. I change their oil on Saturdays, give them pills for their dogs. I wear work boots and blue jeans. There is mud on my sweatshirt from wrestling down a calf that afternoon. Ruth beside me is dark and lithe; her hair spills down around her shoulders, she wears a sweater buttoned up to her neck, large amber earrings. I touch my finger to a wisp of hair along her brow, smooth it back. Beside us a pool cue cracks against a ball. Someone puts a dollar in the juke box, selects a song. Emmylou Harris floods the room. I pull Ruth to her feet without even thinking about it. We dance in the empty darkness, our heads touching, our arms around each other's waists, whiskey in our brains. There is a freedom in a small town—nobody bothers anybody else. No one really gives a shit, as long as you don't bother them. I put my hands on either side of Ruth's face, bend my face to hers. She sighs against me, tightens her hands around my waist. Times have changed.

Sunset comes late in summer, sends its rays along the streets like sentries, like scouts sent on to prepare the way. We sit on our front porch and drink scotch, rocking in our rocking chairs, not talking, just watching the light change, spill out into the air as if it were shaking itself out, preparing like a dog for sleep. The roses bloom around our front steps, a few mosquitoes hover in the air, fended off by the citronella candle that burns on the table between us. The night is quiet, the air calm. Our neighbors are asleep, at rest, quiet. Behind our house the fields stretch all the way back to the trees, green and golden and rolling with hills. We rock in our chairs with our heads back, let the night breeze touch our throats, ease through our hair. We rock in silence, through the night, and somewhere my mother moves through her life, locked into its confines, and no one will ever let her out, no one will ever slow down and pull to the side and open her door, because I have the key, safe in my hand, safe in my heart, buried deep within my cunt where even Ruth cannot go, and I will never give it up, never slow down and give her the chance. I close my eyes, reach for Ruth's hand, and together we rock, the silent air around us like a soft quilt, holding us together.

Proper Names

by Karen A. Tschannen

Today we have company for lunch. Roseanne has made tuna sandwiches and lemonade and set out flowered place mats and the good glasses on the dining room table. And folded four blue napkins into neat stand-up crowns from directions she found in my *Better Homes & Gardens Magazine*. Our table is Scandinavian teak, oiled to look rich. But here and there white flecks show where the veneer has separated along the grain. On the table a squat pitcher glazed deep blue is filled with bright yellow daffodils, so bright on this gray day they glow, small suns. Yesterday they were translucent, a tender new-spring yellow. Their yellow has deepened, become more dense, saturated, their scent pungent. Tomorrow I will discard them and clean the pollen dust from the blue mat where it collects like freckles.

Our young visitor, Andrea, poet at thirteen, says they are beautiful but doesn't know their name. She tells us with great passion that knowing the proper names of things is very important to a poet. "Daffodils," I say, "*Narcissus pseudo-narcissus*." She writes this down carefully in her poet's notebook. I think I will find daffodils in the next poem she brings us . . . or perhaps narcissus.

Was I ever that young? So young even the name daffodil was new? At thirteen I lived with a passion for horses. Once I could name each breed, their characteristics, the lineage of the famous. But I didn't know the names of common flowers then, city girl bounded by paved and numbered streets, only the untended rose bush of baby pinks wilding across our back fence. With my sister in the spring I picked each barely opened bud and made thorned wreaths to crown the classroom statues of the Virgin at Star of the Sea Grammar School. Oh, and the sweet peas! The fragile sweet peas we bought in mixed bunches from green plastic pots at Pinelli's Flower Shop on Eighth Avenue because they were lovely and pliable and cost little. We wove the fragile whites and lavenders into chaplets and offered them up each May Day in the great processional from school yard to church. *Oh Mary, we crown thee with blossoms today, Queen of the Rosary, Queen of the May,* we sang, and I prayed it would be my crown, *this* crown chosen for the Virgin. I was young then and passionate in my beliefs.

At thirteen my nipples started to itch and burn. At fourteen a boy named Robert Rosen put his tongue in my mouth. At fifteen I stopped dreaming of horses. At sixteen I ran away with a man who brought me flowers. He stroked me with long slow hands, called me his pony, his bud, his little calla lily. One day I woke up and he was gone. He left me a daughter but not his name.

My daughter at thirteen had twice read the complete Walter Farley *Black Stallion* series. For her piano recital at fourteen, she played MacDowell's "To a Wild Rose" with only one mistake. At fifteen a red-haired boy named Michael Canby brought her a corsage of gardenia and baby's breath. He kissed her good night at our front door. At sixteen, she ran away and lived with a man whose last name I never learned, a man who beat her. She named her daughter Roseanne and brought her home to live with me.

Desire

by Jennifer Tseng

this desire
is a kind of sleeping,
a kind of forgetting,
a lost childhood.
I see myself as a skin cave
dark, without details
you and I are there having tea
stirring the tea with our bones
each with our own bones

I would drink your reflection
but I cannot find the cup
I cannot find my hands.

The Suburbs of Eden

*Perspective, I soon realized, was a fine commodity,
but utterly useless when I was in the thick of things.*
—Ingrid Bengis

*If you can't be a good example, then you'll
just have to be a horrible warning.*
—Catherine Aird

Seduction

by Jeanne McDonald

Have I told you this story?

Even if I have, it bears repeating, because you might hear something you missed the first time. You might look at it from a new perspective.

It started in church. That's important, because this is a story about sacrifice and redemption. Sacrifice, yes. Women are used to that. But they endure. Men have taught us that. Over and over again they refuse us, they close their faces against us, they shake their heads and try to make us feel ashamed. But we endure. Otherwise, why would I have sat all those Sundays in the church pew, making promises to Jesus, my bones aching against the curved oak?

And Dennis would be up there in the pulpit, his skin stretched tight across his cheekbones like a fine, pale silk. Behind his blue eyes there seemed to be light glowing, and his voice was husky and compelling. He was all angles, his long body a cross-hatching of bones and hollows, but there was power there, too, and energy that electrified the congregation.

From the first row, I watched Dennis and bargained with God. *Just let him look at me*, I prayed. *Give me a sign. Just let him smile or say that he will drive up to the house to see Mother this week, and then I will have him to myself.* One day, as a bribe, I dropped into the pewter collection plate an unmarked envelope containing all the money I had saved that month from my teaching, everything I had left after paying for the groceries and Mother's medicine. *Please God let him love me, I will pay anything.*

"Let us speak today, my friends," said Dennis, "of the seduction of women." Lovingly, he stroked the worn cover of his Bible where the edges had softened and peeled from years of handling. "'And the rib, which the Lord God had taken from man, made he a woman, and brought her unto the man. And Adam said, This is now bone of my bones and flesh of my flesh: she shall be called Woman, because she was taken out of man.' "

Bone of my bones. A woman carved from bone.

When the preacher spoke the next line he looked directly at me. " 'And the Lord God said unto the woman, What is this that thou hast done? And the woman said, The serpent beguiled me, and I did eat.' " Blood pounded in my ears, but I stared back directly into his eyes. They were translucent, sapphire. I knew that the others were watching me—my mother, the other women, Clara. She was his fiancée—Clara Waters. It was different, though, the way she watched me. She seemed to know something. After church she stood beside Dennis at the door and held so tightly to his arm that he had to gently pry her fingers away in order to shake my hand.

"Shame, shame, Rebecca," my mother said as I helped her into the car that day. "People saw the way you were looking at him." The skin of her bony elbow was as soft and loose as velvet in my hand.

I closed her door carefully, making sure not to catch her long print skirt. "A preacher is a man, Mother, subject to the same passions as every other man." I started the motor and pulled out onto the dusty road.

"But he belongs to Clara," she said. "Or soon will. So don't go getting ideas. You'll only be hurt." She wrapped her lace scarf closer around her neck, though the air was parched. Her hands trembled a little as she adjusted the pin at her throat.

"He likes me, I can tell," I said. "Who else is there suitable for me in this town?"

She looked away. "If it weren't for me . . ."

"Don't start, Mother. Anyway, you'll soon be better." Both of us knew this was a lie, but we ignored it, letting it sit between us like an uninvited guest. We drove past the old church cemetery and the parsonage where Dennis lived. Though there were only woods and a field between his house and ours, it was miles around by the highway. If Mother had been stronger, we could have walked across the field to church.

For a while we rode wrapped in our separate silences, stitched in by the threads of our separate dreams. *For a long time now I have not dreamed.* Finally, we turned into the long road that led to our farm, where the oaks were floured with the fine grit of the dry summer. My mother's feeble hand against my knee was like a withered leaf. "How did you like the sermon today?"

I laughed. "The seduction of women. Was there ever a woman who wrote even a single verse of the Bible? Did any of them get to tell their side?"

Her eyes moved across the fields, as if they had found some memory there. "It's always been that way, Rebecca," she said. "Men want to keep us ignorant. What is it people say about a little knowledge?"

"It's dangerous," I said, "a dangerous thing."

The time the baby died, when I lived up north, my mother came to care for me.

She brought me a necklace of Tennessee pearls. They remind me of your teeth, she told me, you have such pretty teeth.

A dangerous thing. I knew about men. I knew the rush of a man's breath, his warm hands, the soft, flat pads of his fingers moving across my wrists.

Dennis came to the house one afternoon when my mother was asleep. I had drawn the heavy green blinds in the house just high enough so that the breeze could enter the rooms. Then I set the electric fan on the windowsill in Mother's bedroom and tiptoed out. She was already snoring, pulling the hot afternoon air across the roof of her mouth and down her throat. I was in the parlor, listening to a symphony on the radio, when a car pulled into the driveway. I looked out and saw the preacher coming up the walk. He was fanning himself against the unrelenting heat, but his fingers were cool when he shook my hand. His eyes moved quickly over my thin blue cotton sundress, my bare feet.

"Mother's asleep," I said, "but you can visit with me for a minute. Come into the living room, it's cooler." I opened the screen door, but he hesitated. "Don't worry," I said. "We're chaperoned. Everyone knows my mother is always at home."

He followed me in and sank down in the chintz-covered armchair. I sat across from him in the rocker, pulling my legs up under me and covering my knees with my skirt. With his fingertips, Dennis tapped the arm of the chair while he glanced around. He seemed afraid to look at me directly. Somehow he seemed smaller here in my house than he did in church. "I won't be staying if your mother is asleep," he said.

I leaned forward. There was something unyielding in him that made me want to test him. "Shall I wake her, then?"

"No, no," he said quickly, frowning. Despite the heat, he wore a black suit that was stained under the arms with dark half-moons of sweat. His blond hair clung to his smooth, broad forehead.

"A glass of tea, then," I said, untangling my legs. Though I didn't look back, I could sense that he was watching me as I walked into the kitchen. With Dennis in the house I was suddenly aware of the color and texture of everything, the grain in the bare wooden floor beneath my feet, the sharp, bitter smell of the lemon I sliced, the gritty scrape of the sugar against the silver spoon, my mother's soft snores.

When I carried in the tea, Dennis was standing at the bookshelf. Music from the symphony soared behind him. "Have you read all these?" he asked, sweeping his hand across the books. It was a question one of my pupils might have asked.

"Most," I said. I stared at him, and he turned away again. I liked looking at his profile, though he would have profited from a mustache, I thought. I brushed his arm as I reached over to tap the spine of a biography. "Most of these are my mother's."

He edged away from my arm and picked up a dark, leather-bound volume.

"Flaubert. Strange books for a farmer's wife."

"She wasn't always a farmer's wife," I said. "She went to the university. When Grandfather died she came home and married my father."

"And you?" He walked over to the window, pulled aside the blind, and peered out over the fields. I studied the angular slant of his shoulders, the straight line of his nose.

"A tenant farmer works this land," I said. "I wasn't meant for farming." Dennis let the blind fall back into place. We stood so close, he could have touched me, and no one would have seen. His eyes swept the room, the books, the paintings. He looked everywhere but at me. "How long did you teach up north?"

"Twelve years," I said. "I'm older than you, if that's what you want to know." The fan sputtered. Blood thrummed in my ears.

Color flooded his cheeks. "Why would I want to know that?" he said. "What would it matter?" He was still holding the Flaubert.

"Do you want to borrow that book?"

"I don't have time for novels," he said.

I smiled. "Only the Word."

"Yes," he said. "The Word." He put the book on the piano where the tea tray still sat and hurried out, letting the screen door slam behind him. In his haste he skipped every other step to the walkway. It was the first time he had ever looked young to me.

The sermon the next Sunday was on humility. Matthew 11:29. "'God resisteth the proud, but giveth grace unto the humble. Humble yourself in the sight of the Lord, and he shall lift you up.'" Near the end of the sermon Dennis turned his face toward me and his hoarse whisper sifted through the church: "'If thou hast done foolishly in lifting up thyself, or if thou hast thought evil, lay thine hand upon thy mouth.'"

My skin prickled. I wondered if anyone else could hear the pounding that reverberated in my chest. I glanced obliquely at Clara Waters and saw a crooked smile pulling at the corner of her mouth. Mother sat with her eyes lowered. Finally, Dennis raised his arms as he always did to call the congregation to prayer. There was the rustle of silk dresses and the scrape of starched collars as heads lowered, but as always, I watched Dennis. His brows pulled down fiercely and his shoulders tightened, as though he were preparing to be transported.

And that was when it happened. As if he could not control it. Without even the slightest change in his voice, still reciting his prayer, he opened his eyes and looked directly down at me.

I knew then that I would have him. Sooner or later, I would have him.

The next day while Mother slept, I walked across the field to the church. There wasn't much time for me, I was well past thirty. I opened the heavy oak door and let myself into the sanctuary. It smelled of mustiness and righteousness, of ruined candles, spilled wine, and wilted lilies. A blue light drifted through the stained-glass windows.

Dennis was in the study, writing his sermon. I stood for a moment in the doorway, watching him, and when he finally sensed my presence, he looked up, startled. He wore a crumpled white shirt, open at the throat, the sleeves pushed up. In that stifling little room, I could smell his body—sweet and earthy, like the newly turned soil in the fields.

"Rebecca." He hesitated, then pushed back his chair. "Is your mother worse?"

"No. She's the same." I motioned for him to stay seated. "It's you I came to talk about." I moved to his desk. "I saw the way you looked at me during the prayer yesterday."

Dennis laughed. He made a full circle in his swivel chair, then spun around to face me. "I looked at you during prayer? You must have imagined that."

"No. You looked at me. I saw you. And tell me this. Why do you always single me out? Why do you preach only to me?"

He smiled. "Rebecca. Surely you don't believe that. There are almost a hundred people in our congregation. How could I preach only to you?"

"It's true," I said. "You think I'm a sinner. Why else would you treat me so badly?" I had not planned to cry, but my voice began to quiver.

"Please, Rebecca." He opened his hands.

It was the sign I had waited for. I walked slowly around his desk. When I touched his shoulder he reached out suddenly and pulled me into his lap. I could feel the tension in his arms. I could smell the musty pink-edged paper of the old hymnals piled on the shelf behind me, see dust motes spinning in the yellow light. In Dennis' throat there was a sound like a mournful song as he rocked in the chair, holding me. But when I moved my hands along his shoulders, he pushed me from his lap. "Get up," he said. "This is God's house."

"Why, Dennis?" I cried. "Why won't you let yourself love me?"

He hurried to the other side of the desk and began to stack his papers in an orderly pile, but his fingers were shaking. "You know as well as I do what the reasons are. Clara, for one thing. You know that we are engaged, have been engaged since you came home, yet you persist. . . ." His voice ripped at the edges, his shoulders heaved. Then he stared at me directly. "Clara told me about what happened to you up north."

"You would condemn me for that? I am punished for that every day that I wake up. A child who was born and died in the same day."

"We are given choice," he said. "There is right and wrong."

"And there is forgiveness of sins."

"For God's sake, be reasonable. I'm a minister. I have to remain above suspicion." He turned away from me. In the heat his rumpled shirt clung to his back in damp pleats. "Go," he whispered. "Have mercy on me."

The dog days began. Sirius rose and set with the sun. The sky hummed with heat. Dennis never came to the house. Sometimes I dialed his number, but only to hear his voice, because I never spoke when he answered. Mother grew weaker, and I walked to services alone. Heat baked the red clay of the roads. Leaves burned on the trees. Crops withered in the fields. I waited for a respite— rain, my mother's death, a call from Dennis. He had held me, I had not imagined that. I had felt his warm breath on my neck, his arms around me.

By August Mother was too weak to leave her bed. While she slept in the afternoons, I roamed the fields, gathering yarrow and grasses and joe-pye weed for winter bouquets. At night I dreamed of a white coffin. Sometimes the face inside it would be my own, sometimes my mother's, sometimes the face of a newly born child. Sometimes I heard crying, but in the morning I could never remember whether it had been Mother or me.

After dark I would cross the field to the parsonage and stand beneath the shadow of the apple tree by Dennis' window. The limbs drooped with their burden of ripe fruit, weaving a dark canopy that obscured me. Occasionally Clara would be there, knitting, while Dennis wrote his sermons. Some nights Dennis was alone, reading by the open window. Once, very late, when he was asleep, I walked onto the shadowed porch and pushed open the screen. Inside I saw his Bible on the table, and beside it, his china cup. I put it to my lips and swallowed the cold, bitter coffee he had left. I moved noiselessly through the dark hallway and found his bedroom. His clothes were draped over the chair. I held his soft, wrinkled shirt to my face, then slipped my arms into the sleeves. Dennis lay on his side, under a rumpled sheet, his hand tucked under his cheek. For a second he wakened briefly, opened his eyes, and looked me full in the face. Then he turned over and slept again. Finally I left him and walked home across the field. I was still wearing his shirt.

Mother died in her sleep the next night. In the churchyard a few days later, Dennis stood in the afternoon sun and read from the Scripture. Later he supported me while I tossed a single white rose onto Mother's casket. Then he drove me home. He followed me through the rooms as I opened windows, threw back draperies. "Why don't you rest?" he said. "You must be exhausted." I lay down on my bed and Dennis sat beside me, smoothing my hair. "Be glad," he said softly. "She has been delivered from pain."

He brought my hand to his lips. Then he leaned across the bed and kissed the tears on my cheeks. He still smelled of the sun. I had never loved him so much as at that moment. I moved his hand to my breast. He drew me toward him and held me, rocking me back and forth in his arms.

Then I sat up and pulled my black dress, my mourning dress, over my head and he lay down with me and held me and my fingers worked at his clothes until they touched flesh and he pushed into me quickly. I wept in his arms, not for the suffering my mother had endured, but for her loss of this life, the quickening, the surge of blood, the swiftness of breath. Dennis held me and crooned, stroking my hair, my face, my shoulders. "There, there," he whispered. And then his arms tensed.

My eyes flew open. "What is it?"

He was staring at the chair beside my bed, where his rumpled white shirt had hung for months.

"I thought I had dreamed it," he said.

"I love you, Dennis," I cried.

He jumped up and pulled the sheet over himself. "How many times did you come there?"

"Just once, I swear it. The other times I only watched from under the tree."

He was pulling on his clothes. "You *watched?* And what did you see?"

"Nothing," I said, "nothing." I grasped his arm as he pulled on his trousers. "My God," he whispered, "my God." He was pulling on his shoes, looking frantically around the room as if he had lost something.

"Please, Dennis," I said. "Forgive me. What did it hurt?"

He looked away from me, toward the bone button of his shirt as he closed his cuff. "We must never be alone together again," he said. He snatched the stolen shirt from the chair and ran out.

Rain came late that night, and wind turned the weather cool as swiftly as a breeze shows the silver underside of a leaf. I lay on my bed in the dark and listened to the rain move against the windows in swift, pleated sheets, fanned by the wind. I thought of my mother's fresh grave, the red mound pressed with hundreds, thousands of fingerprints of rain.

Autumn gave way to winter, and at Christmastime Dennis announced his wedding day. He never looked at me anymore, and after services each Sunday I left by the back door and hurried home across the frozen field.

The wedding was in April, on a day so tender the air wafted through the trees like a length of transparent silk. I waited in the woods behind the parsonage for the guests to leave. The sun went down and darkness filled up the yard, though it was not too dark to see the rose petals still scattered across the lawn. Then I walked slowly through the damp grass and stood outside Dennis' bedroom. I watched as he unfastened the buttons of Clara's stiff brocade dress. I heard his breathing, the girl's high, wavering voice. "You're only tired, Dennis, that's all," she said. "Really, don't worry. We have our whole life ahead of us."

Each evening at sundown I crossed the field and waited in the woods. When the moon was behind me I stood against the tree. Other times I stayed within the shadow of the house. Even when Dennis leaned against the windowsill and peered out into the darkness, he never saw me. He stared into the black night, as if searching for something.

On the seventh night I watched as Clara opened her arms to Dennis. She pulled her thin nightgown over her head and stood naked before him. He shook his head and turned away.

And then the crying began.

I slipped away from the window and began to run through the woods. *I am the true bride,* I was thinking.

Stumbling across the field, I felt the rich red earth, still warm from the sun, pushing up between my bare toes.

I am the true bride.

I tripped over rocks, furrows grown soft with crowns of new grass.

I am the true bride.

In my bedroom I lit the candles that had gathered dust over the long winter. On the bedside table was a bouquet of dried flowers—butterfly weed and gypsophila—and beside that, my mother's old china pitcher, rose-patterned, a pitcher from which I had poured water so many times the gold leaf had disappeared from its handle and worked into the palm of my hand, had mingled with the dark blood in my veins and found its way to my heart. I turned back the soft linens on the bed and went to the door to wait.

I knew he would come after Clara had fallen asleep. And if she woke and found him gone, she would never speak of it, she would be afraid. Finally I saw him running across the field in the dark, his white shirt flying out behind him, translucent, a soft, billowing cloud, his face a pale moon. I lay down on my bed and then he moved through the doorway and fell across my body.

Women endure. Did I say that? Women know how to make things work, to weave patterns and routines out of everyday threads of hope. Every day I drive to the schoolhouse and teach the lessons. Every Sunday I walk across the field to church. Dennis avoids my eyes, but Clara watches me always. Her face is pinched these days, mean and bitter. There have been no children, not in three years.

I sleep very little now, and for a long time I have not dreamed. Every night I stand at the window and look out, in winter at the dark branches etched against the cold gray sky, in summer at the silver rain pearling on the tender, transparent leaves.

From the porch I can see the woods and the overgrown field across which Dennis comes to me at night. I lean against the peeling, yellowed wallpaper and I think how grateful I should be, because this is what I wanted.

God has answered my prayers.

Sometimes, I think of Clara. Sometimes I think of her waking at night to discover that Dennis is gone from her bed. And I imagine her moving through the rooms of the parsonage, calling softly, calling out his name in the dark.

Tristan and Isolde

by Maura Stanton

They were standing on the cool steps of the cathedral, in the shadow cast by its high façade of red brick and black lava. Inside the massive Romanesque building, they had squinted up through the gloom at the famous Black Virgin in her lace veil and satin gown. Christopher had jotted down a few notes on the sculptured capitals of the cloister, while Sylvie had wandered around, looking at the side chapels. Back at the main altar, she had stopped to cross herself, surprised that she still remembered the gesture after all these years, and not understanding why she did it. The last mass she had attended was the one performed at her own wedding when she was twenty-two. She and her first husband, Russell, both graduate students at the time, had decided on a church wedding in order to get as many presents as possible. She remembered the satirical expression on Russell's face as he knelt beside her during the ceremony. Right afterwards, he had ducked out to smoke a joint in the parking lot.

"You look sad," Christopher said now, putting his arm around Sylvie's waist.

"I feel like we're prisoners on a holiday," she said. "I keep thinking about having to go back."

"Prisoners don't get holidays," he said. "You mustn't think like that."

For the past week, Sylvie and Christopher had been pressed up against each other in the back seat of an overloaded Citroën station wagon. In order to be comfortable, and avoid knocking her elbow into a tripod, Sylvie had leaned against Christopher's shoulder. They were both wearing shorts, and their bare knees had accidentally touched. Several times they had been thrown hard into each other on a curve.

95

Sylvie's husband, Mark, insisted on doing all the driving. Sylvie couldn't drive a stick shift, and he didn't trust Christopher, who had been involved in several minor accidents. He had seemed relieved when Christopher broke his glasses, making driving out of the question for him. Christopher's wife, Johanna, suffered from a bad back. She could only sit in the front, with the seat tilted down, a pillow behind her neck.

Two days before, in a little village in Burgundy where they had stopped overnight, black thunderheads had moved rapidly across the vineyards below the terrace of the hotel where they were finishing dinner, heading straight toward them.

Sylvie had been terrified. She stood up, her coffee untasted, trembling. The wind began to blow. She had seen a tornado blow the roof off a barn when she was a child, and she had never forgotten the sight. She knew that they didn't have tornados in France, but she could still taste fear in the back of her throat.

"It won't rain for ten minutes," Mark said, pulling at his beard, a narrow reddish grey fringe that surrounded his jaw. "Drink your coffee."

Thunder roared. Sylvie gasped, and took a step backwards.

"You're acting like a fool, Sylvie," Mark said.

"She's frightened," Christopher said.

Johanna laughed. She learned back in her chair as the wind whipped her short blond hair around her face. Her long, crystal earrings swung back and forth. "Isn't it beautiful?"

Lightning split the sky. Sylvie gave a little cry. She looked at Mark. He was sipping his coffee, his face clenched and stubborn, his arched eyebrows drawn together. She knew he wouldn't move until he began to get wet. She backed away.

"For Christ's sake," Mark shouted at her over the thunder. "Don't be such an idiot, Sylvie. Sit down."

People at other tables were gathering up their belongings. Waiters were running out, hurriedly clearing the tables. Tablecloths were flapping. Napkins had been blown across the flagged terrace.

Sylvie stood there, hugging her arms together.

Then Christopher jumped up. He put his arm around her shoulders. "I'll go in with you, Sylvie," he said. He had hurried her across the terrace and through the glass doors. Lights were flickering in the lobby. They had looked at each other. She shivered. How long had she been living without tenderness?

A loud din shook the hotel. Hail hit the windows. Sylvie flinched. Christopher leaned down and kissed her hard.

The next morning, Sylvie was afraid to look into Christopher's eyes. But she couldn't help herself. He was looking at her in the same tender way. They held hands under the unfolded map as they gave Mark directions to Le Puy.

Now Johanna was flat on her back in the ancient Grand Hotel Lafayette. They were going to have to wait a couple of days until she could travel again.

She had been seeing doctors and orthopedists and chiropractors for years about her back. The diagnosis kept changing. Privately, Sylvie thought it was all psychosomatic.

It was only ten o'clock in the morning, but the sun was blazing. Christopher and Sylvie left the steps and turned into the shadow of a narrow, medieval street. Above them, arrow-shaped windows were tightly shut. No one was in sight. Christopher pulled Sylvie against him, and kissed her.

"What are we going to do?" he sighed, stroking Sylvie's curly brown hair back from her forehead.

She kissed him back. "I don't know. But I can't bear this anymore."

"Me neither."

"We could go to my room. Mark's out with the camera."

"But he could come back any minute," Christopher said. "We've got to do something, though. This is the first time we've been alone for more than five minutes."

"I know. It's hard to get away from them." Sylvie looked up at Christopher. She liked the way his long lashes shadowed his cheek. "Do you still believe in love, Chris?"

Christopher smiled. "You mean true love? Like Tristan and Isolde? Sure I do."

"Isolde was married to King Mark, wasn't she?" Sylvie said. She gave Christopher a tight hug. "You know, we could get a room in another hotel."

"That little one we passed?"

"Right," she said. "Let's go."

But as soon as they left the old town and stepped into the square, they saw Mark coming toward them with his camera case slung over his shoulder. They both smiled brightly.

"I got lost," he said. "It's a maze in there. I never found my way up to the Rocher." He pointed behind him, where the statue of the Virgin rose up above the town on a red volcanic rock.

"We were looking at the cathedral," Sylvie said.

"I'll get down to some serious work this afternoon," Mark said.

"We were just going to have a beer," Christopher said.

"Sounds good." Mark came up beside Sylvie. He took her arm, forcing Christopher to follow them. Sylvie looked over her shoulder. Christopher was running his hands wearily through his thick, black hair.

Mark picked out a table back under a shaded arcade and they ordered beers. The waiter brought out three foaming glasses and set them on cork coasters.

"How's Johanna this morning?" Mark said. Sylvie could see the large flat disks of his contact lenses floating in his blue eyes.

"I think it's just one of her spasms," Christopher said. "She's taking painkillers, and if she stays in bed for a day or two, and doesn't upset herself, she'll be all right."

"Isn't she bored up there by herself?" Mark picked up his beer and sipped cautiously. Sylvie and Christopher were almost finished.

"She kicked me out of the room. She wanted to read."

"Well, tell her not to worry about me," Mark said. "This is a great town for a photographer. I could stay here a week." He looked at Sylvie. "Do you want to come with me today?"

Sylvie stiffened. "To the cathedral? No, I've just seen it. I'd only get in your way." She yawned elaborately. "This heat makes me tired. Maybe I'll nap after lunch."

Mark frowned. "Have you written those postcards?"

"What postcards?"

"To the boys. Look, Sylvie, what else have you got to do? I asked you to send those postcards three days ago."

Sylvie flushed. "I forgot."

"And you could do some laundry this afternoon, too. It's piling up in the suitcase. You haven't been much help on this trip."

Sylvie bit back an angry reply. Last winter, when Mark saw a PBS documentary on Romanesque art, and talked vaguely of going to France and Spain, it was Sylvie who had pushed for a book, hoping it would cinch the trip. She was desperate to get away. She had put him in touch with an editor at the university press where she worked part-time. And she had suggested her old friend Christopher as the person to write the text that would accompany Mark's pictures. She knew Christopher was paid next to nothing for teaching one class in Old French.

Sylvie had not expected to fall in love with Christopher, though years ago, before she married Russell, she'd had a brief crush on him. She merely thought it would be fun to see him and his wife Johanna again and go to Europe. Usually she and Mark spent the summer on a mosquito-ridden lake in Maine taking care of Mark's sons from his first marriage.

Right from the first, though, she had been struck by the grown-up somberness of Christopher's handsome, narrow face, once so open and boyish, and by his constant attentiveness to Johanna. Johanna was still pretty, with her silk scarves and dangling earrings, but there were dark shadows under her eyes, and deep frown lines etched into her forehead.

"The Chateau du Polignac is around here somewhere," Christopher said to Mark after an uncomfortable pause. "I've always wanted to see it."

"Too bad neither of you can drive the car," Mark said. "I'll be busy all afternoon."

"What's Polignac?" Sylvie asked.

"A ruined castle," Christopher said. "I've read a lot about it when I took that colloquium on the troubadours. The most powerful family in this part of the Auvergne used to live there." He smiled suddenly at Mark. "But I think it's only about three miles away. In a little village. We could walk, couldn't we, Sylvie?"

"In this heat?" Mark laughed.

Sylvie looked carefully at Christopher. "Maybe," she said, pretending to yawn again. "I'll see how I feel."

Mark finished his beer in two big gulps. He stood up, looking down at Sylvie. "Your nose is sunburned. You'd better stay out of the sun today."

She put her hand automatically to her face. She had pale skin that freckled easily in the sun. She didn't say anything.

"See you later," Mark said. "Don't look for me at lunchtime. I'll pick up a sandwich somewhere."

They watched him cross the square. Unlike Christopher, he seldom wore shorts, and his long legs were still white under the matted brown hair.

"Let's get out of here," Christopher said, signalling the waiter. He paid the bill, then looked at Sylvie. "Do you think he's noticed?"

"I don't think so."

The Hotel Voyageurs was right around the corner. They stepped nervously into a bar without any customers. Behind the bar was a rack of pegs with a few large keys hanging on it. A middle-aged woman came out from the kitchen, smoothing her flowered skirt.

Christopher cleared his throat and asked for a room. The woman smiled, nodded, then said something else. Christopher frowned.

"What is it?" Sylvie asked.

"She says the room won't be ready until two o'clock. They're still cleaning."

"Jesus Christ," Sylvie said.

He spoke to the woman again, who shrugged her shoulders and turned away. "Come on," he said to Sylvie.

Outside in the street, Sylvie took a deep breath. "Mark said he wasn't coming back for lunch. You heard him."

"All right," Christopher said. "We'll risk it."

Back at their hotel, no one was at the desk, and the box slots for room keys were all empty.

"They're cleaning here, too," Sylvie groaned.

"Maybe they're finished," Christopher said. "Sometimes they leave the key in the door."

The elevator at the Grand Hotel Lafayette, an iron cage which looked as if it dated from the twenties, was permanently out of order. Sylvie and Christopher climbed the wide stairs to the fourth floor. At the end of the dim hall, a figure stepped out of a doorway. They both jumped. Then Sylvie realized it was a maid. As they got closer, she saw that the door to her room was standing open. The maid had gone back inside and was making the bed.

"Shit, shit, shit," Sylvie muttered under her breath.

"Not our day," Christopher whispered.

A door snapped open across the hall.

"Oh, there you are," a small voice said. Sylvie turned. Johanna was looking out through the half-open door.

"Johanna," Christopher said. "What are you doing up?"

"I heard the maids," she said in a quavering tone. "I wanted to tell them not to clean the room today."

"I'll tell them," Christopher said. "Don't worry. You go back to bed now. Can I bring you anything?"

"A glass of water," she said. She seemed to make a great effort to smile. "Hello, Sylvie. How are you this morning?"

"Oh, I'm fine," Sylvie said. "Are you any better today, Johanna?"

Johanna shook her head. "Come in a minute," she said. She opened the door wider. She was wearing a purple silk kimono, and had tied a ribbon of some silvery stuff around her forehead. Sylvie followed her inside. She heard Christopher talking to the maid.

The room smelled of cigarette smoke and jasmine incense, which Johanna liked to burn for her headaches. The unmade bed was piled with books and papers. There were little bottles of pills and jars of ointments on the table beside the bed. Johanna got back under the sheet.

"I've been working on my new book," she said. "But I can only sit up for about ten minutes at a time."

Sylvie sat down on a worn velvet chair with carved finials. It still surprised her—and depressed her, too—that Johanna, with her frail little body, constantly sick or on the verge of being sick, had published two books, while Sylvie was still thinking about revising her dissertation, and Christopher had never even finished writing his own. Johanna had been offered a professorship right out of graduate school, while Sylvie, after several promising interviews, had ended up with nothing.

Christopher hurried back into the room. He turned on the tap of the sink in the corner, and brought Johanna a glass of water. She looked at him with widening eyes.

"You know I can't drink that," she said.

Christopher flushed. "Right," he said. "I'll see if they have any mineral water downstairs."

He poured the water into the sink. At the doorway he turned back. "What would you like for lunch, Johanna?"

She gave a little shudder. "I'm not hungry."

"You've got to eat something."

"I have my fruit," she said. She pointed to a basket of apricots.

"What about some cheese?"

"Oh, no." She leaned back on her pillow with a sigh. "It would just give me indigestion."

Christopher disappeared. Johanna closed her eyes and Sylvie wondered if she had fallen asleep. She looked around the room. Johanna had more luggage than all the rest of them combined. Her bags and baskets and bundles were spread everywhere. She had a traveling teapot, an orange squeezer, a steamer iron, a laptop computer, and several dozen heavy books.

"Where's Mark?" Johanna said suddenly, opening her eyes.

Sylvie jumped. She had been looking at Christopher's bathrobe thrown across a chair.

"We just had a beer with him. He's out with the camera."

"You're really sweet to put up with me. You must be bored to tears, stuck here with nothing to do. Would you like to borrow something to read?" She pointed to her stack of books. "There's a new linguistic study of the *Roman de la Rose*."

Sylvie shook her head. "I'm fine."

"What's keeping Christopher?" Johanna raised herself up on her elbow. "I'm so thirsty. The pills make me thirsty."

Christopher appeared just then. He carried a large bottle of Vittel covered with a glass.

Johanna frowned. "Didn't they have any Evian?"

"This is all they had." He poured out a glass for Johanna and set the bottle on her bedside table.

"It's not cold," she said, putting it to her lips.

"I'm sorry," Christopher said, a little curtly. "They didn't have any cold."

"Would you open the shutters just a bit?" Johanna asked after a couple of sips. "Not too much, now. I need some air, but I don't want any sun."

"How's this?"

"Good," she said.

"Is there anything else I can get you now?"

"Fluff up my pillow," she said. "And bring the computer over here."

"I'll get the pillow," Sylvie said, slipping it out from behind Johanna. She smacked it a few times, letting feathers fly.

"No wonder my head is stopped up," Johanna cried. "Feathers! Bring me one of my own pillows, would you, Sylvie? Over on that chair. Take that thing away."

Sylvie arranged the pillow behind Johanna's back, and Christopher set up the computer across her lap. After he had brought the three books she needed, a yellow legal pad, a felt pen and a box of tissues, he kissed her on the forehead.

"I'm fine now," she said. "I may be able to come down for dinner."

"Good." Christopher backed toward the door where Sylvie was standing.

"Where are you going?" Johanna asked.

"Sylvie and I thought we might walk out to the Chateau du Polignac," Christopher said quickly. "It's not far."

Johanna nodded. She switched on her computer.

"See you later, Johanna," Sylvie said, as Christopher shut the door. Out in the hall, they stood looking at each other. The maid had left Sylvie's room, and the key was in the lock.

"Not here," Christopher said.

"Polignac," Sylvie said determinedly.

The ruins of the chateau sat on a red hill which they could see across two miles of blond wheat fields from the outskirts of Le Puy. An occasional car or truck swept past them as they walked along the shoulder of the highway. Crows were circling overhead, and cicadas thrummed in the dry thickets. The sun was like a white-hot skillet.

As soon as Le Puy had disappeared behind a jagged ridge, Christopher took Sylvie's hand, but his face was gloomy.

"What's wrong?" she asked.

"I don't know. I guess I've gotten used to being miserable all the time."

"We didn't use to be miserable. What happened?"

He shook his head.

"Remember when all of us—you and Johanna and Russell and me—went on that picnic? I'd been married to Russell for only a year, and you'd just met Johanna. We went skinny-dipping, then sat on that rock drying off, and drank two bottles of wine. We were happy, weren't we?"

"I guess we were."

"Johanna's back was fine—or else she just never talked about it. She could swim like a fish. And Russell didn't seem to be drinking more than the rest of us." Sylvie sighed. "I joked about how I was going to get a job at Harvard, but underneath it wasn't a joke. I secretly thought I would."

"Why did you marry Mark?"

"He was teaching that photography class I took to keep my mind off things when I was getting the divorce. His wife had just left him. He kept asking me to go bird-watching with him. Then when I couldn't find a job, I guess I panicked. It was easy to marry him. I didn't know it would be so hard afterwards."

"But he's a decent guy, isn't he? A little impatient, maybe."

"My life doesn't belong to me," Sylvie said, looking away. "He found me the job at the press. It's his house, his furniture—he doesn't want to buy anything new because he thinks it's a waste of money. Sometimes I think I was hired to provide sex, go shopping, and clean the fish his kids catch in the summer."

"Sylvie," Christopher said, squeezing her hand. "You're exaggerating."

"No, I'm not. I'll tell you something horrible. I forgot my pills four nights in a row last year, and I thought I was pregnant. I was sure I was—and I was actually happy about it. Then Mark told me I couldn't be pregnant unless I was having an affair—because he'd had a vasectomy! He'd had a vasectomy before we were married and he never told me. But he let me keep on taking pills just as if . . . I was so angry. Then I got my period and that was that. But I've kept on taking the pill," she added. "Just to spite him."

"You could leave him," Christopher said.

Sylvie looked at him, nodding. "What about Johanna?" she added. "Is her back really that bad?"

She saw him stiffen. "She's in real pain, Sylvie."

"But she gets a lot of work done while she's in real pain."

Christopher sighed. "She needs me, though."

Sylvie said nothing. They were walking alongside a pasture, and she looked at the cows, peacefully chewing grass. A rabbit flitted through the brush. The ruined castle was much closer now, and she could make out the red roofs of the village that tumbled down the hillside below it. At a crossroads, they ran into more cars, and had to stay further over on the shoulder. The cars were full of well-dressed people, women in hats and men in suits.

"Must be a wedding," Christopher said. "It's Saturday."

"Isn't this a shortcut?" Sylvie asked, pointing to a steep path that ran up the side of the hill.

"Good. We can go straight up to the castle and avoid the village."

At the top of the hill Sylvie could see volcanic spires of rock jutting up across the countryside for miles around. The two distant peaks of Le Puy, with the statue of the Virgin on one pinnacle and the chapel of Saint Michel on the other, stood out sharply, though Christopher complained that they were only vague shapes to him. The path crossed a meadow of dried grass and thistles to the chateau, a three-story brick tower surrounded by ruined walls and out-buildings.

Christopher hurried ahead. He ducked through a door in the tower.

"It's cool in here," he called. "Watch your head."

A damp chill enveloped Sylvie when she stepped inside. Christopher put his arms around her. He kissed her throat. She leaned against him, her eyes closed.

"We're in a castle," she whispered. "A real castle. You're Tristan and I'm Isolde."

"I hope not," Christopher said, nuzzling her ear. "They never made love to each other, you know."

"But they never forgot each other. They died for each other."

Christopher laughed softly, putting his hands up under her T-shirt. "It was that love potion they drank by mistake."

"It wasn't just that," Sylvie said.

A child shrieked somewhere, and they both jumped. In a moment two little boys had poked their head inside the tower. They said something to each other in German. Sylvie could hear adults talking outside now.

"Fucking Christ," Christopher said. He dropped his arm away from Sylvie.

"Let's go down to the village," she said. "There must be some rooms to rent."

They stepped back out into the sun, nodding politely at the German family who were gathered in a circle, reading their green Michelin Guide. Sylvie found another path on the other side of the castle which led down around a cemetery, and they reached the cobbled streets of the village.

In the main square, across from the church where people were gathering for the wedding, they saw two cafés. Some teenage boys in blue jeans were sitting at one, listening to loud rock music as they drank beer and scowled at the bridal party, just getting out of cars at the door of the church. The other café, its umbrella tables empty, had a sign stuck on the half-timbered plaster above the door—*Chambres*.

Sylvie and Christopher hurried inside. A woman was washing glasses behind the bar. Christopher asked for a room. The woman dried her hands and took a key down from a peg, smiling broadly. Christopher pulled out his passport but she waved it away. She pointed to the wooden staircase.

After he shut and locked the door of their room, Christopher took Sylvie by the shoulders.

"My God," he said. "I didn't think we'd ever find a place to be alone."

She pressed against him. Then they fell onto the bed, tangled together, kissing and stroking each other, forgetting that they were still wearing clothes. But in a few minutes Christopher began to pull off her T-shirt, and she started tearing off his shorts. They were both sweaty from the long walk. The bed creaked and knocked against the wall.

After they'd made love, Sylvie lay with her head on Christopher's chest. For the first time she noticed the room. The shutters were still latched, so it was dim and quiet. There seemed to be flowered wallpaper, and an old gilt-bordered mirror next to a massive oak armoire. Sometimes she could hear distant voices or gusts of music out on the square.

Her eyes closed. She longed to go to sleep and wake up and be with Christopher forever.

Christopher shifted. "I almost fell asleep," he said.

"Me, too. That's all right."

"If we fall asleep, we'll be late getting back."

"I don't care," Sylvie said sleepily. "Can't we run away?"

He sat up and kissed her breast. "No," he said.

She drew back a little, looking at him. He averted his eyes.

"Chris?"

"Why don't I go down and see if I can get some wine? Wouldn't a bottle of cold white wine—or even beer if that's all they have—be perfect right now?"

"Yes," she said. She reached over the side of her bed for her underpants.

"Don't get dressed," he said, pulling on his shorts. "I'll be right back."

"I'm going to open the shutters," she said. "It's hot in here."

Christopher went out. Sylvie crumpled her nylon underpants in her hand. She caught a glimpse of herself in the old mirror—in the gloom of the shuttered room, her hips rising above the carved headboard, she thought she looked like a mermaid. Her hair was stuck to her damp forehead in wet curls.

She opened the window and unlatched the shutters, pushing them open a little way. She held the white film of the lace curtain over her body and leaned out. The wedding was over and bells were ringing. People streamed out of the church, laughing and talking. Two bridesmaids in blue organdy dresses and picture hats stood chatting with groomsmen in tuxedos.

Suddenly everyone turned, shouting and clapping. Flashbulbs went off. Fistfuls of rice rose up and fell shimmering through the air. The bride and groom, ducking and laughing, ran outside.

The bride wore a white silk gown with tight sleeves and a seed-pearl bodice. Her long lace veil was fastened to her head with a crown of white flowers. She stood at the bottom of the church steps, holding the groom's hand.

Sylvie winced. She thought of the cigarette burn she had found in the train of her own white dress the day after her marriage to Russell; she remembered the corsage of browning orchids she had worn on her suit when she married Mark at the courthouse. Mark had bought them for her a day early, and they hadn't lasted.

She watched the groom lean down and kiss the bride. Then she glanced across the square where the teenage boys in blue jeans were still drinking beer, their distant rock music drowned out by the pealing bells.

The joyous ringing of the bells soothed her. Perhaps Christopher would return with a dusty bottle of wine, centuries old. They would drink it and belong to each other forever.

All at once Sylvie drew back with a shiver. A tall man with a reddish fringe of beard had just entered the square from a side street. Now he was hesitating at the edge of the crowd. It was Mark. He began to circle around the crowd, moving in her direction.

She pulled the shutter closed and locked it. She heard a step in the hall. Christopher opened the door. He was carrying a bottle of wine and two glasses. He looked pale.

"Mark," she said.

"I saw him. I stepped out the door for a minute, and I recognized him even without my glasses."

"Did he see you?"

Christopher shook his head. "But we've got to get out of here. He's looking for us, of course. He's probably been up at the castle already."

"Let's not be afraid," Sylvie said, her heart beating. "Why should we be afraid? Let's just stay here and drink our wine. He'll go away."

"I'm going outside to get a table," Christopher said. "You get dressed and come down in a few minutes. Pretend you've been to the bathroom. I'll pay the woman for the room when I get a chance."

"Wait," she said, as he turned to go.

"What?"

"Don't go. Kiss me."

"Sylvie, we can't let them know."

"Why not?"

"Please, Sylvie."

"Are you worried about us not having enough money?"

'Of course not," he said.

"Then what?"

"We can't hurt them, Sylvie." He turned abruptly and left the room. Sylvie heard him going downstairs.

She grabbed her clothes off the floor and got dressed, trying not to glance at the crumpled, stained sheets where she had been happy for an hour. When she stepped outside on the terrace, blinking against the bright sun, she saw that Mark and Christopher were sitting at a table together, drinking the wine.

Christopher waved to her. "Look who I found, Sylvie!"

"Hello, Mark," she said, walking slowly over and pulling out a chair. "What are you doing here?"

"I drove over so I could give you a ride back," Mark said. He was smiling, but his eyes were cold, the contact lenses floating like pieces of ice. "I couldn't believe it when Johanna said you'd walked to Polignac. You've really got a sunburn, Sylvie. I warned you."

Across the table, Christopher lifted his wine glass to his lips. Sylvie had to turn her face away so that he would not see how the expression of revulsion in her eyes included him.

Woman Looking at van Gogh

by Silvia Curbelo

The way you tell it it's not
that blue is the heaviest color
but that the moment you lay it down
the paint begins to crack from the sheer
weight of the air we're breathing.
So life is hard.
So tell me something I don't know
already.
       I know, for instance,
that the heart rises against
the weight of logic. I know he lights
her cigarettes and can't stand smoke,
so how do you figure?
Japanese businessmen
will pay millions for a painting
they'll never understand
and call it *speculation*
on supply and demand.
The world is a mystery far beyond
cheap flowers in a vase
or some sad bridge in Arles.
Or love. We all *invest* in something.
It all comes down to some guy
we meet in a train station,

107

in a bar. Desire is the light falling
on his face, and in the end
we die of want, of darkness.
The way you tell it
even the most tender scenes are cast
in a harsh light.
                But it's always
that going back to the one moment,
the simplest colors coming together at the scene.
The way I saw them together one night
in a café, in a crowd of tourists,
not like in some European painting
but completely themselves,
rendered precisely in the flat
light of the facts.
                The fact is I saw what I saw.
But God, they were beautiful, even I had
to admit that, sitting together
hand in hand, the air around them
drenched in blue, perfectly cool
the way that passion can be cool sometimes,
irradiating from an icy center,
the blue heart of the flame or
her cool hand around
his cock. Desire is gravity

without a place to land.
                            Still, there's
nothing more exquisite than
the artificial moment coming
to life, the dying stem
of each ten cent flower, or love's
fraying colors. Red nails
raking the skin. Something
you could really cut off an ear for.
In my favorite painting snow seems
to be falling even now, a denser,
cooler white, the color of some
cast-off cigarette. Strike
another match for love.
                            I know in the end
we're all floundering, living against
the grain of light, of shadow,
covering our tracks, erasing what we touch.
We all get painted into such white corners.
I keep thinking about the way
he lights her cigarettes, bright red
nails and those pale eyes opening.
So maybe in his own way he loves me.
Smoke all over his clothes.

The Ins and Outs of Committing Adultery

by Binnie Kirshenbaum

"You're home early," my husband says from behind the newspaper. For all he knows, I could be a cat burglar, or a succubus, coming in the door instead of a window.

"It's almost seven." I take off my coat. "Did you have dinner?"

"A sandwich."

"Did you save me some Jarlsberg?"

"There's plenty left." He turns a page, the paper rustles.

I'm slicing a tomato when the phone rings. I cradle the receiver between my ear and my hunched shoulder. My hands are free to spread mayonnaise on bread, to unwrap the Jarlsberg while I talk with the multimedia artist.

I hang up the phone, carry my sandwich to the living room.

"No plate?" My husband watches crumbs from the French bread fall like a light snow.

"That was the multimedia artist." I offer information.

"Who?"

"The multimedia artist. My friend who paints, sculpts, writes, composes, all in one ball. He invited me to an opening tomorrow night. Uptown. One of the Fifty-seventh Street galleries."

"Sounds nice," my husband says.

The best method, the cleanest, the safest way to commit adultery is this: As often as possible, within reason, tell the truth.

The truth is straight, up-front, liberating, not apt to do me in. The truth within bounds, that is. I'm not a well-intended fool. I'd never say to my husband, "I'm going to be with my lover, one of my lovers. We're going to spend the night fucking our heads loose."

However, I never invent distressed friends, sick aunts. Nor would I say I've signed up for an Italian language class that meets on Wednesday nights, for surely the day would come when my husband would say: *All'ora, cara mia, parla un po' d'italiano per me*.

Lies, outright lies, have a way of tangling, looping to make a noose to fit snugly around your neck. Or they wind, twisting, over and under your ankles like a Chinese jump rope tripping you up.

Before you marry, it's best to be square with yourself on this question: Am I a run-around?

Picking the right husband hinges on the answer. You have to get a husband who allows for extramarital entertainment. Not one of those open-marriage jobs where you, your date, and your husband all breakfast together the morning after. That's messy. Rather, a husband who likes that you have your own friends, your own doings, your own hobbies.

Adultery is impossible if your husband is a pet ferret, snooping, sniffing, curious.

Pick a husband who is absorbed with his career, with a sport, or with a mistress.

Keep your adultery clean, streamlined.

It will be with impunity that I will meet the multimedia artist tomorrow night. I will stand around, drink wine, listen to pretentious commentary without looking over my shoulder. As big as the city is, circles can run small, overlap. But if it happens that I meet someone I know, there will be no cause for panic. No dash for the door. No need to hide out in the bathroom. I have not been duplicitous. I have nothing to fear.

Lighthearted, carefree, I will return home, and my husband will ask, "How was it?"

And I'll say, "They served that lovely cheese. The kind with volcanic ash layered through the middle."

"Mobier." My husband knows his cheeses.

"Yes," I'll say. And then I'll confess, "I didn't understand the paintings. Afterwards, we went back to the multimedia artist's loft, hung around, and he explained them, but frankly, I still don't get them."

"Well, it sounds like you had a good time." My husband will be anxious to get back to whatever he was doing.

I'll screw up my face and say, "It was okay. Nothing special." That too will be so near to the truth, it will be honest.

It Was Humdrum

by Ann Harleman

S he picks up the phone on the second ring. She is in the kitchen anyway. "Hello?" she says.

"Hi, babe." Juan's voice, frayed from too many cigarettes too late at night.

"I'm sorry. You have the wrong number," Maude says. She hangs up. It's their signal for when she can't talk; but he will hate it anyway. She had to do it. Roger and Mary Lynn are both in the living room, within earshot.

Maude goes back to the sink, where she was scrubbing potatoes. She holds them in the slant of light from the window, not bothering to cut out the eyes. On the window frame above the sink she has tacked a postcard, a reproduction of a painting. A brightly colored ship, flat as paper, on a dark green sea; in one corner a red arrow points straight out of the painting. It is called *The Ship Ready for Departure*.

Roger comes into the kitchen to get some cat food for the turtles. He walks slowly with his fists clenched at his sides, the way Lynnie used to do to keep her balance when she was first learning to walk. He does not touch Maude—pat her or rub her shoulder as he usually does—communicating by this omission that he is annoyed with her. He crouches down and reaches around her without saying anything, pulls the sack out from under the sink, and goes.

She hates it when they fight without her even knowing it. She tries to work out what the fight is about. She said something wrong at breakfast. What was it? Her hands move automatically over the roast, rubbing salt and pepper into it. It was the detective, that was it: the detective Roger hired to find his mother. Maude has always thought of her as the "Long Lost Mother," L.L.M. for short. She left when Roger was two. He hasn't seen or heard from her since, except once when he was ten or so, a card with no return address, only the Florida postmark. That was it: Maude should not have said, "When they find the L.L.M., we'll have her up for a visit." Roger wanted the "L.L.M." explained.

It must be terrible to lose your mother like that—or rather, have her lose you, like an umbrella or a single glove. Even Maude's mother hung around. Maude tumbles everything, meat and potatoes, into the oven. She goes to the doorway and watches Roger feed the turtles.

His back is toward her. He throws pellets of cat food into the big tank and the turtles waver to the surface and snap at them. Before Maude and Mary Lynn moved in, they were nameless. Now, courtesy of Lynnie, they are No Name and Buttercup. No Name is the size of Roger's hand; Buttercup is twice as big. They started out as ordinary dime-store turtles, no bigger than a silver dollar. Knowing and sinister, they have corrugated shells and skin wrinkled like hands that have been in water too long.

Roger finishes, closes the bag deliberately, carefully folding the top over and over. Roger is a systems analyst. He is a good man, a good father: her deliberate, methodical husband. That's why she chose him, after years of crazy lovers, after Mary Lynn's crazy father. So why, now, is she betraying him (that would be his word) for crazy Juan? Maude thinks of the story about the duck and the scorpion. Needing to cross the river, the scorpion asks the duck to carry her on his back. No, says the duck; you will sting me and kill me. Why would I do such a stupid thing, says the scorpion reasonably. Then I would drown. Persuaded, the duck agrees to ferry her across. Halfway out into the river, the scorpion stings him. As they both go down, he asks her, Why did you do it? She says: Because it is my nature.

Who is she hurting, after all? Roger doesn't know; Juan doesn't care. The image of quicksilver Juan interposes itself between her and Roger. The two of them together add up to a whole person.

When she drives in to see Juan the next afternoon, the air is heavy and sultry. All day it has been about to rain. Maude likes South Street, the crowds, black faces, noise. Getting out of the car on Spring Garden Street, remembering to lock it (it must not get stolen: that would be very hard to explain), she breathes acrid city air, life, danger.

Juan's apartment is on the second floor, three rooms opening one into the other railroad-fashion, full of stained-glass windows and wood paneling and gilt-framed mirrors that reflect uncertain images like questions. The wavery light gives the whole place an underwater quality. It is full of odd thrift-shop objects: as in an aquarium, you get the feeling everything is trying to look like something else.

Maude lets herself in. The kitchen is empty. She edges around the grand piano in the middle room and finds him in the back room, in bed, already naked. She always comes at one, when Mary Lynn goes to afternoon daycamp.

"Hi, babe." He is languorous, already most of the way through a joint. The little sudden lurches of the heart when she first sees him or hears his voice on the phone have largely abated by now. But there is still something: direct, visceral, as breathtaking as a hand on her genitals. She doesn't love him. She knows that, for an affair, it's better to choose someone you can't possibly love; though even then it's tricky. Sex makes its own bond, one that can even sometimes (she believes this but has never experienced it) generate love.

She undresses quickly—Lynnie will be home at four—and slides into bed beside him. Juan kisses her, running his hand over her belly, hands her the last of the joint. He gets up to get another one. She watches him cross the room, his small tight buttocks round as apples. He is, simply, beautiful. In public, people turn and stare. Reflected in the huge mirror, his erection points stiffly in front of him, wavering from side to side like a divining rod. Maude thinks of marble genitals, throngs of them, museums in Rome, in Florence.

She looks down the length of her own body, stretched out straight like a medieval knight on a tombstone: belly round and a little slack since Lynnie, wide thighs, feet long and slender. She is thirty to Juan's twenty-two, a fact which only seems to matter when she isn't with him. As he gets back into bed, a line from a poem comes to mind. "I like my body when it is with your / body."

She decides not to say it out loud. Juan isn't much interested in poetry, and certainly not at this moment. She fingers the small quick pulse at the base of his throat. He makes a thready noise like a wasp. Light coming in through the colored glass of the window over the bed stains their flesh deep velvety hues, like the behinds of baboons at the zoo.

Afterwards, beached, they smoke another joint, passing it back and forth between them, faintly damp. Juan gets up and plays for her, sitting naked at the grand piano. "We're a musical people," he says when he catches her looking at him, and rolls his eyes. He keeps playing: not the things he plays in restaurants, but Gershwin, Rodgers, Kern, drifting in and out of jazz. His eyes are deep brown and strong, with glistening whites. His mother was Puerto Rican; his father, *quien sabe?*

The music makes her want to dance, but her body is too heavy after making love. It would be like trying to run under water. Listening to the music, riding on it, Maude rests in the moment like a hang glider on a current of air. With Juan she never has to come up with a plausible algorithm to explain, step-by-step, how she got from wherever she was to wherever she is. He never asks, Why anything. *Al-go-RITHM—is not—RHYTHM*, she thinks, in time to the music. Here she has rhythm; at home, algorithm. She laughs out loud.

When she leaves, Juan walks her to the door, bare-chested in jeans, his glossy hairless skin like polished leather. She thinks, driving home, what if she just stayed there. Stayed with Juan. She could get a job, Mary Lynn could go to school in the city; she would never have to explain anything.

The traffic makes her late. When she pulls up outside their row house, Mary Lynn is sitting on the steps, trying to entice some sparrows with crusts she must have hidden in her pockets at lunch.

"Mary Lynn, *don't* do that." But Mary Lynn's attention has already moved on.

"Look, Ma." Lately she has taken to calling Maude that. "Look, Ma. That's nature." A black ant, shiny and fat, crawls slowly across the stoop, drugged by the heat. "Can I go under the sprinkler? It's so hot." Mary Lynn looks straight up at Maude, her forehead corrugating with the intensity of her desire. She has Maude's wild red hair, her father's brown eyes.

"Yes. Run up and change, and I'll turn it on."

Mary Lynn glitters under the fine spray, drops flashing off her arrow-straight body as she jumps and turns. At six, she is as straight up and down as a boy. "Come in," she cries and beckons with quick stiff gestures. Maude laughs, shakes her head. It's more pleasurable just to look at Lynnie. She remembers the pure sensual joy of having a very small child, the feel and smell of Lynnie at one and two and three, a hundred small daily pleasures. How could the L.L.M. have relinquished that?

When Mary Lynn has had enough, they go in. Mary Lynn takes off her bathing suit. Maude dries her small body and wraps it in a towel. She puts on "Saturday Night Fever." They sit in the kitchen drinking Kool-Aid the same violent pink as Mary Lynn's bathing suit.

"Let's dance," says Mary Lynn when they finish. They push the table and chairs into the corner and dance wildly, twirling and flinging each other around. *Oh, oh, oh, oh: stayin' alive. Stayin' alive.* When the song ends, they collapse together on the floor, breathless. Maude rewraps the naked Mary Lynn in her towel.

"Okay, Bean-Bag. Go get dressed." She gives her a thump on her toweled behind.

"Don't call me that. I'm too old."

"Oh," Maude sighs. She buries her face in her daughter's damp hair. "What'll I do when you grow up and leave me?"

"You and Roger have your chother." When Mary Lynn was smaller, she heard the phrase "each other" as "our chother"; she still thinks of a chother as some mysterious secretion that grows between two people and cements them together. She adds craftily, "You could have another baby."

"Nothing doing."

The front door opens. Mary Lynn struggles free and runs to greet Roger. The record clicks off.

The sudden silence is gummy and bland. There is so much silence in Maude's life with Roger. Whole happenings go on inside it, subterranean complications and resolutions that Maude never even knows about until they're over. Sometimes he tells her there was something wrong between them last week, or last month, but everything's all right now. It's like finding half a worm in an apple.

Roger comes into the kitchen. He turns his lips inside out when he kisses her. She hopes she doesn't smell of marijuana. He always kisses her hello and good-bye: it's part of his algorithm. "How was your day?" she says.

He tells her in detail while she gets out a beer for him. (She does not have to ask what he wants.) Maude feels as if she has been absorbed; she feels contained, like a ship in a bottle, like Jonah in the belly of the whale. She thinks, He has swallowed me.

"Have you heard anything about—" she catches herself in time, "your mother?"

"No." He looks grim. She is sorry she asked. He goes and lies on their bed and stares out the window. He has run out of conversation anyway, all the routine inquiries ticked off. She thinks of Juan—passionately, volubly (erratically, untruthfully) communicative.

Even in dreams, Roger doesn't speak. Maude does. At first she was afraid she would say Juan's name in her sleep; but as time goes by, and she apparently doesn't, she relaxes. The thought occurs to her: perhaps she has said it, and Roger hasn't wanted to bring it up. Sometimes she thinks it's not that Roger doesn't understand her, but that he understands her too well. (She imagines a traveling salesman trying to pick up a woman with the plea, "My wife understands me.")

Now, lying beside Roger while he sleeps, Maude hears the occasional thump of the turtles moving in the tank, lurching off the rocks. Her thoughts spiral out into the darkness. Often now, she feels unfaithful when she makes love with her husband. Sometimes she pretends he's Juan. She exchanges his crisp, curly hair for Juan's silky stuff, his hairy chest for Juan's smoothness. But something always breaks the spell. She feels his beard; or her eyes open inadvertently. Then she just hangs on and tries to remember the algorithm for making love. Afterwards, the kisses, small pats, the murmurs of endearment and sighs of success are hard.

She gets up and takes a shower. Then she goes into the kitchen and makes a cup of tea and sits at the narrow counter with it. She looks at her reflection in the dark windows of the old row house, the glass grainy with age like taffeta. Maybe if Roger weren't *around* so much. He's always there, wants to spend all their free time together, comes home early to be with her. Closing the bathroom door makes him uneasy: she can feel his heavy presence outside, waiting. She feels as if she were pushing him through life in a shopping cart, pointing out this delight, wheeling him up to that pleasure. His first wife left him for somebody else, just like that, no warning. He came home one day and she was gone. "She was young and restless," Roger said when he told Maude about it. He made it sound like a tautology, as if youth and restlessness were the same thing. Maude pictures her bounding, freckled, with bright hair in a single thick braid down her back. Thinking about her makes Maude feel old.

Whereas Roger makes her feel young. "Listen, Mother," she said when she called to say she was getting married at last. "He isn't young, and he isn't pretty." By that time her mother's standards had fined down to minimal: a husband (any husband) for her daughter; a father for her granddaughter who, miraculously she felt, was not black.

"Your father would be so glad. A steady man. A good steady job." Maude doesn't remember her father, who died when she was six. Just an outline, like the line drawings you see painted on city sidewalks: burly, broad-shouldered, big hands. Maude imagines that Roger is about the same size and shape as her father was.

Really, Maude thinks now, Mother thought we would live in Fort Washington or somewhere, and have a pair of golden retrievers with golden, stupid eyes. She puts her cup in the sink and turns out the light. She thinks of all the men, her lovers, a long chain stretching across the years of high school, college, dropping out, odd jobs. She lost count somewhere around thirty; jobs, sooner than that. All the changing, the different selves; and at each juncture a man would appear who represented the next self, the next Maude. Lynnie's father was the last in the chain. Intense, passionate, unpredictable, sometimes he would hit Maude, then afterwards sprawl on the floor in an agony of contrition, seizing her ankles, while the baby watched with wide eyes. By the time he left, Maude had already met Roger.

Maude goes back to bed. In the night she dreams of Juan's underwater cave of an apartment, of the two of them swimming strongly in the tangled sheets.

They hear from the detective. They get a card from the L.L.M herself. It is a diffident, impersonal card with a prefabricated greeting, "Thinking of You." Inside are the time and day and flight number, with the handwritten message, "Dear Son, Am looking forward to seeing You again after so Many Years."

Roger lies on the bed and looks out the window. He sleeps a lot, sleeping at Maude's, who can't figure out what she's done. The phrase "L.L.M." hasn't crossed her lips since the detective's phone call. She has been careful how she refers to this woman who now looms enormous in their lives, dwarfing everything else.

Mary Lynn tries to work out what to call her. Harriet, since she's not a blood relation, just as she calls Roger Roger and not Daddy? Lately Mary Lynn has been interested in blood. On the other hand, she'd like another grandmother. Grandmothers buy you Barbie dolls and tell you you swim better than the boys. Mary Lynn makes Maude help her draw a family tree. Red for blood relationships: Maude, Maude's mother; green for "Steps": Roger, Harriet. Black, wonders Maude, for absent members? Her father; Lynnie's?

A week before she's due to arrive in Philadelphia, the L.L.M. sends a photograph. It shows a young woman of nineteen or twenty in a glamor pose, full length, one leg curving inward at the knee. She is wearing a bathing suit, draped and boned in the style of the forties, and her hair marches across her head in precisely crimped formation. Her full lips are very dark. Contemplating this Betty Grable image with Mary Lynn looking over her shoulder, Maude cannot reconcile it with that of the seventy-year-old woman living on the edge of poverty in a tiny Florida town. The detective has told Roger her story: fourth (*fourth*? thinks Maude) husband dead, no insurance, no pension. When she was young, the L.L.M. was a singer. She sang with bands in Cleveland and

Pittsburgh and Cincinnati.

In the days before she comes, the silence between Maude and Roger grows thick and sluggish as the late summer weather. It spreads and fills the corners of the house. Maude tries, as hard as Roger himself usually does, not to fight. Fighting with him, even a small fight over nothing, would be like opening a door onto an elevator shaft. She would end up telling him about Juan, thrusting at him the fact of her lover, in anger or in guilt, she's not sure which. If they start at all, she will find herself falling, falling.

With relief she sees Roger drive off to the airport. The weather breaks at last, the heavy August sky cracks open and releases rain.

When they get back, it is the tail end of the thunderstorm. For hours the rain has been beating city dirt into the pavement and hurling itself against the old windows of the row house. It is very late. The weather delayed the plane, made the drive back on the Schuylkill Expressway a nightmare. Maude barely has time to register how small she is, this woman who has dominated their lives for weeks—how thin and small her outstretched hand is. Harriet is very tired: they will talk tomorrow.

When Maude comes downstairs in the morning, Harriet is already up, fully dressed, sitting in one of the straight-backed chairs in the living room. Her back hardly touches the chair; her hands make fists on the chair arms. Maude can't think for a minute who she reminds her of. Then she remembers: that's how Roger walks.

"Good morning," Maude says. "Did you sleep well?"

"Yes, thank you. Very well."

At a loss, they look at each other. Morning light washes the room, gold overlaid with green. What can they possibly say? Everything, words that touch the heart's core, or nothing. Decisions made four decades ago, before Maude existed, flower in the gap between them. Harriet smiles. Her skin, pale as parchment, stretches precariously over the brittle armature of bone. She reminds Maude of something Lynnie brought home from art class in the spring, made of tissue paper over a framework of toothpicks.

Maude goes into the kitchen to start the coffee, comes back and asks, "How was the trip?" The flight was rough; the weather. And the whole trip took longer than Harriet expected. She smokes as if she were knitting, transferring the cigarette from hand to hand, back and forth to her mouth, in an intricate semaphore. Otherwise she sits motionless. When she talks she makes no gestures, no waving to show how fast, no spreading of her hands to show how big. Maude thinks that she is, not relaxed, but contained: in one piece, all of a piece.

When Mary Lynn comes down, Maude goes back into the kitchen. It's Saturday, so they'll have eggs and bacon and fruit. She is so hard, Maude thinks. *Crack!* She hits an egg on the side of the bowl and drops it in. Imagines a baby's skull. *Crack!* I can't stay with this husband. *Crack!* Not this one either. In her mind a picture forms of Harriet in Florida. Palm trees rise abruptly through the shimmering heat. Exotic birds make their exotic noises: parrots, macaws with glittering beaks. Harriet has friends, women alone like her; they play bridge on Saturday afternoons. She goes to the supermarket in elastic stockings, into the cold slap of air-conditioned air, pushing the cart slowly up and down the aisles.

Maude looks down into the bowl. The yolks stare facelessly up at her. She counts them—ten eggs for four people? She sees the picture of Saint Lucy, virgin martyr, on the calendar of her childhood. When Lucy refused to yield (her body, not her soul), they put out her eyes. In the picture, she holds a platter with her eyes on it like two fried eggs. From the dining room Maude hears Mary Lynn's thin tuneless whistle, her voice explaining Harriet to the turtles. They are feeding them grapes, which Roger has asked her not to do. Maude puts rice in the saltshaker as Roger has taught her, so that the humidity doesn't keep it from flowing, picking up the fine grains carefully between her fingernails. She admires them in passing: long nails, smooth as ivory, smooth hands that would not make anyone think of parchment.

At breakfast Harriet sits across from Mary Lynn, Maude across from Roger. Mary Lynn and Maude are still in their bathrobes. Harriet sits straight in her careful blue knit suit with a darned place over one elbow and her careful hair, protected last night by a plastic hat pleated like an accordion.

"What's that painting there?" she asks. "Who did it?"

"Guy Anderson." Roger is pleased to be asked. He turns and looks at the painting with satisfaction. When he bought it, the gallery registered him as the owner. He has papers on it, like a pedigreed animal.

"Very nice." Harriet looks around, making a gesture with her eyes only, to include everything in the room. "You have a nice home."

Maude looks at Roger, then at Harriet. She is his mother. It's a connection that you can't break, that you can always resume, like the Law of Return in Israel. Maude thinks of the word for it: inalienable.

She wonders if Roger will ask the question. Maybe he's decided not to disturb things. The first maxim of computer programming, he has told her, is: If it works, don't touch it.

As if he's read her thoughts, Roger says into a lull, "Mother." Harriet looks up. "Why did you leave—my father?" He doesn't say me.

She hesitates. Her hands make a sudden small motion. She says, "It was humdrum."

Maude's stomach gives a sympathetic throb, like a bass fiddle. Roger turns to look at her as if he feels the vibration. His eyes move from her face to his mother's. They hold an emotion she cannot read.

After breakfast Roger and Mary Lynn and Harriet leave for the zoo, Lynnie holding Harriet's hand. If they hurry, Lynnie tells her grandmother, they'll be in time to see the nocturnal mammals get their dish of blood.

Alone, Maude stands in the quiet house. Harriet is whole. Like the scorpion, she has followed her nature. Whole-hearted; hard-hearted. Are the two things the same? And she, Maude—is she split in two, living her life on two parallel tracks that never meet, while Roger watches from his shell of silence, keeping her safe, waiting for her to leave?

When the dishes are done, she leaves them gleaming in the rack and goes into the living room. She puts on "Saturday Night Fever" and turns the volume up high. Walls and floors and furniture vibrate faintly to the deepest rhythms. Slowly and deliberately she takes off her clothes and lays them across one end of the sofa. She runs her hands through her hair. She dances in the green-gold light.

French Twist

by Susan McIver

Madeleine entered my life in the merry month of May. She arrived via the office door. "I'm sorry to be late, but so many students come to see me," she said in a French accent thick as onion soup.

I was delighted to discover that my three-o'clock appointment was a tantalizing woman: tall, willowy, dressed in a clingy fuchsia top, white pants and sandals. A wisp of hair hung over one eye.

"Do come in," I replied, trying not to stumble over my own feet. I showed her to the comfortable chairs I used for informal meetings.

Since I was a university administrator and the chair of a presidential advisory committee on gender issues, it was not uncommon for female faculty to seek my help on problems.

"I understand you're concerned about your salary," I said, remembering to keep my eyes above shoulder level.

"*Oui!* The department chairman and the dean are such bastards," she lamented. She gave that quick little exhale of breath the French do so well.

"I am a good teacher. I write many scholarly books, and all they do is screw me," she complained.

I can understand that, I thought, sneaking a peek at her shapely legs. With an effort I arranged my face in a sympathetic expression. "Please tell me all about it," I said. When she finished, I promised to investigate the matter and get back to her.

"What are your books about?" I asked, in an attempt to extend her visit.

"Theoretical lesbianism," she answered.

The confusion in my pragmatic meat-and-potatoes soul must have been evident on my face. As if speaking to a particularly slow three-year-old,

Madeleine explained, "For the French, theory, philosophy, LIFE are important." She cast her eyes heavenward.

"Oh," I replied, hoping I sounded suitably profound. I wondered if "theoretical heterosexualism" had been part of Elizabeth Taylor's training. But then . . . she wasn't French.

I watched Madeleine's curvaceous backside disappear through my door. It was then that I decided to give her the opportunity to apply her theoretical concepts.

Later that week I asked her to join me in seeing a documentary film on the importance of gender-free language. Several well-known lesbian writers were being featured, a couple of whom wrote in French. Madeleine accepted readily.

On the appointed evening I picked up Madeleine at her home in the country. As we drove toward the city, she asked, "Do you know the book *Bear*, by Marian Engel?"

"Yes," I replied, recalling the story of a city woman who spent the summer alone at an estate in the Canadian woods and while there, developed an intimate relationship with a large pet male bear. To be more specific, the bear frequently performed cunnilingus on the woman. In their last tryst of the summer the bear finally had an erection. To accommodate her impassioned furry lover the woman dropped on all fours, whereupon the bear clawed the shit out of her back.

"Why do you ask?" I queried, finding it distinctly odd that Madeleine would mention this particular book for no apparent reason.

"It's such a lovely story," she replied. "And so highly regarded in literary circles."

Personally I thought the story was the best argument I'd ever heard for homospeciesism as well as homosexuality.

Madeleine continued, "The woman's search for inner freedom and strength is so moving. And to achieve such communion with other living creatures! How beautiful."

"How bizarre," I wanted to reply. But this was our first date, so reticence prevailed and I was quiet.

For the rest of the drive we chatted about ordinary things like where we had spent our holidays that year, our families, my cats, Jane and Helen, and her dog, Banff.

The film and subsequent panel discussion were excellent. On our way home our conversation became mellow. I mentioned that I was a lesbian, not any sort of theoretical one, mind you, just an ordinary down-to-earth dyke. The conversation never skipped a beat. Things were looking good. At her doorstep I got a hug, a kiss on the cheek, and a syrupy "*Bonne nuit!*"

Spring turned to summer and Madeleine, Banff, a large black Labrador retriever, and I went for long walks in the country. Some famous guy once said that power is the ultimate aphrodisiac. Perhaps it was for him, but fresh air, sunshine, and a picnic on a blanket under a shady tree do wonders for my libido.

I watched Madeleine as she fondled Banff's ears and fed him delectable morsels. How I wished it were me. In my imagination I could feel her fingers run through my hair and taste the succulent grapes as she slipped them seductively into my mouth.

During one of our blanket chats Madeleine stroked Banff's muzzle and told me that whilst she was a theoretical lesbian she was straight in application. I suggested that she might want to heed the advice of Sherlock Holmes' creator, namely, "It is a capital mistake to theorize before one has data."

"No fear of that," she said, playing with the top button of my blouse.

One Saturday evening Madeleine arrived at my house for dinner. After the meal, we relaxed in the living room with coffee. Putting on an old Elvis record, I said, "This should bring back memories."

She listened to "You ain't nothin' but a hound dog," turned off the lights, and put her arms around my neck. Pressing herself against me, she whispered, "*Ma chère*, the music of our youth. It makes me want to . . ."

She breathed deeply.

"To dance."

Hot diggity dog, I thought. This is it! We moved slowly around the room, entwined in each other's arms. She welcomed my caresses. At the end of the record we collapsed in a fevered pile on the chesterfield. I slid my hand under her loose top and onto a braless breast. I heard the catch in her breathing. "Oh Madeleine," I murmured, my throat dry with desire.

As if struck by lightning, she pushed me away. With eyes flashing she snarled, "You devil! You made me feel this way."

In total bewilderment I stared at her. "Huh?" was all I could say.

"I feel like an animal in heat," she said, quivering from head to toe. She glared at me, thrust her pelvis forward, and declared, "I could screw a telephone pole! And it's all your fault."

"But—" I started to say.

"No, no, no," she snapped back, "There aren't any buts. I'm going home." And she did.

Late the next afternoon my telephone rang. It was Madeleine, sweet and innocent, asking me to come over that evening to hear her new classical tape.

"I'd love to," I said. She's changed her mind, I thought, as I hung up the receiver.

A couple of hours later I presented myself at Madeleine's door. She and Banff greeted me. "Please come in, come in," she said, indicating a large comfy sofa. She put on the tape and lit a candle.

"I'll just slip into something comfortable." Expecting her to go into the bedroom, I picked up a magazine to await her return. Instead she changed right there in front of me!

Madeleine gave me a slow-burn smile as she removed her slacks and pullover and slid into a slinky robe. Reaching under her robe, she slipped off her panties. I was melting faster than the candle!

Madeleine curled up on the sofa. "The only thing nicer than the feel of silk," she said, sensually fingering the material of her robe, "is when I stretch out naked in my bed against Banff." She reached down to caress the dog's ears. "It's delicious, no, my little bear?"

Banff put his head in Madeleine's lap, nosed open her robe, and started to lick. Holy Jesus, I thought. The book! The look in Banff's eyes confirmed my worst suspicion. I mean, I love my cats, but not in that way!

"I like to get to bed early on Sunday night," I said and bolted for the door. Was she really suggesting a ménage à trois with Banff? Being next in line after a dog sure wasn't in my game plan!

I was in bed early that night and every other night after that for some time to come. Eventually I met Anne, a nice straightforward, practical woman. My only moment of hesitation came when she told me she had a dog. However, one look at her rickety old miniature poodle and I knew that owner and dog had never considered such a thing.

I did see Madeleine one more time before Anne and I moved to Salt Spring Island. She was walking down the sidewalk accompanied by Banff and two very frisky puppies panting at her heels.

Steam Until Tender

by Frances Cherman

Before brussels sprouts infiltrated Bokey Bender's life, she never would have thought it remotely possible that she would come home from work one night with the intention of turning tricks on Hollywood Boulevard. Well, yes, she'd had the fantasy from time to time, ever since she'd read the article about a housewife from Salt Lake City who'd just picked up and done it—left the seven kids and the husband and the church and took a Greyhound to New York and walked the streets for three days and went home a happier woman with a little extra spending money, though her husband wouldn't let her back in the house. But an idle daydream was all it had been for Bokey. Until tonight.

Simplicity. That's all she craved. A project that begins and ends with clarity and is over in a matter of minutes—not months. No questions. No names. No politics. No Bokey. Just for one evening. Was that so much to ask? Shouldn't anyone in her position be entitled to a few hours of escape?

Then why was her hand shaking? She couldn't get the eyeliner right because of it. The basketball ad—that was the last straw. That and Paul's *au revoir* on the phone last night. All because of that cursed account. It had her drinking more than six cups of coffee a day lately. That's why her hand was shaking, of course. She was out of practice, too. She sighed, resting her elbows on the tile counter and took another gulp of chardonnay. The last time she'd worn eyeliner was in the sixties, along with white lips, scoop-neck poor boys and Nancy Sinatra boots. She studied her face in the bright dressing room mirror, noting the furrows of anxiety, and grabbed a Kleenex. Screw the eyeliner. She thought she looked slutty enough without it.

She tried lowering her violet eyes seductively and pursed her maroon lips like she'd seen Nastassia Kinski do in *Tess of the D'Urbervilles*, thinking, as she did it, that all it had done for Nastassia Kinski was to get her raped. She opened her mouth slightly to accentuate her blush-contoured cheekbones, then raised her eyes slowly to the mirror. Morticia Addams. But she didn't give up. She stood with one knee drawn up slightly so just the toe of her black high-heeled pump rested on the carpet. She angled the knee playfully back and forth across the other leg like she'd seen the hookers do on the police shows. The black spandex skirt was good. She had even put on a garter belt and stockings to help her feel sexy. She learned forward with her hands on the edge of the tile. If she stood just right, she could produce some cleavage at the deep neckline of the spandex top. Well, maybe a hint of cleavage.

No, she didn't think anyone would miss the eyeliner. She was more than attractive enough without it, and not all whores wore eyeliner, anyway, did they? But she had to have jewelry. Jewelry was crucial. Jewelry said a lot. The right earrings would tell them what she was there for. Then maybe she wouldn't have to.

She pushed aside the velvet cases of gold "office" jewelry—necklaces, earrings, and bracelets—and dug around in her basket of old costume jewelry looking for the giant silver hoops she'd bought but never worn. That was when her hand fell on the sprout. She knew it without even seeing it. Nothing felt like that damn sprout.

It had been a joke. Another stupid joke from the morons in the creative department. "I've got brussels sprouts coming out of my ears!" she'd complained at the end of another day of frustration. It was a mistake. You didn't say things like that to people like Brent or Marilyn, even if they *were* being more obtuse than usual. You didn't say things like that to *anyone* at Myers, Ruskin & Burke, in fact. You never knew when they might turn it into a headline. Or a pair of earrings.

They had appeared on her desk the next morning. Brent wouldn't admit it, but she knew it must have been him. She wore them all day, just to spite them, just to say, "See . . . I can take it," then she threw them into her junk jewelry basket and never took them out again.

Brussels sprouts. She used to like them. She would still like them if they hadn't taken over her life. They were there from the very beginning—at the interview.

"Brussels sprouts?" she'd said. She knew they were a small agency—only $1.2 million in billings—but she didn't know they were that small. Brussels sprouts.

"Do you have a problem with that?"

"No . . . I mean, of course not. Who could have a problem with brussels sprouts?"

"Just about everyone," Alexander said.

"Really?"

"Yes." He furrowed his brow. "We've done three comprehensive marketing studies, and brussels sprouts consistently rank as the vegetable people hate most. Even worse than rutabagas."

"Well," she smiled weakly, "I guess a lot of people aren't crazy about them. . . ."

"HATE them!" he barked. Bokey jumped. "They *hate* them! Number one on the list. And that's what we have in front of us. That's the challenge of this position. That's what we're all here for."

Bokey picked at the leather cover of her Day-Timer and glanced around the room. What was the deal here? Was she really considering joining an ad agency whose key client, whose big money-maker, was the California Association of Brussels Sprout Growers?

"People don't understand sprouts," Alexander went on. "Little cabbages, we've tried to tell them. They're just like little cabbages. The problem is, people don't like cabbage either. Grapes are cute. Prunes have an underdog sort of appeal, like VWs, if you know what I mean. But brussels sprouts—now there's a marketing challenge even Stanford can't conquer!"

When the VP finished, his eyes were fastened on some distant point in the heavens, or at least somewhere between the Georgia O'Keeffe framed print and the fluorescent fixture on the ceiling.

Bokey was silent for several seconds, afraid to intrude too suddenly upon whatever it was he was seeing. Finally, she ventured, "I like them, myself."

Alexander offered her the job and Bokey went ahead and took it. Brussels sprouts or not, it was a smart career move. When you've got barely a year's experience under your belt in a job market like L.A., and you're offered a job as the only media planner at a growing agency, you don't turn it down because the product isn't glamorous. You pay your dues like everyone else. Later on you can go for the BBDOs and Chiat Days or maybe even the J. Walter Thompsons. Now she would take her lumps—and her brussels sprouts—without complaint.

But from the first week at Myers, Ruskin & Burke, she'd begun to wonder how long she would last.

"Bokey?" each of them said when she was introduced. "Is that really your name?"

"Well, Brenda, actually," she said. "But I prefer Bokey."

"Brenda Bender? You've got to be kidding."

"That's why I like Bokey better," she sighed.

But if the creative staff were lacking in tact, she soon found they were even less possessed of something far more crucial: the ability to combine creativity with common sense. In the months that followed, she found that putting up with the teasing was nothing compared with placing the ads. That was a major nightmare.

Where could you run ads for brussels sprouts? She'd tried *Vegetarian Times*. Disastrous. Brussels sprouts apparently were not a cool vegetable even for vegetarians. In fact, vegetarians didn't really eat vegetables all that often, the magazine's ad rep finally confessed. No, they preferred processed foods with names like miso and macho and something called a vegie burger that didn't actually contain a single vegetable. One of the magazine's subscribers even had the nerve to write a letter of complaint, which the magazine published, accusing the growers of genetically altering the sprouts to make them grow bigger.

She thought *Home & Hearth* might be a good vehicle, but the magazine turned their ad down. Incredible! Three insertions at $3000 each—$9000 and they turned it down.

"Not appropriate for our readership," they said. It was Friday, the end of a long day, and most of the agency staff had gone home. She wasn't ready for this.

"What's not appropriate about brussels sprouts?" She had practically shouted into the phone. "They don't cause cancer, you know. No one ever got arrested for driving under the influence of vegetables. Gas, maybe. That's the worst they can give you. A little gas."

She wasn't supposed to say things like that about their key client's product, but she seemed to be losing control more and more often. Jeez! Who would think little cabbages could be so controversial?

Or embarrassing. At cocktail parties given by friends outside the industry, she heard it all too often.

"Madeleine tells me you work for an ad agency."

"That's right. I'm a media planner for Myers, Ruskin & Burke. And what do you . . ."

"How exciting," they'd say. "I've always thought it would be fun to work in advertising. Do you make those ads for Toyota?"

"No."

"I just love those ads," they continued. "They make me laugh. Don't you love those Toyota ads, Hal?"

People seemed to think there was one great big ad agency that produced all the ads for major companies. And only TV ads—only the ones that entertained them. They had no idea that most advertising was stuff they would never see on TV. Or never see at all. Trade-magazine ads that sold carpeting to retail stores. Ads that sold imitation raspberry filling to bakers. Ads for computer cables. Direct-mail pieces targeted at people who bought printing services.

"How about the ads for McDonald's? Do you do those?"

"No," Bokey answered.

Finally, with a hint of impatience, they'd ask, "Well, what kind *do* you do then?"

"Brussels sprouts, mainly."

"Brussels sprouts?" She heard the echo of her own voice at the interview. "Yep."

"You mean there are ads for brussels sprouts?"

" 'Fraid so," she'd say.

"Oh." And they'd edge away toward someone with an occupation they understood.

And then last week's clincher—the basketball ad. A cartoon treatment of a burly basketball player shoving a brussels sprout through a hoop, where it fell with a great splash into a bowl of sour-cream-and-onion dip. SLIM DUNK the headline said.

Just where did they think she was going to place an ad like that—*Sprouts Illustrated?*

And was it so unthinkable, after dealing with episodes like that all week, that last night when Paul was trying to map out the European vacation they were planning for October, she found herself saying, "Anywhere but Brussels."

"Bokey, you've gotten just too damn neurotic," he said.

"Anyone would be a little neurotic if they had to do what I do," she argued. But he had finally had enough. *Au revoir.*

She put the finishing touches on her face and tossed back the rest of the wine. This was it. The silver hoops caught the light when she turned her head to grab her purse.

Each time she pulled up at a signal along Highland, she turned a nervous glance to the car next to her. She took this route to work every day, but tonight things were different. Do they know? she wondered. Of course not. How could they know? She was being paranoid. Like back in college when she smoked pot. She'd go out for a pizza and everyone *knew.* No, if they noticed her at all in her inconspicuous Honda, they probably saw a pleasant-looking twenty-eight-year-old woman heading toward Hollywood dressed for a night on the town.

The corner of Hollywood and Highland was mobbed with traffic, as always. There were the usual tourists from Minnesota and Wyoming, the jocks who were just leaving Hollywood High, having stayed late for a game, and the hundreds of others, young and old, who actually lived in L.A. but came to Hollywood once or twice a year to walk the boulevard, poke into Frederick's and the tacky souvenir shops, and see how far the place had fallen of late.

She managed after twenty minutes of driving around to find a parking space on Gower. Her heart was beating fast as she checked her makeup one last time in the Accord's rearview mirror. Was she serious? Was she crazy? Was she really now going to get out of her car, walk alone to the corner of Gower and Hollywood Boulevard on a Friday night and do it? What if she saw someone she knew? Someone from the agency? That was ridiculous, she told herself. No one from the agency would ever come here. She thought of the Salt Lake City housewife. If that woman could get on a Greyhound and go all the way to New York, Bokey could certainly get out of her own car in her own town.

The August night was warm, humid, but she took her black lambskin jacket anyway. She'd seen them wearing leather on "Police Story." Her spike heels caught in the weedy cracks of the sidewalk. At work, she wore low-heeled Bandolino pumps or flats. At work. Stop thinking about it, she commanded.

There is no agency tonight. There never has to be an agency again. She had no job, no apartment. She didn't live anywhere but right here. Her name was not Bokey; it would be—she looked up at the street sign—Holly. Her name was Holly. No last name. And whatever it was they wanted, Holly would. She groaned. The job was definitely getting to her.

The boulevard hummed with people in motion. Long-haired aging hippies in tie-dye. Middle-aged couples looking frightened in a thrilled sort of way. Teenagers in Reeboks and sweats. Bumper-to-bumper cars in both directions. Everyone was there. Everyone except the hookers. Where were they?

She walked a block or two and didn't see any and wondered if she had misunderstood the rules. Surely, they had their stations. But, though she saw many women dressed more sleazily than herself, they were all on the move, all looked like they had places to go, appointments to keep. None of them looked as if she might willingly jump into a car with a stranger as Bokey was planning to do.

She decided to park herself between Frederick's and The Wild Pair shoe store where—ironically, she thought—she had bought the shoes that were now making her wobble like a newborn colt. But what to do after she'd stopped walking? Should she lean against the window? Try to look as if she were shopping? (That was out—the stores had just closed.) Wander a few feet this way, then back a few feet that way? And what would she do if and when someone did approach her? What would he say—"How much?" She hasn't thought about a price. And where would they go? She couldn't see herself in some seedy hotel—in fact, didn't even *know* of any. She realized uneasily she had imagined this event only to the point of her standing on the street. If she had to go beyond that . . . She shivered nervously.

She needn't have worried though, because over the next hour and a half, no long Lincolns pulled to the curb. No men stopped to say, "How much?" Even the police cars passed her by without a glance. Was she that obvious?

There was one young man—a clean-cut accountant-type with glasses— who passed her by once, smiled shyly, then a few minutes later passed her again going in the other direction. The third time he paused by a window of Frederick's. His posture suggested he was examining a pointy-breasted manne- quin in a gold lamé jumpsuit, but Bokey could see he was looking at her. He edged closer. Bokey shrunk into her jacket. Finally, he was so close, she heard him clear his throat and saw beads of sweat on his forehead. Was he waiting for her to say something? Wasn't he supposed to speak first? He seemed as uncertain as she was, and finally, he backed away from the window and halfway down the block before turning and almost running into a lamppost.

She had a single, brief moment of glory when a polyester-clad family of four walked by—obviously tourists, probably from Iowa or Indiana or one of the other "I" states—and the woman clutched her husband's arm. "Isn't that terrible, the way they do that!" she whispered furiously with a grimace of such distaste, Bokey felt her face fill with something akin to pride. She had passed, if only with people who, like herself, had learned everything they knew about hookers from watching TV.

Finally, near midnight, a shiny Ford sedan pulled to the curb. A window was lowered, and the driver leaned toward her. But when he beckoned, she was so overwhelmed with terror, she turned her back on him and pretended to search for something in her purse.

From the corner of her eye, she saw him make an angry gesture, and when he screeched away, she winced. Who could blame him for being mad? She had deceived him—and herself, too. She was not going to turn tricks tonight or ever. She was not going to be Holly nobody. She was Bokey. She had a job, which she hated, and a roomy old apartment, which she loved. How did she think she could run away, even for a single night? She walked back to her car, pulled a parking ticket off the windshield, and dropped into the seat. Her feet were aching. The evening was a complete waste. She didn't want to go home, but where else could she go? Her feet were too sore to go dancing. Besides, everyone would think she was there to get picked up. She laughed at the irony.

She had almost decided to call it a night when she thought of Ralph's. The twenty-four-hour supermarket on the corner of Sunset and Highland wasn't exactly a Hollywood hot spot, but it was bright, always open, and cheerful in its sterile way. It was relatively safe, if you didn't mind the weirdos who hung out in the feminine-hygiene aisle or wandered all night without buying and who got weirder and fewer as the hour got later. In fact, she needed to get a few things. She had been using dish detergent on her hair for the past three days because she hadn't had time to buy shampoo—another benefit of the job—and her pantry was almost empty except for some condiments and cans of garbanzo beans and sliced beets that dated back to her first week in the apartment three years ago.

The store's loudspeaker system played a Muzak version of "Purple Haze" as she strolled the aisles. Only in Hollywood, she thought, humming along. She put the Jhirmack shampoo in her cart and wandered past the yogurts. Should she buy the one made from all-natural ingredients that cost three times more? Or should she buy the economical Ralph's brand, probably made from macerated extract of cow's hooves? There was no hurry now, and she weighed her decision carefully before choosing the Ralph's.

Mr. Walker was only trying to help her find some fresher asparagus. The few stalks she had found under the asparagus sign (after closing her eyes past the brussels sprouts) were pale and fat and seemed tired. Mr. Walker had been hosing down the lettuce, and he smiled, showing a row of even, white teeth, when she said, "Excuse me . . ."

He looked a little like a young Robert Mitchum, maybe forty, with wavy lips and a disarming, boyish smile. His dark hair kept falling over his right eye, and he swept it away impatiently.

She followed him through the rubber-lipped doors into the warehouse. He seemed almost courtly as he led her around the stack of cantaloupe crates, warning her to watch that she didn't snag her jacket on the wire, and as he offered his hand to help her over the blades of the forklift. He parted the vinyl strips to the cooler where the boxes of asparagus were stacked, and swept his arm in front of him, almost bowing, then laughing at himself. Though the light was dim, Bokey thought she saw him blush. He shook the lid off one of the boxes and she murmured thanks as she scooped out a loose handful of spears that seemed strong and bursting with life. She thought of Paul and shivered. Her jacket was no match for the chill of the produce room.

"Just a few minutes of steam," Mr. Walker was saying. "You lay 'em down nice and gentle in a pan—I use a fry pan. Keep 'em raised up out of the water, and you just want to steam 'em 'til they're tender and bright green. You gotta baby 'em or they'll overcook before you know it." She nodded agreement. If there was one thing she understood, it was vegetables.

"Yep, just about anything you want back here," Mr. Walker said with that boyish smile as they stepped back into the warehouse. The doorway was narrow and their shoulders almost touched. She picked up the faint scent of his after-shave: English Leather, one of her favorites. She looked around the dark, damp warehouse. There were boxes of Idaho potatoes stacked three high. Crates of honeydew melons. Ventilated boxes of lettuce and, yes, even brussels sprouts over in the corner. The boxes, crates and equipment made tall dividers that turned the giant space into a maze of small, almost cozy rooms. He led her through them now, pointing out where the various procedures took place, answering the questions she asked with genuine interest. Maybe it was because exhaustion had settled over her like a kind of haze, but she found herself soothed by the sound of his voice, and, as she trailed in the wake of his after-shave, she relaxed for the first time in weeks. She could have followed him around all night.

At the back of the warehouse, behind a wall of carrot boxes, a conveyor belt sat idle. Draped over it was a rectangular section of green produce-bin liner—the thin, plastic grid that kept the vegetables raised and dry. Bits of lettuce and broccoli flowerets dotted the rubber belt. She idly wondered what it would be like working in this world every day instead of an office where people refused $9000 just like that.

Mr. Walker was next to her then, pointing at something down the belt, and his scent was coming to her in small waves, the way rocks give off heat at night. She noticed his forearms, dark and muscled, and then his hands, large with rough knuckles and a crisscross of faint scars—scars from wooden crates and sharp, corrugated cardboard, no doubt. Short, square fingers with something dark, maybe rutabaga remnants, maybe old parsley, under the fingernails. He wasn't wearing a wedding ring.

He was so close now she could feel the moist edges of his breath, and she noticed, as he kissed her at last, that his lips were as tender and soft as his hands were rough, and they were so warm that as she backed up against the conveyor belt she hardly felt the cold of the steel edge against her thighs. And when he rocked her back onto the rubber belt, even that distant chill was gone, and her skirt was gone too, up around her waist, and she and Mr. Walker were gone. Images swam in and out of her half-closed eyes. A green apron hanging on a hook. A box of plastic numbers. A push broom leaning up against the wall. A hand-lettered sign for shallots, $1.19/lb. Not a single brussels sprout clouded her vision.

Then—minutes later, or was it hours?—Mr. Walker was helping her off the conveyor belt, helping her stand on her shaky legs, and they were both flushed and laughing and looking in different directions. And without thinking about it, Bokey was letting him tuck something into her hand.

Finally, out in the bright aisle with her cart in front of her again and Mr. Walker out of sight, his face still fresh in her mind, she looked and realized that it was money. He had given her two twenties and a ten. She stared at the bills as if they were foreign. He'd paid her. She was wondering how to feel about that, what it all meant, when the images and sensations of a few moments ago swept over her again. She smiled and pushed her cart down the aisle.

She made her way down canned vegetables, trying to look like a normal late-night shopper, then was suddenly sure she had a row of Day-Glo orange sale-price stickers across the back of her spandex skirt. Turning to check, she found no price stickers but was horrified to find that she did have a perfect and deep impression of the produce-bin liner's distinctive diamond pattern down the backs of both thighs. The produce clerks and cashiers would know instantly what it was, she was certain, and would also know exactly how it got there. She tried massaging the marks away as she walked, but realized she was attracting the attention of a man she'd noticed earlier—one of the few men in the store who looked as if he were actually shopping for groceries.

A young man at the register rang her up and Bokey handed over the bills she had absently crumpled into a ball not unlike a huge brussels sprout. The cashier pulled them apart and looked at them curiously. Bokey's heart thumped. He knew. But how? Was it possible that Mr. Walker's money somehow carried his smell?

"Um . . ." he said. She braced herself. "It only comes to $5.43." Bokey laughed. Of course! She'd given him way too much money. That was all. The cashier kept his eyes on her as he handed back the two twenties and made change for the ten. Then he closed the cash drawer just a little too fast.

On the way home, some questions occurred to her. Did all store produce managers behave like this? Did all media planners? Could she make a living this way—between the lunch meats and the frozen desserts?

She let herself into the apartment. There were three or four calls on the machine, but she was in no mood to hear them. She took off her jacket and was reaching for the wooden hanger when she saw it. Clinging to the back of the jacket was a thin, shriveled leaf of iceberg lettuce, looking exactly like a used condom. Bokey laughed softly. Shaking her head, she peeled off the leaf and put it aside for her scrapbook. Then she fell onto the bed. She would get the calls later. Tell them she'd been out doing market research. Yes, she thought as she drifted off, she could live through another year of brussels sprouts. A million-point-two definitely put them on the front burner.

Weehawken

by Susan Volchok

Despite the classic ad campaign—you could see posters in the subway for years afterward—Sonia feels sure she's one of only a fortunate few to have ever gotten a real job through a blind ad in the *New York Times*. And credits a combination of nerve and sheer luck: lacking any qualifications for the position, she'd fired off an audacious letter ("Just give me a chance! . . ."); against all odds, it had actually intrigued the man in charge enough to arrange an interview. And the most improbable upshot of their first meeting was her being hired on the spot. Installing Sonia in his own office— as it turned out, they were the entire copywriting department—Dennis patiently demonstrated the art of producing the direct-mail pieces Viesel Science Press favors. Within a week, she is boiling down books on even the most arid subjects to colorful, catchily written flyers. Two weeks more and Dennis is inviting her out to an Irish saloon for lunch, revealing over hamburgers that he is unhappily married to an accountant named Janet, and confessing over coffee that he thinks he's fallen in love with his new colleague. Work, which has seemed satisfyingly simple, is about to become more complicated.

She scarcely has time, overnight, to wonder or worry about this new twist. Her excitement doesn't surprise her (though, lying in bed, sleepless, secretly exulting, she tries to be stern, to tell herself, Slow down, girl!). She's been alone quite a while. And now, it turns out that if he's not exactly single, he's not exactly taken either. Definitely an interesting situation.

Yet the next day, having gone for a drink with him after work, she panics when he seizes her hand as she laughs at some remark, drawing it to his lips in a way that seems absurdly fervent, out of place in the empty Blarney Stone.

135

"Don't," she says, her voice altogether too whispery to mean business.

"Why not?" Dennis asks. "I want to. You make me want to. You're wonderful."

She reddens. Clears her throat. "Oh, come on. You hardly know me." A cool rebuff seems like the right, the smart, thing to offer. As continued resistance to her own attraction and sense of intrigue seems smart.

"I know all I need to know," he says simply. "I believe in chemistry." What a line, she thinks, even as she feels his dark eyes devouring her. Simultaneously, she can sense her cherished skepticism shuddering on the brink.

"Why me?" she persists.

"Why not?" comes the echo. But it's measured, full of meaning. There's nothing insouciant about his words, or about him. In fact, she realizes, it is just his subtle but insistent melancholy, some heavyheartedness only hinted at by those brown eyes, that touches her in spite of herself. She wants to tenderly smooth the back of her hand along the lean, tense jaw beginning to go bluish with beard shadow. She picks up her wine glass instead and sips, surveying the seedy place he's chosen for the start of their romance. Shit: now she's going to have to get him to tell her more about Janet, about what's happened to make him so unhappy that he's looking around. Looking at her. With that look. He hasn't let go of her hand, either.

"You can't have been miserable the whole time, can you?" she wonders. He's told how they met, married: he's mentioned that it's been seven years and some since. She hates to sound so suspicious of his suddenly conceived passion for *her*. But if it's only an inevitable itch he's scratching, then he's got to expect to have some explaining to do.

"No, we were all right once; pretty happy, actually," he concedes. "Things have been impossible just this last year or so." He sighs, withdraws his hand, presses his palms together as if praying for her dispensation. "Where to start. You know I play piano. But I want to do more with my music than amuse friends at cocktail parties." He opens his hands, holds them out toward her. They're huge, hungry. She hesitates, then places both her hands in his. He lowers his voice. "My ultimate plan is to quit publishing, to compose and perform full-time."

She nods sagely, reflecting on the evidence she's already gathered. Classic pop standards playing eight hours a day in their shared office. The concentrated doodling in music manuscript spirals, lunch hours, after-hours. The half-unconscious humming, dark head swaying to keep time, big fine-boned hands working out complex fingerings on the edge of his desk. She can't judge his musicianship: if he's recorded himself at the piano, he hasn't brought that tape in yet. His erudition, though, is unmistakable, and his ardor infectious. Already, she's learned to hum along with the obscure intros and tricky bridges to songs she thought she knew all about, knowing only their famous lead melodies.

"It's a tough business," she comments, imagining the cliché might cushion the implicit challenge: what makes you think you can make it?

"Every business is tough," he says. "But I'm good; I'm damn good. I'm too good to—" He stops himself, smiles deprecatingly, shaking his head. Sonia wouldn't have been insulted if he'd finished the thought. He's a little older, had put in his time already; probably, he is wasting himself at Viesel. Really, when it came right down to it, how *could* a man stay there, doing more or less the exact, easily mastered thing as she, for four years? She didn't expect to stick around that long herself. This music thing, though, this personal ambition, makes him seem substantial, and at the same time interesting, original. Besides, she likes a man who believes in himself, as she believes in her own destiny. It encourages a certain sense of security. She can feel her shoulders relax, her body tip slightly toward him in some surer sympathy, if not, yet, surrender.

"Unfortunately, my wife doesn't share my confidence," he continues. "To say the least. No, Janet tells me this idea of turning professional is stupid, a self-indulgent dream. Which are all deadly sins, in her book." He scowls, a truly black look, then seems encouraged by Sonia's small answering frown and shrugs a shoulder nonchalantly as his face smooths itself again. "Besides, she couldn't care less about my music. I mean, it's a big-deal favor, her listening to me work up material for the few gigs I do manage to make time for. Bores her to death." He lowers Sonia's cradled hands to the table, the tips of his long, pianist's fingers stroking the sensitive underside of her wrists. Not like you, she imagines him thinking; not like you.

"The truth is, we've been heading toward this dead end awhile now, both of us losing interest and unhappy without noticing. When you've been together for years, you tend to just go on. And on. Anyhow, she's finally let me know, in no uncertain terms, I won't have her support making the transition." His hands open again on the table, releasing her if she wants to go; his importunate gaze falters. "Who knows, maybe she's right."

Sonia doesn't move, barely blinks. It's a throwaway line, the coda to what she recognizes all too clearly as a variation on the well-worn theme My Wife Doesn't Understand Me. But none of it seems any less real for that. And it strikes a chord, certainly. Even if she didn't love music as she does, *she* could never condemn a man to sit at a battered desk in a cramped office if he belonged behind the grand piano of an elegant supper club.

She squeezes one of his hands, smiles, at the same time inwardly acknowledging her own absurdity. Of course, she knows nothing more about his talent or prospects than she did when they started.

"Sometimes, you just go on, until . . ." He kisses her then, quickly but full on the lips, drawing back as if dazzled by her presence, her hands in his.

And what he might be or become seems suddenly beside the point. He's persuaded her of something more essential, perhaps most of all by making such little apparent effort to persuade. Something's settled between them, some consonance, complicity; something's begun. If she doesn't yet believe in him, still she knows that deep down she believes in chemistry, too. And in making destiny happen. Time might very well qualify this little Q&A session as their first date. Whatever else she may have wished it to be, Sonia tells herself she's done her best to encourage a certain openness. She can only hope she'll know what she needs to know.

On the other hand, she doesn't want her relationship with Dennis—"or whatever this is we're getting into," as she describes it to herself, just to be on the safely cynical side—any more out in the open, or moving any faster, at least for the moment. On the basic level of public perceptions, she hates the idea of people figuring her for someone who has a thing about married men. Which she doesn't; or, hasn't had before. In point of fact, their staid old firm un-officially frowns on even single colleagues coupling off.

But Sonia has her own, more private scruples. If Dennis is unhappy (her thinking goes) his wanting me is all right. Why not? And my wanting him: it's not as if I'm breaking up his marriage, stealing him from her or something. Still, I won't go out with him—except, maybe, for working lunches—until he says he's definitely splitting. And sleeping with him—well, that's strictly on hold, until he's got a place of his own.

Not that she had these ground rules ready; she's frankly never found herself in the midst of anything like this before. And they're as much about self-defense as self-righteousness: suddenly, setting some such conditions seems the only way to get a grip. Who (she wonders) could have foreseen that the physical constraints of office life would actually work to turn up the heat?

Temporarily prevented from acting, Dennis teases, tempts, endlessly telling Sonia what he wants to do to her. Now. Here. Never having cheated before doesn't seem to have crimped his imagination.

". . . that sweet spot . . . playing you, like . . ."

The images are vividly graphic, without a trace of vulgarity. And they work on her as even the women's erotica she's seen doesn't, as if he's somehow projecting her most intimate fantasies, purely her pleasure in mind. When she complains (pretty lamely, it's true) that she can't think or write with him talking nonsense, he laughs at her lack of conviction, launches into another squirmy scenario. Or sometimes, instead, presents another piece of his detailed plan for their future together.

"We'll spend this first summer trying different beaches every weekend, up at the Cape, out on the Island, down the Jersey Shore, see where we want to settle."

She gets up, walks stiffly past his desk and out of the office, feeling his gaze following, heavy as a long-fingered hand on her backside.

"Imagine doing it out in a deck chair at sunset," he hisses after her.

Catching up to her later at the coffee machine, he sulkily whispers, "I *want* you."

And the next morning, leaning into her as they walk down a long, empty corridor toward the weekly editorial conference, he moans, "I can't stand being so close to you without being able to hold you."

There's no question: weaving a web of words, he's getting to her, daily, hourly. It's ridiculous, she thinks. But when an afternoon goes by with no sighing from his side of the room, no delirious daydreams breathed across the small space between them, she's disappointed—almost dejected. He's getting to me, all right, she realizes. And realizes that he realizes it too.

It isn't all talk, either; he has, she thinks, a real gift for romantic gesture. One gray January afternoon, she comes upon him lost in the embrace of her heavy tweed coat where it hangs on the back of their door. His eyes are closed as he breathes in her phantom fragrance, and he seems insensible to her approach, as if he were in a swoon. She stands there, swaying a little herself, stunned by the whole idea, no less by the sight of him staging it—even as the suspicion that it has been staged, for her, sinks in.

On a Friday evening not long after, as she's buttoning that coat, he shuts the door, falls to his knees, and begs her (as if he had to beg! and there are tears in his eyes, she sees, amazed all over again), "Please; please don't go yet. Can't you work a little late tonight?"

"Oh for God's sake, Dennis, get up!" she laughs. But, God! he was so intense! And all so that they could walk the single short block to Grand Central together, away from the office full of waggling tongues. Who would think we're totally nuts, she reflects afterward, recalling their brief clasping of hands for good-bye. It isn't as if they take the same train, or even the same staircase: she rides the East Side IRT just a few stops uptown, while he shuttles over to the West Side to catch a commuter bus bound for New Jersey. Weehawken! The fact that he lives there, works on his music there, is the only thing that keeps her from sneering at the silly, small-time sound of the name.

Eventually, he offers her a chance to hear the work, sliding a cassette onto her desk one morning before hurrying off to a meeting of department heads. The label on the tape inside is hand-inscribed with two song titles and a brief note: "S., How I love you! D."

No mention is made of this on his return, and she doesn't listen to it until very late that night. There's anticipation in the delaying, but also anxiety, a genuine dread that the tape will be so awful she'll want to call off the whole affair. Finally, she undresses, wraps herself in the old chenille robe, starts up the tape deck, and settles into the armchair, still edgy but ready for anything. The sound of the piano is slightly muffled; his voice, though, is uncannily clear, a pure, strong tenor.

" 'Ah, penny, brown penny, brown penny, I am looped in the loops of her hair.' " She'd worried, at the time, that handing him the typed-up bit of young Yeats (half-recalled from her own younger days, copied out of a tattered Complete Works) was a mistake: would he take it too seriously, or (worse, much worse) think she was too serious, Miss English Major totally gone? But now, she's moved to hear the melody, preternaturally unmelodic, he's made to fit "Brown Penny."

"Sonia's Song" is even less tonal, and more haunting. Or haunted. As are the lyrics, apparently also his own. "I will watch you cross the river, you will walk across the river, through the glittering snow." Unsettlingly strange stuff; she has no idea what any of it means, except for the chorus, her name as banshee cry, three keening syllables: *Son . . . i . . . a.* It has a starved-out sound, nothing left but hopeless longing and who knows, even love. It's too tender, too tormented; she can hardly stand to hear it. She plays it over and over. Then she pops the tape out of the machine, brings it to the bedside table, slides it into her Walkman. And falls asleep with the headset on, safe in the close, familiar darkness, chilled and fired both by his faraway call. " 'O love is the crooked thing. . . .' *Son . . . i . . . a . . .*"

Shortly after, they begin kissing themselves breathless behind the closed office door, holding one another so tightly Sonia can feel his sex stir against her, hear a whimper escape him. It's torture moving apart, almost impossible to sit down to work again, swollen and sore. Soon, she lets him slip his hand inside her sweater to cover a breast as he stands behind her desk chair, surveying her latest work; soon lets him slide her skirt up, work both hands down behind. "You have the *most* adorable ass," he tells her, squeezing a little, then a little harder, his grin almost goofy with affection. He must know how weak her knees go, how wet she gets. She doesn't have to put her hand on him to know how excited he is by the liberty, by the fact that they're going this far on despised Viesel territory. This is, though, about as far as they can go, just now. She's still set on their waiting for his separation. There's no way he can imagine it's any easier for her. And no question in her mind it will be worth the wait.

It takes Dennis something less than a month to decide that he has to leave Janet once and for all.

"It's for me," he assures Sonia, "not just for us." (She's most scrupulous about this, wanting him to be sure of his own motives, unwilling to take full blame if things don't pan out.) They celebrate by going down to Little Italy for dinner, eating family style in a noisy, garishly decorated joint. Afterward, they walk along dark Grand Street with their arms around one another, then sit holding hands in a small café. As they finish their espressos and he signals for a check, she impulsively leans over to press her mouth to his temple, then whispers that she'd like him to come up when he drives her home.

"Not for coffee," he muses. "We've done coffee."

"We've done coffee," she agrees. "Maybe, um, a nightcap?" The word sounds so implausible on her lips she begins to laugh, bending toward him until her forehead brushes his chest. Then, she feels his hands close on her upper arms, and he draws her up, holds her away for a moment, gives her a little shake, his expression so sober it scares her.

"What?" she asks. "What is it?"

"I love you so much, it's—"

He shakes his head, doesn't say What. His face looks strained, intent on unseen things. It hasn't really occurred to her, until tonight, that this must be even riskier, more complicated, for him, wanting her, walking away from his marriage, and still not entirely sure what she wanted, what was going to happen. The drive uptown seems to relax him, though; he pulls her closer as they climb the narrow staircase to her apartment, second floor, front.

"Nice place," he comments, sitting back on the mattress she's made up as a day-bed, and looking around the sparsely furnished studio.

"Huh," she says disparagingly, throwing one leg over an arm of the homely embroidered chair that had been her grandmother's. Most of the furniture is similarly family castoffs. But it's a cozy enough home for her, it's fine, for the time being. Smiling over at him, she's struck by how right he looks, lounging against the bolster pillows.

"Come here," he says. She gets up, goes to him, more than ready to relax the rules tonight. They lie on the bed kissing, urgently but unfrantically, their first coming together this far from the office, and all by themselves.

"I adore you," he tells her. "You're incredible, the absolute best thing that's ever happened to me."

She blinks, bites her underlip to keep from protesting.

"You have no idea how badly I want you," he breathes in her ear for the thousandth time. "I want you so much my balls hurt, my whole body aches with it. I want you, want you, want you." It's like a spell. They roll over and over until she's on top again. She sits up, straddling him, gazing down at his painfully pleasured face, and moves more deliberately, thinking that, since it's just a matter of time before he's free, it might be all right to let him. It would be her decision, now. And then, he could stay until morning; he wouldn't have to leave her alone.

"I'd better go," he's saying.

"Oh no. Are you sure?" she asks. She doesn't want to say, Stay. But she wants him to know she's thinking, Don't go.

"Yeah, I think I'd better," he says. She leans over to kiss him again, but his lips are set in a taut line, and his mouth has hardly met hers before he eases her off and sits up. He tucks in his shirt, slips his loafers back on. She sits on the edge of the bed beside him, puts her arm around his shoulders. He isn't a big man, only inches taller than she, but his body is solid, smoothly muscled. Beautiful.

"You know, you don't have to go, not yet," she says softly. Still noncommittal enough.

"I want to," he says.

"Oh." She can't keep her voice from sounding small, hurt.

"Silly," he says, turning, taking her chin in his palm, tilting her head up a bit. "I mean, look, you said it yourself, we want to do this the right way. So let's not ruin everything by rushing it now." He kisses away the crease between her eyebrows, strokes her cheek with his back-curved thumb. Funny, she thinks, the way he'd taken on her point of view just as she was on the verge of abandoning it. The effect is that she feels a last remnant of hesitation evaporate, trailing away like a dream.

"You're right. It'll be wonderful, when it's time." The thought that he would still be going home to a wife in New Jersey occurs to her only after he has kissed her lightly at the door and gone. She even wonders, momentarily, whether he'd promised to be back at a certain hour, before reassuring herself that he could have slept with her and then taken off if he'd wanted to be a sneaky shit.

Another few weeks of playing office games: sometimes now they manage to sneak out to the elevator bank at the same time and commandeer a car, frantically tonguing and pinching and stroking as the rattling cabin goes all the way up and all the way down without stopping anywhere. And there are a few more excruciating weekend dates, parking in the narrow front seat of the vintage VW, parting at her front door with more kisses, promises. Impossible to wait any longer.

On the first Monday night in March, Dennis calls her at home for the first time.

"Guess what?" His high happiness in her ear sets her body humming.

"You found a place."

"I found a place," he confirms. "For us."

Somehow, she'd imagined that if and when he finally made the break, he would move right into the city. But she should have known he wouldn't want to trade down to the kind of New York apartment he could afford. Besides, he'd naturally be trying to cut expenses to the bone now, maybe even put money by before kicking off his new career. No, the move isn't going to be much in miles.

And he must know Weehawken disappoints: first thing, he raves about all the space he'll have for less than half what a convertible one-bedroom in Manhattan runs.

"I'll be settled in by the end of this week," he crows. "I've got a van for the few big things, and I'll drive my own stuff over in the bug. Susie too, of course."

"Of course!" Among all the elements of his domestic drama, Sonia has most closely followed the sticky subplot involving Dennis' dog, Susie. He'd brought the aging black Labrador into the marriage, but Janet had balked at giving her back, claiming she couldn't live in their house all by herself. Though they both knew this was pure spite, he'd had to buy her a pricey Doberman puppy, and promise to pay for its future training, before she'd agree to let Susie go. Once again, Sonia is agreeably struck by his devotion to the dog. And by secret relief that he and Janet don't have any real children to bicker about, or bargain for custody of.

"I've even gotten piano movers who promise the baby grand will be in place by Friday," he continues. "And I want you to be here with me, this weekend. You've got to come! I'll make dinner for us, and I'll finally be able to play for you. And then . . ."

Their audible sighs suit the overheated, overgrown adolescents they've been impersonating.

"Can you wait, my beautiful wild girl?" he teases.

"I'm not sure I can," she says, blithe now that the waiting is almost over. "We'll see."

Strangely (or maybe not so, when she stops to consider it) they both seem eager to buckle down to work for the rest of the week, as though the existence of the apartment, the certain prospect of some consummation, has really resolved things. Sonia notices that even her breathing seems steadier, more collected, as if she's come down from the thin ozone of a mountaintop to an atmosphere that supports real life.

"See you Monday," Dennis says, as they emerge from the elevator Friday evening with a crowd of chattering secretaries and editors.

"Have a good one," calls Sonia gaily. She has the directions in her purse.

Saturday, there's snow in the air, and by afternoon the sky is a steel dome. Sonia wanders around the Port Authority Terminal, killing time before the 4:35 to Weehawken. There are as many hookers, druggies, homeless as usual, and she decides, after all, that it might be wiser to wait upstairs on the platform; in fact, the bus is a 4:25, ready to take off when she reaches the top of the escalator. She rushes on, grabbing a seat near the back, and glances at the tired, closed faces of the other passengers. So strange, she thinks: she's probably never been as happy and hopeful as she is today, riding a bus to Weehawken, New Jersey, to sleep with someone she can now begin to think of as her lover, a man with whom she is, maybe, in love.

The late afternoon light is gone by the time the bus pulls into town and stops at a streetside shelter to let her off. Snowflakes flurry around her head, and the wind tangles her hair. She walks two blocks before noticing that the numbers are going down instead of up; not one for omens, or for panicking at the thought of being lost in the Jersey dusk, she trudges back, worrying more about the mascara that must be running down her cheeks with the tears the stinging wind has wrung from her eyes.

He doesn't ask who it is before buzzing her in. She pauses in the dismal lobby, trying to make herself presentable without a mirror, then takes the elevator to the top floor.

A door at one end of the short corridor is open, piano music drifting out. She pushes against the door with her fingertips, and as it swings slowly in, she can see him, outlined against snow-whitened casement windows, seated behind the instrument whose sonorous voice and massive mahogany case fill the narrow living room. The sounding board is fully uncovered; the song that surrounds her is one of his favorites, "The Way You Look Tonight." It's a ravishing arrangement, further proof of his artistry, if she needs any. And of his affection.

She steps over the threshold, stops; his efforts to make the newly tenanted setting seem lovely, too, are everywhere evident, and enchanting. Candles glow on the piano, the windowsills, the small table set back in a dining alcove; she imagines she can see their soft lights flickering even from the bedroom beyond. There are flower-filled vases scattered around the room, a bottle of champagne and two crystal flutes waiting on an end table. It's all perfect, she thinks; perfect.

"My God, at last," he says huskily as the chords die under his hands. "You're here. You're actually here."

"I'm here."

Then, arms tight around her, he's kissing her, fierce kisses, almost frightening. Most of the men she's known have been much cooler, far less direct, even when it came to desire, as if disdaining the idea of needing anything from her. Whereas Dennis' need is so undisguised she's sometimes felt it's what most defines him. She pulls away, finally, lightly protesting, "At least let me get my coat off, maniac!" He obligingly helps her out of it, supports her elbow as she kicks off her boots.

A large black dog ambles out of the kitchen, makes straight for her, snuffling her outstretched palm.

"You must be Susie," she says, kneeling to pat the dog's graying head and look into its sleepy face.

"She hangs out in the kitchen when the oven's on," Dennis explains. "The heat's not the greatest here." He kisses the top of Sonia's head, murmurs into her hair. "But I'll keep you warm, I promise." He holds out his hand and pulls her to her feet, while Susie gives a parting snort and pads back to her own post, heavy hips swaying, tail sweeping against the worn wood floor.

"So, what do you think?" he demands, lacing his fingers through hers.

"This . . . it's beautiful," she says. To her eyes, the apartment itself already appears less spacious and impressive than his enthusiastic descriptions had suggested. What is beautiful and moving is his sense of the occasion, how painstakingly he's prepared for her coming.

"Champagne now?" he asks. "Or with dinner."

"Oh, I don't know," she answers, then adds, "Now."

She stands beside him as he fills the champagne flutes, hands her one. The stem trembles slightly between her fingers.

"To us," he declares. "Starting over." He sits down, sinking slightly into the seat cushions of the dilapidated couch. She settles on its threadbare arm, swallows a crisp mouthful, her free hand playing with the thick, dark hair brushing the back of his turtleneck. His eyelids appear almost closed from this angle, lashes velvet against sharp cheekbones. She sighs, thinking of later, of how much she enjoys watching a man drift off after lovemaking. Especially the first time. He starts up, eyes brightening with some mischief.

"I'd better see about dinner," he says. "I'm starting to feel like I might just pull out the sofa bed and throw you down on it." She expects he'll kiss her again, make her forget about eating. But he goes straight into the kitchen, and soon she hears him bustling around like a seasoned housekeeper, all the while humming something, what is it?

"Can I help you?" she calls.

He hums another few bars. "Embraceable You." She holds her arms out to an invisible partner, glides a few steps forward.

"No thanks, nothing to it," he finally answers. Then: "Well, actually, how long do you cook a piece of frozen turbot?"

It isn't a total disaster, all things considered. Sonia manages to partially defrost the fishy ice block under running water, trusting his electric broiler-oven and liberal doses of lemon and butter to do the rest. The vegetables, too, are from the freezer section of the supermarket, but at least he hadn't grabbed the first succotash bargain bag he saw. The Fiesta Combo looks cheerful on their chipped white plates. And Dennis has baked the potatoes himself, he assures her, disappointed that she wants to eat hers plain, without the sour cream he's remembered to buy specially.

"It's fine, I like it this way," she says, picking at the dried-out skin. She smiles contentedly at him through the grouping of candles set on unmatched saucers at the table's center. It's all so funny, so sweet. He refills their champagne glasses, and she wordlessly raises hers to him. The way to a woman's heart (this woman's, anyway) isn't through her stomach. They could have sat on the bare living room floor, licking their fingers over a bucket of KFC, for all she cares about the food.

He tops off her champagne once more, pushes away from the table, takes his original seat at the piano. This might have been the awkward interval, the meal over, table ready to be cleared, and both of them standing around, wondering how much longer they should delay. He offers a deftly arranged medley of "As Time Goes By" and "I Only Have Eyes For You." Then he moves into something extravagantly lyrical, yet without lyrics, something she doesn't recognize.

"'Sonia by Starlight,'" he teasingly retitles it, swaying over the dramatic progressions. She'd begun to collect the silverware and stack the plates but slips up behind him, her hands on his shoulders.

"Come to bed," she whispers, working her thumbs into the tense muscles of his back. The sound of her own voice asking him makes her shiver.

The bedroom is a floral-papered box off the living room, furnished with a brand-new double bed and a man's dresser newly separated from the marital bedroom set. Dennis stoops to blow out a guttering candle, then switches on a lamp sitting on a folding chair between the bed and the grimy leaded window. Sonia can see snowflakes sailing by.

He half turns from her and strips to white briefs so instantly there isn't time to feel surprised. Another awkward moment averted. He slides between the sheets and watches as she undoes her blouse. She watches her fingers work the pearl buttons instead of watching him. She unzips the slim black woolen skirt, steps out, carefully hanging it over the back of the chair. She's aware of the exaggerated thrust of her breasts in the lacy, black underwire bra, conscious of flattening out the curve of her belly as she stands near the foot of the bed and works the black patterned hose down over her hips. She isn't used to putting on a show. Is dark, coordinated lingerie really sexy, or just silly? She leaves the bikini pants on. The parquet floor is cold. He throws aside the covers; she gets into bed and sinks back against a pillow, closing her eyes as he draws her to him, kisses her forehead, eyelids, lips, nuzzles the hollow between her breasts.

"You are so beautiful, so incredibly beautiful," he says, sliding one hand down between her legs, pressing insistently there. "Beautiful . . . beautiful . . ." He continues to speak in an urgent undertone between kisses. She finds the words he uses on her more supple and insinuating than his fingers, reminding her of how helplessly aroused his soft, suggestive voice has often left her at work. She can feel her body, her whole self, opening and opening to him.

"I love the way you make love to me," she murmurs, tentatively moving her hand to touch him, cupping her fingers beneath, rubbing her thumb up along the ridged cotton pouch. He isn't ready, not nearly. Selfish, letting him do everything. "Let me." She slides her palm across his abdomen and under the waistband; his eyes close and his voice is stopped by a sharp intake of breath. "I want you inside me," she whispers, tender, too, toward her own sense of the newness of everything. He lies under her grasp; it's up to her, now, to end the waiting.

He pulls the briefs over his hips and off. They kiss, but he doesn't touch her anymore, just lies back, gives her the power; she rocks herself open against his hip, letting her breasts brush his rib cage, her fingers steadily working. And nothing happens. Oh, he might seem to be coming to life for a moment; then he retreats into himself again, small, fragile, hesitating. Quick inventory of her small bag of tricks, where some slight pressure might be applied, where to try a teasing finger: nothing. She can feel her grip growing tense, impatient, around him.

Then, gracefully as she can, she releases him and sits up, kneeling over his body. He's so still, lifeless, she might be a night nurse about to administer artificial respiration. As she sweeps her hair to one side and bends toward him, he opens his eyes and seizes the arm that steadies her. "Don't."

Her smile is meant to be sly, self-assured. "I want to," she says. "I want to, Dennis." There's pleasure for her in the simple saying of it, the offering of herself. "This is what I want to do for you."

"Well, don't," he warns. "I don't want you to. What I want is, just stop, okay? I want you to stop." He puts out his other hand to keep her from touching him again. Then he shifts his hips so that he's out of her reach. "Stop it!" In another instant, he's sitting up.

"What's going on, Dennis?" She herself can plainly hear the fear behind the question. He isn't even looking at her, as he sits hugging his knees to his chest, rocking slightly.

"Nothing's going on. Or haven't you noticed?" Like a slap. She's never before heard this nasty edge in his voice.

"It's okay; I mean, it's *okay.*" Isn't reassurance the thing to offer? "Let me try to—"

"You don't get it! I don't want you to try anymore, you've tried and you've tried and—" He makes a gesture of sheer futility, his face almost distorted by a grimace of disgust.

"And what?" Her voice is more remote, a little colder: scared cold.

"It's no use. Get it? It's no good." He stares at her as he might at someone seen for the first time, some utter stranger. "The thing is, I don't think I'm really attracted to you." There is a small, deafening silence, in which she sees something like a smirk blossoming on his so serious, persuasive lips.

"*What?*" It may be the most ferocious sound she's ever made in her life. She lunges across the bed, seizes his shoulder. "What the hell are you saying?" He seems to shrink under her hand and the force of her shouting. But only for an instant; then he shrugs her off, starts talking at her.

"I'm saying that I wanted this to happen, I willed it to happen, but it's not happening because—because it's not, that's all." His voice is as matter-of-fact as if he were explaining some step of the publishing process. "Something's missing, I don't know, the attraction, the chemistry, whatever you want to call it. Let's just say you don't do it for me." He scarcely flinches as her hand flies up toward his face, a sharp crack across one cheek that brightens the sallow skin.

"Liar!" Closing her throbbing hand, she lands four or five blows with both fists across his chest before he even bothers to catch her wrists. He won't hit her back, she knows without knowing how. He isn't *in* it, somehow; not exactly here.

"If you hadn't been so up for this yourself, you would've sensed something," he tells her, holding her at arm's length, a stray cat. "Even so, you should have realized something was wrong. You should have known."

She tries to twist away; his hands on her now, rude, restraining, are horrible. She'd nearly forgotten her nakedness, how appallingly exposed she is.

"What should I have known? *You* were all over *me*, all over me from day one." She's trembling, her eyes sting. But she knows what she knows. Doesn't she? "You got hard enough in the office."

"I didn't. I never did, that's the point."

Unbelievable; but it unnerves her. "No, that's more bullshit," she manages, not even sure she can trust her voice to mean it. "What are you really telling me, that you can't get it up when it counts? Is that what I should have known?" She summons this as the harshest, most hurtful way to say it, to defend the truth—the real story—from what he's trying to do to it now. And it's as pathetic as hitting him. It doesn't even make her feel better. As for him, he just shakes his head, rolls his hound-dog eyes.

"Oh, I can get it up all right." Smiling again, expansive, he lets her go. "I can get it up just fine, thanks."

"Right. And this has never, ever happened before," she comments, crossing her arms over her breasts, her eyes stony. But she's left too many openings.

"If it has, it's been—reversible," he returns easily. "There's no problem when there's, you know, a spark. But with us . . ." He raises his hands, palms flat up and empty, nothing left to say.

" 'Us.' " She takes up the scornful refrain. "What about us? What's the problem?" She can't really be asking, asking for more. But she still doesn't understand. And understanding things is crucial, it's everything. How can it be over, before anything's happened?

"I've told you, *it's not happening*. And, sorry, you can't make it happen. Neither can I; it's just one of those things. I guess I should have stopped trying to get it going without that energy being there. You really can't make something out of nothing."

Nothing. The word itself is a numbing nothingness; a white noise fills the space, flooding her head, silencing her. But he's still talking. "I always thought a woman could tell what's what. You should have known."

Every time you held me in your arms, every time you kissed me, every time you told me how it was going to be? Later, she would think, That must be how couples kill each other when there's a gun in the night table. But she doesn't even have the energy to swing at him again. "You liar, you miserable, goddamn liar," she says. Only, less incredulously this time. Whether he'd lied all along— with his words, music, his ravenous eyes and hands, everything he had—or whether he's lying now, she has no way of knowing. He's not talking anymore. He draws the twisted sheet up toward his chest, pinning it with a muscular arm: case closed.

She's struck by the sudden insight that his melancholy is a mere accident of nature, that pensive look, that somber face, no more than a mask; his natural mask, certainly, but still, a trick, an illusion: part of the seduction. Seeing it, believing in it, you wanted to hold him, comfort him, make him laugh, give him your love. But she had seen him laugh, hadn't she, seen her love reflected in his eyes day after day for months, and now he was saying there was nothing to that, nothing at all behind it, whatever she'd dreamed she'd seen. This is crazy, she thinks, crazy: He feels *nothing*? None of that desperate desire, not even remorse for this outrageous ending?

Crazy or true or neither, let it go, she tells herself; let it go, and get out of here. He'd been eager enough to assure her he didn't want her, after all: pressing him beyond that—there's a limit to what she can stand. And, likely, no limit to what he might say. Or be able to make her believe.

Shaking with the cold now, she turns abruptly from him to retrieve her clothing. She knows he's watching as she dresses; her movements feel unco-ordinated, her fingers too stiff to swiftly secure buttons, zippers. She breathes deeply, concentrating on getting ready to be gone. Before she has a chance to ask, his calm, caressing voice informs her that there are no more buses into the city until morning.

"Where's the phone? I'll call a cab," she says briskly, glancing around. Whatever it costs, it will be more than worth it. Home, in her own little place, her own little bed, alone and allowed to cry until she can't cry anymore: she'd give anything for that.

Though he has the decency to wind the sheet around himself before he swings his body out of bed, he sounds less than decently regretful as he announces, "No way a cab can get through this blizzard." The brittle snap of the metallic slats irritates her as much as his casual tone.

"So I'm just stuck." She imagines it's what he really wants to say.

"I guess you are." In his flimsy toga, his bare feet pale, his raven hair falling over his forehead, he looks boyish, beautiful in an unthreatening, uncomplicated way again. But boys are the cruelest, whatever their intentions; they can't help it, that's their nature. She doesn't know if he can help it; he'll never tell. Besides, he isn't a boy, though he hasn't acted the way she imagines a man would.

"It's not so bad, really; you can stay in here, and I'll sleep on the couch."

Annoyance replaces rage, allowing her a moment of control.

"How very gallant of you."

"Well," he murmurs, almost contrite. Then, as if heartened by the thought, he asks, brightly, "What are your choices?"

It brings her straight back to reality. She has no choice, is in control of nothing but herself here. And how certain is that? Face-to-face in the near darkness, the air seems electric again with possibility. Or impossibility. For an instant, it seems that the slightest sign either way could prompt her to open her arms to him, or provoke her to bloody his sad-eyed face with her fist.

He doesn't give a sign, just shows her where the extra blankets are stowed, pulling one out for himself. She doesn't move, doesn't speak, only follows his movements with her eyes. All right; get the hell out, then! She needs, suddenly, to lie down, oh, just to lie down. She'll have to wait until tomorrow (Sunday, of course, only the loneliest day of the week would do) to lie in her own, lonely bed, feel how bad it had been, know exactly what the damage is.

"Good night, Sonia." He stands in the doorway, draped and dignified as a Roman. Shameful, disgusting, to want him, to wish, to imagine What if. She doesn't answer, but stands stubbornly watching, waiting until he's gone before moving to sit on the edge of the mattress. Frigid air leaks through the rotting window frame. She curls up beneath the covers, a child in a strange, stone-cold bed.

She can't sleep; of course not. The plummeting temperature alone guarantees wakefulness. After a time, when she thinks he—with his cloudy face and clear conscience—must be far away in dreamland, she steps out into the little hall behind the living room. She imagines she can hear his steady breathing and steals past, thankful that he lies buried so far beneath the bedding there's nothing of him to be seen, not a silky hair, nor a skillful finger.

Nothing.

In the kitchen, she nearly stumbles over Susie, sprawled on a rag rug between the still-radiant stove and the refrigerator, which gives off some heat at its base, she discovers, as she sits down beside the dog. Sonia massages the special place behind Susie's ears, strokes her palm along the dog's spiky back.

"Wake up, little Susie, wake up," she softly sings. *Thump, thump, thump thump*, the tail beats the time, and the dog sits up on its haunches and licks her cheek. Then the tears come, and she can't stop them, and not even Susie's huge, pink tongue can wick them away as fast as they fall. She puts both arms around the barrel-shaped body and buries her face in the coarse black coat. The dog sits stolidly, perfectly still, patient as a mother while the woman sobs and shakes. Every so often, a little cry rises in Susie's throat, a reflexive response so subtle that only Sonia, with her ear near the dog's breastbone, can feel the vibration, or hear the sound.

Beyond the ice-edged kitchen window, the season's last snowfall is smothering the town. Watching it, Sonia can almost feel its hushing weight; she wonders whether the warmth that seems to be penetrating her body is an hallucination, the kind they say overcomes you as you freeze to death. But that's silly: a dog would know better than to lie down and freeze on a kitchen floor. Even if some people do die in unheated apartments every winter. Is not caring part of the delusion? Maybe it would be better to go back to bed, but this time with Susie to huddle against.

"C'mon Suse, let's go," she whispers, half rising and noiselessly snapping her fingers. The dog won't budge, not even when Sonia tugs gently on the worn leather collar. She stands beside the sturdy, unmoving shape, hesitating, calculating: the icy bed sheets, the funky braided rug; alone and awake in the freezing dark, awake and comforted by some creaturely warmth.

"Let me at least get us a blanket," she concludes. Susie greets her return by sniffing uncertainly at the green-plaid wool, then sighing companionably as Sonia settles herself against the wall, tucks the blanket about them.

Poor old girl, she thinks, you should have a bed out here every night. But though Susie finally consents to ease her full weight to the floor and wear the tartan cape, though she occasionally rests her head on Sonia's thigh, she seems never to close her eyes again, not even when her loyal muzzle is stroked, her noble brow rubbed. Sonia surprises herself by dozing off for long moments. But whenever she looks down, the dog is watching her, easily alert, unwavering.

Rescued, she thinks drowsily. Stupid storm, making everything even more stupidly difficult and dramatic. But truly, it's as if the brave Labrador had been sent ahead by the search party to track down survivors. And found her. If only Dennis doesn't discover them stiff and senseless in the morning, everything will be all right, she'll be fine. It's only a matter, now, of making it through this last long night, the courageous black bitch standing guard beside her, watching through the drifts for the rescue vehicles, which would surely be rolling out again come dawn to carry her back across the river through the glittering snow.

Appomattox

by Ai

The bus was full the rainy afternoon
we sat across the aisle from one another
and unashamed, I stared at you.
You had a choirboy's face,
tempered by the promise of sin.
I thought you were a pretty man,
the kind who was too dangerous
for anything but friendship.
When I got off, I was surprised
to find you matching my stride
through the pools of standing water.
One block, two blocks,
upstairs to my apartment.
I still remember the slow, sweet time
before the foreplay ended.
We never spoke.
We kept our separate war and peace to ourselves,
until one day, you broke the spell.

I'm James, you said
and I told you the intimacy of names
was still too much to ask of me,
but you insisted,
and we lost the game of keeping things simple
and plain as a Shaker hatbox,
where we could store our past
poor failures at loving.
I don't want to see you anymore, I said, one day
as you were leaving,
but suddenly, I wanted to suck your fingertips
and twist those long strands of your hair
in my hands until you begged me
to make love to you again,
so I pulled you back inside.
I wish the floor had opened up
and swallowed me,
but here we are five years from then,
locked in our wedded misery.
Sex without responsibility could have saved us
from disaster,
but now it's too late,
now love's a letter stamped "return to sender,"
stamped "surrender" on delivery.

Counting

by Lisa Vice

S teve, Rita thinks. Steve makes nine. But there had been three Steves and whenever she comes to the first one as she counts, she inevitably thinks of the other two. The first Steve was shorter than Rita and had long thick black hair that spilled over his shoulders and the smooth hairless skin of a young girl. He had a dog named Love with blue eyes and a wolf's face. The dog lay at the foot of the bed whimpering until the bedsprings stopped rocking. The second Steve had seemed so sweet, with his blond hair tucked under a bandanna. How was she supposed to know he'd end up taking too much acid the way he did? How could she know he'd end up standing under her apartment window singing "Wild Horses" until the neighbors called the police and they took him away? She could still hear his soft faltering voice singing, "We'll ride them some day." The last Steve, the one she'd seen off and on for years, called himself an aging hippie. He kept his curly graying red hair under a green felt cap. This Steve washed windows on Mass. Ave. and once won a bet that he could sample every liqueur behind the bar at Jack's and still balance his washing stick on the tip of his index finger when he finished.

It was a familiar ritual, this counting of men she had slept with. It was what Rita did when she couldn't sleep, which happened more and more, even though she would crawl into bed exhausted from the work of the farm. That day she had pushed the hand cultivator up and down between the rows of peas and every muscle in her body ached. But she knew as soon as she lay on the bed that she was not going to be able to sleep. She couldn't even close her eyes and stared instead at the thin sliver of a moon rising up over the hills. She tried to imagine that she had a huge broom to sweep away all the thoughts in her mind. The worries about money. Always, would there be enough? Her concern about the weather. What would they do if it didn't rain? Could they afford to irrigate? Was it too late? In the past, sometimes just the sweeping sound of the straw across wood relaxed her enough to sleep. But tonight it doesn't work. She presses a pillow over her face and tries to picture herself sleeping soundly, tries to envision herself lying on the bed with her eyes peacefully shut, her arms at her sides, her chest rising and falling rhythmically. But tonight, with Neil beside her snoring softly and her daughter, Rain, in her bed on the other side of the kitchen singing the ABC song in a whispered voice, she ends up turning to her last resort.

As Rita counts the men she has slept with, she tries to remember details about each one. Lonnie Elder, the boy who'd lived in a pink-painted cinder-block house on the other side of the small town where Rita grew up. Medora, Indiana, where old men sit on the bench in front of The Covered Bridge Cafe waiting for their wives to emerge from the Hornet's Nest across the street, their blue-tinted white hair whipped like spun sugar around their heads. Where the children buy penny candy from Randy's Market, a grocery stocked with stale crackers and bread, lunch meat and cheese. A row of soda pop machines lined up on the wooden porch for after-hours, which comes at six. Randy's Market, where swallows' nests dangle like whiskers from between the corrugated tin roof and the rafters, and, when the screen door slaps behind you, it is easy to navigate the wide aisles since you are the only one walking down the wooden floors that creak as you look for a can of corn or a bottle of vinegar.

Medora, Indiana: a town ringed with cornfields and grain silos, divvied up by railroad tracks. A plastics plant on the outskirts beside the cramped trailer park. A town that smells of trash burning. Where on summer days barefoot girls in shorts and halters ride their bikes hoping for a breeze. Most of the shopping that is done takes place at Bob's, where the shelves are loaded with bottles of hard liquor and cheap wine.

Lonnie had eyed Rita on the school bus and started walking her home, then later to the edge of town where they would lie in the snowy cornfields, the wind howling around them, his face red and wet as he kissed her, his breath tasting of the chocolate bars he ate by the dozens. He lay on top of her, pressing her down, grinding his hips into her until finally he talked her into coming home with him to lie on a cot in the basement of his house, in a room they called the rec room, which until years later, reading it in a book, Rita had thought of as a wreck room, it was such a mess of broken-down furniture, rusty lawn-mower parts, and piles of newspapers. On a cot in a corner with her bare thighs pressed up next to the damp wall, Lonnie reached his goal. That being to get "it" inside her.

What Rita remembers most about that moment is Lonnie's mother's car pulling up beside the narrow casement window, the tires crunching across the gravel, the slam of the car door as Rita pushed Lonnie away and yanked her jeans back up.

Lonnie wasn't the first, as he liked to think and as he told all the boys at school. There was no stain of blood on the mattress ticking. Rita's father had already seen to that. Before she was old enough to know what he was taking, he would come in the night, his rough callused hands touching her in places she'd never dared touch herself. With his thick gray horse-tail hair brushing her face and the sour wine smell of his sweat cold on her body, he would push himself into her while Rita pretended to sleep, praying her little sister, who was inches away, would not wake up and be scared.

Rita got out of town the first chance she had. That was after Phil, a boy from the college in Bloomington, drove into Medora on a hot day in July. He was sight-seeing, he said. He saw Rita sitting on the bench in front of the grocery store drinking a Coke and offered her a ride in his red Chevy. She had gone with him without another thought but Take me away. They went clear to Sparksville, driving fast along the White River with all the windows down, the radio blaring, competing with the locusts that whined and whirred in the corn. They had kissed in the graveyard till Rita's lips ached.

Afterwards, Phil told her about his hopes of becoming an entrepreneur. Rita did not ask what that was. She leaned her head against the soft red upholstery and let him touch her under her blouse. The idea that a person could spend his whole life without ever seeing corn grow amazed her. That he found it beautiful and commented on the sweet smell of the earth baking in the sun. To Rita, corn was like the air she breathed, and she had completely taken its presence for granted. Later, when her mother threatened to have her locked up if she didn't quit with that good-for-nothing city boy who only wanted one thing, Phil gave Rita bus fare to Boston and the name of a girl she could stay with. It was 1968. All over the country, girls like Rita, who had been lucky enough not to get knocked up but not lucky enough to figure out what else to do, had begun running away from home. She knew if she stayed, she would soon be one of those women with a tired shuffle and a bad perm who pushed a rickety baby carriage up and down the roadside.

Rita feels tired thinking of Phil, but not tired enough to sleep. She remembers how he gave her all of his Lawrence Durrell books. She had read the books, but to this day couldn't say what they were about. She remembers the name of the place where the characters were: Alexandria. Nothing more. Phil sent her a few postcards after she left Indiana, then nothing. But by then it didn't matter. Rita had a job in downtown Boston cutting fabric, and a room in an apartment on Beacon Hill.

She continues to count. The man whose name she can't remember. The one who wore white jeans and a white shirt. Whose back had been covered with a thick carpet of hair. He had thrust himself into her rapidly two or three times and then sighed and said, "The pause that refreshes."

Then Bobby, who sat on the front steps of their building playing his trumpet, his head tilted back, his eyes half shut. Bobby, who convinced Rita his girlfriend Shelly, who went out of town to visit her folks for the weekend, had an open mind. But when Shelly came home she stood under Rita's window screaming that she couldn't live in the same building with someone who had slept with her boyfriend and either Rita or she had to go. Rita moved across the river to Brighton, swearing she would never sleep with another man again, but then there was the last Steve, whom she saw off and on for years, until that last time, the time after a party at his house, when he talked her into sleeping with him and another couple. A man and woman she'd never seen before. Hadn't even noticed until he pointed them out. The man looked her right in the eye. He had round gold-rimmed glasses on. The woman pulled at the split ends of her long brown hair and seemed bored. Rita still cringes as she remembers turning away from the strange man who had pushed in and out of her slowly, stopping every few minutes to kiss his girlfriend who moaned beside them. When he rolled off Rita, Steve pulled her into his arms. She still cringes when she thinks of the other woman beside her staring up at the ceiling as the strange man pushed himself into her. She had wanted to take this woman by the hand and say Let's get out of here.

George always jumped up to wash himself when he finished. He never held her. He was the first man, she realizes with a start, who made her understand that she wanted to be held more than anything. After George came Elias. Rain's father. Rita had never met a black man before. Had never even seen a black person until she moved to the city. I was old enough to know better, she thinks. Twenty years old. But he was tall and thin and looked at her so intently when they passed on the street Rita felt her face blush clear up into her scalp. She had stopped and turned around, as if pulled by an invisible magnet, and he had been waiting for her. "Where are you headed?" he asked. Rita thought if anybody could understand what hell her life had been, it would be a black person. Hadn't they suffered like she had? Wouldn't that be something to finally share? What Rita remembers most is Elias sitting cross-legged on her bed eating an orange after the first time they made love. His thin dark fingers picked the sections apart carefully; his white teeth bit the juicy fruit. He leaned towards her and tucked a piece into her mouth, brushed her hair away from her eyes. They saw each other every day for two weeks. It was the closest Rita had ever felt to being in love. More than anything, the hope of some shared history kept her wanting him. Her body did not respond the way she had begun to hear a woman's could.

Later, when men took to asking her, "Did you come?", she would nod and assure them she had, though she had no idea what it meant. But back then, nobody asked. Least of all Elias, who had stripped her clothes off with the same precision he had peeled the orange.

At the end of two weeks, he told her he was married. That his wife and boys had been away, visiting family down south. That this was the end of what he called a pleasant time. Rita didn't even know his last name. She didn't know where he lived or what his phone number was. When she discovered she was pregnant, she would walk the streets looking for him, but she never saw him again.

After Elias, that was it. Never again. It wasn't worth it. But of course now there was Neil.

Rita feels like a worn towel being squeezed through a wringer. Neil, who has no idea he is number twenty-two, turns on his side, his erection bumping her thigh. Now here I am, she thinks, biting her lip and sighing as she moves to the edge of the bed. Trapped. As trapped as I was in Medora.

Love bears no resemblance to that malarkey they feed you in the picture shows, her mother had often said when Rita was growing up. What is it then? Rita wants to know. Men passing over her body like she is one more bridge to get to the other side of?

Rita has never felt so much as a shiver of desire for any of the men she has been with though she knows that none of them would ever guess this. Making love, having sex, coupling—whatever you decide to call it—feels to Rita like her body has been invited to a party while the rest of her has stayed home in flannel pajamas watching reruns.

With a child depending on her, with a kid to always think of, she feels as trapped as when she lived back home. She knows if she could cry, she could sleep. But she is afraid Neil will wake up and hear her. Neil, she thinks. If I can't work it out with him, that'll be that. Already the thought of sex with Neil makes her sick inside. He has what he calls his technique. Three kisses, one for each eyelid, one for her mouth. Then he kneads her breasts and tells her he loves her before he crouches over her whispering, "Are you ready?" Ready for what, Rita wants to say. But she always gives him what he wants. It's easier than saying no and having to live with his sullen moods. She moves underneath him in the way she knows will make him finish. And afterwards, when he moans and whispers, "Did you have one?" she always says "Yes."

Rita crosses her arms across her chest, hugging herself. An image of her father's rough hands reaching up under her nightgown, of how he would spit into his hand to make her wet, flashes by like a slide being projected on a screen in her mind. But Rita is thinking of the rows of strawberries they will plant next spring. She is thinking of the baskets of peas they will bring to farmer's market on Friday. She is thinking of the blackberry jam she will make in August, already counting the jars lined up above the sink, planning how they will open the jars all through the winter, smear the thick purple jam across toast. The cat, sensing she is awake, inches slowly up the bed and flops beside her, purring loudly. Rita puts an arm over him, hugging the soft furry body close. She can hear the broom straw scratching across the unfinished shed floor. In her mind, she is sweeping and sweeping, slower and slower, counting the men, one by one, till their faces blur.

Watching Out

by Deborah Shouse

It takes all my courage to walk into the coffeehouse alone. In the three months since Andrew and I broke up, I have either cloistered myself at home or cushioned myself with a circle of women friends.

The walls are rough and clothed in black paint, the pipes above are orange. I wind through the small round tables, clotted with twosomes leaning close, sipping iced cappuccino, talking earnestly.

Near the makeshift stage, I take an empty table and open my book.

I am reading *To Kill a Mockingbird* for the twenty-third time, my own private psalm. I skip to the middle and read about Boo hiding, the brilliant ghost whom no one understands. I ignore the shadow that falls across my book. The shadow robs light from my pages, then diminishes. Someone touches my hand and I jump.

"Sorry to startle you," the man standing beside my table says. "But I was asking if this chair is available." The man's face shines with the excitement of a child ripping open a present. His eyes are the color of fallen pine needles. I want to brush the slice of coffee-colored hair from his forehead and press my finger into the frayed opening on the knee of his jeans.

"Sure, sit down," I say.

Laughter splashes above the serious rumble of conversation and the espresso-machine hisses. A thin balding man taps on the microphone and clears his throat. "Thank you for coming to our first poetry and prose reading," he says, playing with the fringe on his purple vest while he speaks.

"Six, seven, eight . . ." The man beside me is counting a stack of papers. I watch until he reaches twenty. He looks up and smiles.

"I compulsively count my pages before I read," he explains. "I have this fear

158

that I'll get deep into a story, then suddenly, a page will be gone. I'll lose my train of thought and the audience will think I'm an idiot."

"And now, I'd like you all to help me welcome Peter Algeme," the microphone man says.

The man beside me tosses his hair and stands, smiling at the applause. His steps are certain and strong and his hands steady as he takes the microphone.

He reads aloud from his unfinished novella. He writes about short women with brown curly hair who dress like schoolteachers and turn into fierce lovers once the room is darkened. He writes of cowboys who sit outside empty buildings waiting for something to change. I listen and know the echo of his chest under my ear though I have not yet touched his wrist.

He finishes reading and hangs his head during the applause. Then he hurries to my table.

"You were great," I say and touch his arm.

He looks at me with such openness that my words freeze. He puts his hand over mine.

"Thank you," he says. His voice is the sun breaking pink against the sky. I inch my chair closer.

Peter talks about how Faulkner has shaped his own work. He has lived a few hours from my growing-up town, haunting the Ole Miss campus while his father taught piano theory to sophomores.

"I used every typewriter on the campus," he says. "A secretary would go out to lunch and I'd commandeer her desk. I knew even then I wanted to write."

"While you were becoming brilliant and literary, I was working at Jennings Fruit Market, adding up produce. But I didn't know I would end up as an accountant," I say.

I am conscious of leaning toward him, breathing him in. I wait until it's quite late before I stand up to go.

"Let's meet again," Peter says. He stands too. When I look into his eyes I am flung out of my abyss and into the light. "How about Monday afternoon?" he says.

"I work until five-thirty," I tell him.

"Six then," he says, holding out his hand for me to shake. I am strong, so I do not bend and kiss each knuckle. I do not press his hand against my mouth and allow him closer to me. I shake firmly and bump into only two chairs on my way out.

At our third meeting, a fly nudges my bagel. Peter waves a lazy hand and brushes my face. The tips of his fingers on my cheek feel like fire. As he talks I imagine pressing my lips against his right nipple. I imagine the sound he might make as he talks about Truman Capote's influence on his writing. I lean closer.

After coffee, he walks me home. He walks backwards in front of me, not minding the rain on his face. He watches me while he talks about Anaïs Nin's journals. He weaves words into castles and invites me inside.

"What do you do to make a living?" I ask him.

"Talk and write and walk." He raises both arms to the sky and laughs.

"Where do you live?" I ask.

"Mid-town."

He is so pure, so happy, that to poke him with questions makes me feel like a nagging mother. I loosen my stride to walk near him. I unclench my arms. I wear purple socks instead of panty hose and swirling gauze skirts instead of straight wool.

The last man who borrowed my heart wore grey suits and lived on his Gold Card. He said, "Our relationship will yield large dividends."

Peter pays his way with crumpled dollar bills. He has the comfortable look of someone who sits on the porch steps, bare feet lolling in the dust, waiting for me to roller-skate by.

"Who is this person?" Gerda asks. "Why haven't I met him?"

"He's mysterious," I say.

"Where does he live? What does he do for a living? What are the names of his former wives? What kind of childhood did he have? Is he in therapy?" Gerda throws out the questions I have bitten back.

"I know his favorite authors," I tell her.

She pats my hand and says, "Watch out." She gives me a look for emphasis as she picks up the income-statement analysis.

I watch out my window and imagine Peter walking past, seeing me and dashing into the imposing building, conquering the elevator, mastering the long grey corridor to my office. I imagine him bursting through my office door and opening his arms to me. The cash flow sits stagnant while I watch out for him.

My heart doesn't start beating until five-thirty on Tuesdays and Thursdays, when I've left work, walking, skipping toward the cafe where I meet Peter. Then I dare to take a deep breath, and longing, love, and excitement tumble out of me like spilled marbles. I rush past them, hoping not to trip.

Peter bends over his writing tablet, a mug of coffee at his elbow. I sit across from him and he reads to me. His heroine wears my hair and now has an accounting job. She is beautiful and I imagine Peter dreams of me while he writes.

"Do you want to come with me Saturday to my boss's anniversary party?" I ask.

"I can't," he says. He offers no more and I am ashamed to question him. So far, we have been together only in this coffeehouse or walking me home. His life is a bright-globed mystery and I want its map. I want to mark his movements with black crayon so I can be sure to find him.

The other men I loved had routes and systems. They traveled in straight lines and easy trajectories. But Peter is untrackable.

He strokes the inside of my thumb, then moves his fingers down my wrist. His touch is the ending of the world, both fire and ice. Closing my eyes, I hold my breath and lose myself.

"You take pleasure so easily," he says, smiling.

"Yes," I answer, though I had not known it before.

Yes, I say to all that he tells me. Yes, my hair looks reddish in the light of sunset. Yes, I have a strong way of walking. Yes, I easily understand the insides of a poem. He gives me missing pieces of myself and I collect them gratefully.

Gerda persuades me to go out for a drink.

"You seem so withdrawn since you've started seeing this Peter character," she says. The sports bar where Andrew and I used to go now seems alien. I can't remember what I used to drink and embarrass Gerda by ordering hot tea.

"We don't serve tea," the young bartender says. His hair is porcupine-stiff and he is moving, pouring, mixing while he waits for a more appropriate response.

"Perrier," I say.

"If you like this guy so much," Gerda says, leaning her elbows on the bar, "how come you never actually go anywhere with him?"

"We go to the coffeehouse," I say.

"I never heard of anyone going to just one place. Are you sure he isn't married or anything?"

"He's not married." A calm spreads through me thinking of Peter. His drawing-room approach enthralls me. He moves toward me like a nineteenth-century gentleman, touching my hand, my arms, brushing against me, inciting me without hurry. Andrew had grabbed me and run with me as though I were his ticket to a touchdown. He dashed toward dating, lovemaking, living together, then he dropped me triumphantly and walked away.

With Peter, I am the one who yearns for more. He colors every corner of my mind. I carry his words, his gestures, his casual touch with me everywhere, like a puzzle with missing pieces.

"Well, Bob in liabilities asked if you were going with anyone," Gerda says. "What should I tell him?"

I see Peter's face, forming like a developing picture from clear liquid and blank paper. His hair, hiding one eyebrow, his eyes demanding to know more, his mouth, forming elegant syllables.

"Tell Bob I'm in love," I say.

The Saturday Peter finally invites me to his house, I spend all morning trying on underwear in front of my bathroom mirror. To see myself, I balance on the rim of the old tub. Usually I wear dusty white cotton, plain as a line of numbers. But since I met Peter, I've bought a drawerful of richly colored lingerie. I imagine Peter arching his hands over the cool pink satin or the purple silk. Or would he be more pleased with black lace?

His house gently blends into tall trees and old apartment buildings. We sit on his porch swing and he strokes the crook of my elbow and looks at me while I talk. He catches every word as though it were the last drop of a vintage wine.

When he lifts my hand and kisses it, I feel like a diver, shooting to the ocean surface for a gulp of air.

In the yard, a large dog roots around in the peonies. On the sidewalk, a bent woman wrestles with a shopping cart. Peter talks about the tricky ending of his novel. I run out of words. My mouth is a desert.

"I need a drink of water," I say.

Peter takes my hand and leads me inside. Books are stacked on both sides of the sofa. I picture him lying on the couch, facing the window, a sofa cushion jammed underneath his head, the light texturing the pages of his book. I imagine his bare feet, the nails slightly crooked.

He hands me a glass and I drink. When I am done, he puts the glass on the bookshelf.

"You are so wondrous," he says, reaching for me, guiding me to the sofa.

He lays me down and touches me gently. The words that fill me are: "I too have drunk and seen the spider." The spider inches across my mind and shrivels as I feel Peter's chest and hear the hard thrust of his heart.

Everything in me wants him. I reach to unbutton his shirt and travel my hands down his chest. His skin electrifies my palms; his moan unties my heart.

A ballet, his hands as he tenderly undresses me, his mouth a sonnet as he revels in my body. By the time he moves to my breasts, I am floating, lost in viscous swirls of purples and reds.

I reach to unzip his jeans and he catches both my hands. I pull him down and bury my mouth in his. I press him hard against me and his belt buckle jabs me.

"Peter, I love you," I say. I feel like I am running down a secret path deep into forest as he suckles my breast. I lose myself in the tug of his mouth, melting into pools of musky want.

My nipples stiffen into pebbles. I slide my hand through his richly tousled hair and hear a raspy breathing.

"Peter? Are you all right?"

His mouth releases my breast and I realize Peter is asleep.

"Peter?" Loneliness floods all my open places. I stare at the ceiling. I wish I were dressed, sitting beside him, listening to him talk. I wish he was telling me how the sparkle of my eyes in the candlelight reminded him of Proust.

A man who is toothpick fragile walks into the room. Peter is sleeping soundly. I reach for a shirt, a blanket, to cover myself.

"Who are you?" I ask the man.

"I'm Robert, his roommate." The man shakes his head. "He sleeps like he does everything else, intensely. I love that about him." Robert touches Peter's head. Peter's face breaks awake, then clouds over when he recognizes me.

"I'll be back," Peter says to me. He motions for Robert to walk ahead of him.

For a moment, I cannot move or think. I try to dress, but my fingers can't fit the button into the unyielding white slit. Kneeling, I look at the stack of books next to the bookcase. All Faulkner, all hardback. I feel sticky and tired and hurt.

Before I have finished dressing, Peter returns, looking crumpled and embarrassed.

"I'm sorry Robert barged in like that," he says.

I wrap my arms across my chest and realize I wear Peter's roomy white shirt, instead of my own narrow ivory silk.

"Are you lovers?" I ask.

"Do you know the poem 'Give crowns and pounds and rubies, but not your heart away'?" Peter says. "My father recited that to me every night the year after my mother divorced him."

"Are you lovers?" I repeat. I stare at him and point the question like a dagger.

Peter nods.

I dig my fingernails into my palm. I had already imagined our life together: long literary walks during moist overcast days; reading cozily with a glass of dark red wine; making love in twilight with the window open.

"Why were you touching me?" I say.

Peter's face looks dark. "I was attracted to you. I thought maybe, it could work."

I walk over and pull on the neck of his shirt with both hands, trying to rip the fabric into imperfect halves. The cloth only stretches.

"I thought you loved me," I say, tugging, wanting to feel something unravel.

"I do." Peter reaches out but I step back.

Robert walks into the room and over to Peter. I think about slamming my fist into Robert's mouth. Instead, I walk down the hallway and into the bathroom, which is clean and sweet-smelling, like a girl. Next to the cold water spigot, I find a pair of scissors.

I sit on the toilet and cut off a strand of my hair. Then I reach for one of the thick mauve monogrammed towels, which hang neatly over a brass rack. The scissors are dull, so it takes me a while to cut Robert's initials out of the towel. I throw the scrap of terry cloth on the floor and sprinkle my hairs over it. I leave without flushing, feeling a dangerous emptiness, as if explosion is the only thing that can fill me.

I let the door slam behind me. As I walk away, I imagine Peter saying, "You have a nice stride. You move with a great sense of purpose." But now, I have no reason, no purpose except to get home without falling or spilling into tears. As I run, I remember what I've left behind, my pink satin underwear, my ivory silk shirt and the closest I've ever come to the softness of love.

Instants

by Christina Sunley

T he sun was a ninety-pound weakling but at least it was shining.
I hadn't been stupid enough to leave my apartment without my big
black overcoat but at least I could unbutton it.

Month-old scabs of snow still clogged the gutters but at least they were
melting. Where there is slush there is hope.

I was ready for hope. It was the first day of spring in New York and I was
happy, in my way, but longing, too. Spooky's love wasn't enough, not after my
first winter in the city, my heart like one of those fish you'd see frozen into the
lakes back home, back where I knew how to find other women, how to talk to
them. I didn't know how to talk to women in New York. They were everywhere, all right, but they were picky. Where I came from we were few and far
between: short hair, a cute grin, and you were in. Here it was taken for granted,
being queer. Something extra was expected, something I didn't seem to have,
and I spent most of my free time walking Spooky.

But spring would be different. I could see it in people's faces as I walked to
Tompkin Square Park, their heads lifted up and their shoulders back, not
hunched against the cold. I found an empty bench to sit on, closed my eyes,
and offered my anemic face to the anemic sun while Spooky ventured off to
gobble trash, sniff mutt butt, and frolic in the makeshift ways of all urban
creatures.

Click, click, click.

A woman was taking my photograph. Shaved head, gold nose ring, ripped
jeans. I felt my heart begin to thaw, flipping and flopping and slapping its tail
against my belly, up to its slippery tricks again. She was an angel, a waif, a punk,
a brat, and out of everyone and everything in New York City she was

photographing *me*. I pretended to doze but watched her furtively, blurrily, through the slits of my eyes. Most people look scary with shaved heads, but hers was perfect, round and small. She had a drifty way of moving, like she was reaching into our world from another dimension, unable to materialize completely, except when she'd snap a picture. In those instants she'd solidify, skinny and serious and utterly beautiful. I shut my eyes, adjusted my profile, and let our whole life together flash before me.

The clicks grew louder, closer, as if she was photographing my feet. I opened my eyes all the way, and that's when I realized she hadn't been taking *my* picture—she was photographing my dog, who was hiding underneath the very bench upon which I sat, shredding up a used diaper.

"NO SHIT!" I screamed, yanking Spooky out by the tail. I grabbed hold of his muzzle and smacked him under the chin. He whimpered loudly, then scampered off to the nearest Dumpster, spraying slush in his wake. I stood up. The sun was gone, melted snow was leaking into the holes in the soles of my high-tops, and the beautiful girl with the camera, the girl with the shaved head, the girl I wanted, was giving me a dirty look.

"I know it seems cruel." I tried to sound informative. "But that's what the monks say to do, these monks upstate who train dogs at their monastery. You're only supposed to hit the dog if it commits a canine sin, and eating human shit is definitely a sin—it could kill him. And Spooky loves shit. If you gave him a choice between a juicy steak and a steaming pile of shit, Spooky would pick the shit, no question."

She wiped the slush off her lens with a tissue. Her fingers were short and bitten down at the nails. "Why should I care if you hit your dog?" she asked, without looking up. But she didn't sound sarcastic—her voice was too flat, too toneless—so I decided she actually wanted to know.

"Because he's beautiful, that's why. He's purebred dalmatian, the breeder says he could show, he's got the right number of spots per inch. And he's got one blue eye and one brown, that's very rare. And he's psychic. He runs to the phone seconds before it rings."

She nodded, still without looking at me, a ghost of a smile on her wide thin lips. Then she knelt down and took aim at Spooky again, bare knee poking through the hole in her jeans and resting on a patch of ice. No feeling whatsoever.

Spooky has terrible taste in bitches. He was trying to hump a miniature terrier, the kind with long grimy hair that trails on the ground, a snippy nose, red bow. His paws clutched her belly but there was such a huge difference in their heights that he ended up humping a piece of air about twelve inches away from her tail.

The girl I wanted crawled closer and closer to them, farther and farther from me. True, Spooky was nothing but an image to her, shimmying polka dot in motion, but at least she *saw* him. Me, I was a spectrum of light too pale to register. I couldn't get over the injustice of it. I was tired of women coming up to me in the park, "Oooh, what's his name, can I pet him?" Me, I'd want to say. Pet *me*.

"You want pictures of my dog, you pay for pictures of my dog."

She shook her head like I was crazy. She must have taken a dozen pictures of Spooky and that bitch. By the time she was done, he had no dignity left.

I accepted payment in blintzes. We sat in the window seat at Odessa, a Ukrainian diner across from the park. I felt shaky, like I'd been drinking coffee all day and couldn't stop. I figured I didn't have much time before she'd pay the check and be gone, so I made my eyes like a camera, click click click, hoping I could store her in my brain for later: eyelashes longer than the hair on her head, skinny lips that made her look about six, nail-bitten finger lightly circling the rim of her coffee cup.

Bess.

California.

Twelfth Street.

Photo lab.

She answered all my questions, didn't ask me one. I felt like I was looking at her through a one-way mirror, speaking a language she didn't understand. It made me frantic, I started doubting my judgment. I'd made mistakes before. And she seemed so dainty suddenly, spreading sour cream over the greasy folds of the blintzes. I had to make sure. "Do you sleep with women?" I asked.

"Of course I sleep with women, what do you think I am?" She laid her knife on her plate and for the first time looked me straight on. "Do I seem like I don't sleep with women?"

"I don't know." I wanted to keep her worrying. "You seem like maybe you don't sleep with anybody."

"Well I do. Just not right now. Right now I'm not sleeping with anybody, OK?"

"OK," I said, like it had nothing to do with me. The funny thing was, I didn't feel too terrible. Hopelessness breeds its own kind of hope. I told her Spooky and I were going to Coney Island on Saturday and she could come and take pictures of him if she wanted, free of charge.

Spooky riding the F train in a milk crate, Spooky ripping apart a dead horseshoe crab on the beach, Spooky shaking hands with a twelve-year-old Puerto Rican hustler. Finally I asked her, would she take a picture of me?

While she adjusted the focus I stared at the boardwalk. Old Russian ladies sat on benches, bundled in heavy wool coats, looking out to sea, toward the Old Country. My eyes drifted down beneath them, to the underside of the boardwalk. That's when I saw them, two men groping for each other. Their shadows merged, split apart, then merged again; above them, the old women mused and chatted.

"Do you think they know?" I asked Bess.

"Who?"

"The old ladies. Look below."

She lowered the camera and a smile stretched across her face. "They know, they know!"

In an instant she forgot about me and turned her camera on them. I could see the shot she was framing, the silhouette of one man kneeling at the feet of another, directly above them an old woman knitting in a splotch of late afternoon sunlight. It reminded me of me, of the way I was with Bess, faded on the outside, steamy underneath.

When she let the camera swing back against her chest I could see she wasn't laughing anymore. She was crying. "What's wrong?" I asked. "What did I do?"

She sat down in the sand, back turned against the boardwalk. I sat next to her, but not too close. The sea was the same gray color as the sky and the sand felt cold and hard. Bess piled it over her sneakers, packing it into mounds. She didn't look at me, she addressed all her words to those two mounds. She'd had a brother, a year older. He'd moved in with her while he was sick, then gone back to their parents in California to die, last spring.

"How?" I asked, to make sure.

"How else?"

She looked like she was about to say more, but just then Spooky started digging a hole, right next to us, spewing sand into our faces. He does that when he gets sick of my staying in one place for too long. I yelled at him to stop but he kept digging.

"Asshole!" I screamed, and suddenly I was throwing sand at him, shoving at him with both my feet. All I could think of was wanting to kill Bess' brother for dying, for making her heart go somewhere so far away I might never get to it.

"Stop," Bess said, grabbing my arm. As soon as she touched me all the thoughts flew out of my head. There was the sea, still and calm, there was Bess' hand, circling my wrist. I thought she might be mad but she wasn't, she was smiling.

"The monks wouldn't like you doing that," she said. "It's not a canine sin, digging a hole in the sand."

Spooky gave me a sandy lick on the cheek, begging forgiveness for my having gone crazy mad at him. Dogs are like that. We stood up and headed back across the beach. It was windy and almost dark and Bess and I walked close, bumping against each other accidentally, again and again. It surprised me, that she remembered about the monks. It gave me a little hope. At least she was listening.

The week after Coney Island she called and asked if I wanted to come see the photographs. I picked out a couple of Spooky and the terrier bitch and the one of the old woman on the boardwalk. There weren't any of me.

The only furniture in the room was a futon on the floor and Bess was lying on it. I didn't have much choice so I sat on the edge of it, looking at the photographs on the walls. They were all of her brother. You could see him getting thinner and thinner in the photographs, wasting, so it looked like his eyes were growing larger. You could see him losing his hair too, from one picture to the next, until it was completely gone.

"I remember flying into San Francisco for his funeral." Her hands lay on her chest, tracing the ridges of her collarbones. "When the plane started its descent it looked like we were going to land right in the water. I had a window seat, I kept watching the water coming closer and closer. But there were no announcements from the pilot, no stewardesses strapping on oxygen masks, no panic. We were about to plunge into the water and nobody seemed scared. But that didn't surprise me, I just figured everyone else felt the way I did. My life would be over in a few seconds. There was nothing I could do. I was so happy."

She rolled onto her stomach. Her hair was beginning to grow back and she looked like an eight-year-old boy with a crew cut, napping. When she spoke again she didn't turn over, and her voice was almost inaudible, muffled by the mattress. "Then the plane turned and land tipped into sight and I felt the wheels bump onto the stupid fucking runway."

There was nothing I could say to that. I stared at one of the photographs of her brother. With his shaved head and his skinny body, he looked just like her. She looked like him. I understood then. She didn't want him to come back. She wanted to be with him where he was.

I didn't know whether to touch her or not, whether it was something she needed. But I didn't think it could hurt her, I didn't think I was capable of hurting her. I was an instant. I reached over and with one finger I stroked the wisps of hair growing in on the back of her neck. She shivered. I put my lips there.

"Lie on me."

I could hear Spooky scratching at the door, like he needed to go out, bad. Desperate. But out was six floors down, so I ignored him. I climbed onto her, I covered her completely. She felt so little beneath me, I was afraid of crushing her, but I couldn't roll off. I could feel her skin getting warmer, the pulse in her neck quickening against my cheek. But all of this was internal, changes happening inside her, beyond her control. She needed my body the way a starfish needs the rock it clings to, slowly regenerating itself. She never actually moved, she lay still while I touched her. She wanted me to give her back that moment on the plane.

That's why I bit her. Hard, on her shoulder, where the skin was thick enough to take it. Not deep enough to break the skin but steady, making the pain bore through, in, until it met up with the other pain that was boring its way out, like two sides of a tunnel opening onto each other and letting in a flood of light and earth and water. I could feel her trembling, crying, but I knew not to stop. I didn't stop until she jerked away and pushed me off.

"Are you happy now?" She meant it, she wanted to know.

I thought of saying, *Yes, because you asked, finally*. But it wasn't true, it wasn't enough. I could see the deep red marks of my teeth on her shoulder. I could hear Spooky whining at the door.

The Divorcée and Gin

by Kim Addonizio

I love the frosted pints you come in,
and the tall bottles with their uniformed men;
the bars where you're poured chilled
into shallow glasses, the taste of drowned olives,
and the scrawled benches where I see you
passed impatiently from one mouth
to another, the bag twisted tight around
your neck, the hand that holds you
shaking a little from its need
which is the true source of desire, God, I love
what you do to me at night when we're alone,
how you wait for me to take you into me
until I'm so confused with you I can't
stand up anymore. I know you want me
helpless, each cell whimpering, and I give
you that, letting you have me just the way
you like it. And when you're finished
you turn your face to the wall while I curl
around you again, and enter another morning
with aspirin and the useless ache
that comes from loving, too well,
those who, under the guise of pleasure,
destroy everything they touch.

Love Art

by Debra Martens

She should have been locked up, too. To keep going back to him—she was just as mad as Jack. When he tried it on me, calling "Laurie, come here" and flashing the knife at me, that was it. He wasn't my lover anymore.

He'd always been a bit rough. Throwing me around as if I were a rag doll. Biting me. Like a kid in the school yard who doesn't know his own strength. And he had this thing about putting objects inside me. He called it hide-and-seek—let's play hide-and-seek. Over the few months I was with him, he'd inserted a pot handle, vegetables, a hammer handle, cardboard poster rolls, a doll's leg. I let him put bottles in despite the story I'd heard about a bottle getting stuck by suction and breaking inside. I indulged his curiosity. I brought him things to try: an oval stone, hard Italian biscuits, a blunt-nosed umbrella, a bottle brush. But a knife, no way. I didn't wait around to find out what he wanted to do with it.

He liked to cut her skin. Not deep slashes, merely nicks. It was a good sharp knife, one of those wide Henckels. All he had to do was touch the tip of the blade to her skin. Nora's skin was so firm it would break with a whispered pop. I was there sometimes. Yes, the three of us. It's not that easy to say good-bye to a lover. Although I wouldn't let him touch me with the knife, I started looking at women in tight skirts, the flesh pushing against the fabric, wondering if that was the attraction for him, the tension of the flesh pushing against the skin, demanding release.

They found each other at a concert. There were three bands at the old dance hall by the waterfront, the place that burned down last summer. We were dancing together, our gang from the warehouse, and Nora suddenly turned

171

away from whoever she was dancing with, and started dancing with Jack. She said something that made him bend down. His dark curls touched her cheek, her neck, as he put his ear to her mouth. He nodded. After he stood up and started dancing, I raised my eyebrows to Jack, to find out what pearls of wisdom had dropped from her red lips.

"Great band." That was it. Small talk. I don't want to sound like a snob or anything, but there were a lot of bridge-and-tunnel people there that night. The kids who came in from the suburbs, with their studded wristbands and wide leather belts, with their careful punk attire. Peacocks. Not that I'm innocent; I remember distinctly what we were wearing that night. Jack was dressed like an angel, he always dressed like an angel, in white. Dirty white, mind you, but white all the same: he was wearing white jeans with a leather vest, a white, round-collared shirt with long loose sleeves, and a cap. I was wearing my purple silk harem trousers, with my orange Hawaiian shirt. Nora was in black, from her tits to her toes.

She might have been a groupie, one of the kids who'd piss their pants if they knew that Martha, the singer in the first band, was a friend of ours. They didn't have Martha's band storing their equipment in the loft down the hall from them, didn't have a band practicing at three in the morning. Don't get me wrong, I love Martha and her band. By this time I'd been living and working in my loft for five years, and maybe that was too long to be in the same space, but I was starting to get work—commissions, and illustrations in magazines. Jack had been painting only a year or so, little burgundy torsos in muddy fields, so he was broke, poorer even than the arts students who hung around, waiting for one of us to die of an overdose or something so they could have the loft.

Not that they would want Jack's loft. He lived at the bottom of the back stairwell of our warehouse, in what used to be a loading area. He'd closed off his space, to make a room around the flight of stairs. Under the stairs was a pile of debris, things that had followed him home like stray pups, things that might be useful for his work. On one side of the stairs was the bed. On the other side, his nest. Here were the castoffs of his daily life. Clothes, dirty and clean together, were heaped with newspapers and books and cassettes and shoes and empty bags and used Kleenex and scarves and coats. The chair, which faced the stairs, was sometimes shaken clear for guests. The bed was the only neat corner of his loft.

I had trouble letting Jack go because I couldn't believe this stuff with the knife. I'd look at him and see my Jack, the picture of innocence, like an English country boy on the postcards you buy in secondhand bookstores. One day he was plain old Jack, and the next, he was turning psycho.

The only words that ever came out of his mouth were kind words, friendly words, curious words. If you wanted to talk bands, he would talk bands. If you wanted to talk dope, he would talk dope. Or art, or food, or friends. If you didn't talk, he wouldn't talk. We in the warehouse swapped personal horror stories, but Jack never talked about his past, unless you count the funny stories he told us about his shrinks. Yet no hate came out of his mouth. No words that resembled his paintings.

If anyone seemed like they would greet their lover with a knife, it was Nora. She was deeply and quietly angry: her black clothes and studded belt were surface signs, the way an ooze of oil on the ground was evidence of a toxic dump site below. She was a small thing, and her blonde hair was close-cropped, spiked. She was no groupie: she sang. She'd cut hair and waitressed her way through singing lessons, and now she was getting paid to sing. And she could. She could sing. Even if she couldn't sing, she would've become a singer, she was that determined.

Around her, he hardly talked at all.

He liked to nick her skin so that when they made love, her blood would leave marks on the sheets. When he started with the knife, he cut her at the back of her neck. After they'd made love, the first time he cut her skin, he stood over the bed, gazing at the patterns the blood made on the sheets. He'd rolled Nora out of the way, as if she were a log obstructing his view. He called the stained sheets love art.

Over the weeks, his cuts moved around to the front of her neck, slowly down past her collarbone. Before she let him put the knife near her breasts, though, she made him do her limbs first. He was happy with her arms and legs for a long time. Their lovemaking tousled the sheets; it hardly mattered what position he fucked her in, or where the nicks were, as long as there were some front and back.

In the mornings, he'd throw her out of bed. She'd go around the corner for coffee and Danish, bring them back warm from the bakery. She'd dawdle on the way, talking to the people coming out of their lofts. While she was gone, he'd make the bed. He'd pull the sheet tight across the mattress, and admire the old and new bloodstains. He'd shake out the top sheet, let it billow over the mattress, pull it smooth, and admire.

I liked Nora almost right away. The night of the dance, she came home with Jack. Because we still thought she was one of those suburban jerks playing at being tough, that she wouldn't last, Henry made a point of walking in on her when she was using the toilet down the hall the next morning (the door barely closed, never mind locked). Later that day, she came upstairs to visit me. Right away, she saw my books—Gertrude Stein, Brautigan, Hesse, Nietzsche. Most people who came to my loft simply didn't see the books, and certainly never talked about them or asked to borrow one. She offered to lend me hers—Robbe-Grillet, Marquis de Sade, Anaïs Nin. Only after she saw the books did she go to look at the feathers.

A friend of a friend told me where I could pick up thirty flats of antique feathers. I bought them not knowing what to do with them. They were for hats, for costumes. I thought they were beautiful. After they sat in their flats in my loft for three days, I painted all the walls in my loft white, and I painted the ceiling and the floor black. I chose the wall across from the windows for the feathers. I drilled a zillion tiny holes, spiralling outward from a small wing shape, and I stuck the feathers into the wall, close together. All of them together made a giant multicolored wing on the wall.

That's what people see when they come to my loft; they see the feathers, not the books. They have to ask about the feathers. Where'd you get them, what'd you put them up for, aren't they dusty, don't they take up too much space sticking out, aren't you afraid you'll get paint on them, great shadow on the wall, and so on.

Nora had a good long look at them. She turned to me, where I was sitting at the table, and said, "Why'd you paint the floor black?"

White came out of Jack's mouth, too. White lies. Jack never told Nora about the shrinks, that he was being checked by the shrinks all his life. When they let him out of the loony bin, where he'd disappeared for a while, not much changed. Nora came back. Come to think of it, no one knew where she went to, either, nor where she lived before she moved in with Jack. When she wasn't singing or waitressing, she was at his place. His mound spread to cover more and more of the floor, as her things got mixed in with his.

The only daylight came from the skylight above the door at the top of the stairs. They stayed down there, living and fucking like rats. We kept an eye on them. Made sure they ate. Sometimes opened the door at the top of the stairs to look down into their nest. He told me his shrink told him to seek out normal human intercourse. Jack wasn't sure what this meant (he told me like it was a joke), and neither was I. I thought maybe it was eating and talking.

One morning, on my way out, I heard Jack shouting. He was chanting, "Talk, so talk, talk, so talk." From Nora, the sound of gagging. I opened the door of the stairwell landing and looked down. She was lying half on the floor, half on the wall. Her legs were up the wall, but her head was below her torso, at the bottom of a mound of clothes. Jack was pushing the neck of a bottle down her throat, jerking it in and out in time to his chant.

I hollered, "Jack, take it out, Jack, stop."

He did, as if he had been woken from a dream. But from her mouth came a bloody froth, and laughter. She laughed.

She was in love with him because he didn't try to protect her. She was sick to death of men who tried to take care of her, tell her what was good for her, claim her as their own, as if they were her fucking parents. Jack didn't do that. He let her come and go. He didn't even have a telephone number to call her when she wasn't there. He would watch her sing, but he wouldn't interfere. She said he was the only guy she knew who seemed not to have one ounce of jealousy in him. All the same, she thought Jack was fragile.

And I think he was besotted by her love. She was the first lover he'd had who didn't pick fights with him for not calling, for not seeming to care. When they were in public, you couldn't tell they were together. If he left the room, say to get a beer, and if he passed her, he never touched her. No stray caresses. He never reached for her hand when they walked together. One night, at my place, Henry insulted Nora, and Jack didn't say anything; he watched Nora to see what she would do, like he was watching a play, like he'd never met her before.

Around this time she let him start nicking her torso. Up to three nicks a day. The nicks were two finger-widths apart at first, as he worked down from her collarbone. He stopped short of the nipples, and made tracks around to the back, where he worked his way up to her shoulders, and then down, rib by rib, to the small of her back, to her buttocks.

One of the nicks was too deep. She sat down to dinner at one of the upstairs lofts, and when she got up, there was a stain on her pants where no stain should be. We argued about whether to call his shrink. It was only because I liked Nora that I convinced them. Jack was locked up again. Nora disappeared.

I didn't tell anyone about Nora, about her being as bad off as him. Jack used to be my lover. He was happier with her than I'd ever known him. She made him happy. I could see that. I thought maybe she was playing at Anaïs Nin, you know, her erotica. I was afraid she'd let him put the knife to her cunt next.

The shrink suggested that Jack might be able to control himself if he had order in his life. Between me and the other warehouse people, I managed to find some of the stuff I needed to clean Jack's place.

The mound had spread. I found the bed only because I knew where it should be. Under the dirty clothes, the sheets were neatly tucked, and blood encrusted. The love art was taking on the contours of an oil painting.

I shook the apple cores from pockets, chips from creases. I shook all their clothes into plastic bags and took them to the Laundromat. I swept. I put out garbage. I folded all the clothes, and put them neatly into milk crates stacked along one wall.

I didn't wash the sheets. I didn't touch the bed.

When he came back, Jack asked for Nora right away. She was there the same day, with a package of new sheets. How did she know he was back? He stripped the bed. And then, if you can believe it, he pulled an iron and ironing board out from the junk under the stairs, and he ironed the sheets. Then he hung the old sheets up on the wall. As if it were a finished work.

They tried hard to be good. The knife was gone. They made love in a clean bed in a neat room. The sheets were only bloodied when she had her period. He was painting, and she got to her studio on time; she was putting together a record. We stopped keeping an eye on them.

Some months later, a little mound of shed clothing began to grow. At first, only some socks and underwear. Nora was too busy waitressing and singing to do the laundry, and Jack never had the habit. A few more socks in the corner. By that time, I had stopped coming down to see them. Gradually, they took up where they had left off. She brought a knife home from the restaurant, not as good as a Henckels. He had to press harder. New blood patterns started.

You see the stains on the floor, on the walls. When he pressed the dull knife into her vital vein, did he do it on purpose? Had he made love to her while she bled to death? Their bodies slippery with blood, blood flying off in every direction as they moved. As if he were trying for a Pollock effect, clots and rivers of blood on the messy canvas of the bed sheet. Blood soaked through to the mattress, spilled over to the floor. And then Jack trying to warm her body, holding her in his arms, bracing his slit wrists against her back. Everything slick with blood. The sheets, the bed, the floor, even the walls. Them. Nora. Jack.

That's how I found them, the morning I came down, drawn by the butcher-shop smell.

After their bodies had been taken away, I put all the sheets into the incinerator. The love art was not for public viewing. Everything else, I left as it was, for the time being.

The Suburbs of Eden

by Katharine Coles

Mario has always pretended to believe me.

I was sitting for him; I had got restless and Mario, right then, was looking at Ace walking back and forth over my shoulders, fluffing his wings, preening, letting out the occasional ear-grating screech. I had Mario's bone-handled knife—in the pose, I held it loosely in my palm, but now I was using it to cut a button from the front of the white shirt I was wearing open. I sawed lightly at first, then harder.

The blade was a keen blue. I was thinking only about results, my own light touch on the handle of the knife. The bunch of threads held, and held. Ace rubbed his head against my nape, took my earring and earlobe gently in his beak, pulled, then let go and right there next to my ear loosed a shriek. I pulled up on the knife; the clump of threads gave.

Looking back, I can feel the blade slip, can feel the combination of surprise and exultation and sudden pain—surprisingly abstract—and despair as it slid over my finger to the bone and into my sternum. The ease. The way it took my breath away. I looked down for a second; then, because I couldn't think what else to do, because I couldn't at that moment remember how long the blade was, how much of its cold length was inside my body, I pulled it out.

I said, "Oh, shit," and Mario looked up from his easel where he was dabbing the blue into Ace's wing, his one lit side, and said, "Maureen, what the fuck," and right then I realized there was blood everywhere on his wife's white carpet and chair—this was Mario's truest infidelity, to paint me there—and the blood was mine.

He said, "I told you not to move."

I said, "I'm sorry."

Later, after the emergency room and the surgery and the three-night stay, after the police who kept looking at Mario and saying to me, "You did this yourself?" and asking me to repeat the story again, just as it happened, Mario took me in a cab back to my apartment. He said, "What the hell were you doing?"

But I must have known something. While I healed, he brought me tea and chocolate and little sandalwood soaps from the Chinese market on the corner. He lied to my mother, all the way across mountains and prairies on the western slope of the Rockies, endlessly, tenderly on the phone.

He said to her, "She's fine, I'm here." He said, "I love her." When the bandages came off he kissed the tip of the finger I would never feel again, and he made love to me gently, curled against my back, until I could bear his whole weight.

Then, when he had decided I was well enough, he showed me the painting: the white face and black hair; the eyes lowered to the hand holding the knife; the slumped shoulders and casually spread knees; and behind the open man's shirt just the gray shadow of a body from which, over the shirt's white cotton, the red stain spread. It was difficult to tell if the red on the knife was a stain itself or a reflection, so pure a surface had he rendered for it. The bird was unfinished but still, as Mario said, complete: almost oriental, those bare strokes of blue and the baleful red eye.

Though he'd been paying for my apartment for a long time, since soon after I began to sit for him, it was at this moment I realized I was not his lover but his mistress.

I said, "I like the shirt right here"—I pointed—"where the folds are."

He said, "It's a breakthrough." He was looking at the painting. He said, "I'll leave her." He said, "We'll have thirteen children."

I said, "Like hell." I didn't believe any of it anyway.

I stopped pretending to paint, myself. I left everything—failed canvases, paints and brushes—just where it was.

Mario started staying the night, then every night. And then my mother's call came, and later we sat drinking gin on the fire escape and watching the soot settle on my white shirt, and I said, "I'm going back."

He said, "To that cow town?"

I said, "You won't believe the light."

He said, "I'm not finished with you."

I breathed in. I said, "Then come on."

I never claim to know what's true. I know only what I've been told. The one story my mother ever told me about herself as mother she relayed as if it were an ordinary one, with only the usual amount of bloodshed and anguish. She said, "It's the same everywhere. Only the details change."

Here is the story. It was morning. Every day at dawn my mother had carried the bulk of her stomach, of me, to the dig, up the dry wash and even up the cliff face on the ancient, precarious carved-out hand- and foot-holds.

But today, still ten days from due, she had stayed behind at camp while the others went ahead up to the site. For weeks, they had been urging her to go back to town. They had said, "It's almost time."

She got up early that morning and after the others left she washed her hair in the river. It was hard to bend over; she had brought a pan, she told me, to scoop the water up over her head. All the night before she'd been turning more and more inward, she told me years later, as if listening to me and my movements, to what in my impatience I was saying, there in the dark: Pay attention.

When she was done washing, she took a blanket and laid it out in the soft sand under the juniper. She set out her army knife open to its sharpest blade. She filled a pail from the river and put it nearby to warm in the sun and folded a clean towel next to it.

Like anyone, she must have been afraid—in her case, maybe, as much of a kind of revealed disarray as of any pain. She must have worried about the time, about whether she could be finished before the others came back. She must have been afraid of loss, too, and of blood and of cutting the tough cord herself.

And then, for as long as she could be attentive to them and me at once, she went back to her fragments of painted clay, sorting, arranging, assembling, blowing the dust from their rough surfaces, running her fingers along their edges. And then she lay down under the tree.

I wonder, still, how long she would have lain there afterwards, her child on her stomach and their shared blood drying in the sharp air, exhausted, drifting in and out of sleep, trying to reassemble herself from the long push into pain and back out the other side, before she roused herself and reached for the bucket and the towel. By the time the others returned at sunset we were lying washed on a clean blanket, just as she had wanted; within a week she was climbing the cliffs again, with me knotted into an old man's shirt tied by its sleeves to her back, a weight she was already used to.

My mother was not a teller of tales, not a person to peel back layers of time and events to reveal herself. It was the archetypal dead who interested her.

"I didn't want to miss anything," she said, the one time she told me this story.

Now I think of my birth as if it's my own memory: I can see the canyon, identify the tree and the particular shady blue of the blanket. I don't know any more what parts of it are true.

The reason I'm going back: my mother, suddenly, is old.

When she called, I could imagine her on the other end, one hand on the receiver and the other over her faulty heart as if touching herself there would help her describe what has gone wrong. Between New York and the Rockies I pictured the phone line snaking over hills, through cornfields, across open plains and mountains. Such an attenuated connection, her voice growing thinner with each electronic mile. Still, though I can't say how she's escaped it, my mother doesn't know yet what I know: even she is doomed.

And so, driving back west is nothing like driving into my childhood—not with Mario next to me asleep, his black lashes curved like wings at rest over his cheeks; and the bird cage in the back seat; and Ace's cackle over the stereo.

I even know why there has opened such a rift, this break between the present and that mythical childhood spent under blue skies, in a desert where I watched my mother bend her head over the reemerging bones of the long dead. I believed for years, even after I left, that if I could watch her hard enough she would lift her eyes and look at me; she would take me back to the green lawns and ordered cabinets of home. But she will never lift her eyes from the past she holds in her hand. And she will not find what she is looking for; there can't, I think, be yet another new lost city out in the American desert where she roams. Even that space could not be so vast.

She must know this, but she keeps looking for signs of that city anyway. In her mind, at every crossroads, under every piece of ground where her foot falls, lies somebody with a history. She thinks any risk, any accident of man or nature, can be survived into myth.

I don't know about Mario. He's sleeping with his head propped on a pillow against the window. He's gone slack-jawed, but when I let up a little on the accelerator, he opens his eyes and shuts his mouth. He says, "Slow down."

I say, "I'm not going to try to stop her."

Mario yawns and looks at me sideways.

I say, "She can die out there if she wants. I just want to save the house." And it's true, I want to save something, and the house is there. I think I can recover it from the slow degeneration of our long-time tenants, the Quales; I believe I can restore it to what it was, its old innocence and its lushness.

He says, "Leave her alone."

I say, "She's sick." I say, "Things are different out here."

And this too is true: living in the city, the big city, where the violence is human and metallic and mechanized and unavoidable, where there are always witnesses, however speechless, I would shut my eyes in front of my empty canvas and just envision, for example, the sunlight flashing off the back of a snake, the delicately raised quills of a porcupine, a white bone, cliffs rising out of the desert. I know how to tell if a lost people might have lived once, centuries ago, behind where the cliff face is shaded over with branches.

I might picture the way a river would begin to slide almost imperceptibly faster, glittering, toward its falls. Lightning a hundred miles away, dancing over the desert. A hand turning a human skull or a fragment of a pot as if they had the same value. All as if danger itself composed a kind of paradise.

I know where I learned this.

I would reach out my brush toward the easel then, but by the time the bristles touched down too often it would all be lost—only the gray sky, the gray buildings and everywhere man-made dirt. What I wanted was that old seduction—brilliant, frank, but only if you knew how to read the signs.

And all the time my mother growing older in the usual, still shocking ways.

In town, the first thing we do is ride in the padded elevator with the bird and the suitcases up to her new condo.

My mother takes the blanket off the cage and opens up the cage door for Ace and starts to murmur at him. She thinks she's going to teach him to talk, or at least to be a companion, to sit on her shoulder and gently nibble her jawbone. She believes, here as with everything, there's some tenderness that can accomplish what she desires.

I say, "It's no good. He was taken out of the jungle."

She looks at me.

I say, "I didn't know until later. He won't talk."

Ace just hunkers down on his perch with his shoulders up around his ears. It's been a long trip.

She says, "Maureen. You're here to stay."

I say, "That depends on the Quales." I say, "We'll be back for supper."

She says, "I'm leaving Monday. I'll just be gone a few days."

It's starting already. I say, "You could stay in a motel."

She says, "Not where I'm going." She laughs and brushes my bangs off my forehead.

I shake my head. I say, "It's not like there's anything out there. Not that matters."

She says, "This country is smaller than you think."

Then Mario and I take the elevator back down and get in the car again and drive by the old house. I pull up in front and turn off the ignition. "Here it is," I say.

Mario says, "This is nostalgia. It's shit, pure and simple."

I say, "The Quales have never done well."

Mario has sensibilities. Intrusions pain him. I'm different: I can't concentrate on one thing—everything I see reminds me of something else. This is why, according to Mario, I'll never get anywhere as a painter.

"The world can't be bigger than the canvas," he says. He says, "No wonder you don't paint. Where would you start?"

Mario believes in the pure inviolability of the closed form. Mostly, he believes in his own ideas, in how they emerge whole, one at a time. I'd thought his certainty would have been shaken by now—not, I suppose, by the roil and dirt of Manhattan, which must have made him what he is, but by seeing the way the land unfolds from the man-made coastline as if shaking itself free of something, through the rumpled hills of West Virginia and Ohio into Nebraska, flat and calm and terrifying, and then under Wyoming's high, explosive sky and into the mountainous west.

But Mario has kept to himself. I suppose this is what vision is. This is how he has become successful: by, he says, maintaining his integrity. By never changing his mind.

And so he is famous, in a small way, for his portraits of women askew, with pieces missing but implied. The absence of these body parts, he says, is the same as their presence, but better. The absence makes the bodies more complete. I understand what he tells me.

And for my appearances in his work I have my own small bit of fame. His other model, at least at first, was his wife, Dorothy, whom he always painted wearing a white terry bathrobe, or with the robe tossed over her shoulder or lap. Me he paints always with Ace, in the background or in the foreground, wings outstretched or folded, looking at the canvas through one eye, looking at himself in a mirror that reflects him back. Ace is always the one bright spot against my extreme black-and-white, my pale skin and dark hair and eyes.

I admit, I liked the idea at first, the notion of being that kind of object, even of sharing the galleries with Dorothy, as if between the two of us he portrayed his whole life. I had no illusions then about fidelity or my own occasional impulses toward family unity. I knew where I had come from. I couldn't predict my little act of violence, how it would throw him my way.

So in the beginning, I sat for him feeling whole, self-contained. We were embarking together on something new. Piece by piece, I watched myself being dismantled. I tried to imagine what he was seeing, what wholeness or flaw or defect or gap. I wondered how he could break me open just by looking.

He'd say, "They're not portraits. They have nothing to do with you."

I stopped painting altogether. Instead I'd look at his paintings of me for what they said about form and the world. What, if anything, they said about my life.

Now he says, "You're opening up a can of worms, if you ask me."

Me, I just sit there behind the steering wheel and look across him toward the old house, which, when my mother moved us to a smaller house up the hill, we rented out rather than sold to the Quales because the place had been in the family for almost a century, which out here is a long time, and besides the Quales couldn't afford to buy and my mother felt sorry for them. Now the paint is peeling off in strips and little chunks, white over the brick and a faded blue on the wood shutters and front door.

I say, "It hasn't been painted since we moved out."

Mario doesn't say anything.

I say, "It's been years."

Mario settles further down in the seat. He has his Caterpillar ventilated hat pulled down over his face.

I know what's eating at me. I say, "You know, when she goes out like this it's a serious thing."

He says, "Yeah."

I say, "She doesn't know what she's looking for."

He says, "Who does?"

I say, "That's not what I mean."

But Mario's just seen my mother for the first time. She is tall and thin and elegant with silver hair. She was wearing a suit she made look like a Chanel though it probably wasn't. When she pursed her lips at Ace, she looked prim and composed, and the bird looked, next to her, sloppy, ill-mannered, unmade. In other words, Mario has no reason to believe me.

He says, "You worry too much."

I say, "No marshmallows. No pastoral." I say, "We're talking about the desert here. She climbs cliffs looking for bones. She goes alone. She doesn't use ropes. You have no idea."

I am thinking of myself, too.

The junipers edging the front yard are now overrun completely with morning glories. I used to comfort myself by imagining we were staying in town under this real roof, that we would begin a normal life. I can't blame the Quales, really, for letting the shrubs go. But the morning glories are climbing the honeysuckle by the porch, the pyracantha under the windows. It is late morning, and the white trumpets of flowers are still half open, pale and innocent looking.

I say, "They're poisonous." I am surprised to see, through the leafy vines, a little juniper green here and there. Signs of survival, too small and blotted with brown to be triumphant or even hopeful, but indicative of something nonetheless.

I want, at least, to take that little sign as a positive one, though I think I'm old enough to know surviving isn't always the point. I want some indication to stand against the crabgrass in the yard and the refrigerator and scrap lumber and pieces of rusting old gutter, signs of projects begun and abandoned, in the driveway and carport. There's nothing left of what I yearned for, all those years ago. Something's been building up here. Most of us work to keep it at bay: this going back to the earth before our eyes.

I think of my mother's tidiness, her precision, the decorum with which she shuts the door or backs out from under the tent flap. The way in which her smallest gesture has meaning, if only one can learn to read the signs.

To Mario, I say, "Mr. Quale has been ill for years."

He says, "That's no excuse for filth."

Most of us no longer speak from the heart. We are reasonable beings.

Sometimes my mother does what I tell her, though the results are not necessarily what I imagined. Her new condominium, for example, built right up on the mountain, a high rise, the last building on the highest road, is not what I had in mind when I told her even the small house was too much for her—too much, I meant, for me to let her stay in. Last Christmas, when I was back, it snowed seventeen inches in one afternoon, and she insisted on driving us down the mountain to the grocery store in the middle of the storm. Outside the car was a cloud of snow from which, as we approached, lights and houses emerged briefly before fading back into the white background.

My mother was driving fast. She looked over at me; I was holding tight to my purse in my lap. She said, "Watch this," then gunned her four-wheel-drive wagon, put it in neutral, turned the wheel, braked hard, and slid half-sideways all the way down the hill. Her leather-gloved hands rested delicately on the wheel; her face wore a look of unmixed glee.

Her condo is on the tenth floor; spread out below her, the city looks peaceful and just. There have been rumors that the slope beneath the building is not stable, and my mother knows them to be true. She paid a lot to live here anyway.

My mother got her Ph.D. in anthropology back when women were thought to be uninterested in the insensate or the academic.

She used to say, when called upon to explain herself, "I never married," with her eyebrows raised a little and a slight smile on her face, and though she said it quietly as she said everything, my grandmother, if she were there, would say "Miriam, hush," as if she were reprimanding a boast. Even I read in my mother's expression such pride I'd repeat the phrase myself—"My mother never married"—with the same little smile, until I started school.

For years I've kept a photo on my bedstand: my mother stands on a terrace overlooking the sea. She's in Cuba. I can't quite remember why. Her specialty was the Anasazi, and in this photo for once she is not dressed for work. She is turned a little sideways; she has her hip cocked like a model's. It is late in the day. Her hair is the same honey color as the sun on the rocks behind her. A breeze lifts her white chiffon skirt and sash, and the man next to her has lifted his hand to catch the sash's end flying into his face. He is dark, wearing a tuxedo. He is laughing and looking at her while she looks right at the camera.

This is what I have.

When people said, talking low where she could overhear, "The child has no father," my mother would break in and say, "Of course she has. He just isn't here."

Now she stands on her balcony like any woman and says, "Just look at the view."

Her decor is pristine, all in whites and pearl grays. Against the pale walls and above the glass cases filled with the scraps and debris of dead peoples— potsherds, chipped stone, pieces of rock worn with use, the inevitable bones— my paintings look lush, overgrown, chaotic, unfamiliar. It took me a minute to recognize them as mine. It's been a long time.

Ace, too, adds a touch of the exotic. He's settled in now, perched on the top of his cage. Whenever anyone walks by, he leans far out in the opposite direction and cackles.

"Just like you told me," she says, "and you were right."

I say, "How do you feel?"

She puts her hand over her chest and says, "It's like something is opening there, something I could fall into. It takes my breath away, literally." She smiles, as if this satisfies her. She says, "I feel fine."

I say, "Don't go." I don't want her to stuff a pack with a sleeping bag and food and water for days in the desert and carry it where no car can reach her. I say, "There's nothing out there."

"Except axe-murderers," Mario says.

I roll my eyes, say, "This is not New York."

"*Adventure Magazine*," he says.

I say, "Well."

My mother says, "He's right. You never know." I can tell she likes the idea. She says, "Those stories are supposed to be true, aren't they, dear?" She's talking to Mario.

I want to say, act your age. I want her to sit in a chair by the window.

"This Mario," she says, tilting her head toward him, "is he all right?"

He looks at me with his eyebrows raised. He doesn't know what I will say. I think of the red scar, still angry, on my sternum; the scars behind that one, in the dark where I cannot see; the scar on the finger I will never feel again.

I think of his hands on me, of Dorothy, his wife, in her white terry robe, which in fact she was wearing the one time we met, when Mario and I picked up his last boxes before we left town.

"He's good," I say. I mean it. I say, "But here, he won't last."

He rolls his eyes.

She says, "Why don't you have a baby?" She looks at me, says, "You don't have a whole lot of time."

Eulalie Quale has dirty brown hair pulled back in an elastic. She's only maybe forty-five, but she's wearing one of those print housecoats from the fifties.

Real low, she says, "Mr. Quale is resting." She doesn't stand aside for us to come in.

I say, "I'd like to work this out."

"We had an agreement," she says. "Your mother never liked us, but she's been good to us anyway." She says, "I know what's right. I know it's been a year since we paid." She tilts her head back and looks at me. She says, "I know all of it. There's nothing you can pull on me."

I didn't know any of this. I lean against the doorjamb. I say, "I could give you another chance." I'm seeing the place as Mario would, decrepit, nothing but work. And the whole town: hills going brown now in late summer, the slight haze, the way there's no city, not really—or maybe it's that the city is everywhere, not in any one ideal eroding heart but embodied in each neighborhood. It's suburbs on suburbs, Mario says. A sprawling small town. Even what used to be downtown, quaint and old-fashioned with its

Woolworths and old Mormon co-op all the way through my childhood, is now just two big malls. The old iron co-op facade was restored and built right into the outside of one of the malls, but everyone just parks in the indoor parking terraces and walks into the stores from there, so nobody sees the regilded iron arches. It's not the same.

Every evening, Mario says, "Where do you go at night?"

Now Eulalie Quale says, "It's too much for him anyway, all of this." She gestures out at the overgrown yard, the choking tams and the building materials leaned moldering against the carport wall. "It only makes him worse to see it. There's nothing here he'll ever finish." She says, "I have a sister up north."

Even from here, just on the first bench of the foothills, I can see all the way across the valley to the Oquirrh Mountains. The day is so bright I have to squint to raise my eyes to look.

I lower my eyes again and shrug at her. "Whenever you're ready," I say.

She says, "I'm ashamed it's come to this."

She stands aside and I walk in.

"Just so you know," she says.

Nothing is changed except it's all older and dirtier—grime on the windowsills, on the white-painted iron banister curving upward, ground into the old figured carpeting. It's all smaller but I am ready for that.

Mr. Quale is lying on the couch in what used to be my playroom. There is still the wall of built-in cabinets where I kept my toys, but their white paint is grayed with dirt and age. Mr. Quale's eyes are wide open, staring at the ceiling. He doesn't move to look at me when we come in. The room smells of sweat and the accumulated oils of the human body, too rich and spoiled and thick to breathe in.

Mrs. Quale shrugs and gestures around her. "It's been all I could do," she says.

I say, "Of course," as if I understand. I touch her shoulder. "You just let me know," I say.

She says, "We'll leave most of it. I've been ready"—she gestures around her—"a long time. We'll be out by tomorrow."

I say, "I know the way. We'll let ourselves out."

When we get back, my mother is sitting next to the window, looking out at the lights of the city below. She says, "It's just like I told you."

Mario and I stand in the doorway behind her and watch. She looks the way I think she should.

I say, "I think I'm in love," and Mario puts his hands on the front of my T-shirt and kisses me. In my ear, he whispers, "What is this shit?"

My mother says, "The trick is to stop waiting."

Mario says, "What?"

She's still not looking at us. She shrugs her shoulders.

I wonder what she knows. I say, "You're being a child."

She says, "Yes."

Mario still has his hands on the front of my T-shirt. He leans down, puts his forehead against mine, says, "I'm getting a divorce."

My mother turns around, eyebrows raised, and says, "You're married?"

I say, "Not to me."

"Of course," she says.

I say, "We can put a studio in the attic. We can punch out skylights." Suddenly, now that the possibility is there, I want him to stay. I say, "We'll put Ace up there, in the sun." I want to know what we would be like if we had this much space between us.

We are on the front lawn of the old house. The Quales are gone, as promised. It looks like they've left most everything behind. I am lying on my back; Mario is sitting propped up on his elbows.

He says, "There's room for kids."

I look over at him. He's wearing a faded black T-shirt and his black leather vest.

I can imagine Mario staying long enough to get the test results. He would be happy, I know. He would stand behind me and cup my belly in his hands. He would close his eyes and picture what he held there. He would go to Lionel Toy World and walk the aisles for hours and come home with a carload of basketballs and dolls and little plastic automatic weapons.

And I can see me holding a child in a high room with skylights, a cradle and an easel. The room has white walls and is filled with sunlight. On the walls are all the framed posters with which, as a younger woman, I surrounded myself: movie stars, the glamorous, fated ones. I liked their imperturbable loneliness, their turbulent affairs, their sense of being watched, the way they were composed within the frames. All they had, and all they never expected. Marilyn Monroe. Rita Hayworth. Ann-Margret, looking down at me. These were what I began with, all the way back in junior high, when I started to paint: not art from life, but art from still life, from the posters of famous, distant faces.

The canvas on the easel is white.

In my head I split the picture: the nursery on one side, blindingly bright, and Mario on the other. On his side it is night in New York. The streets he stands on are black and wet and shining. This is easy.

"I don't know," I say.

I think of my mother, beautiful and innocent and alone, high up in her quiet rooms smelling of new carpet. She's on her knees in the living room, stuffing her sleeping bag into its little red sack. She is going out into the dark.

I say, "I have enough to worry about."

I say, "Maybe it's only me. What I remember about childhood is how dangerous it was. We were monstrous." I'm not thinking about myself.

He says, "She can't just stop."

I say, "Maybe we're right to resist."

When we make love that night on the filthy rugs of the old house, I leave out my diaphragm and Mario, usually an efficient lover, can't get enough.

"Baby," he keeps saying, "come here."

I help my mother load up the car. I see it as the only way I can keep an eye on her. Though she'll be walking under its weight for four days, I take her backpack from her and carry it in the elevator down to the garage.

I say, "Do you have enough food? Water bottles?"

She smiles a little, says, "Yes."

I want her to say, "Yes, dear." Her voice sounds too young. She looks like a little silver-haired lady, but under the hair her face has almost no lines. I wonder what on earth happened.

I say, "Who else is going?"

She says, "I've done this before."

I say, "That's not the point."

She says, "You could come along."

I say, "No."

She says, "It doesn't matter, you know, if I come back empty-handed."

I say, "No." I lean over and kiss her on the forehead. I say, "Hurry back."

This is not a dream, though it haunts my sleep.

It's my bedtime. My mother has come with a book to read to me. I am a child and she is still young, her hair in a gold braid down her back. I'm in a cot in a large tent, big enough to stand up and move around in. In the middle of the tent is a table with a lantern on it and a tin mug with my mother's brandy. In its light the tent feels cozy, enclosed, like a real room, but we know the lantern casts our shadows against the canvas, a domestic scene for everyone to watch: the cook, the archaeologists, the graduate students passing on the way to their own tents.

The book my mother has brought is a picture book, but one for adults, with photographs and text about dead cities, all lost to some great, careless gesture of nature or man, or just to a natural winding down of something that once held tight. Now these cities, buried for centuries or millennia, are being dug painstakingly back into the light.

My mother opens to the section on Pompeii. "See," she says, "how perfectly preserved it is." I'm looking at the pictures. I can't imagine why we would want to know about this, why we would go to all this effort. The people in the pictures have been burned permanently into their own shapes, at the same time unrecognizable and all too acutely recognizable as human. Some are sitting, some lying down. Two of them prop their elbows on a table, where they lean over some kind of game. The walls are still brilliantly painted.

She shows me pictures of the tools, some of them as delicate as dentist's tools, with which the anthropologist carves the bodies back out of the earth.

I have seen them all before in my mother's thin hands, flashing in the sun.

With her finger, my mother traces a map of the city, the district where the markets were, the brothels. "Here are the suburbs," she says. She laughs, but I don't know what about. She looks up at the ceiling of the tent, shuts her eyes. "A discovery like that," she says.

I look back down at the book. The absolute, lifelike gesture held still for centuries. Street upon street, a whole city.

I will never walk over the surface of the world safely again. These figures are everywhere under our feet, whether we find them or not. There, under my cot, in this tent full of warm yellow lantern light.

My mother leans close to me, her mouth in my hair, her hand tight on my upper arm. "Any one of these," she says, closing the book. She says, "This is what we mean when we say 'Eden.'" She says, "But they've got it wrong. Nothing is ever lost."

And this is where the dream takes over: at that moment, I hear rain on the tent, the wind slapping it against the canvas, and I know the river is rising, filling with red dust from the desert, water rushing in rivulets, through washes, from all over the desert toward us. We can't escape.

I say to Mario, "You don't know what we've survived out there."

"And here you are," Mario says. He is holding me in the crook of his arm. I say, "Yes."

Looking at him, I can see he has no idea.

I think of the first time I took a subway from downtown, 10 A.M. and the station deserted except me and one man. The station smelled of human urine and I thought, this is it, I'm here. I sat down at the other end of the bench from the man and looked at him. He was leaning forward over his crooked arm and fist, like Rodin's *Thinker*, I thought at first, and then he let go of the rubber tube in his teeth and pulled the syringe out and leaned back into himself.

I thought, This is it. I stayed right where I was, waiting for the train.

I say, "That was only one time, I guess. That's what it was like, is all."

The next day, I call a guy who advertises in the classifieds to haul the Quales' trash. "Bring your friends," I say. I want it gone tomorrow.

I say to Mario, "You wouldn't believe what she put me through." I say, "You don't know what it's like out there. It's not only the flash floods. The land can get you, or the scorpions. Avalanches. Lightning. Poisonous snakes." I am thinking of her bending down, putting her hand flat on the earth. I think of her reaching her hand up over the top of the cliff, not knowing what might be there. I say, "She could have a heart attack, and that would be it."

He says, "She told me it's not that serious. A murmur, that's all."

I say, "Of course that's what she told you."

I say, "I've seen them all in a single day. When the water rises, down there, it turns red as blood."

He says, "She'll be fine."

On Sunday, the trash is gone from the yard and house—every artifact hauled away, only the layers of dirt left to remove. Mario and I start in the attic and work down: ceilings, walls, windows, windowsills, baseboards, wood floors, stairs. Mario pries open windows, tightens the screws on towel racks, drills holes, carries buckets of hot, fresh water. I have never seen him like this. When he turns the screwdriver, the muscles in his forearms clench.

We are at my mother's, waiting for her to get back. Sometimes I get up and go out on the balcony, but I have no way of knowing if any of the cars on the road below are hers. We've been watching a news show: someone has just discovered a new lost city in the Andes. The camera shows him with his hands full of gold jewelry, little carved charms. He will never, he says, stop looking. This ruin he found in a dream, and then he went where the dream told him and there it was.

Mario is sitting forward, his elbows on his knees. He keeps saying "Jesus," every time the camera focuses on a house, a temple, an observatory for watching the skies. Everything has been overgrown. On the TV, we see Peruvian peasants, shirtless and sweating, hacking at vines and foliage with machetes, pulling densely leaved branches away from the faces of statues. Mario reaches for me.

There is the sound of the key in the lock. We don't get up; we just turn to the door. My mother is standing there, looking like she always does but smaller. Her white shirt is pink from being soaked in the red water but still it looks somehow pristine. She has a panama hat in her hand. She throws it down on the couch.

I say, "I'm sorry." She looks exhausted; her face is gray and has wrinkles I've never noticed, but there's something she's holding back.

She says, "I'm going to bed."

I say, "What?" I think she's been listening to the radio.

She says, "It's okay."

I say, "Go to bed." She's breathing a little fast.

Mario says, "Maureen."

My mother says, "It's okay." She raises an eyebrow. She looks, suddenly, the way she always did, except for that way she's breathing, like she came up the stairs instead of the elevator.

I say, "It's possible."

My mother looks at me and winks. She says, "Thanks for waiting up."

Back at the house, Mario and I zip together our sleeping bags and spread them on the floor of what will be the bedroom. We lie down.

Mario says, "It doesn't matter."

We make love again, this time quietly, slowly. I try to feel, deep inside me, if anything takes.

And then he is asleep, his head on my shoulder, and I am looking out into the dark, feeling the house tick around us.

I keep imagining the high room and the canvas: first it is pure white, and then the vines begin to curl in with their pearlescent flowers, the hint of limbs underneath. There are an empty white bathrobe; the wedge of sky stitched by lightning, a cool blue; Ace's wings stretched out; a couple playing cards; a couple with their mouths pressed together; water rising redder and faster and washing the dirt away.

What emerges: a city at the crossroads—I know none of this is right, but it's what I see here, on the edge of sleep—its inhabitants waking refreshed and going about their business of cooking, weaving, nursing their babies.

The whole flat earth and what it holds. The world of the body, all around, waiting for us to put a name to it. Waiting for us to recover.

I turn to him again. I will wake him up. I will wake him.

War of Hearts

Love is a fire. But whether it is going to warm your hearth or burn down your house, you can never tell.
—Joan Crawford

The only courage that matters is the kind that gets you from one minute to the next.
—Mignon McLaughlin

When We Fight

by Lesléa Newman

milk curdle in coffee
toast burn
hot water run out
shampoo empty
tire flat
bus late
rain come
umbrella break
shoelace snap
stocking run
button fall off coat
glove disappear
pocketbook vanish
earring break
nail polish chip
typewriter key stick
white out spill
xerox machine jam
envelope don't seal
stamps stuck together
check bounce

pizza burn mouth
tomato sauce on white blouse
heel break off left shoe
key fall down sewer
mail box empty
answering machine silent
cat miss litter box
dog vomit
toilet overflow
lettuce rot in crisper
finger cut instead of onion
meat spoil
bread green
soda flat
newspaper don't come
TV fuzzy
plant on window sill die
pages fall out of book
pen run dry
light bulb burn out
heart stop

The Cram-It-In Method

by Cris Mazza

Maybe Annie's father never taught her (like mine drilled into my head) that force doesn't make anything work easier. This morning I had to refold all her grocery bags because she doesn't flatten them along the seam so that they'll stand upright between the refrigerator and cabinet. She tries to smash them in there without folding first—the cram-it-in method. Also the trash can was overflowing, a deluxe-pizza box wedged in and a Coke bottle balancing on top of that. She could've emptied the trash and started over instead of just pushing in more than it can hold.

I guess I've been living with her for almost a year, but I've managed to never see her. She answered my ad for a roommate and we settled the details by phone. I told her to feel free to go about her usual business. I certainly never wanted to be a witness to anything. Don't I have my own problems to worry about? I stayed in my room when she moved in. I'm in my room whenever she's home. I'll be here when she leaves in her white dress and veil. She wasn't engaged when she moved in, just a college girl in her final year, with (I thought) no worries farther ahead than Saturday night's lover. I didn't know—when she moved her stereo and four speakers, double bed and television into the apartment; nor when I first saw her makeup remover, three kinds of shampoo, tampons and minipads, and her diaphragm kit (which she sometimes leaves on the sink shelf, and I have to see it there, then it disappears again)—I didn't know then (and never wanted to know) that Annie was going to have an even bigger problem than the yeast infection in her crotch (which she treated with yogurt, marked "not for internal use" in the refrigerator, and which some of the boys she screwed mistook for a social disease and were angry about—one guy with sensitive skin actually caught it). Maybe I saw it coming when she pointed

196

out to someone on the phone, "What can anyone *do* with a sociology degree, especially if I don't want to go to graduate school, which my parents want me to, but I don't. I'd rather take time off from school for a while . . . but still, what can I do—? My parents, of course, would also like to see me married, which I wouldn't mind, but there's no one to marry. All of a sudden I seem to know less boys now than ever (just Mick every other Saturday, but that'll never amount to anything). It's scary—what if I don't meet someone *this* year?"

When she studies, she does it in the living room or kitchen. She keeps a mail-order catalogue on the coffee table with her schoolbooks, and one night while reading, she took a break to order some underwear with lace. She always washes them by hand and leaves them hanging to dry in the bathroom where I have to see them. *Scary.* I thought it was funny how she used that word. No, I never meant *funny.*

A few months ago I was in the living room when I heard her key in the lock, so I went to my bedroom before she came in. She had a low voice with her. After making sure they weren't talking about me, I didn't really listen. They giggled a while and they turned the stereo on, then some silence, except an ad on the radio for control-top panty hose, interrupted by talking and a few more giggles, on and off—put my teeth on edge, the giggling, but thought I was handling it, covered my head with a pillow—then they went into the bedroom, bounced on the bed a few moments, and they left the apartment together. I came out to use the toilet. I shivered in the bathroom and noticed the soggy condom I didn't want to see in the trash can, half-hidden among crumpled tissues.

Later that night she called a friend. "Let me tell you what happened today, something that only happens on television. I was walking to a class and this guy was waiting outside the building, watching girls—you can always tell when a guy is watching girls—so when I went by he said something like "Hi cutie," or something, then he walked me to my class, and when class was over, I came out and he was waiting for me and he walked me to the next class, and after that class he was there again, waiting for me. I was going home then, so he waked me home, and we got talking. Listen to this, he's good-looking. Well, his hair's real short, but that won't be forever 'cause right now he's in ROTC and National Guard Reserve, and as soon as he serves four years as an officer after graduation, he'll be out and can let his hair grow. The army pays him, though, and also he gets social security 'cause his mother died when he was little. Anyway, he stayed and we talked and horsed around a little—we danced and I stood on his feet, then we roughhoused on the living room floor. He's strong, too, he works out. Huh? . . . Oh, his name's Zack. But this is the part that's really weird, listen: We got carried away, after he kissed me a few times, and we wrestled around—we almost did it in the living room, but we made it to the bedroom, and he was a *virgin!* That's right. Well, he seemed to know what to do, technically he seemed to know, then afterwards he told me he'd never really gone all the way before, but he must've known something 'cause he was *fast!* It was over in two minutes, I swear, not more than two minutes. I didn't say anything this time, I could tell he didn't want me to be the leader, he's in the ROTC. Then he gave me his dog tags—no one's done that to me since high school rings. It's sort of sweet, you know? I guess I'll play along with him, it's been a long time, since I dumped Roger in the tenth grade, remember that? . . . Okay, he dumped me, if you want to get technical. What? . . . Yeah, maybe he just needs experience. He calls me the all-American girl and says he's the all-American boy. But he noticed my tummy and says I have a little pot, and he was poking it. I like my tummy, he embarrassed me. . . . Anyway, he wants us to be the all-American boy and girl. I guess I'm going to have a boyfriend for a while."

She called all her friends, in order of importance. The story got shorter every time, but she never forgot to tell the parts about his virginity and the ROTC. Sometimes one amazed her more than the other, then vice versa on the next call.

Three weeks or a month later she went through the whole phone list again to tell them all she was engaged. "We're telling my relatives we've known each other for five or six months. . . . Probably in June. Then he'll be an officer in the army. Oh—Julie's doing the engagement party, and I think Carol has the shower. I'll probably have a shower with my mother's friends too. Yes, you'll be a bridesmaid." That's when the cards started coming, and Annie tapes them to the outside of her bedroom door where I have to see them too. Most of them are silhouettes of people in a sunset, a few close-ups of hands holding each other. One card is a couple of gold rings on a little pillow next to two glasses of pink champagne.

This is Friday evening and Zack has gone to a military fraternity meeting after being here all afternoon, locked with Annie in her dank bedroom. (I've gone in there a few times when she's not home—only to look for the dictionary which she uses as padding between the bed and the wall, otherwise she causes all that banging when she screws because the headboard slaps the wall between our bedrooms. As it is, the dictionary usually slips free halfway through. Her bedroom smells of stale clothes and not-often-changed sheets and is damp because she keeps a pan of water on the radiator.) Whoever's on the other end of the phone is being updated. "Zack's still too fast and I don't know how to tell him without hurting his ego. I figured out he thinks it's more macho to be fast like that. But really, how can you tell someone they aren't doing sex right. . . . No, I'm not getting anything out of it. I'm not sure he knows that I'm supposed to. . . . Yeah, I'll have to tell him somehow. I've still got my books from my human sexuality class—I'll put them on the nightstand. The other thing is now that he's tried it without a rubber, he likes it better that way. Huh? . . . I'd get another abortion. . . . It's not his decision to make. . . . Yeah, he'll have to realize that if he doesn't want to wear one, at least I've got to know in advance so I can get prepared. . . . Yeah, I decided on six bridesmaids."

In the morning Zack is here again. I can hear his voice through the wall, so I use the toilet quickly before they come out of the bedroom. But they talk a long time in there today, then the bed creaks pretty steadily. She must have the dictionary—the headboard isn't knocking on the wall. Voices again, mostly hers, like the sound of a Morse code telegraph machine. I keep hearing the same strings of dots and dashes. I can't understand her—don't want to understand her.

When they do come out, they go into the kitchen and I wouldn't be able to hear them if Annie wasn't half screaming. "My parents will have to take out a loan for a big wedding! Listen, I want a small, simple ceremony, maybe a hundred to a hundred fifty couples, a band, liquor, a small supper, six bridesmaids, six ushers. . . . I don't care if it's free, I don't *want* a military wedding. I'm the one getting married, I get to plan it, it can be just as nice if it's small. . . . *I'm* the bride and the bride makes the plans. Listen: A band, a hundred fifty, two hundred couples—it'll be plenty, the liquor alone will cost five hundred dollars, my parents'll probably ask your father to pay part of it. . . . Why not, you're getting married too. You're supposed to pay for the flowers and booze at least, that's in all the books, but listen, a couple hundred couples, a band, we'll find a hall, that'll be plenty big enough, we don't need it any bigger."

After they're gone, I go out to eat and find their broken eggshells and the empty tub of real butter, and there, forced into the loaded trash can, is the milk carton that was almost full yesterday. She always pours the milk down the drain on the morning of the date that's stamped on the carton. On the table is a copy of *Modern Bride*, the spring issue, all the brides in white, every single one of them.

If I'm already asleep I don't hear them come in at night until the headboard starts banging the wall. I needed the dictionary today. Sometimes the headboard pounds like a heartbeat, then it goes back to a single downbeat, or sometimes it misses a beat. But no voices at all, not even loud breathing. It's like hammering nails, a carpenter on the job all night, his work never finished.

I can hear cartoons on the tube while Annie's in the kitchen frying something. I smell butter. She yells "Breakfast" twice, and at the end of a cartoon the TV goes off and they're both in the kitchen. He eats in five minutes, then goes out to a morning class and she heads for the telephone. The floors creak, different pitches in different parts of the room. The boards near the phone always groan when she picks up the receiver.

"You'll never believe it," she says. "No, *worse* . . . I told him, then we read about it together. I didn't want to just come out and say he stinks in bed! It's hard to hide the fact that I know more about sex than he does. I can't help it, I took a class. But he pretends everything I know is from that *class*, not from experience, so I'm careful to never say, When this happened to me before, or, I know a guy who does this or that. I have to say I read it somewhere. . . . Yeah, well, he seemed to understand, but—Huh? . . . No, just the opposite! Now he can't *finish!* . . . No, I can tell when I take my diaphragm out that he didn't. . . . Actually no, it's not much fun because that's all he worries about—he says he has to make it in order to prove he loves me, so that's all he's trying to do, and, well, the harder he tries. . . . Exactly, I showed him in the book, but—Huh? . . . Well, yeah, but I don't want to be his goddamn sex therapist!"

When I return the dictionary later, I spot the sex manual on the night stand, not opened. I flip through it, but she hasn't highlighted or underlined anything. One of the positions is called female-superior . . . her on top, doesn't look like it would make much noise. There are some dead plants in her room, but the bed is made and the dirty clothes are all piled on one chair. A fishnet is mounted on the wall over the bed as a decoration.

When she comes home, she takes the phone to the kitchen, so I shouldn't have to hear too much. But the longer she talks, the faster; and faster always makes louder. So by the time the usual greetings are over, I can hear every word. "Well, it's a big mess, listen: His father wants to give us some money, right? He's been saving it for Zack since Zack was little, but his father wants us to put it away or let him invest it for us for a nest egg. My parents want Zack's father to pay for half the wedding, but I'm afraid if he does that, that's where the money'll go, which is why he doesn't want to help pay for the wedding because he wants us to invest the money so when Zack is out of the army we'll have something put away. Anyway, *I* want to use some of it for the honeymoon— I decided on the Virgin Islands, and we can get a couple of weeks there easy for what he planned to give us—they sent a brochure and I've already decided on it, I'm making reservations. His father doesn't know yet, and tomorrow we're all having dinner together—my parents are planning to ask him to pay for half the wedding, especially since Zack's the one who wants it big, but I've already told him two hundred fifty couples tops, a hundred fifty will be mine and he gets a hundred—we made our lists—so I told him not to meet any more people this term because we won't be able to invite them and they'll wonder why. He wanted to wait until some people said they couldn't come and then send out more invitations to fill the empty places, but I said no, the invitations are sent once, maybe a month or six weeks ahead of the date, then no more go out, so don't meet any more people, I told him, we can't afford it."

I can smell macaroni 'n' cheese. When she goes back out for her afternoon classes, she leaves the pan on the stove, half full of yellow-orange noodles. I put the stuff into a freezer container. I can tell there's real butter in it. Then I wash the dishes from this morning. Looks like eggs again. Zack uses a lot of ketchup on his. She's left a few new magazines here. In the *Bridebook* I find a questionnaire, already filled out. *How long have you known the groom-to-be? Where do you intend to live? Do you already own stainless cookware? What type of honeymoon?* It's a multiple-choice test. *How much will your wedding dress cost?* She checked the middle choice, between two and three hundred dollars. *Who will do the cooking? Who will manage the budget and pay the bills? What kind of literature have you found most helpful in planning your new life?*

On the phone late Sunday morning, she says she has to do some studying and write a paper. She's found a dress, she says, which she wants all the bridesmaids to look at in Macy's, it's only fifty dollars. "Well," she says, "I recognize what phase he's in, I went through it too—but I was in high school, you know, when I first did it. Now he's going through that phase—you know, he wants to experiment. It's only fair, I guess, to let him have his turn, but really, I got over all that, you know he reads about something and he wants to try it. I remember when I was doing that, because everything was new, but now it's only new to *him*. Well, I go along with it because it's only fair."

When he gets here, they have strong-smelling fish for dinner, then they leave the kitchen and go into her bedroom. They turn the stereo on to try to hide their noises, but they end up drowning out the music. Like two carpenters not hitting their nails at the same time. Then one carpenter finishes his nail and the other is left banging all alone. When that one stops there's just the music, but they turn that off too, and there's silence, until Annie starts talking. I'm pretty sure she's not talking about me. Her voice goes faster and faster, shriller and higher, and I can't understand any words. She has plenty to say, or if she forgets where she is, she starts over. Then she screeches, "I hate you," and something thumps like a butt on the floor or a head against the door, and her voice starts again, jabbering, a record on the wrong speed. His voice is there too—he's not taking this lying down—but his voice is a weird high falsetto, a breathless cartoon voice. The next thing I can understand is when she screams "Get outta here," and more thumping. But the door doesn't open and no one creaks footsteps on the living room floorboards. I've lost track of time. One of the carpenters starts hammering again, so the other shuts up.

She doesn't get to make any more calls until the next afternoon when Zack leaves for close-order drill. She says, "Hi. Ready for the latest? You know, his mother's dead and all. Well, Saturday night he takes me into his father's attic and gets out this trunk. . . . Yeah, like a horror movie. And he pulls out this dress wrapped in plastic and mothballs and holds it up. His mother's wedding dress, see. . . . It was okay, nothing great, it might've once been white, high neck and sleeves to the wrist. Then last night he tells me he wants me to wear it when we get married. He said it's the way he always pictured his wedding. I told him it won't save any money because we'd have to have it tailored to fit me, and cleaned and pressed, and somehow get rid of the mothball smell. Yeah, well, I didn't make any promises."

She sleeps most of the day until her father arrives to take her home for a family supper. Later she comes back to the apartment howling, walking around crying—not hitting anything or stomping or throwing anything, but she cries like an ambulance. Not sorrow, but absolute terror. When Zack comes in—he has his own key—the siren stops without a grumble. Maybe she was singing, it could've been singing. I can hear her showing him vacation brochures. "Look at this—this is the one I've chosen, Virgin Islands, see, you get a private bungalow, sauna, meals included, there's a pool and boats and the rooms are modern and air-conditioned, fully staffed and private. I'll make reservations."

When I use the toilet after they go to bed, I find his shaving gear piled on the sink shelf. I take my toothbrush and soap back to my room.

It's not until Friday that she finally has time to call her bridesmaids again. "Yeah, for another two hundred down we could've gotten a later time in a different hall. Anyway. . . . No, he doesn't care, know what he's been doing? Listen, we get along together and start fooling around, then he says, Let's play teacher and student, and he makes me pretend I'm his student and he's a teacher, and he's teaching me how to do it, and I'm supposed to pretend I never have and he's showing me. I have to say stuff like, Oh, is that where it goes? and say *Eeek* when I see it. . . . Well, if it'll help . . ."

I have to go to the bathroom!

I can't hear as well from here, but I notice she washed her control-top panty hose and hung them on the towel rod where I have to see them. By the time I come out, she already has another bridesmaid on the phone. "Well, at least with the earlier time we won't have to rush to the airport. We'll have all afternoon to get ready and relax. You know, the ceremony will probably be exhausting for both of us. . . . Yeah, we're going to need those two weeks alone together. . . . Not exactly, but today he wanted to play two kids experimenting, so we had to pretend we didn't know anything about it and were finding out about it together, like we're both surprised when it gets big, all that stuff. I don't know. . . . Yeah, I ordered those dresses at Macy's."

When I finally have a chance to come out of my room, I can't find the dictionary, so I look through her pile of schoolbooks on the coffee table. No dictionary, but in *House Beautiful* magazine there's an article on solutions to age-old room-divider problems, and here's another little magazine, *Handbook of Creative Lifestyle*, a marker in the chapter called "Daddy and Mommy," but the mommy wears spike heels and fishnet stockings and a gunbelt with bullets, breasts disguised as gold-tipped missiles, and the daddy sucks a bullet-shaped pacifier. Why did I have to see this?

Can't really say I'm on the outside looking in. It *is* our living room window—four windows up, two over—but I can't see inside. The drapes are closed. I call from the corner drugstore in a booth with no door and snow underfoot. She answers after one ring—half a ring, and she's already on the line, eager, breathless. . . . "Who is this?"

It sounds so different to hear her *through* the phone. Last time she spoke on the phone—this morning, to her mother—she screamed and stamped her feet, then lowered her voice and talked quickly, almost a hissing whisper, almost positive I heard my name.

"Hello? Hello?" she says. "Anyone there?"

It's been a long time since she's said anything was scary. I can't remember what her voice sounded like when she said it. Not any louder or faster or less intense. Just more like a real voice.

"Hello!" she calls. "I know you're there, I hear you breathing."

Is that a laugh? She's laughed before, but not like this—brittle and metallic and thin. Hard to listen to, makes my ear feel frozen to the receiver which will have to be ripped away, leaving my ear bleeding.

"Roger, is that you, you weirdo? You got the wedding announcement I sent, didn't you?"

If she looked out the window, she might see me at the phone booth, not that there'd be any new flicker of recognition in her voice. What difference would it make if she did?

"I know it's you, Roger. Zack wanted to send the announcement, as a joke, he asked who my last real boyfriend had been. What'sa matter, it make you jealous?"

Lots of other times I couldn't understand every word like this.

I just noticed the milk carton has tomorrow's date, February 15, the expiration date. I'll pour it out and save her the trouble. But the phone is ringing and I'm about to answer it the same time she comes in the door. I get back to my room just in time, still holding onto the half-full milk carton. She's alone. "Just got in," she says. "What? Oh, Zack's all upset 'cause his father wants to move out but Zack doesn't want his father to sell the house. He grew up there. Huh? No, I can't, I'm going into the city to price some rings. . . . Well, he was going to come too, but he has National Guard duty, and then tonight he shows me this little ring box with his parents' wedding rings and he says he wants to use them. He said his dad said it's okay. His father hasn't worn his in years, and Zack says he would like me to have his mother's wedding ring. . . . No, it was kind of plain. I didn't try it on. I sort of want my own, you know, braided gold, a wider band, maybe something set in it, something special. . . . I said we've got a while to decide. Want to come with me tomorrow? . . . Wait, Zack's at the door. What's he doing here? Anyway, I'll speak to you tomorrow."

Her bedroom door squeaks and their voices mumble together in there. The bedsprings whine and the headboard rattles against the wall, and their voices mumble again. They may be talking about me. But they finish talking before I can hear, and the bed bounces and the headboard knocks and very soon, very soon Annie breathes eagerly. I can hear her little voice in every breath, on the verge of a sneeze. . . . Then something crashes, and the headboard rat-a-tats out of rhythm, and Annie's voice is oh-oh-oh-oh, higher and higher. No sound from Zack, no grunting, just his carpenter noises and her piercing scream, screaming and screaming, the headboard like a machine gun now, and Annie screaming, like the scene of a crime, but I plug my ears with my fingers and I think I'm crying . . . or maybe it's her crying (at last) and *I'm* the one (finally) screaming my head off.

Not Me

by Kate Velten

S onya presses her body against a clammy, grit-encrusted lamppost and
watches a mother and son chase each other down the sidewalk, mother
in front, son in front, back and forth like pistons. Each carries two heavy
parcels, wrapped in brown paper, tied with string. They have broad behinds.
Their torsos are thrust forward urgently. Their legs scurry.

Pinprick drizzle scratches Sonya's neck and face, but she's not going to
move now. This is her first chance to be on the sidewalk with these two, whom
she sees through her windows all the time.

They live two houses from her and take the bus everywhere. She has no
idea what their names are but the woman looks like one of those sorry old
actresses from an old movie. There is no father. Jimmy, her husband, says
they're two crazies and if she ever tries talking to them they'll scare her like
everything does, and she'll have no one to blame but herself.

Jimmy always ridicules them from the living room window. He stands, legs
wide apart, cracking his knuckles and making wise remarks. Sonya wonders
what secrets Jimmy knows about them. She wonders if he is the boy's father.
Sonya doesn't bother to wonder unless she has a good reason. Jimmy has taught
her that—if she has an opinion she'd better be able to stand by it. "Don't tell
me what you think," he says, "unless you are ready to defend it to the death."

Well, this is her opinion ever since the day she watched him from behind,
his back scrunched up making him like someone small, climb over the back
fence between their home and the neighbor's, and then over the chain-link
between the neighbor's and that woman. She couldn't believe he didn't rip his
pants.

Leaning into the doorway, Sonya had watched Jimmy standing there for a long time, bent forward stiff as wood, except he'd jut back his shoulders once in a while the way he did when something bothered him. What's he doing? Then she saw him raise his hand to a striking position and automatically she cringed and caught her breath. But Jimmy stopped, hand stuck up in the air, and stayed like that until Sonya wanted to laugh at how silly it looked.

Suddenly a hand from in front of Jimmy reached up and pushed Jimmy's arm even higher and then shoved him so hard he was pressed against the fence. She geared up to bolt. Then Jimmy turned sideways sharply and shook someone loose. It was that woman craning her neck to see up as high as Jimmy's chin and shaking her finger right in his face.

The woman was scolding Jimmy hard, nonstop, and Jimmy was keeping still! Sonya felt queasy. Stop, stop, she wanted to shout. Leave my husband alone. Instead Sonya backed quickly into the doorway, feeling suddenly exposed. What if Jimmy saw her watching him? It would shame him, she knew, and she'd pay for it. He'd beat her hard. She bit her lip, and went back into the kitchen.

Later, when he came home, he was muttering to himself. Sonya wanted to ask him what was wrong but that was always a chancy thing to do. Sometimes he just got angrier. She went into the bathroom instead and gently closed the door. Jimmy usually didn't mind when she was in there, as long as she was quiet.

After a while she emerged and Jimmy was slumped into the living room couch. "You know, Sonya," he said, "it's too bad that there aren't ropes slung from trees everywhere. It'd be damn nice to string up any sucker who tried to rub your nose in shit." He glared toward her. "Man or woman," he said.

Since he hadn't caught her, Sonya watched a few more times when Jimmy would leap the fences. Sonya found out she was fascinated by the woman's effect on Jimmy, that he was never the one in charge. He was just like a kid getting scolded. Once the boy was out there too. The woman had him by the ear and was tugging at it while she talked vehemently at Jimmy. Each time he'd come back and stand smoking in the backyard a while before entering their house. Sometimes when he came in he'd say something to her about no kids. That's why Sonya guessed Jimmy was the kid's father. Why with her? She wasn't even pretty. And Jimmy was so handsome. One thing, it was pretty damn brave of her. Or stupid. But then, no, because as far as Sonya could see, Jimmy acted like he was almost afraid of her. Isn't that something, Sonya thought. I'm sweet as cream to him, and look how he treats me.

When they got married Jimmy told her if she got pregnant she could kiss him good-bye. She used to think it was worth it; he was such a catch. And she used to believe it was because Jimmy has eleven brothers and sisters, and he had to watch them when he was young, and work to support them when he was old enough. She'd told herself, "I have the best and most handsome man around. I don't need kids." Now she tells herself it wouldn't be such a hot idea to bring a baby home with Jimmy as mean as he is sometimes.

She can't get angry at him because there are times when he's gentle like he was when they dated. Sonya believes it's a sickness, that Jimmy gets so cruel. She remembers the TV movie she saw advertised where the woman had two black eyes. Sonya was home by herself the night the movie played, but she didn't dare watch. If Jimmy came home and caught her he'd kill her. And even if he didn't show up, he might try to trick her later into talking about it. If she didn't watch, she couldn't make a mistake. Sonya did not want the movie to set her thinking wrong, the way her mother, who had always been against him, was trying to do.

"Did he hit you again?" she'd ask whenever she called. And Sonya always answered, "Mama, Jimmy doesn't hit me." She knew her mother didn't believe her. Sonya told Jimmy once in an argument that her mother could tell that he hit her. That was a mistake. He smashed her head against the bathroom radiator. He told her not to visit her mother ever again unless he was with her.

Sonya and her mother meet at the mall sometimes. Once Sonya's arms were bruised, once her neck was ringed with black and blue like beads. She said she'd walked into an open door to explain her arms, and that she had hickeys on her neck. Her mother's eyes opened wide and she looked cold as steel. "Sonya," was all she said. The problem with her mother is that she only sees what's wrong. She doesn't believe that Jimmy really wants to be good but sometimes bad just explodes out of him. She says every man is his own god, and gods think women are their creation to do with what they will. She says, "Sonya, I'm beginning to believe you're never going to get as smart as I tried so hard to raise you." Then she sighs and stares out over Sonya's shoulder.

When her mother telephones and Jimmy answers, he's sweet as pie, but after passing the phone to Sonya, he'll stay right next to her listening and keeping his hand on her shoulder.

Sonya has figured out many ways to keep Jimmy appeased. They don't always work but that's just the way it is with Jimmy, he has these troubles and sometimes they come out. One of her tricks is that whenever Jimmy makes mean remarks about people, she chimes in. Sonya can come up with some very nasty lines. Her tongue is quick, which Jimmy appreciates, except sometimes he laughs at something she said, but then later he thinks about it and decides she's made fun of him. That's one of the reasons she knows he has troubles, because he takes something he liked, something good, and turns it to bad. He can't help it. So she should. She should try harder to make it easy for him. Why can't she get any better at it?

Yesterday Jimmy came home balancing a narrow box on his palm. It was very long and he had to dip it forward to get in the doorway.

"New cue," Jimmy said.

From across the kitchen Sonya hunched her shoulders and shivered.

Jimmy slid the box onto the kitchen table. The end close to Sonya extended well over the edge like a diving board.

Trying not to look at the box, Sonya stared at her husband's jaw, her lips pressed together, her fingers crossed at her sides. Embedded in the cracks where the kitchen floor and walls meet, there were slivers of wood from his old cue. She could not dig them out. She tried with the point of her nail file, but they did not budge. When he'd whacked that stick across her back it broke in two. Sonya screamed so loud Jimmy'd rammed the jagged piece he still held into her thigh.

Jimmy stood beside the table, arms folded across his chest. His tongue protruded slightly out of the corner of his mouth, and more pain rattled down Sonya's spine. She dared not move. She started to pray inside but was afraid she might forget and say the prayer out loud so she stopped.

In the silence she could hear the pilot flame in her stove and the parkway traffic three blocks away.

"What'd you do today, doll?" Jimmy asked, his words dripping with a hive's worth of honey. "Did you buy that Fleischmann's you forgot yesterday?"

Sonya nodded, running her tongue behind her teeth.

Jimmy didn't say anything else, just stared at her and rocked on his heels, then pulled a beer out of the refrigerator and leaned against the sink. Maybe he didn't remember how the other cue broke. There were things he forgot, and when he forgot Sonya was relieved. Because when Jimmy said, "Do you remember the time?" Sonya cringed. Jimmy only remembered bad things. Most of the time those things never happened except somewhere in his head. That's the sickness.

Quietly she watched Jimmy guzzle the beer, his Adam's apple jumping. He reached in the refrigerator for another. She watched him down that one. He paid no attention to the new cue.

After a while Sonya began to relax.

The ground is damp from rain that ended only an hour ago. Sonya's sneakers feel soggy and cold at the toes. The bandage at the place where her neck meets her collarbone pulls, tearing at her skin. Sonya tries to tamp it in place carefully because it's her last one and Jimmy hates when she buys bandages. He tells her she's throwing things in his face and why can't she respect him. Every time Sonya moves her shoulder the bandage pulls away again. She wants to listen to these two; she wants to hear their names.

Their voices are rising.

"Watch what you're doing. Look! You're going to wreck the wrapping!" She stops short. "Don't drop them!"

"I'm not!" The boy pulls up.

Sonya can see the packages slipping from his grip. She curls her toes.

The mother stares at the boy. "Tub of lard. Even if a corner touches the ground, you'll be sorry. Get me?" She raises a fist and turns away. "I'll chase you until you fall," she shouts over her shoulder. "Beat you to a pulp!"

The boy stomps his foot, splattering his mother. She stops again, rises to her toes and turns so red Sonya can see it from across the street. Sonya shudders.

The woman spreads her arms wide, dangling the packages like clubs on either side.

"You idiot!" She glares down at her water-spattered legs, then back up at the boy. "Look! Look! You've ruined my stockings!" She swings a package toward the boy's head. He ducks.

"No!" Sonya screams.

Across the street the woman and her son stop in their tracks and lean into each other, watching her. But Sonya doesn't stop; doesn't care if they see. She just keeps on screaming.

Resurrection

by Ellen Terry Kessler

I will rise above this cold tile floor
I will imagine the Lord
My body is not pressed into a corner
You are not beating my face and my breasts
I am walking down a street
Where the wind is a caress
I am going to the movies
To watch other people suffer

Do It Yourself

by Gail Donovan

"**L**et me tell you about how you were born," Arty said. He stroked the puppy's stomach; she fit perfectly in his lap. "Just as Wilson's dog, that's your mother, went into labor, I was talking to Susan on the telephone. She'd gone to New York for the weekend–can you believe me? She *had* to see some dude with a big trust fund. I told her how much more terrific I was, but did she listen?" Arty slammed his fist down on the table. "No." The coffee cups jangled and Ruth twitched.

"Pardon me," he said, stroking her quivering body. "I digress." He rubbed her belly. "Okay, Mom is starting to breathe heavy. She's panting. Then all of a sudden—squirt. Out you slide. Wilson said, 'It's a girl, Arty.'

"'It's a girl, Susan,' I said. She said, 'What color is she?' Wilson was rubbing you with a towel"—here Ruth stood and circled around, her rough pads tickling Arty's bare legs, and settled in the exact same position—"wiping off all the gook. 'She's black and white,' I said. 'We'll take her,' she said. 'Tell him we want that one.'"

Ruth licked his kneecap. "How many times do I have to tell you?" said Arty. "*No licking.*" Abruptly, he stood. His legs vertical, his lap gone, Ruth crashed to the floor.

Cranking open the window, Arty threw the remnants of his breakfast, a banana peel, outside. The yellow skin landed in the grass. Wildflowers— daisies, black-eyed Susans, and gloriosas—dotted the overgrown yard. He ought to buy a mower, plant grass, turn it into a real lawn. "Spread compost," he explained to the dog. "More efficient. It's how the French do it."

Arty aimed his remote-control device at the television. Big Money! Big

210

Money! He pushed a button, and three men swiveled in chairs: a pale and pudgy funeral director, a cremation expert, and the host. It's the only alternative, the cremation guy said. The host tried to pick a fight by getting the burial guy to list his prices. How much for the ebony wood, velvet-lined model?

"I'm telling you, I'm going to make a fortune with this coffin concept." Arty aimed the remote control at the dog. "Be a rottweiler," he said. "Be a poodle." She wagged her tail and launched a running leap toward him.

Open caskets, said the pudgy man, allow many to *confront* their grief.

Ruth settled in his lap. Arty aimed at the window. "Click," he said. The birch trees still curved into the sky at the edge of the yard; his pickup truck still stood where he'd parked it that morning, when he got back from bringing Susan to the emergency room. The grass was still littered with the remnants of his spread-compost technique: fruit skins, coffee grounds, vegetable peelings. "Click," he repeated, causing a Volkswagen to chug up the long dirt drive, and Susan to step from the driver's seat, flawless, intact.

Your soft carpets, your velvet, your lilies, said Mr. Cremation. The death monopoly has gone on long enough. The host announced they would break for station identification.

"See, I *told* you so. The time is right," Arty explained to the dog. "I have the tools, I have the technology. I just need some funds, and a place to sell them." Searching for something to work on during the slow winter months, Arty had tried birdhouses, dollhouses. Then he'd hit upon affordable coffins. Through January and February, Arty had designed and built several coffins, as yet unsold, which he used around the house. A child-size served as a kindling box. Susan had filled one with potting soil; she wanted to put in pink geraniums. Arty intended to sell reasonably priced caskets, or he could cut the pieces to size and sell them as do-it-yourself economy packages. There was a market; there was a need.

"No!" Arty cried. "Bad dog!" He belted her; she cowered. He rolled her over onto her spine and slapped her under her chin, twice. Ruth crouched on the floor, trembling. Arty grabbed her forelegs and shook her. "No!" He pointed to her pillow. "Go lie down," he said, "scoot." When she wouldn't move, he kicked her toward the kitchen.

Arty threw some paper towels on her shit. He wiped the feces from his left foot. It stuck between his toes, cold and wet. He hobbled upstairs, trying not to let that foot touch the floor, and stuck his foot under the tub faucet.

The morning after he and Susan first slept together, last summer, she'd driven off in her Volkswagen after breakfast, and Arty had gone upstairs to shower. He'd walked, dripping wet from the bathroom, and sat down on the bed. There were no clean towels; he'd just drip dry. He pulled down the covers.

"Oh my god," he said. "Oh god."

There were smears of colors. Susan was twenty, but it couldn't be possible. He tried to reconstruct the previous night. She was a friend of a friend. They'd often been partners at country dances. Last night they had dinner, and she came home with him. He tried to remember if there'd been an innocence, a naïveté he'd been too dim-witted to observe. But on the contrary, she was comfortable in bed, playful. When she lifted up her dress, momentarily cloaking her face and long sandy hair, her black slip shimmered.

Then what had happened? Sitting down on the mattress, she took a cosmos flower from the vase on the bedside table. He hadn't been positive she would sleep with him, but just in case, he wanted her to see what kind of person he was, someone who set out fresh flowers for company. Señor, she said, the long stem in her teeth.

Arty turned off the water and sat down on the toilet lid. He towelled his foot dry, first the ankle and arch, then the dark crevices between each toe, the places where disease sprouted. Arty got excited just remembering, how he took the flower from her mouth to kiss her, leading the stem behind her small ear, the maroon petals curled against her cheek. Señor, she said, rubbing the silky slip against him, oh señor. She ran the blossom all along his body.

Ruth trotted into the bathroom. She wagged her tail uncertainly. "Stupid!" Arty realized he'd said the word aloud. Stupid was what he had shouted that morning, stripping off the covers and throwing them on the floor. The long slender cosmos stem lay at the foot of the bed, blossomless; its petals had been torn off under their embraces, squished into the sheets. He hadn't hurt her. "That purple-red color," he told Ruth, who stood on her hind legs, paws on his thigh. "It was just flower juice."

She rushed at him, growling and baring her teeth. She tried to run behind him, but he circled with her, holding the mirror in front of him. "Ruthy—who's that? Ruf! Ruf!" Arty barked, and in a frenzy Ruth yapped, pranced, and whined. The hackles bristled upright on her shoulders. "I find it hard," Arty sang, "to believe you don't know, the beauty you are. I'll be your mirror. I'll be your mirror." At the sound of Arty singing, Ruth stood still, looked at him quizzically, her head tilted to one side. "Woof?" asked Arty . "Bowwow?" He propped the mirror against a chair and pulled Ruth into his lap. "It's this language barrier," he said. "*Talk* to me, baby."

The kettle whistled; he was pouring the water onto the coffee grounds when he heard a crash.

The chair was on its side, its legs stretched uselessly into the air; mirror fragments lay scattered on the floor—some silver and reflective, others, the glass-coated backside, flat gray. "Ruthy!" Arty said. "Careful." He scooped her up. "Those are dangerous." He dropped her onto the oily, overstuffed couch. "Stay," he said. Kneeling, he began to gather the sharp-edged pieces into a pile. The south wall of this room was mostly windows. Birds used to fly into them. He'd found sparrows with broken necks, limp yellow finches in the grass.

"Arthur, why don't you do something?" Susan had asked. "Poor things," she crooned over their bodies, "poor things." The orange-pink insulation hung uncovered on the walls, and the front step was a tree stump. "Do it yourself," he said. "I don't have time." She hung red strips from the middle of each large pane. When the wind blew, they fluttered. Now they hung straight down.

"Arty boy?" Wilson's voice preceded him into the room, which served as both workshop and living room, since it was here the big cast-iron stove stood. He waved two small pieces of paper in his hand. "Old Orchard Beach," he said. "Come on. Triple A ball game, beers, the time of your life. Get your coat." He wiped his face with the bottom of his paint-splattered T-shirt and sat down next to Ruth on the couch, setting his boots on the coffee table, an extra-wide pine casket, painted black. "Hey," Wilson said. "What happened here?"

"I think she ran behind the mirror and pushed it over, or jumped on the chair or something. She doesn't know what a reflection is." Arty placed each piece gingerly into a brown paper bag.

"Nice," said Wilson, pointing to Arty's T-shirt: We killed Flipper, now Bambi must go. He stared at it for a few seconds, humming, then asked, "How did that song go?"

"Flipper," Arty answered. "Flipper." Wilson, recognizing the old TV theme song, joined in and together they sang, "King of the sea."

"Did she do that, too?" Wilson pointed to the middle of the floor. An overturned lamp, the contents of the coffee table—fashion magazines, a wine glass, some Polaroid snapshots—a ripped shirt, and a single sneaker lay scattered on the braided rug.

"I'm a little behind on my housecleaning," Arty grinned sheepishly. "Pay no attention to that man behind the curtain."

Wilson waved the tickets. "They're playing Pawtucket. If we leave now, we could stop at Aqua Park and check out the young ladies. Oh god," he groaned. "They'll whizz down the slides. Oh!" he shrieked in imitation. "Zoom! Their bikini tops will get all messed up." He readjusted an imaginary bathing suit top, patting his chest and giggling. He sighed. "I know," he glared at Arty. "I *know*. But no harm in you just looking. Come on. Let's split this scene. Some mess."

Arty placed the last diamond-shaped piece of mirror in the bag. "Can't," he said. "Stay for lunch?"

"No," said Wilson, pausing on his way out. "Susan waitressing today?"

Arty stepped outside for the first time since dawn. The heat and mosquitoes attacked him. "Oh," he said. "Yeah." They trod through the daisies and clover, the fruit skins, wood chips, empty buckets, and dog shit, toward Wilson's car. "Be good," Arty called, as Wilson backed down the drive. The day was dry and clear, and he bet if he was high up on a ladder, shingling, he could see Sugarloaf.

"Shush," Arty had hissed last night, "silence," as he opened the door and Ruth began to yelp. Moonlight eased through the big southern windows, paling the thick stars. Pines loomed against the black sky, and gleaming birch, their young trunks white and slender, stood before them.

"It's okay, I'm awake," Susan had said in the dark. "Over here. In the coffee table."

"Baby," he said. "Why aren't you in bed?"

"You're drunk."

"Am not."

"Are so." From beneath her patchwork quilt, Susan lifted her arms and reached out from the model casket. "Kiss, kiss." She touched his face with a moist palm. "Why don't you come on in here?"

Arty felt her brow. "You're all sweaty." Often in the night she woke, clammy and hot, thrusting the covers from her, and he would pad downstairs and bring her a glass of water with ice.

"Where were you? I couldn't get to sleep without you in bed. You know I'm going to New York tomorrow. To see my sister."

"And who else?" he demanded.

"Beautiful. You go out drinking so you can brood about something that's *over*."

"Don't go."

"Be real." She began twisting strands of dark blonde hair around her fingers. "You're the only guy for me, padre. Why don't you come, too?"

"No money," he said. "And what about Ruth?"

"What do you mean, money? I have two weeks of tips. I can cover you."

"You shouldn't spend it in New York," Arty said. "Maybe you should try paying your way around here, for once."

"I buy groceries. I pay bills. I bought all those dishes so we wouldn't have to eat off paper plates. You own the damn house. Who asked who to move in?" She let out a deep breath, and spoke again, her voice lower, less shrill. "Let's just drop it."

Arty squatted by the long box. How did their conversations escalate into arguments? Instead of wiping her brow, instead of cupping his hand over her warm belly, he grabbed her by the shoulders. He accused her of using money she rightfully owed him to cheat on him. Kneeling, leaning over the coffin, he towered above her. First wet with perspiration, her face now glistened with tears, and when he seized the hand she struck at him, it was sticky with mucus.

"Go away," she finally cried, "get away," as she turned from him and tucked the quilt around her.

Arty closed the lid. He sat on the slick black surface, which vibrated with her pounds. Ruth jumped up and began whining. When Susan called in a muffled voice that she couldn't breathe, he asked why she was in there in the first place. She answered, I just wanted to feel the feeling. In a way, Arty reasoned, he'd been buying time. He wanted to hurt her; she was safe in there, for the time being. Ruth's whimpering and Susan's pounding incensed him— he was only trying to stop her from provoking him further, only trying to protect her. In a minute, she ceased banging. If she was willing to drop it, so was he. As he stood, she pushed the lid open, rose up, and laying her hand on the casket's edge, gasped, "I'm leaving now." It was then, her body lit by the moon, one leg in and one lifted midair, pale limbs against the black pine, breasts dangling like blossoms of white foxglove, that Arty had rammed the lid down on the spine of her crouched body.

Arty pulled the planks toward him, through the radial, cutting them to length. White pine, since it was soft, and wouldn't warp, or split. "Wait till you see," he told Ruth. "Just you wait." Setting each cut board on the bench, he threw the leftover scraps into a pile for kindling. The edges were warm.

By 3 P.M., he had the parts glued and clamped. He turned on "General Hospital." It was Susan's favorite; he could tell her everything that happened, when she came home. He sat down in the easy chair in the kitchen, with a liverwurst sandwich and a beer. The ambulances raced around the corner and the sirens wailed. Ruth sat on the floor, thumping her tail whenever he looked at her. He threw her a piece of liverwurst.

All the women on the program looked alike. They all had big hair, long and bouncy, and everyone was all dressed up. He thought of Susan's straggly, dirty blonde hair, the way she leaned over in the summer to get it off her neck, then flipped her head back, "for the windblown look," she explained. He'd never seen a woman with hair light like hers, but such dark brown eyes.

Oh Rick, she sighed. Oh Monica, he panted. Arty bit his sandwich, took a gulp of beer. She had feelings for him; he wanted her. It looked like they were going to do it, but they kept kissing and breathing heavy. Their love blared on the TV. It was sort of funny, Arty thought, that Susan couldn't watch "General Hospital" because she was in one. "Asshole," he said, aiming the remote control toward the screen, touching the volume button, reducing their moans to whispers.

Pulling the black telephone into his lap, Arty dialled the hospital. He waited for them to connect him to Susan's room, observing the swarms of tiny midges—she always called them "no-see-ems"—that hovered outside. "Is this Susan Morgan? Mr. Wonder is on the line," Arty squeaked in falsetto, then began to sing, "I just called to say I love you." The bugs vibrated, flitting together, like a cloud. Rubbing his stubbly, unshaven face, he stared out the window, focusing on the insect schools. "No way," he said. "I couldn't have. No way—a broken rib?" Arty poked a finger into the beginnings of his beer belly; he tugged at the fuzzy black hairs on his legs. "Your mother? Your *mother's* picking you up? Call me," he said, "if you change your mind. Call me anytime."

The sirens cried; the show was over. "Shazam," he said. He pushed the off button.

Arty kicked open the screen door and walked out into the yard. A flock of the gnatlike insects surrounded him, darting into his eyes and ears. A second later, emerging from their swarm, he spit one from his mouth. Overhead, puffy, bulbous clouds blew through the sky. Pines encompassed his house, shielding the insects from the strong wind above, which flushed the clouds, turning them into a herd of stampeding animals. Arty dropped the crusts of his liverwurst sandwich into the grass. As soon as he walked away, a crow came swooping down, snatched one, and flapped off.

Arty could sense the faintest dimming of light. It was still hours until sunset, but the sun wasn't shining straight down, it had to make its way through the wood, between the pines. Twelve hours ago he'd bundled Susan into the pickup. It was just the opposite then, he could sense the impending dawn, the whirrs and chirps of activity. Now a lull hung over the yard. The air was still blue, but opaque, not brilliant.

"Ruth," Arty called. He tilted the Gravy Train bag; brown chunks tumbled into her bowl. "Not yet." He carried it to the sink, turned the tap. The water turned brown. He set the dish on the floor.

Arty listened to the lap-lap below him. Her tail beat against his leg. He began rummaging through the kitchen shelves. He peered behind the Bisquick, the Spaghetti-Os, and the grape jelly; he picked up the cornflakes and set them down. Then he spied the little tin, behind the sardines.

He pried off the lid. It used to have candy in it, but now an inch-long fish lay inside, the blue of its flattened eye still distinct. The gill, pressed and dried, was gray.

Last summer, he and Susan had taken a day trip down to the coast. In the channel, zillions of little fish glittered in the water. They poked into you as they slithered past. Arty shooed a whole school toward Susan. Some swam blindly into the sand bank, and lay there, silver and gasping, until they writhed back into deeper water. Susan was wearing a bikini, and when she ran shrieking from the channel, her breasts flopped up and down. He'd felt his erection pushing against his cutoffs.

When they got back to the house, drunk and sunburned, they plopped down on his bed. They kissed, touched; she tore off his shorts. Later, they found the fish, dead in the sheets.

Arty stuck the candy tin back on the shelf. Outside, the blue faded into blue-gray, and the trees merged into a single dark mass. He stared down at the dog. Ruth was wolfing down her food and wagging her short white tail. He bent over to scratch her ears. She bolted, slunk into a corner. "Hey," he said. "What's wrong with you?"

As he planed the sharp edges, the shavings curled and fell onto the floor like wet ringlets of cut hair. Arty went into the kitchen to get the time, but the stove clock had stopped. Turning the knob for the left front burner, he held his hand over the black coils. He felt his fingers warming just as the rings began to glow faintly orange. It was just the clock. "Piece of shit," he muttered. The Sears man had been there just a month ago.

By the darkness and the crickets, he judged it was around 9 P.M. "Ruthy," he called. "I've got something for you." They walked into the main room; her toenails clicked across the floor. Arty thought of the cosmos flower laced through Susan's pubic hair, its purple stain on the sheets, her black slip; he remembered her breasts swinging as she ran, the minnows fluttering on the banks and the one that had slipped into his pocket in the channel, then out into the bed.

On the way to the hospital he'd sung for her the theme songs to every TV show he could remember. "Here's the story," he sang, "of a lovely lady." He was pushing the Chevy faster than it could go, and the steering wheel trembled in his grip. They drove past farmhouses with tin roofs just beginning to shine in the dawn, past dewy pastures, and geese sleeping beside dirty man-made ponds. The gearshift rattled, he took one hand off the wheel and silenced it within his fist. The sun rose just as they neared Skowhegan.

"C'mere, Ruthy," Arty called again, squatting. "Go on." He pointed inside the doghouse. "It's for you." He shoved her gently through the door. She circled a few times, then plopped down, her head on the threshold. "You like?" Wandering over to the coffee table, Arty sat down, stretched out his legs, and lay full length on the lid. The dog followed him with her dark eyes. Arty tapped his chest; she rushed from her house, put her front paws on the edge of the casket, snuffling at his clothes, then cocking her head and gazing at him. Her eyes shone, her nose quivered. "Okay," he said. She leapt up, her paws sinking into his stomach before she settled down on his chest. Her name tag clanked faintly against her collar. The made-to-order, bone-shaped tag read, "Ruth. I belong to Susan Morgan. Please call 371-0952." He'd used her name, his number. "Don't worry." He felt her cold nose nuzzling his face. "She'll come back for you." Her tongue darted out, warm, as she began lapping his cheeks.

Best Friends

by Brenda Bankhead

They lived in Echo Park, the hills magnifying their loud music three times as it traveled up to the houses on top overlooking the city. But who cared? It was his birthday and they were there to party. Alfonso held Delia's hands as they danced to the hard beat, their palms sweaty in each other's fingers as she glided and he staggered around the floor. She was a heavy woman but light on her feet. He was so full of cocaine and pot and liquor he lurched each time he took a step. Delia laughed as she supported him. She did not see the dark young woman who watched them from the corner of the room. Did not see her clearly until after Delia had bloodied her nose and yanked Alfonso's dick hard in her hands, her fingers wanting to draw blood. The same fingers that were intertwined within his large rough hands now. Alfonso was a drummer, had his own band. They were starting to get gigs all over the city now, and not just weddings and receptions but in rock clubs that had a name. They were going places and Delia was delighted. She'd been with Alfonso when they'd both lived in that rat hole in Hollywood, stayed with him through his drinking days and his coking days, tried to change him and given up. But here they were, in this cute little Spanish stucco, still together, and that's what counted. They were a couple.

Delia suddenly felt Alfonso's full weight against her body. "Oooh, baby. I think you need to sit down." She lugged him over to a cream-colored couch in the corner. Alfonso groaned and leaned back. His olive skin had a green pallor and his thinning brown hair had come loose from his ponytail. Delia watched his face closely. She hoped he didn't throw up. This was a new couch, the first new couch she'd ever been able to buy, with the first credit card she'd ever owned, J. C. Penney, and she was proud of it. If Alfonso threw up on it,

218

it would be ruined and Delia couldn't afford a new one. She worked as a receptionist and money was tight. All of Alfonso's money went to coke. Or to buy new CDs. The stereo system was his. The speakers were almost as tall as Delia.

The song stopped and no one bothered to put on a new one. Delia looked around at her guests. Most were sprawled around her living room, next to bottles of beer, or drinks, or half-eaten pieces of birthday cake and cigarettes. It was 4:00 A.M. She was exhausted but she knew she wouldn't be able to fall asleep if she went to bed now. She had to unwind.

"You be all right?" Delia asked Alfonso. He didn't answer. "I'm going upstairs for a few minutes. Be right back."

Delia threaded her way through the prone bodies on the floor. She grabbed a cold bottle of beer from a sink full of ice in the kitchen and kept moving. When she reached her bathroom upstairs she grimaced in the mirror at her face. Her makeup seemed to be lifting off her skin in a layer of oil, her black eyeliner smudged way past the corners of her eyes. Strands of her straight black hair were plastered to the side of her face. Delia reached for the bar of soap on the basin and lathered her whole face, including her eyes. "Better," she said to the mirror when she looked at her clean face. "I didn't like all that shit on my face anyway." She patted the front of her bright pink blouse with a towel. She never could rinse without wetting the whole front of her. She had very large breasts. She envied women who had little ones, who could do without underwire bras that left friction scars all over their chests. Delia laughed to herself. Those sheer nighties at Victoria's Secret, with the thin little shoulder straps and no support, were obviously not made for women like her. Those places pretended that she didn't exist. But they could go to hell. Alfonso said he liked her big breasts. Although she had to admit she'd been pricing breast-reduction operations for years now.

Delia walked into her bedroom and sprawled her body out on her bed. She picked up the phone and punched in the number of her best friend.

"Linda? You up?"

"What the hell are you doing calling me at this hour of the morning?"

"Oh please. I know you. You sound good," Delia laughed, "you must be working."

"If I was working I'd come over there right now and shoot you for interrupting me."

Linda had painted since Delia knew her in high school. Her work was in a group show of multicultural artists that was touring the city. Delia was proud of her but she wasn't about to let her know *that* right now.

"So aren't you going to ask me how it went?" Delia said.

"No."

"Damn. You're cold."

"Delia, what do you want me to say? I'm sorry I missed the party? I'm not. I told you, I can't hang around that shit anymore. *Yo estoy harta.* I'm through."

"But I'm your best friend. You could've come for me. I haven't seen you in so long." Delia felt like she was whining and she hit the bed with her fist. She did not want to whine. "Besides you know I don't do drugs."

"Where's Alfonso?" Linda asked. "No, let me guess. He's out cold or throwing up or worse."

"No," Delia lied, "he's dancing."

"I always know when you're lying. He needs help. And so do you."

"Please. Spare me the preaching, OK? I just called to see how you were doing, not to get a lecture."

There was a long pause before Linda spoke again. "Why don't you call me tomorrow? I'm really tired right now."

"Should I make an appointment?"

"Look, Delia, I care about you, I really do, but do me a favor. Call me after you've dumped Alfonso, all right? Or after he's dumped you, if you're that lucky. Bye for now." Linda hung up.

"Bye," Delia whispered. She placed the receiver very gently back on the phone. Her stomach was tight. She was afraid to be as mad at Linda as she wanted to be. Linda knew that she couldn't leave Alfonso. She knew that. He needed her.

Delia uncapped the beer bottle and took a long noisy suck on it until her throat was stinging. Damn Linda. She knew how it was. Delia was dug in. She was in debt up to her ass. Moving to the new place had cost her every cent she had. And she'd fixed it up real nice, too. New furniture, new linens, lots of plants. She was tired of living in a dump. Ever since she was a kid she'd wanted a nice place. A nice, safe place where she could raise a family in peace and quiet. Her childhood had certainly never been like that. Thinking about family made her stomach knot up again. She took another long swig of beer. Alfonso had gotten her out of all that. He'd jumped on her father when the old man had started beating on her that final time, had held him down as she packed. She still felt satisfaction when she thought of the look on her father's face as he struggled to be free from a bigger, stronger opponent. He had finally gotten a taste of his own medicine.

Someone put another song on the stereo and the floor vibrated with the strong, slow pulse of its beat. Delia got off the bed and began to slow-dance with herself. "Grinding music" she and Linda had called it in high school. Close and tight in the arms of some boy they liked. That's where Delia had met Alfonso, at one of her high school dances almost two decades ago. The basement hall of the high school had been dark and stuffy. Delia had been one of the girls on the sidelines watching the bodies shifting slowly on the dance floor. She'd gone outside to the parking lot for air and that's where she'd seen him, leaning against the side of a brown Thunderbird, smoking a cigarette. The slouch of his thin body had seemed graceful and self-assured to her. His hair was long even then, slicked back from his angular face, falling straight down the back of his neck. He'd had a mustache, a thin one that sent long brown strands down each side of his mouth, and when he'd smiled at her the corners of his mouth had pushed the mustache into two peaks pointing at his cheeks. Delia thought it looked like a tiny bird flexing its wings. She stared so long at it that she embarrassed him.

"I got a feeling we're gonna be best friends," Alfonso laughed. And he asked her to dance.

When he held her he made her feel wanted. And that was something she'd never felt before. Not at home or at school. Nowhere. Alfonso made a place for her. He later said that he would have picked her out of the crowd. He could tell she needed him.

And now he needed her. They were a team. She kept him healthy. She made him take megadoses of vitamins. She made sure he ate well when she could. Although that was getting harder and harder. They were beginning to argue bitterly about his weight loss. He'd always been thin but now he was looking gaunt and Delia didn't like it one bit.

She ran the cold, damp glass of the beer bottle over her arms, cooling her skin. She enjoyed the goose bumps it gave her, enjoyed rubbing her hand over her arms until the bumps went away. Delia put the bottle down and caressed her breasts under her blouse until her nipples hardened. This was the closest she'd been to sex in months. Alfonso had been so busy with the band lately that they hadn't slept together for a long time. But that was the price of success, right? It ran you ragged for a while but eventually you caught up with it and then, well then, you had a good time. Delia suddenly wanted another beer. She looked at her watch. The music was still blaring and none of the neighbors had called the police like they usually did. She walked back into the bathroom, opened all the drawers and put back on her makeup. She wanted to look good for Alfonso. She found a piece of spearmint gum in a drawer and popped it into her mouth. She thought of his tongue playing against the hardness of her teeth as the gum filled her mouth with its sweetness. The painted wood of the bannister felt almost satiny to her fingers as she descended the stairs. And that's when she saw them. Alfonso and the dark young woman, half-naked in the corner, on her new J. C. Penney couch, humping each other.

"You shouldn't have done that." Alfonso's words were slightly slurred.
"What?"
"You shouldn't have done that."
"What?"
"You should have respected me more than that."
"What?"
"You shouldn't have pulled my dick like that."

Delia stared at Alfonso in disbelief. She stopped herself from saying what again. But it was the only word she could think of right now. She felt as if she had cotton stuffed in her ears.

Things had calmed down considerably. Delia faced Alfonso alone in the backyard. Their separate crowds of supporters had retired back into the house and left them to themselves. Delia stood in the center of the overgrown garden. Her eyes felt tight in her head from crying. Alfonso gripped the chain-link fence for support, his long fingers spread out on the cold steel. He turned his body slightly away from her. But even in this posture he pointed his finger at her accusingly.

"Respect," he said.

"Respect? You're talking to me about respect? You didn't even have the courtesy to take it upstairs!" Delia began to cry again.

Alfonso leaned more heavily against the fence. "I'm drunk."

"What?"

"I'm drunk."

"Are you saying you didn't do this? Are you saying your drinking did it? Like you weren't even there?"

"I'm drunk. I got horny. She was there."

"I don't blame her. I blame you. Yeah, I lost my temper, I apologize. At least I can admit when I make a mistake."

Alfonso folded his arms across his white T-shirt. It had the image of a leopard emblazoned across the front of it. It was a birthday gift from Delia.

"Sorry," he said.

"You're not sorry you did it. You're sorry I caught you."

"What more do you want me to say? I said I was sorry."

"You tell me how you would feel?"

"This is stupid."

"You think a woman doesn't have needs, too? You think I haven't had opportunities?"

Alfonso was quiet. He looked Delia in the eyes a little too long. Her face flushed a bright red.

"You know I never . . ."

"You're the one."

"I love your gall. I love your fucking gall." She was crying again. "You pushed. I went without . . . Admit it. I've been there for you. You just can't handle success. Is that it?"

"I don't wanna hear this. I'm telling you it doesn't mean what you think it means. She was there."

Delia's face got redder. She brushed tears away from her cheeks roughly with the flat of her hand.

"What I want to know is how you got it up? You being so high you can't even stand still now. How'd you get it up? You haven't touched me in months!"

Alfonso's face got red now. "She's not fat," he countered, staring at her eyes again. "You're an elephant."

"Oh, is that it?" Delia sneered, but she was as hurt as he wanted her to be. "I'm not woman enough for you because I'm fat? Is that the lie you're telling me? I was woman enough to give up that baby I wanted for you, for you!" Delia choked. "Linda told me not to do it . . ."

"Linda's fat, too."

"What did you say?"

"She's a sloppy pig."

Delia stood there, shaking with rage. "Linda's like a sister to me. If you call her that again, I'm gonna hit you."

Alfonso turned around and began to make his way unsteadily down the driveway on the side of the house. Delia didn't know if he was dismissing her or if he was afraid. She followed him.

"That's right. That's what you're good at. Run. Run. You're the pig. Wee, wee, wee! All the way home."

They both stopped on the short grass of the front lawn, facing each other in the gray light.

"I want you to stand there and look me in the eye and say it was worth it," Delia said. "I want to hear you say you don't want me anymore."

She wanted him to stay. She wanted him to say that he was sorry and mean it so that she could gather him in her arms like a little boy and hold him to her breast, so that she could try to believe him. But Alfonso didn't say anything. He just swayed back and forth in the chill air and looked around him as if he was surprised that it was morning. Delia found herself swaying back and forth in rhythm with him.

The woman Delia had hit came out of the house. She wore a short black dress that hugged her body. She was beautiful, a mix of Black and Latin. Her hair rode in long kinky waves to her ass. The side of her face was swollen and red from where Delia had smacked her. The woman walked on shoes that were backless and low-heeled to a black Mazda parked in front of the house. Her heels made quick, panicked clicks against the cement. She searched in a large handbag for her keys and once she found them she looked up at Alfonso.

"You coming?" she asked. She slid her keys into the slot.

The realization hit Delia like ice water being thrown in her face. This wasn't the first time they'd done it. This had been going on for some time. Delia's fingers twitched. She wished she'd hit the bitch harder. Alfonso staggered toward the car. Delia took two heavy steps toward him, wishing that she *was* an elephant so that she could take her huge leg and crush them in the car, wishing that she was a hippo so that she could swallow them in the huge maw of her mouth.

The young woman moved quickly into the car. "Lock your door," she told Alfonso. "Roll up your window."

Delia went to the driver's side. "You'll see," she said. "You'll see. What have you got to offer so he can use it all up? He'll use you up. He'll swallow you whole. You're his next meal, baby."

The woman stared wide-eyed at Delia through the car window.

"Yeah, you're cute. You're real cute," Delia continued, "but that's not the only reason he wants you. You got money? You got a job so you can take care of him? You got the abortion papers in your purse? Cause he won't give you nothing you want. He'll use you up. You'll see."

The two women's eyes met for a moment. Delia suddenly placed her palm flat against the window. "I didn't mean it. I didn't mean it. I'm empty without you. Empty. Please don't leave me."

The other woman's eyes flickered in confusion for a second. She thought Delia was still speaking to her. When she realized she wasn't she turned the key in the ignition.

Delia grabbed a handful of dirt from the garden and threw it after them as the car pulled away from the curb. She watched the cloud of dirt descend into the empty space the car left. She was too stunned even to cry, she just stood there staring at the ground. Eventually, she walked to the backyard and found herself in front of a fig tree whose fruit was ripe to the point of falling to the ants below. The heavy figs hung like purple scrotums on the tree. Delia began to pick one piece of fruit after the other, biting out the softest, plumpest middle of each then dropping the remains in the dirt, like bruised disemboweled carcasses. When she couldn't eat any more she wiped her sticky fingers on the front of her blouse and went back into the house. Everyone else was still crashed out on the floor, sleeping off their stupors. Delia went into the kitchen and sat down. She picked up the phone and dialed.

The Woman I'd Like to Eliminate

by Laura Chester

"**I** just don't wanna talk about it," I say to Jelena. "I'm not one of those love-too-much women. Not anymore."

We're raking up the chicken yard, and this one bird's got his head cocked around as if he'd just heard something. My boys are too busy to help me. They even sleep fast. While Jelena here is aiming to marry my ex-husband and needs some information. Me too.

Jelena's no flirt so it's hard for her to understand that Tyler and I were always soft on somebody. "But I never *did* anything, see?" I explain. "I just used it as a kind of inspiration." Love always put me in the mood for my music. "But with him now, he had to go through with it, and I had one hell of a nose."

Jelena is right furious with Ty. Her black wavy hair seems to kink up in coils, as if her thoughts were electrifying her. It certainly makes her work good, and I do like company when I've got a job.

"So how's all the plans for the wedding?" I ask. I figure she's got something brewing.

"There ain't gonna be no wedding. Tyler's in love."

"Oh no," I say. Poor Jelena. She must know it's his only defense. It couldn't mean a thing, not really.

"It's the girl who types his things up in Lexington."

I immediately picture someone pretty like my sister, with all that luxurious gold hair. "What does she look like?" I ask.

"She looks exactly like you," Jelena says. "About fifteen years ago."

She means, not unkindly, when I was twenty pounds lighter, tall, thin, straight long dark brown hair. Secretly, I'm a little pleased. But how can Jelena not hate me?

225

"He sits around with head in his hands, as if I'm s'posed to feel sorry. I just wanna *kill him!*"

I believe she is serious. But I don't want her doing that in front of my children.

Daniel's been telling me not to eat so much so fast, but the younger one's on my side—"She's just good with a fork!" I got my reasons to put food away.

But lately I've been wondering about this woman named Judith, and today is the day I mean to find out. Judith is this K mart clothes designer, who always had a crush on Ty. He thought if he was real outright I wouldn't suspect, but you don't go sharing a cigarette with somebody, placing it back in her mouth.

Well, he always pretended there was nothing there, that Judith simply gave him clothes, seconds on sweaters she had some peons knit up for her, big faggoty pants, way too stylish for him. He looked best in a pair of worn Levi's, a soft flannel shirt. I didn't like him looking too prissy. But he was her high school sweetheart—said "friend"—and supposedly they had never slept together so they hadn't got it out of their system.

So then I got sick. This was after both boys, but Ben was just a baby. I'd done nursing, and after the milk wore away I still felt this nodule—thought it was a gland. Can you imagine a woman moving in on your family while you're half alive recovering from mastectomy?

"That must be the lowest of the low," she says.

But does Jelena think he's not going to repeat himself? I don't believe that any man's faithful.

"Tyler says I'm being ridiculous, crazy—says he's a writer, just following his nose."

Following his dick more likely.

"Don't you think that by fifty he'd begin to grow up?"

I don't believe you can mature somebody.

"Now he says he don't believe in vows. He broke 'em once with you, so what's the point of it?"

I wonder why she wants to get married to him anyway. It's not like they're gonna have children.

"He says the one thing he likes about me, is how I always leave a toilet roll a paper on the back in case he runs out."

Well, shit, I think, that *is* considerate.

We're both well aware that if he loved her enough he'd want to claim her for his bride and stop acting like a capon. Men are so sensitive about the state of their balls the illusion of freedom seems to be all they can care about.

"Some men can't handle commitment," I tell her, knowing it's that kind who can handle extra helpings of chicken pot pie.

I don't want my ex-husband to move to Lexington, remarry some trash and start another family. Jelena has been good to me, good to my children, but there's always going to be another Judith.

I try to explain it by way of his books. Tyler writes western romance, about

226 · The Woman I'd Like to Eliminate

two a year, and he needs to be in love with his characters, so he has to fabricate up this feeling out of life. Maybe he even loves his book people more than he loves his own folks, or maybe it's just his way of loving parts of himself.

"I don't care!" She stomps her rake and the chickens puff and scatter. "What about *me?*" A question I never asked myself.

I still want more info on Judith. I knew she was a heroine in one sequence of novels, long yellow hair and an excess in jewelry. She got her hair cut off now, well, *haha*. Finally found some man who would marry her, but the baby pulled so hard on those long golden locks she had to buzz it right off, well, too bad. I hope her husband's out screwing the sewing machine girl. Let her sit there with her baby and its donut-grip bottle.

"Oh, yeah, they were carryin' on," Jelena tells me, "while you was still recovering in the hospital. She wanted him to leave you—he wasn't ready for that."

I feel a sting in the dead flesh of my scar. This is my first confirmation.

"You know that woman, she sat at my table," I tell Jelena. "She held hands with my children and sang grace before the meal, said how it was such a nice family ritual."

"Well, she'll fry in Hell," Jelena mutters, as if the chickens had ears. The dust from our rakes runs up along my arms but we're cooking now anyway.

"When I came home from Mount Mercy, she was there, you know, to help with the boys, and I had to seem grateful—I guess I even was, but she was wearing one of Tyler's shirts as a nightgown—I'll never forget that, this blue an' green flannel shirt. She kinda saw my shock and came up with this concept—how she was gonna design a flannel dress sometime with fringe along the bottom, you could cinch at the waist? Sort of western style. She also thought up midcalf jeans. Oh yeah, I said—the pedal-pusher look. Next she'd be getting a ducktail. Wearing red-bandanna petty pants or something. But she acted like her ideas would all be news to me, and me there with a scar burning stitches across my chest, and she didn't even bother to wear a bra, just let her tits hang like insults."

"And *I'm* s'posed to be *nice* to this person?" Jelena asks me.

"You can shoot her along next to Tyler if you want to." I consider this Judith to be a water moccasin, and I just can't *breathe* when there's a snake in the vicinity.

I once told Tyler I thought she looked real cheap, and he said that could be a turn-on. Well, that felt good, one half of me missing and hearing that my man liked sleaze. "And that woman was walkin' my little baby!"

At the time I couldn't lift my arm. All I wanted was to sleep and let the world slide by. I didn't care if they went off to the movies after the kids went to bed, but sometimes I felt left, like an infant.

"At least you know what you're getting," I say to Jelena, no eighteen-year-old bride, banged up beforehand.

I think with Tyler I just always accepted. After the girls grew up, we had these two boys, and whenever I was pregnant, I knew. I could smell it on him, as if the scent of her *stuck* till I named her perfume.

Now Jelena wants to know if the pattern will change.

"He'll come around," I say, meaning the wedding, as I drag the work basket over to the trash bin.

"But do I even *want* a man like that?"

I have no idea, but I suppose so. I want to say—It's none of my business. I don't envy most people their togetherness, always straining on each other. I feel all of a piece. Now my left arm can be used like the other one, and I've come to even like the angry feel of my scar, as if I'm half man and half woman, completed—I run this place like I am, anyhow.

My operation did ruin some things with Tyler. He was always what you'd call a "white meat man." I tried to get him focused on my rear end for instance, but he had this fixation and I couldn't switch that.

Jelena's well built, and I doubt this little typist could compete on that score. I just want to get even with Judith. Here's the thing—what got me thinking is that Judith's coming to town, bringing this big trunk of new designs. We small-town gals are supposed to be impressed, wowed by her line a junk jewelry. Well, Jelena and I are gonna try a couple of things on. Me and Jelena and a couple of our friends, we gonna squeeze our loving asses into some small-ass sizes and split 'em up the cheap-sewn seams! We laugh. And if she dares complain we gonna fucking wrap that stupid head a hers around the closest standing meter on Main.

"But listen now, honey," I say to Jelena. "You gotta figure if you really want him. If you do, you might as well settle on what you have, 'cause there ain't no changing nobody. And since I been alone, I ain't seen no man much different, so you can just stop examining phone bills."

"Well, I want much more than half a nothing," she says, as if she's all done working and wants a drink a real Coke. She is mad 'cause she can't plan her wedding, or pick out a dress.

"Hey, maybe you should get one a Judith's little numbers, tell her it's a gown to marry You-Know-Who. Tell her as if holding a gizzard knife, and maybe she'll consider a discount."

Maybe she'd like a chicken part crammed up her hind end, crawling down the runway with him in the audience. Maybe she'd like a wig to turn her rat's-nest head around so her face can go smother and we wouldn't have to look at her. Maybe she'd like a little barnyard style—right there in public, and he could participate.

Jelena and me, we be stomping in the front seat—*Sock-it-to-her, Sock-it-to-her, Sock-it-to-her, Sock-it-to-her,* then send this so-called woman home.

Differences

by Pamela Gray

i

When the white woman
fell in love
with a Black woman

some of her friends said
*isn't your life
hard enough?*

as if to say

whatever happens
is your own
damned fault

ii

the first thing she noticed
was how people
stared

The second thing she noticed
was the way her friends
hesitated
when she introduced them
to her new lover

The third thing she noticed
was how often
they were seated in the backs
of restaurants
and how often
they received
bad service

The fourth thing she noticed
was an increasing sense
of isolation

The fifth thing she noticed
and the sixth
and the seventh
and the eighth

was every racist thing
anyone anywhere said

and the ninth
and the tenth
and the eleventh . . .

iii

Her family tried to put the world
into neat little boxes for her:
this is the good neighborhood
this is the bad neighborhood

She drives out of the *good*
neighborhood into the *bad*
neighborhood to visit
her lover

She hears the click
of her parents' voices
lock your door
lock your door
and the click
of car door locks
locking shut

She drives into
her lover's neighborhood
with the car doors unlocked
and the windows
open

iv

She remembers racist thoughts
she's had, she remembers
racist words she's said
she remembers racist things
she's done

The memories are toxins
seeping through her pores
She wants to cleanse herself,
flush them out

I am not a racist
I am not a racist

She is afraid
that one night
she will say something racist
in her sleep

v

The white woman's parents told her
she was lucky
she didn't look
Jewish
and she had
a *shikse* nose

The Black woman's parents told her
she was lucky
she was light-skinned
and she had
good hair

vi

Her lover tells her
you're not white
you're Jewish

This is a distinction
the white woman does
and does not
understand

The next time they fight
her lover calls her
white girl

vii

The white woman says

it's not just a matter
of different words
or different meanings

it's that sometimes
we're speaking
two different languages

and we don't even know it

viii

A group of men in a car rushing by them
screams out the window: LEZZIES
seeing only two woman and a gesture
of tenderness, enough
to ascertain at 40 miles per hour
what name to call them, an unpleasant
but necessary reminder
of the one war
they fight together

ix

Sometimes when they were
dancing and watching each other's
eyes, it seemed that they had known
each other for years

Sometimes when they were
feasting on one of the meals
they cooked together,
it seemed that they had found
in each other a lost best friend,
a lost sister

Sometimes when they were
locked together, embracing,
it didn't seem possible
that they had been raised
to hate each other

Sometimes when they were
making love and only moonlight
lit the room, their skin
seemed to have the same color,
or rather, the same absence
of color

x

They sit next to each other
on the couch, watching a T.V.
documentary: white people
killing Black people.

A Black woman weeps, crouching
over the body of a young Black boy
lying in a river of blood.

White people
killing Black people.

The white woman feels the couch
split open
between them.

She wants to touch her lover's hand.
She doesn't.

xi

The Black woman says her hostility
is part of her heritage

she says it's not something
the white woman
can understand

no more white lovers
you're the last one

xii

The Black woman and the white woman
are walking down the street
holding hands.

The Black woman's arm
and the white woman's arm
form a V between them, the wings
of a bird taking flight, wings
like blades cutting the sky
into shreds, shreds like paper
falling on the heads
of all those who witness
this act.

The Black woman and the white woman
are walking down the street
holding hands.

xiii

In the kitchen, the Black woman
slices a challah.
The white woman is cooking
greens, the sweet smell of ham
rising from the pot.

She dreams the exchange
will always be this simple

She dreams
that their differences
will always be a source
of sustenance,
that they will always
feed each other

She dreams
of a long and beautiful
undisrupted feast.

As Needed

by Kathryn Chetkovich

I was sitting on a subway train out of Times Square, fanning myself with a chewed-up copy of *The Great Gatsby* and trying to remember if I had ever been this hot in my life and when that might have been. The subway kept slamming me in all directions and the effort to hold my balance made me so angry I was almost crying. I stared down at the red-and-white striped skirt my mother had made over for me that I had once liked. It was limp and wrinkled and it made me look fat. I wanted to go home and burn it but I could not afford to: I had only four work skirts.

It was 1980, my first year out of college, and I was doing temp work in a law office and writing for an obscure community weekly that no one I knew read. It was not the life I had always imagined. At school my friends and I had longed for the real world, that magical place where we would find meaningful work and in time, we each privately assumed, become famous. At parties we'd stand around the keg on someone's back porch, so hot from dancing that we'd be steaming in the night air like horses, pawing and stamping impatiently for our future to get there. We'd pass cigarettes and joints back and forth and tell each other what it was going to be like.

On the train I opened the book and read the scene where Gatsby is throwing his expensive shirts all over the room. *"They're such beautiful shirts," she sobbed, her voice muffled in the thick folds.* I had once thought this was a lovely, tragic passage; now it struck me as melodramatic and silly. Across from me a woman was engrossed in a book I wished I were reading instead, something with a title that swirled passionately across its cover. She wore nurse's shoes and nylons as thick as tights and she frowned at the print as she read.

The doors squealed open at Seventy-second Street and people pushed each other in and out. A tall man in a dark suit grabbed the bar over my head. I felt the whisper of his pants against my legs. He was trying to manage a newspaper, a briefcase, and a bunch of flowers wrapped in green waxed paper. I met his eyes and saw his lips move.

"What?"

"I said can you beat it? Can you beat this heat?" he said. I thought, all things considered, he looked remarkably cool.

"You could take your jacket off."

"What?"

"Your jacket." I pantomimed. He nodded and winked, something that had not happened to me since I was about five.

He handed me his briefcase and slid gracefully out of his jacket. The leather of the case felt smooth and important on my lap. I ran my fingers over it.

"I'm Carl." In his shirtsleeves, his hand held out towards me, he looked good enough to run for office.

"Emily," I said, shaking his hand. Firmly, I thought.

"Emily," he said. "My mother's name."

I smiled, although I hate that sort of sweet talk.

I looked back at my book, opened now on top of the briefcase. It gave us a peculiar sort of intimacy.

"Great book, right?" He shouted down towards me.

I nodded.

"Never read it," he said. "Saw the movie. Great car."

"You should," I said. "It's a classic."

He nodded. "You even sound like my mother." He winked again and smiled broadly. His whole face seemed to brag about his teeth, which were as white as his shirt, the whitest teeth I had ever seen in my life. I remember thinking absurdly, I will miss those teeth.

The subway threw us all forward at Ninety-sixth Street and knocked us back. We shook our heads and smiled at each other, united in this tiny misery, and he headed towards the door.

I watched him thread his way through the crowd, the briefcase still on my lap.

The elevator in my building was broken. I started climbing the stairs and felt a wall of heat hit me on the fourth-floor landing, where a little girl in underpants was riding a tricycle like a scooter down the hallway, standing on the back step and pushing off with one bare foot against the tiled floor. Plastic tassels fluttered from the handlebar grips.

On my floor my neighbor Ruth had her door propped open as far as the chain would allow. Her cocker spaniel, Charlie, had wedged himself against the opening and I could hear him breathing like an asthmatic in the shadows. Ruth gave him pills for his heart twice a day and fried up hamburger for him at night. In the evening they sat together on the front steps of the apartment building, Ruth cooling them both with a big fan that had cherry trees painted on it.

Kathryn Chetkovich · 237

Charlie whimpered slightly as I coaxed the key into the lock of my door. "It's okay," I said. "It's only me."

My apartment was small enough to memorize in a single glance, and after a year there was no longer anything romantic or courageous about living there. After a long shower, I turned the fan on high and sat on the bed with a beer, drinking for a while and staring at the briefcase.

When I finally nudged the latch, it flipped open with an expensive click, a sound that reminded me of TV movies about successful executives and their unhappy marriages. Inside were a stack of file folders, copies of *Forbes* and *Sports Illustrated*, several pens, a date book, a pack of Camel filters, some breath spray, and an amber-colored prescription bottle. Carl's last name, Wright, was typed on the label, along with the drug's name, which I didn't recognize, and the phrase "As needed."

I pulled a cigarette from the pack and got his number from Information. His voice answered after three rings, instructing me to leave my name and number at the tone, assuring me that he was sorry to have missed my call.

I followed his instructions, then closed the leather case and set it on my desk, where it looked sophisticated and foreign next to the spiral notebooks and battered paperbacks.

In the kitchen I opened the tiny refrigerator and crouched in front of the faint blast of cool air. The lettuce and vegetables looked so difficult in their plastic bags that I settled for a cheese sandwich and ate in front of the television with the plate on my lap. Outside twilight was falling with an eerie brightness that made me think of all the things that were going on in the city and how little I had done that whole long day. I had that confused feeling of wanting the phone to ring and yet not being able to think of anyone I really wanted to talk to.

I had another sandwich and another beer, and when it was finally dark I made myself turn on the light and go to my desk. It was professionally littered with all the information and quotes I needed for an article I was doing for the community paper on rent stabilization and renters' rights. I knew it was an article few people would read; it mostly repeated what had been said a thousand times before. Jerry, the editor, told me we would flag it on the front page and run it with a photo, but with a readership as small as ours I knew this would make little difference. That sort of remark pained him. "Go ahead, Emily. Curse the darkness," he would say, crossing his arms protectively over his chest.

Tonight I sat at the desk with the pack of forbidden Camels and bribed myself through two pages. My head was already light with nicotine when the phone rang around eleven.

"Hello, this is Emily," I said in a flat voice. "I'm sorry I'm not available right now but I *would* like to return your call. Please leave your name and number when you hear the little beep."

I listened to Carl leave his message. He sounded like a talk-radio host— chatty, friendly, vaguely midwestern, someone you could talk to about acid rain or violence in the schools. He sounded like someone who was faking sincerity and almost pulling it off. Almost.

I smoked my way through two more uninspired paragraphs and then turned the lamp off and sat in the dark watching Johnny Carson with the sound off. A pretty woman in a low-cut gown was singing, the sequins on her dress popping like flashbulbs in the lights. Watching her I thought of the hours I had spent in front of my bedroom mirror at home, holding a make-believe microphone in one hand and, to heighten the realism, periodically straightening out the make-believe cord with the other.

At the next set of commercials I called Carl.

"Here you are, a grown woman in New York City, and you don't know a briefcase from an attaché case?" was the first thing he said to me.

"I'm not the one who left whatever you want to call it on a total stranger's lap on the *subway*," I said.

"Hey, don't knock it. I've met a lot of attractive women this way." When I didn't say anything, he said, "I'm kidding, of course. I'm just joking." Another pause. "I'm from Nebraska."

So we talked for a while. He told me he had come to New York to make a fortune in investment banking.

"And is it working?" I said.

"Well, that's the amazing thing," he said, sounding amazed. "It is."

I told him the name of the paper I worked on, trying to make it sound like a paying job without actually lying. He had never heard of it. "But I get the picture," he said. "You're out to save the world from bastards like me."

"More from the system that *creates* bastards like you," I said.

"Thank you," he said. "That helps."

We agreed to meet for breakfast. He thanked me for calling, and then he said, "Good night, Emily."

The sound of my name reeled me in like a fish. He said it in just two syllables, as though he were already used to it, as though he had been saying it for years.

I put the briefcase—attaché case—on the kitchen counter next to the toaster before going to bed, so that the dark bulk of it would not keep me awake. I turned the fan off and noticed that it had grown surprisingly quiet in the street. A single siren, blocks away, rose and weakened to silence within a few seconds, leaving the night so quiet I thought I could hear Charlie whimpering in his sleep next door.

In bed, waiting for sleep, I saw Carl swaying for balance above me, one hand wrapped around the pole and the other clutching a funnel of green waxed paper. I found myself wondering where he had been tonight and who the flowers had been for. Whom.

I bumped through the revolving door with the attaché case and saw him sitting at a booth in the back, his suit jacket hanging on a hook behind him, his newspaper propped up against the sugar dispenser. He looked like an ad for himself, down to the pinpoint of light glinting off his collar bar. In the leftover early-morning heat, he was the only person in the diner who did not look damp and cranky.

I walked towards him behind a waitress who stopped at his table with a plate of food and a coffeepot. He said something I couldn't hear and she smiled.

"Emily," he announced when he saw me, bobbing up as much as the booth would allow.

"Don't get up," I said.

"You smell nice."

"It's soap," I lied.

"Something else here?" the waitress asked. I ordered coffee and she filled my cup and walked away.

"You ought to eat something. Breakfast is an incredibly important meal," Carl said. "Don't tell me you're dieting. Women are always dieting."

I was trying to lose five pounds but I would never have said so. "I'm not hungry. Thank you."

"You look fine. You look great." He waved his fork at me. "Women like you shouldn't be too thin. Here, eat this." He pushed a plate of buttered toast towards me. "Really. I can't eat all this."

"Cuff links?" I stared at his extended arm. I had never been out with a man who wore cuff links.

Carl reached across the table and patted my hand. "If you're good, I'll show you my tie tack later."

"Well, here it is." I patted the attaché case on the seat next to me. It was beginning to feel like mine, like an expensive leather lapdog.

"Great. Super. Thanks," he said. "Look, can't I buy you *something*? An English muffin at least?"

I shook my head. "I'm late for work as it is." I wanted him to know that my life was not unimportant.

He nodded sympathetically. "I guess even exposing injustice and championing the people can get to be a grind after a while." He grinned and I got another look at those fabulous teeth.

"I love my work," I said, forgetting for a moment my many dissatisfactions with the paper and the fact that the work I was late for was the full-time temp job that I hated. "At least I believe in something besides my salary."

I stared at the toast, gone soft in the middle where the butter had melted. I felt a flash of hunger. When I looked up, Carl was still smiling.

"I love earnest women," he said.

"That's interesting. Men like you turn my stomach."

At this he laughed out loud in surprise and I had to bite my cheeks to keep from smiling. We had nothing in common, but we had a strange bond of mistrust: I knew I could count on him to be exactly what I thought he was, and that comforted me.

When I got up to leave he said he would call me and I said, "Why?"

He pointed his finger at me. "I like you, Em. I really do."

I laid a hand on his shoulder and felt the smooth, tight weave of his shirt. "I'm sorry to hear that," I said, and I left.

After work I dropped the story on renters' rights off at the paper. Jerry seemed to like it. "Great. Great," he said, glancing at it. "You really move in for the kill." He looked up from a desk ringed with empty Styrofoam cups.

The story was nowhere near great but he loved the paper enough to wish that it was. I stuck around for a while out of respect for that, and because when you do not really believe, you must work that much harder to prove that you do.

I decided to walk home to try to get back a sense of where I was, passing through neighborhoods instead of underneath them. By the time I got to my building it was dark. Charlie began to whine when he sensed me on the other side of the door, and I could hear Ruth sweep across the room in her bedroom slippers. She was a big woman and her feet barely left the ground when she moved.

"How's the boy?" I asked.

Ruth shook her head and spoke softly, as though she didn't want him to hear. "Cholley's having a bad night. It's this heat. And that g.d. elevator's on the fritz again. We take turns carrying each other on the stairs." She prodded the dog lightly with the toe of her flowered slipper. "Isn't that right, old boy?"

"How about coming next door to watch TV later? The change of scene might do him good."

Ruth looked suspicious for a moment. She plugged her fists into the pockets of her housecoat. "Johnny Carson?"

I nodded. "Whatever."

She looked at Charlie. "We'll be over later," she said.

Ruth brought two Dr. Peppers over and the three of us settled on the bed, Charlie curled against his mistress. He had a reassuring dog smell about him. We watched Johnny Carson, and when Ruth giggled, Charlie's head bobbed in her lap.

That Saturday Ruth and I rode to the vet in a cab, Charlie breathing noisily between us. The vet was a sad-looking man with long sideburns. He lifted the dog onto the stainless-steel examining table and listened to him breathe. "It's time, Ruth," he said, and Ruth nodded and held the dog close.

"I wish I could explain it to him," she said, crying. "I wish I could make him understand."

Ruth held her dog and told him all the things she needed to hear herself say while the vet worked quietly beside her. A dog barked somewhere in the building and Charlie passed from what was left of life to death, Ruth's warm breath against his ear.

On our way home, she stared out the window of the cab. Her black T-shirt and black stretch pants were covered with the dog's blond fur.

"We should never have come," she said, her head still turned away. I could hardly hear her over the traffic sliding around us. "He would still be alive."

"Oh, Ruth," I said. "You did the right thing. He wasn't going to get better.

He was in pain and you helped him."

She turned to look at me. "How do you know?" she said. "It's fine for you to talk about right and wrong. You don't know. You have no idea." She snatched at the fur on her pants. Each time she shook her fingers free of a clump of it, it flew back to her clothes. "I *loved* that dog," she said finally, shutting me out.

I knew I had somehow said the wrong thing, and I felt angry and sad. We each held fast to our own door handles for balance, and between us, where the dog had rested on the ride over, there was now an invisible boundary line that I could not bring myself to cross.

Ruth didn't want company so I went home and sat at my desk rearranging the stacks of papers and notes, organizing the books according to height. The phone rang. It was Carl, asking me if I wanted to go to dinner.

"What's the matter? Did your real date stand you up?"

"Emily, has anyone ever told you what an unusual phone manner you have?"

We agreed to meet at a dressed-up diner in his neighborhood, a place where the booths were equipped with white tablecloths and jukeboxes. I got there early, hoping for the first ten minutes that he wouldn't come and then, for the next ten, fearing it.

He did come, looking like God's idea of civilized man. Just because we're fallen doesn't mean we can't dress well, I thought. He carried a fistful of daisies wrapped in green paper.

"You sounded on the phone like you needed these."

"You shouldn't have done that," I said. I did not feel strong enough to handle that sort of kindness from a man I didn't trust.

We drank wine and talked politics and religion; he called me naive and I called him reactionary.

"I can't believe I'm having dinner with a man who actually voted for Richard Nixon," I said.

"You're having dinner with a man who volunteered for duty in Vietnam."

I did not believe this.

"Want to see my scars?" he said.

"No," I said. "Jesus. No, I do not want to see your scars." I felt that he was somehow turning things to his advantage and it made me feel mean. "What are those pills for, the ones in your attaché case?"

"Those," he said, and when he stopped to take a breath I knew we were headed under the surface of something, "those are what I take when I feel like killing myself. Do you ever have days like that?"

I swallowed and waited to hear my own answer. "No," I said. "But sometimes I think I'm starting."

Neither of us said anything after that, and then he reached in his pocket and handed me a quarter. I picked some Patsy Cline and Nat King Cole, and, blessedly, our food arrived. Carl ate like a high school kid, swallowing his food in big, unconscious bites and wiping his mouth wholesale with a pink napkin from time to time. He didn't seem as much like the enemy, eating. I liked watching him.

We split the check and Carl guided me out of the restaurant with his hand at the small of my back. I had not felt the pressure of a hand there in a long time, and something in me went weak. Outside, it was cooler than it had been in days, and a breeze seemed to be blowing the dead air out. Carl put his arm around me. I leaned into him with a feeling of honest relief, as though I had been running a relay for miles and had finally tagged my partner. For that moment the outcome of the race was unimportant; I was happy simply not to be running.

We made a slow zigzag of the long and short Manhattan blocks and finally Carl stopped in front of an apartment building and said, "This is where I live." A young couple sat on the broad cement steps, smoking. The boy's voice carried in a gentle hum and the girl laughed softly.

Carl turned to face me. "I want you to come up," he said, "but I'm not going to talk you into it."

I wanted something else to pass between us before I went upstairs, some promise or confession, but he moved on ahead of me and stood quietly, holding the glass door open against his back, waiting.

"Come on, Emily," he said finally. He held out his hand.

I took it.

Upstairs he did not bother to show me the apartment or offer me something to drink. We walked through darkened rooms to the bedroom, where he sat me down on the edge of the bed.

We sat breathing for a bit with the awkwardness of it, and then I began to unbutton his shirt. It felt supple and exceptionally smooth in the dark, and in my fear and desire it seemed like the most beautiful material I had ever touched. Underneath, the skin of his chest was marked with ridges like the lines of a map, scars. I traced them with my fingers and tried not to think.

We made something akin to love and once he was asleep I edged myself beyond the reach of his long limbs and crept quietly out of bed. In the next room I turned on a lamp. The attaché case lay centered on the blotter of a huge wooden desk. In the corner were two photographs in heavy silver frames, one of a family gathered around a picnic table, the other of a smiling young woman sitting on a couch, her legs tucked up next to her.

I turned out the light and went back to bed, quieting myself to the sound of Carl's even breathing. I could not tell if the lack I felt was for something that had been lost, or taken from me, or given away. I lay there and thought about going home, and then I realized I had no idea where I was or how, exactly, I had gotten there. It would have to wait until morning. The ceiling disappeared into darkness and I stared up towards it and thought, Dear God, please don't let me die here in this bed, in this apartment.

Afternoons in the Blue Rain

by Lyn Lifshin

when I still wondered
if you'd call   now
those Junes, a cake
of soap made out of
flesh, a lampshade you
can see where a
nipple or tendon
was. I'll wait
in the dark for the
ice you left plunged
in me like a mugger's
knife to melt into
the Hudson River   first
I thought your heart was
in your penis   now I
can see it was in
the leg you saw
torn from you
on the other
side of the
road, Vietnam

Cottonwood Silk

by Carol Turner

I t was June in Nebraska and white clouds of soft cottonwood down flowed silently across the freeway. The countryside was flat and green and quiet.

At the wheel of the Jeep, Glenn looked relaxed and steady, and, for the moment, Audrey felt content. They followed directions in the AAA guide for Cottonwood Flats Campground.

"We should be almost there," Audrey said.

"Who the hell ever heard of going on vacation in Nebraska?" Glenn said.

"They don't have any dangerous mountain roads in Nebraska." Her thigh was a crisscross of scars from the accident and she thought back, trying to remember how long it had been. Her mind was a blank. She'd been having trouble remembering things, and wondered if she'd fractured her skull or something. The doctor had said her head was fine, but Glenn said most doctors were idiots and couldn't be trusted.

Glenn was covered with scars too, but most of them were from his army days. He had white marks across his abdomen, chest, lower back, and she no longer knew which ones were which. He had been a sergeant in the army's airborne rangers and saw action in Grenada, Honduras, Panama. He was discharged with a disability from jumping out of too many airplanes. He often told Audrey how much he liked the emptiness below him, the excitement of knowing he might soon be dead, the deference the pilots showed him before he jumped. Now, because of his back, he could only dream about the earth yawning below and the seductive blast of cold air. He had a drawer full of painkillers in their dresser at home.

"Let me drive," she said, suddenly nervous. "Your eyes look droopy. How many Percocets did you take?"

"One this morning," he lied.

"You're going to drive off the road," she said. "Just like before."

"I didn't drive off the road," he said. "You grabbed the wheel, remember?"

She and Glenn and Audrey's two young sons were lucky to be alive; Audrey remembered a moment as she flew through the air when she was sure no one would survive. They were up on Sugarloaf Road above Boulder, driving home from a big barbecue. A lot of Vietnam vets were there and everyone was drinking heavily and Stan and Jimmy were bored because there weren't any other kids. They had whined and whined until Glenn finally agreed to go. He was not happy about it.

"Want to know the weirdest thing I ever did?" Glenn had said. His voice was low and controlled, like it always sounded when he was really angry.

"No," she said.

In the back of the Jeep, Stan and Jimmy were quiet. Little Stan, only six, looked frightened and he sat close to Jimmy.

"I skinned a monkey." Glenn's eyes glittered. "Do you know what a monkey looks like skinned?"

"No, Glenn. Watch the road!"

"It looks exactly like a little baby." He made a choking sound.

"What's wrong?" she asked, leaning forward, trying to see his face. He opened his mouth as though catching his breath, then rubbed the heel of his palm against his eyes. "Those guys at that party. You just don't get it, do you? You don't understand what they went through in 'Nam. Do you know what they did over there? The nightmares they carry around in their heads?"

"I know, Glenn," she whispered awkwardly, watching the road for him. He was driving too fast. "Take it easy."

"You know I've killed people, don't you?" His voice sounded heavy, like something was stuck in his throat, and he slurred his words.

"Keep your voice down," she whispered. "I don't want them hearing this."

"Did you boys know that? Eh? You want to know who I killed?"

"I don't care!" Jimmy said from the back. He had just turned nine and his father back east had bought him a computer. He was bright and ambitious and he hated Glenn.

"In Grenada, I killed a Cuban kid. He was just a skinny little punk, and I blew his fucking head off. There wasn't any cleanup, so I had to go through his pockets. Have you ever seen what a mess half a head makes? He was so young, he didn't even have a picture of a girlfriend, just a mom and dad standing in front of a yellow house. You know what I mean? I kept thinking about it afterward, that he probably never even had a girl."

Audrey had been listening to this speech, her head swimming from too much wine. She knew Glenn. If she tried to stop him now, he would get louder and might start in again on the Salvadoran refugees. She knew her boys shouldn't hear those things, shouldn't have been at that barbecue or in the Jeep with Glenn driving the way he was. She was blowing it again, and she knew what her ex-husband would say when Jimmy told him.

"Glenn! Watch out!"

The Jeep skidded and spun off the road backwards and landed several hairpin curves down the mountain in someone's driveway. The boys were thrown another seventy feet down. When the paramedics arrived, they found the small battered bodies stacked against a ponderosa pine. All four of them were lifted off the mountain by helicopter and taken to the trauma unit at Denver General. When she woke up in the ICU, she screamed for her boys. Glenn lay moaning in the next bed. A nurse came and told her the boys were all right and their father was with them and could she please keep it down.

Later, she told the judge that she had grabbed the wheel and they went into a spin. Glenn was wiping his eyes, had taken his eyes off the road for a moment, and she had seen another hairpin curve up ahead and she was dizzy from the wine she'd had—nearly a whole bottle—and the last thing she remembered was reaching across . . .

The judge took Stan and Jimmy away from her and gave them to their father.

"Cottonwood Flats Campground!" Audrey pointed at a green sign along the highway.

They took the exit, followed a frontage road, then turned right through a high bank of fluttering cottonwoods.

"Go right again, just past the mailboxes," she read from the AAA guide. "Then turn left at White's Farm."

"I see it," he said. "Piece of cake, babe."

They entered a sudden cloud of cottonwood down and it swirled around the camper. She reached out the window trying to catch it.

"I can't see anything," he said.

She trembled suddenly, brought her arm back in, and hugged her chest. "Looks like heaven," she said softly.

He touched her knee. "What's wrong?"

She rubbed her eyes. "It's the cotton," she said. "I must be allergic."

"Like snow." Glenn sounded faint, dreamy. "Look how it covers everything."

Audrey blinked, moved closer to him. "My mother always called it cottonwood silk." She heard the murmur of her mother's voice somewhere and felt the sweat on her forehead and she was still shaking. She wondered, once again, if she should take just one of his Percocets. Maybe it would help relax her. This was her first vacation without the boys and everything seemed much too quiet, too final. She could hear people talking about her. *She ended up losing her sons.*

Glenn and Audrey weren't married. They had met in a bar three months after Glenn's discharge, six months after Audrey came to Denver to "clear the divorce lawyer's drone out of her head." They had slept together that night, and nearly every night since. The first year they were together, Audrey liked to tell their friends it was love at first sight, but after that, she forgot she'd ever been without him and the subject of their first meeting no longer came up. She considered it a great irony that she had ended up with a soldier, an army lifer until his discharge.

She had been married to an ACLU lawyer, with whom she had demonstrated against every war Glenn fought in. She lived a predictable, virtuous life and loved her two sons. Her husband had elaborate principles and spent long nights in the office. After ten years of marriage, he was a stranger to her.

"Living with you is like listening to the same boring song over and over and over," she told him one day. "Only the lyrics are in another language."

She packed her bags and her boys and left. Her husband, who had often joked at parties that the only personal problem he had was his wife, did not try to win her back.

She changed after she met Glenn. She became soft and sad. Sometimes, she felt like she'd got lost in his pain, that her whole being became dedicated to soothing him, making life a little more tolerable for him. Unlike her husband, who viewed everything intellectually, from a distance, on paper, Glenn had experienced the ugliness and horror of man's world firsthand. Glenn was real.

The cloud of cottonwood down vanished and Glenn turned slowly down a narrow lane, moving past a mailbox marked "White."

"Old Farmer White," he grinned. "We'll be camping in his cow pasture."

"You look stoned," Audrey said irritably.

"I've been driving all day," Glenn said. He didn't say his back was hurting, but she knew. She knew a lot about his back. Sometimes when they made love, or walked together down to the local movie house on Colfax, or simply when she rolled over at 3 A.M. because her arm was asleep, he would wince, or groan, or catch his breath. He usually said nothing about it, but when the pain got really bad, he broke into a sweat and became sullen and ate Percocets like candy. Sometimes he ate them secretly, sometimes in a brash mood, defiant. Long ago, the pills had stopped killing the pain in his back; now he used them to kill the pain in his head. Whenever he ran out, she drove him to the VA hospital where an army doctor again told him his back was hopeless and renewed his prescription.

She had often congratulated herself that she did not take any of his pills.

Last night he had woken up screaming again, didn't recognize Audrey, seemed to think he was in a ditch somewhere. He flailed around in the bed, pushing something off his chest. She knew what it was because he once told her a fellow soldier's leg had been blown off in a field in Grenada and landed on Glenn's chest.

She rolled up her window and rubbed her thumbs against her palms. They were clammy. As soon as they parked, she would set up one of their new green lawn chairs next to the river and sit back with a cold glass of Chablis from the cooler. She hadn't had a drink for six months, not since she lost her boys, but this was her vacation and she needed to relax. The view out the window was too bright, too vivid, and she felt tired suddenly, wished she could just drift off somewhere. She leaned her head against Glenn's shoulder, slipped her arm through his. He didn't seem to notice, and her love for him felt like a burning underneath her skin.

She had given up her boys for him. That's how she saw it anyway, though the judge had taken them away without asking whether she'd leave Glenn. Glenn had stuck with her during the hearing and sometimes she thought he'd been more upset about the verdict than she. That night, he went into a rage. Empty beer cans were lined up on the kitchen counter. "Dead soldiers," he called them. His Percocet bottle lay on its side on the dresser and several of the little yellow-and-blue capsules had rolled off and dropped onto the rug. His back hurt and he stormed about the house like a crazy man, bent over his hated cane and swearing that he would kill that fucking judge. She sat numbly on the couch with a bottle of wine and stayed out of his way. When she finished the bottle, she opened another.

"Come here!" he said then, shaking the cane. "I want to show you something."

Slowly, sleepily, holding the wine, she approached. She wondered, for a moment, where Stan and Jimmy were and worried that they would see him like this. Then she remembered.

He showed her something round and black, the size of an apple, shoving it under her nose.

"Let's do it together," he said.

"What is it?" she asked, but she knew it was a grenade.

"I want to die."

"Put it away for god's sake!"

He let her take it, then laughed. "You're afraid!"

When they moved in together, Glenn had put the grenade on the bookshelf along with his other army things. She had always assumed it was harmless.

"You're an asshole." She put the grenade in a kitchen drawer, then returned to the couch and curled her legs underneath and drank more wine.

The next day she told Glenn she was giving up the booze and would leave him if he didn't do it as well. He gave it up but, because of his back, he couldn't give up the Percocets.

"There's the gate," said Glenn suddenly, and she lifted her head.

Twilight dropped over them gently, and when they drove into the campground, the place had a soft, eerie glow.

"This is weird," Glenn said.

"Look at all the cottonwood silk," Audrey breathed. "It's beautiful."

"I can't see anything."

Through the dim flurry of cotton, she saw the flash of stream. "I want to be next to the water."

Glenn winced. "I'm never going to get to sleep tonight," he said.

They parked and set up the chairs. She took the bottle of cheap wine out of the cooler and set it on the ground near her left foot. Her hand felt sticky after handling the wet bottle and she knew she shouldn't open it. When Glenn saw she had bought wine, he had gone out and bought a case of beer. They had not discussed it.

She held onto his hand, knowing he would start eating Percocets and drink the whole case of beer. Then he would lose himself in another rage. She didn't know if she cared or not.

It was dark now, and the night was filled with ghostly white cottonwood down. It floated over the river, covering the black water. Several tufts landed in her lap and she stared at them. She never wanted to go back home; she wanted to sleep forever.

She knew she had lost herself, but until recently she firmly anticipated getting her life back together. At some point, she realized it was not likely to happen as long as she stayed with Glenn. She never told him, but she had thought theirs would be only a brief affair; she was drunk when she met him, and the truth was she could not remember anything about the love at first sight of that night. A friend warned her that Glenn was bad news, he had "Vietnam envy," and Audrey was too good for him. Audrey had not seen that friend in many months. Glenn loved her the way she needed—he did not care about anything but her, and he made no demands except that she stay. Glenn needed her, and on those nights when he awoke with visions of the leg, or the Cuban boy's mutilated head, or the decomposing bodies of Salvadoran children he had found somewhere in the Honduran jungle, she held him and gave him soothing words until he fell asleep again.

They had not kissed in a long time, Audrey realized. She got up and knelt at his side, but, watching his green eyes, she found it too painful to kiss him. Instead, their lips moved close, touched softly. Audrey turned her face so her cheek rested against the rough stubble of his chin and they clung to each other. Before they separated, Glenn held her face in both hands, stared hard into her eyes.

"We're not going to make it," Audrey said. "Are we?"

Arms

by Jo Dereske

K ate had hooks. Her real arms were torn off in a farm accident back in Michigan when she was nine years old. I've always had an unhealthy curiosity about what they did with her arms, but I'll probably never ask.

Now that times are more modern, Kate could have had a pair of those snappy, electronic, bionic, computerized, flesh-toned silicone-and-poly-something arms. Somebody good saw her pushing Devin's baby carriage once and pretty soon one of the churches wanted to hold a fund-raiser for new arms, make Kate their cause. She graciously declined.

"I don't know, Trish," Kate told me, picking her teeth with the end of her left silver hook. "Why mess with it? I can do whatever I want with the ones I have."

She could, too. She could pin, actually *safety-pin* Devin's diapers on him, as slick as you or me. She drove; she cleaned; she cooked. I once watched her test a pot of green beans by fishing one out of boiling water with her hook. I knew it didn't hurt or anything, but still . . .

You learn things when you have a friend with hooks: that round doorknobs are barriers; that public restrooms pose potential traps; that infants, even tiny ones, can learn to clutch their mother's clothing for dear life; that the majority of people you meet are very nice, perhaps occasionally misguided but they really do mean to be nice.

Kate and I have been friends for four years but a few weeks ago I said to her, "Keep your fingers crossed for me." See, even I forget.

It was January and we were all living cheek to jowl with the countdown to Desert Storm. Bernie and Kate, Stan and I. We sipped Christmas Cointreau

251

and watched Tom Brokaw explain it all.

"Nobody wants another Vietnam," Stan said in his way that tempts you to argue even when you agree with him.

"I don't agree," Bernie said, lightly touching Kate's hair—he was always touching her, watching out: exchanging her glasses for cups, guiding her sweater sleeves so they didn't get caught. "We need a little something to take our minds off the S & L debacle and the economy."

Stan grunted. "How in hell did Saddam get the arms for a war anyway? You can bet that somehow we're at the bottom of it ourselves. Shoot ourselves in the foot."

War hovered, dusting life with inconsequentialities. I went to the studio every morning, rehearsal every afternoon. Our troupe had just won a state grant and we danced with renewed fervor, with purpose, keeping war at bay, not letting it weight our leaps or tip our heads as if we were cautiously listening. Madame even smiled now and then as she ordered us through our paces.

Arms were vital to me, their placement and flow, the beauty of balance and expression. There's a moment when the legs and line of the body mesh with head and arms, as if the whole were more than the sum and the body could take voice, take wing, the perfectly poised arms enabling flight. I turned down a part in *The Rite of Spring* because I felt the arm movements—all the movements for that matter—were ugly, that Stravinsky was playing us for fools. My reluctance was boring, immature, to the others. "C'mon, Trish," I was told wearily. "We need you in this performance. Listen to him a few more times and you'll hear the melody." No, thank you. Record a car accident and listen to it enough times and you'll hear a melody, too, but it'll never be beautiful. Kate attended my performances, sitting between Stan and Bernie. I liked to think I heard her applause like silver chimes as she brought her hooks together.

The taste for war was so palpable it drew down saliva. And so we satisfied it.

After Bernie tucked in Devin and rubbed the back of Kate's neck, he and Stan went together to Jordy's Pub to watch the war in a community of men. Kate and I fixed lattes and had them with a plate of shortbread in her living room. In the sky, live over Israel, Patriots collided with SCUDs, lighting up the city, right there in front of us on Kate's TV.

"Trish," Kate said in a voice that brought my eyes to hers, "I'm thinking of leaving Bernie."

"Why?" I asked, shocked. Leave Bernie?

"I don't think I love him anymore."

Bernie had drilled holes in all their doors and rigged up latches above the doorknobs so she could open them easier. Every time I saw one I felt a little choked up. Such obvious signs of tenderness. So *personal*. He'd made wood-and-wire holders for the pots and changed every round knob in the house for her: TV, stereo, stove.

"What about Devin?" I asked, trying to absorb her announcement. Leave Bernie?

Just then Devin was asleep in his room, sucking his thumb, probably. Kate didn't try to break him of it. "At least he has thumbs," she said. "Let them get acquainted."

"There'll be a nasty fight, I suppose." She shrugged and her hooks raised off her lap a few inches. That was how she moved them, with her back and shoulder muscles. Kate had overdeveloped shoulders, thickening her back like a nascent dowager's hump. She wore her glossy hair long, as if it might camouflage the dense mass of muscle.

SCUD fragments fell to earth onto Israeli homes. We watched rescuers picking their way through the rubble, carrying a litter. "Ohhh," Kate breathed. Blood blotted the white sheet near the victim's upper arms.

I met Kate after reading her ad in the campus paper: "Typing: accurate, reliable, fast. Call Kate."

No kidding. And that's just what she said to me when I brought Stan's smudged, cut-and-pasted thesis notes to her door, back when Stan still had hope, before the illusion of a literary career met the reality.

"No kidding."

I guess I was standing there openmouthed after she said yes, she was Kate. Yes, that's right: Kate the typist.

"I hold a pencil in each one," she explained, holding up her twin silver hooks, pointy ends toward herself. "Eraser end down, of course."

"Not exactly flying fingers," I said. I don't think too clearly when I'm put on the spot and sometimes words just appear and I'll be damned if I can figure out from whence they came.

Kate guffawed and sprayed me with fine saliva. After that we were friends.

"Do you think she takes her hooks off when they do it?" Stan asked me after the first time he met Kate and Bernie.

"That's rude," I told him and didn't answer, but I'd wondered that very thing myself. Who knew what people did when they were alone. Anybody who's slept with more than one person knows nice manners don't count; people surprise you. Hooks in bed didn't sound very sexy, but then to me, leather and handcuffs didn't, either.

Stan must have thought about it, too, because a couple of nights later we were getting all hot and he asked me to take my arms from around his neck and hold them close to my sides, "like you don't have any," he said.

"I can fold my legs up, too," I said sweetly, "and lie here all still like I'm dead."

He got the message.

"I'll bet there's another man," Stan said, pointing a half-slice of French bread at me. The other half was in his mouth.

"She'd have told me."

"Sure?"

"Of course. Bernie's too good to her for her to want anybody else." Scooter meowed beside my legs and I slipped him a piece of chicken. He gulped it and sat on my feet in gratitude.

"Yeah, he treats her like the Queen of Sheba but I'll bet ten bucks there's another man."

Stan always had ideas about other people's lives. "I should've been a novelist," he liked to say, lightly but the regret was truly there, if you knew how to hear it. The only artistic props left were a typewriter with dust in all the little key hollows, and an occasional roaring whiskey drunk which dissolved into maudlin regrets for his wasted life. He was thirty-one years old, for chrissake. Jesus hadn't even settled his career at thirty-one.

Stan and I got together with Bernie and Kate every few weeks. Kate and I were more the friends than Bernie and Stan. But I've always been surprised by how interchangeable men seem to be in the company of one another. Stan and Bernie amiably discussed stocks and sports, and of course the war, those things, pulling in their conversations from an invisible stream. But always Bernie had half an eye and ear out for Kate, whether she might need him.

"'. . . collateral damage caused by incontinent ordnances,'" Stan read to me from the paper. His voice was soft in wonder, lapping at the words.

"What does that mean?" I asked.

He shook the paper and it snapped. "It means that a bomb went off target and killed a bunch of Iraqi citizens."

I shivered at the innocent words, their *deception*.

"I told him," Kate said over the phone. I pictured her, headset tucked between ear and shoulder, hair draping.

"Yeah?" I said. I was pissed—how could she?—and didn't want to give her an inch, let her wiggle through her own opening.

"He took it hard."

"So what'd you expect, he'd say 'fine,' and give you a supply of door latches for your next apartment?"

Bernie rang our doorbell after dinner the next night. It was raining and his hair was slicked to his forehead like Marlon Brando playing Napoleon. Before I opened the door I was happy because I liked it when it rained; it gave me excuses. Bernie was long-boned, slender—"artsy looking," Stan said. I lowered my eyes from his because they were red and wet, not from the rain.

He beelined for Stan. "I have to talk to somebody, Stan. I don't know what to do."

He was shaking; desperation sat on his shoulders. Even Scooter sensed tragedy. He jumped off the arm of the chair and padded to our bedroom, tail twitching a warning: keep that stuff away from me.

Stan gave me a meaningful look and I left the room, too. Light on my feet, almost dancing my sorrow. Right into the kitchen behind the door. I didn't miss a word.

"Kate's seeing another man," Bernie said. His voice was so painful I closed my eyes against it. "She's leaving me."

"Sweet Jesus," Stan said. "Who'd have thought she'd do that?"

Did I detect wonder, an undertow of jealousy? I peeked through the door crack. No, Stan's face was furrowed, simple in seemingly genuine concern. Bernie hunched beside him, staring down at his two long hands lying lax against his thighs. A tear fell, darkening the fabric of his sleeve in a perfect circle, and he covered his face, leaning his elbows on his bony knees.

Stan self-consciously squeezed Bernie's shoulder, twice.

"I don't know why," Bernie sobbed. "I just don't know why."

It's since become clear to me that men rarely do, they don't see it coming, not like women. For men it's a quick one two and crash to the mat, flat out of nowhere.

I was so intent on the tediousness of my *port de bras* I hadn't seen Kate come in. She leaned against the studio wall, her coat buttoned to her throat and her hooks deep in her pockets. We hadn't talked since Bernie's visit and I wasn't sorry for her drawn face and circled eyes.

"Gotta go," I told Madame, grabbing my towel off the bar. She shook her fist at me like a peasant.

"I'm sorry to interrupt," Kate said, "I have to talk to you."

"That's just what Bernie said. You guys oughta talk to each other. Spare your friends."

"Trish, please."

She followed me while I changed into street clothes, accompanied by the rhythmic echo of slippered feet behind us.

"Don't you ever feel like leaving Stan?" she asked, almost shyly.

"Constantly, but I don't do it."

If Kate had had fingers she would have tapped them lightly against the wall, focusing her thoughts. Instead, she placed one hook inside the other in front of her, chaining them. "Bernie's a good man," she said.

I snorted. "You're being trite."

"No, really. I know he is. He's kind and gentle. He's given me Devin. I've been fortunate."

"All he's done for you," I said. My frustration was getting the best of me. "The door handles . . ." I stopped, seeing a barb of contempt flick from Kate's eyes.

"Is that what it comes down to?" she asked. "Door handles? I'm being an ingrate?"

"You know that's not what I meant," I said, hitting her lightly with the damp towel from around my neck.

Out on the sidewalk, she tried again. "I need more of a balance, do you know what I mean?"

"Not really," I admitted.

Kate sighed. "I can't explain, I just know there has to be more balance. I'm suffocating."

"But Bernie . . ." I said.

"I know, I know." She turned to me, touching my wrist. Coolness. "I don't want to lose you, too."

"You don't have to lose anyone." But I wasn't being unkind any longer.

The ground war replaced the air war and I cried at the broken men surrendering in the war-littered desert. It was over before I grew accustomed to "friendly fire" and "tank missiles," before I could grasp just what it was we'd won.

"We hardly got to use any of the good weapons," Stan said regretfully.

"It wasn't a real war like Two was," I heard an aging man claim, shaking his head so the medals on his VFW cap gleamed.

"I saw the guy," Stan told me.

"What guy?"

"Kate's. They were in Johnny's drinking coffee."

"What's he look like?"

"Big, beefy. Not what I expected."

"What about Bernie?" I asked. "Have you seen him?"

Stan shook his head. "I heard he gave it up and left, moved to Renton."

I met him a month later. His name was Joe and they were living together. Devin was with Bernie, "just until summer," Kate said, deflecting any questions, "only until my life is settled. We're still working out the terms."

She'd invited me to stop for coffee on my way to rehearsal and I was a few minutes early.

"Joe's just leaving," she told me. I'd caught them in a farewell clinch at the door. Like Stan said: big, beefy. Bending over Kate, brown eyes.

For a second I thought Kate wasn't wearing her hooks but it was the way he had his arms around her, covering them. When she stepped away, the afternoon sun glinted on silver and I saw that she was complete.

War of Hearts

by Gloria Frym

T he salesclerk announced that there was a war of hearts. I looked at her
with the puzzled expression a person gets when they don't understand
the reference.

"They'll put each other out of business, fast as XYZ," she chuckled.

Is that right, I nodded.

Still, I must have knit my brows together. I'm always doing that, not that
I know I am, but my husband tells me I do it all the time.

The clerk pointed to a locked glass cabinet across the room. I took my time
meandering over to it, busy admiring the chartreuse-and-black salt and pepper
shakers on the counter.

The clerk explained that the hearts were all marked down.

"One jeweler's studio was robbed, you know, then the other's got bombed
in the middle of the night." She stretched her eyes wide open and her eyebrows
shot up. "Seems awfully accidental on purpose, if you know what I mean."

I had, in fact, bought a silver heart some time ago in this very shop, one
that said Forget Me Not. I had no one in mind when I bought it, and perhaps
everyone I knew. Christmas came and the heart seemed corny. I would have
to find the right person.

Mind you, my taste in certain objets d'art has provoked family feuds. In
fact, a favorite cousin refused to talk to me for years because he thought my
wedding present mocked him and his new wife. How was I to know? I searched
through five stores in Manhattan for the perfect music box and finally found
one I'd love to have kept. When you wound it up, the bride moved close to the
groom who then put his arms around her, and embracing, they waltzed to the
tune of "The Anniversary Song," waltzing and waltzing around in a circle until

the music ran out.

My husband who was only my boyfriend at the time helped me pick it out. I don't know why I say "only," he certainly had full status in my life as a boyfriend. I don't think I ever called him "boyfriend." In fact, I think we behaved as though we were married along about our third or fourth date. Anyway, he didn't exactly help me pick it out. He accompanied me, would be more accurate, and completely approved of my choice, I really should say. He's like that. He won't say anything is bad unless it's really terrible.

I wasn't in the mood for hearts today, war or no. I was looking for a bedside stand for my husband, believe it or not. Something skinny and oak. But there seemed to be more hearts and bracelets and dressers in this shop than I remembered. Glass cases full of collectibles. Little deco knickknack boxes, a set of ruby red blown-glass tumblers, sterling combs, jeweled thimbles, brooches shaped like plumed birds. There were 1940s hats on the wall and an abundance of imitation Persian rugs on the floor.

My husband and I had been fighting a lot recently. We never fought before we got married.

It started when the president decided to go to war in the Middle East. I had no idea external events could cause so much tension in a house. We were both much too old to actually be worried about going off to war. But we worried about the war. We talked about it constantly. We were addicted to the news, which was like a sickening liqueur that made us nauseated every night and every morning, but we still kept on drinking. In between we fought.

We didn't fight about the war itself. We were two people with very compatible values. That wasn't the issue. It was as if the war hyperbolized the proportions of who we were, what we each separately felt to be our selves.

For several weeks, our personalities became exaggerated versions of their usual selves. Whatever bothered us about the other person bothered us to distraction so we each couldn't help saying it. After a while, our bodies and our thoughts moved farther and farther away from one another. Then my husband coincidentally went out and bought a king-sized bed. We didn't really need a new bed. But now in the middle of a very rocky time, a giant monument to sleep was delivered to our door one Saturday morning.

That's why I'm looking for a different bedstand, as you probably figured out. The new bed took up the whole bedroom. The only way you could be in the room was to be on the bed. Once you were on the bed, things were very comfortable. But oh the bed was big. In the middle of the first few nights, I woke up several times and glanced over at my husband. He was hugging his side of the bed just like he used to do with the old small bed. The new bed was so big that the center went completely unused, a big gulf between two bodies. Another couple could fit there, the kind of couple that likes to sleep very close to one another.

The worse the war got, the more sarcastic we got with one another.

"Why do you always leave the heat turned up when you leave the house?"

he inquired rhetorically. "Because I'm subsidizing PG&E, why do you think?" I sneered. Or, "There are pieces of black fuzz on the carpet and I just vacuumed," I announced. "Well, if you hadn't picked carpet that showed lint, you'd never notice it."

History in the making had nothing over the senselessness of our recent conversations.

I don't know what came over me. I could no longer do what I'd been doing anymore.

"Listen," I announced one morning to my husband. "I'm tired of cooking, cleaning, shopping, buying gifts, arranging, coordinating, and everything to do with the house. Find someone else to work here."

Not that I make him breakfast, mind you. We get our own. Not that I even make him lunch—he's at work and so am I. Not that he doesn't do things around the house. He does.

I just didn't want to do my share anymore. I didn't want to cook, clean, shop and think about dishes. I wanted something else.

My husband likes dinner. He doesn't mind fixing it but he likes to have it with me. He likes the ceremony. He likes the ritual of doing it the same way almost every night. Or he likes me to be the one to invite people over. He likes a hot meal and he likes to sit in the same chair every night.

I was sick of dinner.

I couldn't tell him nicely. Each time we had a fight, it was over some small, stupid thing, but the real thing was I didn't want to do anything the same anymore.

The war brought that out in me.

This change in attitude always seems like all of a sudden to the other person, but of course it was brewing for a long time.

The next day I didn't do a thing regarding the house. My husband thought I was very angry with him and he didn't speak with me for fear of making me angrier.

Days passed and I didn't do a stitch of housework.

By the end of the week, he started doing everything I'd been doing. He started doing all the things I never thought he even knew I did, like fold the towels so they actually fit on the shelf properly.

But really that wasn't the issue.

"I'm going out," I told my husband before dinner one night during the war. "I probably won't be back before midnight."

You're probably thinking that I went out with another man, that that was the way I was changing my life, and that's why I had gotten sick of the way things were with my husband. But you're wrong. It wasn't that I wanted him to do more housework, or that I thought another man might be better.

I don't know why I took my old violin out of the living room closet where it's rested in its case like a corpse for years. I used to practice every day. I used to play an okay violin. I wasn't an artist, but a worker musician, you know, good in an ensemble, accurate, a decent ear.

The blue velvet lining the inside of the case was plush and soft, protected. I ran the bow across the strings. I could have stuffed everything back behind the sleeping bags. But I didn't.

Lessons. I needed lessons. Someone to teach me what I once knew.

That's where I was going that night.

Then I would go to the university and rent a practice room. My husband, after all, had an office where he conducted business.

My husband never asked where I was, as it was his habit not to ask. He thinks it's none of his business. I've always hated this habit. If I tell, he's glad to listen, even participate. He's a very respectful person, if a little remote.

"Do you want to know where I've been tonight?" I asked him when I got home. You'd think he might wonder why my jaw was a bit red.

He was flicking channels with the remote. Something I hate. Particularly during a war. Each channel had a slightly different version of the same news, watered down to about ten sentences. The only thing that was different was the voice delivering it. And even that wasn't too different. The hairdos of the female news readers varied, though, from channel to channel.

My husband didn't respond. We were speaking again, but we were estranged, as they say.

A month passed and we were still at war. After several lessons, I decided I was playing well enough to join a local orchestra.

I came home one night and told my husband I'd be out a few evenings a week playing music. That I wouldn't be around for dinner those nights.

"Okay," he said impassively. Ordinarily I'd have started a fight with him over his reticence to ask me anything about my comings and goings. But I held myself back, remembering that I'd never change if I acted the same.

The television was showing the charred corpses of children being dragged out of a bomb shelter my country had bombed that morning.

My husband was eating vanilla fudge ice cream right out of the container. In all fairness, it wasn't his fault that the news was even worse than usual.

The orchestra was just a local group of people who loved music and played for civic occasions. It wasn't a symphony or anything, and I made first-chair second violin very quickly. By this time the war had ended. I remember the day. It was the day before my birthday. The headlines read: It's Over. Which only proves that It was so familiar to everyone, so much on everyone's minds, that the papers could take the liberty of using an indefinite pronoun to refer to something that was very definite.

One night my husband and I had just separately come home from work. He was dragging his old cello up the basement stairs when we met in the kitchen. He set the cello down beside me. I looked up from the violin string I'd broken the night before, fretting over how long it would take to replace.

"I'm taking up the cello again," my husband announced. I smiled and said, "Good."

My husband had arranged to play cello, it seemed, on the same nights I was at orchestra practice. Several months passed, conditions in the Middle East were very unstable, and the region could explode again from the literal and psychological combustibles left by the war. Two hundred thousand people perished. The newspapers reported that the region was an ecological disaster. Oil fires were burning and might keep on burning for years. The sky was dark, day and night, and children would be born into a world with intense heat but no visible sun.

Journalists got lyrical about the war, now that it was over. "A dusk-like gloom confuses the birds into singing their twilight songs," one reporter was moved to write. I can't blame him, I guess, for finding poetry in collateral damage.

I was very happy my husband took out his cello, as he used to be a good musician, probably better than I was when we first met. It's what we used to talk about, music. I liked the mournful, deep moodiness of the cello. We were no virtuosos, as I said. We didn't have ambition but we had desire.

We began to speak again of music.

My husband waited until he'd practiced a respectable amount and eventually invited me to join a chamber orchestra with him. I was flattered, but I could see right through his offer. My husband likes to think of himself as someone who is flexible, someone who will bend and change, though really his motivation here was competitive. I knew this, what don't you know about a person after so many years of sleeping in such a small bed together. But in some ways, I didn't care anymore about his motivations. I only wanted change!

I wanted change in myself and I wanted change in him and I didn't want to join the chamber orchestra with him. I liked my own orchestra a lot.

The day before I went on housework strike, my country made two thousand air strikes against another country. Missiles and bombs were dropping on the average of one a second. Not that my country's violent actions had much to do with my disgust for housework, but frankly, such news really put housework on another planet.

We could not go on just the way we were going on. I mean, we *could* go on the way we did, contracting towards death, with the television on for background music, with the remote control endlessly changing the channels which were exactly the same. I was afraid. I was afraid that if I didn't take my life into my own hands, that it might take me farther into a daze. My life might do something terrible to someone else. Or it might just mount up like dishes when you don't push up your sleeves and wash them. Every day. You have to wash them, you know, to keep them at bay, to keep yourself from coming home one day and throwing them all out the window.

Which isn't such a bad idea, sometimes.

Our Lady Has Another Argument

by Nita Penfold

She fumbles with her words like an arthritic woman
trying to close her wool coat—
large circles of buttons never slip easily
through the narrow woven holes,
again and again she fights her swollen fingers
but the thin hard knob misses the slit
and she is left with the cold on her chest.

Things they remember are always
the last ones said, the worst act done;
that point when patience will not withstand anger
and both corks are popped, explosions bursting out
at each other like soda bottles shaken
and then released, the rush of hate held
too long back then surging forward
to drown whatever love is left.

Conflicting Testimony

by Alice K. Boatwright

Elizabeth could never sleep in the country. She lay in bed beside Alan, eyes open, listening to the gentle creaking of the Fullers' house. The sound was peaceful, like the creaking of an old dog's bones as he lay down on the hearth, but it kept her awake. She was used to New York where the silence was punctuated with rapid footsteps in the street, shrieking sirens, backfiring engines. She missed knowing that if sleep eluded her she could slip out into the amberlit world of Second Avenue, cross the broad black street to the lurid fluorescent safety of the 7-11, and eat Snickers, hunched in her leather jacket at the magazine rack by the window, undisturbed by the restless junkies and homeless drifters who wandered in and out under Carlos' sloe-eyed supervision. Here in the country she felt as if every living thing were asleep in its burrow except her.

Beside her in the sagging brass bed, Alan was asleep, wheezing softly, unaware of her wakefulness. Even at home he didn't acknowledge her furtive comings and goings, except perhaps by a low grunt, an arm thrown possessively across her tense streetcold body. He didn't know about the 7-11 and she didn't want him to know.

This secret faithlessness filled her with guilt, stirred her closer to him, until their bodies touched. Alan turned onto his side and nestled his back against her, as if he had forgotten the coldness between them.

"Who is she? Who is that girl?" Elizabeth wanted to know.

The phone had rung just as they were about to leave for the weekend and she answered it.

"Hello, is Alan there?" a young woman asked. Elizabeth recognized the voice. It was one of Alan's students—but not one of the anxious ones, full of excuses. This one phoned often, sounding sure of her right to be calling Alan at home. There was something intimate about the way she spoke his name. Alan. Is Alan there. When Elizabeth held out the receiver to him, Alan's face flushed.

"I'll take it in the bedroom," he said, and Elizabeth's knees went numb even before she could say: "Why?" He left her standing with the phone in her hand, listening for his hello, the girl's soft answering hello. She dropped the receiver into its cradle, not wanting to hear more. She paced the living room, feeling the dirt around her plants with her fingertips, hot in her down coat, waiting, listening to the light happy cadence of Alan's voice through the door.

She didn't need to hear any more.

"Who is that?" she demanded when he came back into the room. He ignored the question, impatiently picking up his jacket.

"Are you ready, Elizabeth?" he asked. As if she had been holding them up.

On the drive up the Taconic from the city to Red Hook, they didn't speak, except to say, "Have you got a quarter?" "Did you shut off the coffee?" Elizabeth stared out the window at the darkening frozen countryside, her palms sweating with resentment.

If he would only just say who she was, tell her some story, Elizabeth would believe him. She would try to believe him. But when he said it was only a student calling about an assignment she knew that wasn't true. She had been accumulating evidence and even though it was still disjointed like clues in a scavenger hunt, she was sure that Alan was leaving her.

His defection had begun that fall with a new enthusiasm for his job. If he drank too much wine at dinner, he became eloquent about the pleasure of teaching young artists. He went to class earlier, held more office hours, spent more time on preparation. He bought new shirts: a black one covered with zippers and a blue iridescent one. Elizabeth made a joke about his change of style and was sharply, surprisingly, rebuked.

The radio incident had occurred in late October. Elizabeth remembered because it had been a warm Indian-summer day, and she had walked home from her office without a coat. She'd flicked on the radio in the kitchen, expecting it to be set, as usual, on WNYC and was assaulted instead by the grating sound of heavy metal.

That didn't seem important until he began bringing home the CDs. He would shut himself in his studio after dinner, to work, he said, and then on came the music. Elizabeth, in the living room trying to proofread galleys, would ask him to please use earphones. Sometimes he would, but often he refused.

One night she threw open his door, ready to tell him she was calling the police, and caught him dancing on a table. He stopped, jumped down, and turned off the music. "You shouldn't come in here," he said, ushering her firmly back out of the room. Elizabeth was so shocked she went to bed and lay in the dark staring at the pattern of light cast on the wall by the streetlight.

Later, he said he was sorry and wanted to make love. He talked about the new piece he was planning, and, turning on the bedside lamp, sketched it for her on a scrap of paper. Elizabeth listened numbly, leaning on her elbow, and wondered why this routine failed to charm her as it had in the past. Why she found herself, for the fourth night in a row, heading out the door at 4 A.M.

That same week he began taking his own clothes to the Laundromat and buying his own yogurt. Elizabeth was glad about the laundry, but the yogurt was puzzling.

"What's that yogurt?" she asked him when she noticed four containers of vanilla honey yogurt in the refrigerator. They had been eating plain yogurt for ten years.

"It's yogurt," he said without looking up from the paper.

"No kidding. Do you want me to start buying that kind?"

"No," he said. "Don't worry about it."

As soon as he was gone, Elizabeth stared at the alien yogurt and, without warning, burst into tears.

It had been Elizabeth's idea to visit Sam and Judy Fuller, as if being with old college friends might bring Alan back to himself. To her. She was lonely living with the stranger he had become.

That evening, as the four of them sat around the big pine table in Sam and Judy's kitchen, the wine and candlelight almost erased the distances between them. Judy made spaghetti with clam sauce, the staple food of their SoHo days, and Sam demonstrated the mechanical toys he'd been making for the neighborhood children. They gossiped about other old friends, told stories, and drank until late in the night.

Alan went out of his way to appear charming and witty, without ever making eye contact with Elizabeth. She wanted to reach him to say: Isn't this nice? Haven't we shared a lot? Aren't we lucky to have such good friends? Aren't we wonderful people? Still.

But it was a waste of time. In spite of her smile, she was sure that all he saw in her face was: Why don't you love me? And: Who is she, Alan?

Oh Alan, Elizabeth said silently, don't do this. Please. We have a whole life. How can you think of throwing it away? How can you imagine your life without me?

She touched his shoulder, then slowly ran her fingers down his back and over his bony hip to his soft sleeping penis.

It lay in her hand, twitching like a diviner's stick. Elizabeth swam beneath the blankets. Spoke to it, her lips direct on its tender flesh.

Tell me. What are your secrets.

His penis nodded, jerked, and lengthened in her mouth, but yielded nothing to her gentle persuasion.

She turned and resurfaced. The house creaked, moaned.

Restlessly her hands roamed Alan's body. It was comforting to touch him and she wished he would wake up, pleased that she had been touching him while he slept. But she knew it was not really love, or even desire, that made her want to arouse him. It was her fear that she wanted him to drive out. She wanted to force affection from him, if that was the only way she could get it.

This, she told herself, was the result of being taken over before you'd had a chance to form yourself.

It was only recently that Elizabeth had begun to describe her relationship with Alan in these terms. Before it had always been destiny. Karma. Her lucky stars.

She had been a freshman at NYU, straight from rural Ohio, when they met. He was in his last year of grad school, already teaching and exhibiting his sculpture. Elizabeth had signed up for his three-dimensional design class because she was interested in photography. She wanted to learn about shape and mass, she said. He told her freshmen were not qualified for the course, and then, when he saw her work, let her in.

After their first conference, Alan asked her out for coffee and began to pursue her with notes, loaned books, little drawings. He listened to what she said in a way no one ever had before. He liked her work; she liked his.

Their romance, set against the backdrop of Manhattan, eclipsed any thought Elizabeth had had of getting an education. On the first night they made love, Alan said they were mates for life. He had known it the first time she walked into his office. Elizabeth was eighteen and she believed him.

By the end of the semester, they were sharing a place. It was that simple. That quick. She had gone from being a shy, dark-haired girl with vague, uncertain ambitions to being Alan Porterfield's mate.

"Your other half," was the way her mother referred to Alan, once they actually got married. Elizabeth thought the expression was disgusting, until one night when she was attending one of Alan's openings. Observing people's anxious attention to him and the blank way that they looked at her, Elizabeth had the sensation that somewhere along the line she had become negative space. Alan was the object; she was merely the space around it. Important aesthetically, but totally defined and created by the object. To be an "other half" suddenly seemed like a long step up.

Of course she had immediately rebelled against this vision of herself. She was not the hole in the doughnut. Although she had given up photography, she had finished a degree in Renaissance history. She'd gone to graduate school, published her thesis, and become history editor at a respected house. She had friends, interests, a life that Alan played only a part in.

So why did she fear sleep, as if morning wouldn't come if she didn't keep watch?

She hugged her knees to her breasts and studied the familiar landscape of

Alan's skin. She knew every mole and crease, every scar, every hair, as well as her own.

You are mine, Alan, she whispered. A part of me. We are inseparable.

But the back curving away from her said: no.

The knees drawn up, the tense buttocks said: no.

The ears that did not hear, the heart that beat without her knowledge, the lungs that emptied and filled regardless of her wishes, said: no.

Who is she, Alan?

Which one of those arrogant girls in your class lusts after my life?

Elizabeth had studied young men. She watched them swagger around the art school, portfolios under their arms, eyes bristling, soft stubble on their cheeks. Their flesh was smooth, like something bred scientifically. Nectarines. What did they know? Nothing. Elizabeth felt only relief, remembering her own adolescence, that she no longer had to deal with them.

She wanted a man tempered with age and use. She wanted her own man. Worn and familiar. She wanted to feel the daily aging of his flesh with her hands. She wanted him to have and to hold all through their lives.

They had agreed on this. Or so she thought.

She touched Alan's shoulder again tentatively. The back was so impersonal. If he were facing her, she could put her cheek into the hollow of his collarbone and know that in response, his arm would automatically curl around her. But this expanse of flesh, as blank as his face had become, offered no resting place.

Alan, do you mean it? Is this it?

Don't be asleep. You can't afford to miss this message.

Stop fucking teenagers!

I won't let you leave me. I swear I won't.

I swear on the bones of my grandmothers. I won't allow it.

Why then, Elizabeth wondered, did she find herself reading "For Rent" ads? Why did she sit in the living room mentally arranging the furniture the way she would have it in her own place? Why did she enjoy imagining scenes from Alan's funeral every time he was late? As Elizabeth tossed and turned from one question to the next, a grey dawn light gradually filled the room and night was over.

Elizabeth threw off her covers with a sense of being released from prison. As she stood up, the cold bare floor sent a shock from her feet to her head. She hopped gingerly across to the window and looked out.

It had been snowing during the night. A gentle snow that blurred the lines of the barns and studios below, capped the fence posts, and blanketed the fields. The mountains had vanished into the sky as if they had been painted out.

Instead of dark and empty, the countryside looked soft and welcoming. Elizabeth had the urge to run out and dive into the snow. To make a heavenly host of snow angels all over the yard that would shout to the world, "I, Elizabeth, am here!" Still.

"What are you doing?"

The voice sliced through the silence. Elizabeth turned to see Alan watching her, his face framed by the jumble of pillows, blankets pulled tight to his chin.

"It's snowing," she said. "I'm looking at the snow. Did you have a good sleep?"

"How could I with you molesting me all night?"

Elizabeth blushed, her head tilted to one side. "You might have enjoyed it."

Alan snorted. "You're nuts. Last night you weren't even speaking to me."

"I was trying to reach you on another level." Elizabeth watched his eyes for a response. They flickered soft/hard/undecided.

"A lower level, as I recall," he said and then he laughed.

Her relief was so great that she laughed too.

He was still hers. She was going to win.

"Why don't you come back to bed," he said, patting the empty space in the bed.

Elizabeth moved toward him swiftly as Alan held up an arc of blankets to enfold her. She was eager to be warm, to have him hold her in his arms, touch her face, her hair. Kiss her. Admit it. He loved her. Nothing could ever change that.

But he only pressed against her, his fingers insistently kneading the soft folds of flesh between her thighs, as if it were clay that needed to be prepared before he could work it. Her lips brushed his cheeks, seeking reassurance, but his eyes were closed and the contact she thought she'd made with him was broken.

Elizabeth tried to concentrate on the sensations of her body. When his penis pushed into her, she felt a sharp release, the connection of belly to belly, and it felt good. Always did, feel good. The joining of their bodies. But it was not what she needed. A respite from isolation.

Alan pushed up on his hands and slanted over her, like a man doing push-ups, to watch his penis sliding in and out of her. Elizabeth watched too, as if it were happening to someone else.

The bed rattled against the wall, reminding her of days when the neighbors banged on the wall for them to quiet down. They didn't care then how much noise they made—they were lovers and they wanted their whole building to know it.

Alan dropped back down on her, his chest glazed with sweat, and came silently. Elizabeth felt his penis go limp, knew it was over, while she was still struggling to find some quiet place in her head that would allow her body to take over.

Who is she, Alan? Is she good?

Alan kissed her mouth. Like a handshake, she thought. A punctuation mark. A series of exclamation points, followed by a period. But what was the message?

He rolled off her, leaving her sweaty, wet between the thighs.

"That's what you wanted, isn't it?" he said.

Even if it had been a genuine question, Elizabeth could not have answered it. She glanced at him and then averted her eyes. Allowed herself to admit for just one moment that maybe it was what she wanted: to feel the hopelessness, to experience his indifference and be humiliated, to know clearly that no matter what she had once thought her relationship to this man was, it was no longer anything that she wanted.

It was over. She had to get out.

Alan had curled up again, this time facing her. He liked to sleep after having sex. It was one of the things she would always know about him.

Elizabeth looked at his face—the way his eyelashes curled against his cheeks, the shape of his nose, the colors in his mustache—and felt the hollow rush of years to come without him.

The pain that formed in her chest was so sharp she had to get up, move around. She stripped off her damp nightgown, rummaged in her bag for her jeans, a thick sweater, warm socks.

When she was dressed, she felt better. She went back to the window and saw that the snow was still falling.

It was not too late. Her whole life was opening up. Free and full of new possibilities.

There was no reason at all for her to believe that she was dying.

If Memory Serves
You Well
1952

by Susan Policoff

Threw he last person I expected to see on my front stoop, apart from my husband Lowell, was Helen Arber. Her bruises had faded to yellow-green, but a white cast encased one arm.

"May I come in, Abigail?"

Her voice is that soft, you have to lean close to hear. She's a bit of a thing, wispy hair, twittering fingers. She has a firm grip on her boy, though. My daughter Kate plays with Jason. Kate's a whirligig, shouting, running, but Jason's solemn. Well, who wouldn't be.

I could hardly say, Why, Helen, I thought surely your long-suffering husband had locked you up again, so I stepped back, and she drifted inside.

She touched each button on her blouse. Doc Arber's rich by the pitiful standards in this corner of Kansas, yet his wife wore a limp skirt, and the collar of her yellowed white blouse had frayed. "I'd love some coffee," she said, wandering toward my kitchen on run-down heels. A cardigan unraveling at the sleeves completed a pathetic picture, unless you'd heard Lucy Tearn, the Reverend's wife, whispering of the sight she'd had of Helen's closet, overflowing with crinolines, cashmere sweater sets, and pastel shirtwaists.

Last year, Helen sent Jason to the opening day of kindergarten in a dress. Lucy Tearn and I had a time explaining that to her Kyle and my Kate. I called Doc to ask if anyone had tried to talk to Jason about it, and he said he'd take care of it. Not many men in his position in Glory pay any heed to small children. He must've eased the boy's mind, too, because according to Kate,

Jason acted like nothing had happened.

"Earl Monty called Jason Mama's Girl at recess and everyone waited to see if Jason would cry, but he didn't," Kate had said, proud as if she'd been the one to face down a tormenter.

"Helen shouldn't have done it," I'd told Lucy, despite Kate's report, not long after that first day of school.

We'd started the conversation over the back fence and had ended up in Lucy's kitchen.

Lucy cited the little girl Helen had miscarried a year earlier, how, afterwards, she'd wilted like a parched flower.

"Two hurts don't cancel each other out," I said.

Lucy clanged a spoon on the side of a pot, the very image of a teacher calling an unruly class to order. "Where's your heart, Abby? She needs our pity."

"We can offer it without excusing her," I said. "That child of hers . . . Unnatural, a six-year-old who doesn't laugh."

"Helen doesn't laugh, either," Lucy had said.

After the episode of Jason and the dress, Doc whisked Helen off to a private clinic in Wichita. She stayed two months. She's been subdued, since. The past ten days, folks have bandied it around that due to her recent encounter with Roy Higgins, she'd be headed back to the clinic.

I stood inside my own kitchen doorway, and studied her. Ignore the bruises and the cast, and she appeared normal, for her, at least.

"Did the fire do much damage, Abigail?" she asked, sounding normal, too.

"Not to the house. Charred the roof, is all. Did make ashes of my marriage," I said, in a tone Lowell had always hated—making fun of what's not funny, he called it—to prove how quickly I'd gotten used to his absence.

"I came to offer my condolences." Helen sat, resting the cast on the table, curling her other hand in her lap, a good child who has recited her piece and hopes her audience is pleased.

"He deserted me, Helen. No need to sound like he died and I'm weeping over his grave."

The hand in Helen's lap uncurled and plucked at a wrinkle in her skirt. "I just meant I was sorry, Abigail."

I reminded myself that this was Helen, not Lucy, and softened my voice. "Thank you, kindly."

She inclined her head graciously. Mutual politeness having smothered the conversation, she examined her cast, and I peeked into the open utility closet at Lowell's black sweater, abandoned on a hook. I had promised myself every morning since the fire that I'd deposit it in the trash.

When I couldn't stand the silence or looking at Lowell's sweater another second, I whirled around the room, collecting paper napkins, tarnished spoons, scattering them on the old table I'd painted yellow. Kate and I eat at it, since I use the dining room and its half-bath for a studio. I'm the official school-district photographer, and in demand for portraits.

Lucy Tearn chides me for my "unwomanly preoccupations," a phrase I just know she got from her husband, Reverend Josiah Tearn, but she tells anybody else who speaks out against me, "Abby's a fine mother."

Her husband has no such divided loyalties. "You've no right to be wrapped up in your frippery concerns. A woman has a duty," he said to me, a few weeks ago. "Only reason your picture-taking doesn't constitute the grave sin of deserting your home is, you work from your house."

After he delivered this speech, in my very own hall, I dashed out to search for a separate studio to rent. I didn't do it, though. I enjoy working at home. I didn't intend to allow the Reverend to destroy my pleasure in it.

The Reverend had showed even less forbearance toward the Stevenson button on my coat. "You want a firmer rein on your wife," he'd lectured Lowell. Lowell didn't care a fig for the Reverend, one of Lowell's finer traits.

Ike's not awful—a little mushy for my tastes—it's Mamie I can't abide, so wifey-wifey. Lucy's the wifey sort, too. Their men have stuck by them, not run off like Lowell, but I could never be the type. Till Lowell left, I never wanted to be.

Hard to say what kind of wife Helen was. Doc was another husband who'd stuck to his marriage close as a wet shirt clings to your skin on a hot day. It couldn't have been easy.

And now she sat in my kitchen, had scarcely moved, didn't so much as blink when I clunked the kettle on the burner. I meant to ask about her garden, Jason, maybe mention the farmer's almanac's prediction of early snow and a bad year for tornados, anything but more talk of husbands.

A second later, my mouth started flapping on its own. "Lowell had a man coming to talk business the afternoon of the fire. He wanted the man to provide funds for Lowell to build a baseball stadium. They'd lure a minor league team to Glory, and be heroes."

Helen contemplated the yellow sheaves of wheat on my wallpaper. "Gordon was a hero in the war. He showed Jason his medals."

"Lowell envied you and Doc, for having a son."

"I envy you your daughter," Helen said.

"I was game for another child, we were trying." If we'd hit the jackpot, would Lowell have stayed? Still, I'm glad Kate was Kate.

"If only Jason had been a girl. Gordon plans to teach him to hunt doves. He knows I love the doves. He talked to Jason about killing them. I locked my bedroom that night."

The kettle screeched. I bustled around, preparing coffee.

Helen twiddled her napkin. "I dreamed Gordon flew away. The doves pecked him, and he flew away. I woke up, and it's your husband, flown."

I couldn't prevent a flinch. "It was on account of the fire," I said. "Right before Lowell's associate was due, the postman delivered a wooden crate from Grandma. Sister said her house wasn't big enough for all Grandma's possessions."

I paused for breath, to let Helen say anything she had to say, and because I'd thought better of putting in that Grandma was sending me stuff as much to rile Lowell as to clear out her bedroom at Sister's house.

"A crate?" Helen asked, more like someone had poked her and whispered, Your cue, than like she cared.

"She sent me a slew of photos of suffragette parades she was in, clippings of speeches she gave. . . ." The clippings were preserved under glass, cushioned in the crate by pine shavings and crumpled newspapers.

I brought out my mismatched china cups. Lucy Tearn wrinkled her nose at them. My grandma raised me and Sister, and she had important matters to attend to, no time for collecting pretty china to pass on, the way Lucy's mama did.

The cups didn't interest Helen, either, but not because of weightier matters. When I set one full of coffee down in front of her, she added sugar. I counted six spoonfuls.

I felt rude staring, so I started talking, faster than before. "Lowell refused to help tote the crate upstairs. Said his business prospect'd be arriving any minute, and he didn't care to get all sweaty. Since it kept sitting there, and I was eager to find out what Grandma had sent me, I pried up the lid. A few shavings spilled out. Nowhere near the amount Lowell claimed. He maintained if I were a proper wife, I'd clean them up."

Helen licked grains of sugar off her spoon. "Gordon said locking my bedroom door against him was a breach of my proper wifely duties. Reverend Tearn agreed."

"Rev. Tearn's a busybody," I said. "Lowell got steamed. Said he doubted anybody'd put up money for a man living in a pigsty. He was bellowing, tearing fistfuls of pine shavings and newspapers out of the crate, strewing them around. Place was a sight when he finally wound down. He scooped up what he'd pulled out of the crate, plus a heap of old *Saturday Evening Posts*, and stuffed the lot in the fireplace. I warned him the fire'd blaze up too hot, too high. Should've saved my breath to blow it out."

Helen stirred her coffee. She hadn't taken even a sip. She caught my eye, and clucked her tongue.

"Sure enough," I said, "the flames shot out the chimney and set fire to the roof shingles. I called the fire department. Lowell grabbed the phone. Said he had an important business appointment, it was a small fire, could they please not use the sirens. The Tearns feared the wind would spread the flames to their roof, and called, too. The trucks zoomed up, sirens blasting. You'd have sworn it was an enemy attack. Lowell's caller arrived on the firemen's heels. Lowell refused to see him. 'Nobody does business with a fool,' he said. 'I'm a cooked goose in Glory, thwarted at every turn.' That night, he up and left."

". . . envy you," Helen murmured.

She must not have heard me, was still fixed on mourning her lack of a daughter.

I'd told my story, had a right to expect Helen to tell hers, but she didn't catch my eye this time, just kept looking at her cup.

Like everyone else, I'd heard the gossip. She'd flirted with Roy Higgins, he'd misinterpreted, it had ended as an assault. I flat out did not believe it till Roy vanished, and even then, the whole thing bedeviled me.

Roy was a teddy bear of a man, with a big grin. He played Santa Claus for the hospital children's ward every Christmas, buying gifts with money Doc provided. Oh, Roy had a reputation—a skirt chaser, Lowell called him. Plenty of women saw fit to let him catch them. Wasn't reasonable he'd mess with Doc's wife. Nor was Helen his type, which ran to high heels and sass.

'Course I had a soft spot for him. A woman does, for her first, 'specially if he's got Roy's sweet and easy manner. Happened the spring of '42, just before he headed overseas. After the war, and the advent of Lowell, Roy still had a wink, a gentleness in his voice for me, and I treasured my memories.

"Did Helen name Roy?" I had demanded of Lucy Tearn, a week ago, in this very kitchen.

"Oh, Abby, she reeled off the tale as though she'd learned it by rote, and said 'he' the whole while, but Doc saw. Josiah heard the whole thing from Judge Nickel. Doc swore it was Roy, and his word's good as gold in Glory. Besides, Roy ran, didn't he?"

I nodded, yet clung to my doubts. If I'd seen Roy attack Helen with my own eyes, I'd have felt the same. Seeing him in that light made everything that had happened between us seem different, too. Of course, the war might have changed him. It changed plenty else. Folks acted hungrier, like they'd starved for years and meant to quick gobble all they could. The war made them willing to risk more to fill the emptiness, and the few years since haven't eased their cravings. I was no different. I went after Lowell. He might've been the shiniest, highest bauble on the Christmas tree, and I could've cared less if other ornaments broke as long as I got him.

With all this weighing on me, and Helen still silent, I didn't shrink from prompting her. "I understand Lowell's not the only man who lit out of Glory recently. I hear Roy's another, and where to's a mystery." I'd no clue where Lowell had gone, either.

Helen stirred yet more sugar into her untouched coffee. She lifted her cup, her fingers crooked like talons, and stared into it, not drinking. "I do enjoy a cup of sweet coffee," she said.

For the sake of those spring nights with Roy, I tried again to prime her pump. "Roy serviced the Packard, didn't he?" Doc had inherited the car, a '30 coupe in beautiful shape, from his daddy, and Roy was the best mechanic in Glory.

"He drove up in the Packard." Helen peered in her spoon, at her distorted reflection. "I was watching the doves. He pinned me in the car. I fought. I fought him. I clawed his wrist and gouged his neck. I drew blood, and I was glad."

I recoiled, something inside me insisting, Not Roy. But the same part of me had believed Lowell would cool down and come home.

I patted Helen's hand. Her lips trembled. For an instant, I was certain she was smiling, but then, I dismissed the fancy.

My doorbell rang, and there was Doc. "Josiah said he saw Helen on your porch."

I ushered him into the hall. He clopped inside in the cowboy boots he loves. He wore a plaid shirt and string tie too, but he does draw the line. He was bareheaded, in a plain navy suit.

Helen must have heard his voice. She flitted out of the kitchen.

"I told you to stay home, Helen," Doc said. "You aren't well enough to be out."

She raised her head, looking straight at him, and that time it wasn't fancy—she flashed an odd, satisfied little smile at Doc.

"Now, Helen, you go on out and get in the car," he said.

She remained where she was, still smiling.

"Helen?"

"Thank you for the coffee, Abigail," she said. She went out on the porch, glanced back over her shoulder at Doc, that odd little smile still hovering on her mouth.

Doc watched her meander toward his car. "Sorry for barging in, Abby, but Helen hasn't been well. How did she seem to you?"

"Maybe a mite distant," I said.

"Was she babbling, or talking sense?"

He sounded anxious. If he were a different sort of man, I'd have patted his shoulder. I repeated Helen's and my conversation. Oh, I omitted her remark about her locked bedroom, common courtesy, and the details of her struggle with Roy. I figured, like me, Doc had had his fill of the story.

"He hurt her," Doc said. "But she brought it on, acting the way she did. I've no idea what to do with her, Abby, and that's a fact." His voice cracked on a baffled note. He whipped a white handkerchief from his pocket and blew his nose.

I felt a twinge of sympathy. He was a man who set store on winning out over obstacles, and his failure with Helen must've cut deep. I rearranged the umbrellas in the walnut stand near the door till he'd refolded the handkerchief into his pocket.

"Sorry to trouble you, Abby." He turned his back to me, and reached for the doorknob. His cuff slid up. I gaped at the big scab on his wrist, chilled by the knowledge that if I was to wrest his collar open, I'd find a similar wound on his neck.

I sped to the Arbers' next morning.

Helen peeked out from behind the front door, her lashes brushing her cheeks. "I'm not to talk to you, Abigail."

I pointed to the garage, empty and open, to the empty drive, testaments to Doc's absence. I coaxed her out on the porch. She wouldn't look at me, kept eyeing the doves winging above us. The attic of Doc's house boasts slits instead of windows, and the doves flew in and out of them, their coos coming at me in waves, OOOoooOOOOoooo, like the sound of a train whistle, but higher and softer.

"The doves warn me when he's coming," she said. "That's why he's going to make Jason help him kill them."

A fat white dove fluttered on the roof. My own roof remained charred. My throat, my chest, all my innards tightened up. The core of my regret was close to home: Kate fatherless; an end to the sweet moments in bed between Lowell and me; even the tattering of his dreams of acclaim; but the ache included Helen's boy, his faced pinched as a pallbearer's, and Roy gone, his name darkened. It included Helen, and Doc's tone of broken bewilderment. . . . The world spun, too fractured for mending.

Helen fumbled in the pocket of her soiled pink dress for a crust of toast, and threw it into the grass. Several doves descended, and she cooed to them while they tussled over the bread.

Her wrists looked so thin, the knobs of them sticking out. My eyes stung. "Helen, about Roy . . ."

She bent over the doves, the fingers of one hand scrabbling in her pocket, but it was empty, she had thrown out all the crumbs.

I tried to fill in her silence: I could imagine Doc paying Roy to leave, but my imagination balked at Roy accepting blame for Helen's injuries. I was convinced Doc must've spun him a tale. 'Course, I'd convinced myself Lowell loved me, when the fact was, he'd been passing through after the war, and halted when I dangled my grandma's house in front of him, and I'd clinched the deal by getting pregnant.

Helen had met Doc after the war. He'd been passing through her hometown, in California. I don't know what she dangled, or if she had believed Doc loved her, but I remember how pale and thin she grew the first winter she spent here as a bride, and how she talked and talked about an orange tree outside her window at home. Nothing here but cottonwoods, and the wind's moaning in them has brought low plenty of women stronger than Helen.

The doves, having eaten all of Helen's crumbs, flew away, and she gazed after them, her mouth all pinched up like that was the only way she could keep from begging them to come back.

"It wasn't Roy who attacked you, was it?"

Helen lowered her head and looked at me, eye to eye for the first time in a long while, and I was taken aback, because she glowed with an expression of triumph.

I didn't see any of the Arbers for a week, till I met Doc and Jason at the Huntsman's Palace. I was buying rain gear. Doc was showing Jason a shotgun big as he was. The boy started like a frightened fawn when his father tried to push the gun into his hands.

"Evening, Abby. Jason's growing like a weed, isn't he? Going to take him dove hunting. Toughen him up. Boy's got to tear loose from Helen's apron strings."

He took my bowed head for agreement, but I was grieving for Helen. Her locked door, what Doc had done in retaliation, hadn't changed anything.

I passed the Arber place the following day, and spotted Helen on the porch. I slowed the car to wave. She raised her hand, and damned if she still wasn't ashine with the radiance of victory.

"You look peaked," Lucy said to me, later that day.

I wanted to tell her about Doc and Helen, but I can never be sure about Lucy, what she will or won't tell that husband of hers.

"Old Doc had a tonic he prescribed for peakedness, but Doc says it was a humbug. My mother took it all the time," Lucy said.

I nodded, half listening, pondering Helen's radiant expression, remembering how Doc had sounded in my hall, a man bested by a foe he'd brushed aside as a serious threat. . . .

Lucy passed me a plate of homemade oatmeal cookies, and I nibbled one.

"Josiah says it's unwomanly to enjoy catching your husband in a mistake," she said. "But really, he was so certain. . . ."

I set down the cookie. I never did hear what the Reverend was wrong about, but Lucy had given me an idea of the kind of victory Helen might have thought she'd won, no more than her knowledge of Doc's lies, and his awareness of it.

Scorn had always tinged my sympathy for Helen, but now it leaked away, leaving a dark sorrow, and something like fear for her. As for Doc, I'd admired the way he tended his patients, tended to Helen, his concern for Jason. All that vanished. I wasn't willing to credit a single good quality to him. I couldn't forgive him for what he'd done to her, to Roy, to my faith in the possibility of truly knowing another.

Doc kept Helen in the house till her broken arm healed. He barred all visitors, and she no longer sat on the porch.

"Kindest thing is to let her be," Lucy said. "Doc says she's raving."

I knew better, but the knowing didn't stir me. I felt worn down from the mean messiness of life. I missed Lowell, missed Roy's bright smile at the gas station, missed knowing for sure who was who and what was what. I couldn't shake my uneasiness about Helen, but I couldn't think what to do about it, and so, I did nothing.

I blame myself for that. I always will. Because the minute the cast came off, Doc shipped Helen to Wichita for six weeks.

Lucy saw Helen first, right after she came back from Wichita, and hurried to my house to report. For once, she didn't sniff at my unmatched cups. "She had shock treatments, Abby."

My fingers numbed. My cup rattled in its saucer. "Can't a body lose their memory from that?"

"She has. She's forgotten the attack, her broken arm, Roy, all of it. Josiah says she's blessed to have lost those recollections. He called it an example of God's undeserved mercy. I guess it is." Lucy banged her cup on the table. Coffee sloshed out, a brown puddle on the yellow wood. Neither of us moved to wipe it up. "But I wish she weren't so quiet," Lucy said.

In my mind, an image of Helen arose, alive with that glow. My throat shut up, tight. I shooed Lucy home, and crawled into bed. Not even Kate roused me. I let her eat cornflakes for supper.

I'd give Helen my remembrances if I could. Twice, I teetered on the verge of telling her the story. I stopped because I read how shock treatments burn out brain cells. To Helen, the events never occurred. Cruel, to return them to her minus their saving resonance.

Now, only Doc and I knew the truth. Awful as his attack on Helen seemed, I might have forgiven it. But I couldn't forgive Doc or myself for retaining our knowledge while Helen's was erased.

I took to driving over to the Arbers'. Helen had grown wispier, paler. She hardly spoke to me.

One day, I found her on the porch in a green metal glider that squeaked when it moved, reading to Jason from a book about the habits of birds. The child sat close to her, and she kept touching his hand. He held his shoulders hunched, and when I stood on the bottom step looking at them, seeing how they'd appear in my camera lens, I thought he was trying to keep his distance by hunching his shoulders that way. He peeped at me, then down. His gaze seemed riveted to a color plate of a big black bird, a magpie or a crow, but he scratched one finger at a streak of rust on the glider's arm, scraping and scraping, a line of green under his fingernail.

Soon as Helen's voice trailed off, Jason leaped up, scurried down the steps, toward the creek at the back of the property.

"Helen?"

She closed the bird book and held it up against her breasts.

Hampered by not knowing what to say, I chitchatted. Grandma would have rolled her eyes to hear me rattle on about cornbread recipes and the children's homework. Helen never did say a word.

"She doesn't seem truly miserable," Lucy said.

We were back in my kitchen. Helen had been home for two weeks.

"There's misery and there's misery," I said. I don't know what Lucy answered, because I was trying to remember something Helen had said to me about misery, back before Lowell left.

He and I had had a quarrel, and I'd made a funny story of it for Lucy and Helen. Helen said, "Abigail, I do admire how you laugh in the face of misery."

"Best medicine in the world is to spit in sorrow's eye," I'd said.

Recalling that proved to be a tonic. I visualized Lowell's face, reddening to purple as he realized he'd set the roof on fire, his mortification when the engines wailed to the curb, and I saw he'd fled not out of anger at me, but in sheer embarrassment.

I felt like a fever had broken, and I laughed at how far folks'll go to avoid seeing themselves stripped of pretense.

"What in the world is so funny?" Lucy asked.

"Nothing," I said, sobered by thinking of Doc. He'd wiped out Helen's memory to preserve his vision of himself, in his own eyes, in Glory's. I felt a shiver of warmth toward Lowell, who had taken away only his own self, not mine.

Helen stayed close to home. I went back once or twice, but she didn't say much, and I couldn't. A day did come though, when everything built up inside me like a head of steam, and I had to do something.

I marched into Doc's office at Glory Memorial Hospital. The acres of glittering white no longer seemed as dazzling as they once had, and the smell of disinfectant roiled my stomach. I mustered an ease of manner that was purely a sham, and plunked down on a straight wooden chair.

"You recollect the day Helen came to my house, while her cast was on? She told me something I didn't mention to you before."

He twirled a pen, regarding me from beneath half-shut lids. "Now, Abby, be a good girl, and run along. I have patients to tend. Whatever Helen said, it was crazy talk. She's better. Let's not go rooting around in the past."

I forced my gaze steady. The rhythm of his pen twirling faltered. Pleased, I said, "She told me she hurt her attacker. Like everyone else in town, I took your word, and assumed she meant Roy. Later, at my door, you had your back to me. Either you figured I couldn't see, or you figured Helen had kept quiet. Except she didn't, and I did see, a mark on your wrist right where she said she'd gouged *him*."

He aimed the pen at me, narrowing his eyes, the picture of a man sighting down a barrel. "Why, Abby, you'd best take care you aren't misunderstood."

I thrust out my chin. "I know what I know."

His eyes gleamed. "Losing Lowell's unbalanced you. You tell folks . . . what you're implying, and everyone'll think you're mad."

I could read his mind—he had practice dealing with a mad woman. I hesitated, my palms clammy. He was Doc Arber. I was nobody, not even a married woman anymore. Roy wasn't there to cheer me, or refute the charge against him. If I battled Doc directly and lost . . .

He was staring at me, and I had the feeling he had seen inside my head, because he suddenly relaxed and leaned back in his chair. "Your contract with the school board to do the district's picture-taking is up for a vote again in the fall, isn't it?"

I ducked my head. "You know it is."

"Sometimes a woman alone has delusions, Abby. Right there, in Freud. Hysteria. Woman like that might not make a very good mother. I surely would hate to be forced into doing anything drastic."

I'd seen a big old hot-air balloon come down from the sky once, found something sad in how quickly it deflated once the gas valve was opened. I imagined I'd felt the bump of hard ground, could hear the hiss of my own breath.

Even so, I had to live with myself. And a stubborn corner of my heart meant to go on cherishing the memories of that brief spring with Roy. How could I do either if I let Doc have it all his way?

"A man must never shrink from bearing witness to the truth," Rev. Tearn had preached once. Well, I was just a woman, and the Reverend hardly had me or Helen's truth in mind, but I sat up straighter, and picked each word carefully.

"I haven't breathed a hint of this to another soul, and I won't." I rose, striding out of Doc's office.

Just beyond the threshold I paused, and peered over my shoulder. Doc had a funny look on his face, like he'd poked a discarded snake skin, and was suddenly fearful he'd spotted fangs.

He wasn't looking at me, though, so to be sure he understood me, I said, "But now you know I know. And I have a very good memory."

Blood darkened his cheeks, reddened his nails where they pressed down on the edge of his desk, and he breathed fast, almost a pant. When I was a girl, I saw a classmate almost drown. He was showing off above a deep hole, part of the quarry outside town, which had filled with water in a big storm. He fell in the hole. We threw him a branch till the grown-ups came to his rescue. Doc reminded me of how that boy had clung to the branch and panted.

I was of no mind to rescue him. Instead, I aimed at him the same smile I'd seen on *her* face that day in my hall, and added, "Give my best to Helen."

Desperate Measures

by Rachel Loden

When at the end
you've cured me of it

and it's all that I can do
to lie there, wasting

a last ragtag band
of brain cells

on some foolishness
or other, like

my next life
as a Wallenda

and the sequined
garters I shall wear,

that's always when
a company of riders

roars down from the mountains,
my mother and her mother

and her mother, with their
killer hair blown loose

and their Celtic eyes
all fire, and not

a whisper of forgiveness
in them anywhere.

Survival in the Wilderness

*It's a good thing to have all the props
pulled out from under us occasionally.
It gives us some sense of what is rock
under our feet, and what is sand.*
—Madeleine L'Engle

I have been in Sorrow's kitchen and licked out all the pots.
—Zora Neale Hurston

The Bird Man

by Susan Ito

Janey Nomura was looking for some chance at excitement on the Co-op bulletin board. Recently she had become unbearably bored with her life: bored with her Intro to Everything classes at college, bored with her plain but practical L. L. Bean wardrobe, bored with the snow that wouldn't melt. She stood in front of the mosaic of colored flyers, chewing on a piece of dried fruit. Consciously and in her bones, she wished for something interesting to happen to her. She thought about some story she had heard, about a sophomore named Sheila.

This Sheila had called some guy who had posted a notice for a ride down to New York City. She drove away in his black Camaro and two weeks later her roommate had gotten a postcard from Florida. Sheila had driven all the way down to the Keys with him and now had a job selling beauty products made from aloe. She got to snorkel every day and lived in some beachfront apartment. She most likely had a spectacular tan. Including the windchill factor, the average temperature on campus was about twenty below zero. Everyone hated Sheila for her unbelievable luck.

Janey pulled off one of the fringes from a flyer advertising a bookcase and stereo for sale, while surreptitiously eyeing the "ride offered" announcements. A voice behind her said, "Ah, Kenwoods are excellent. Can't go wrong there."

She jumped, startled that someone had been watching her, and she felt inexplicably guilty. She turned, her face red and flushed, and stammered quickly, "But . . . it's really just a bookcase I wanted."

It was an older man in maybe his midthirties, with thinning brown hair and a wiry beard with a few white hairs mingled with the dark. He wore an army fatigue jacket with a dove-shaped PEACE patch sewed onto one of the pockets. His eyes were intense, wrinkled at the edges, and a strange color that she couldn't quite place, a translucent greenish gray. His hair was tied with a leather cord into a ponytail the size and shape of a small brown mouse. Janey took all this in quickly, and then she looked back to the bulletin board. *You should be careful about wishing for things,* she told herself.

He tilted his head toward the tag of paper in her hand. "You like to read?"

Janey nodded, trying to look uninterested, but after a few seconds her eyes darted back to look at him. He was still looking at her, and although he wasn't smiling, she could tell that there was a smile there, poised somewhere in the muscles of his face.

"You go to the college up on the hill, don't you?" he said, stroking his beard with his index finger.

She wasn't sure if it was a question or an accusation. She shrugged, her mind scrambling to categorize him, thinking, *Is he homeless? Is he going to ask me for money?* She glanced down at his feet, but they were good, expensive leather boots, recently oiled. She looked up at his face, relieved, and then, almost in spite of herself, *nice eyes.*

"Do you know Jonathan Kominsky?" he asked suddenly. She was startled. Kominsky, the sociology professor? She usually sat in the back row of his class, thrilled and intimidated by his impassioned shouting. They had never spoken.

"Yeah, I'm in his class. Why?"

"He's my best friend from high school. Funny how he never left town."

Janey took a deep breath in and said, "Oh!" Here she was talking to Kominsky's best friend. It was like meeting the relative of a movie star, someone who knew important things. He was talking, saying other things about traveling, being away a long time, his name . . .

"Gordon. Gordon Oaks. And you are . . . ?"

She hesitated a moment, then said, "Jane Nomura. But people call me Janey."

"Nomura-san, I'd like you to have dinner with me." He bowed low and swept his hand out as if she were a princess.

The Japanese title startled her, but his gesture and comment stirred a warm, familiar place inside her. She hadn't heard anyone addressed like that since she'd left her parents' home on Long Island. She wondered if he was teasing. "Dinner? Now?"

"Yes, *now,* right here, at Millie's Garden." He winked at her and laughed. "I guarantee it'll be better than what they feed you in that college cafeteria!"

Gordon opened the door for her, and she walked through, almost in a trance. It was like being in a movie, eating dinner out with a man. She had been out with her family hundreds of times, and had ordered pizza or hamburgers with boys from high school, but this was different. This was the real thing.

It was a vegetarian restaurant with small wooden tables, each one topped with a squat white candle in a porcelain dish, and a Perrier bottle holding a few yellow daisies. The plates were all different, as if the owners had collected them at a series of garage sales.

Gordon ordered a vegetable stew for both of them. Janey ate three rolls while they were waiting, smearing them with butter. A red-haired waitress brought a ceramic casserole dish to the table. The stew was like a painting, studded with chunks of red bell pepper and gleaming purple-black eggplant. Gordon offered a piece to her, passing it across the table on his fork. Its soft flesh dissolved on her tongue, the skin stuck to the roof of her mouth like a leaf.

"Eggplants," Gordon said softly, "the most sensuous food that Mother Earth knew how to create." He looked at her solemnly, but again she could see a twinkling underneath his skin.

Janey blushed and looked down at her plate. "So . . . what kind of work do you do?" she said abruptly.

He told her that he was a high school science teacher, and she thought, *One year ago, I was in high school.* She thought of Mr. Hinkle, her bald, elderly biology teacher with his green bow tie, and a giggle blossomed in her stomach. This Gordon was way too interesting, way too good-looking, to be a colleague of Mr. Hinkle. She looked up at him, smiling as he described his laboratory, where the class had built an aviary. They were breeding doves, he said, and he spread his hands out over the table, making a soft fluttering noise with his mouth. He had names for all of them, strange and mysterious like Moreina and Plym. She thought of her parakeet, Tweetie Bird, at home and suddenly felt embarrassed.

"But I want to learn about you," he was saying. "Why don't you tell me something about Janey-chan?" He called her the same name her grandmother did, but it sounded strange and provocative in his deep, rusty voice.

"I don't know," she protested. "It's a regular life, nothing to say, really."

He pressed her, popping questions like a professor, and she had no choice but to answer. He asked her her favorite smell. *Christmas trees.* He asked her the earliest memory she had of when she was small, what she liked to eat when she felt sad. He was pulling stories out of her that Janey didn't even know still lived in her brain. Stories about her mother's perfume, and her cat Lewis getting electrocuted on a power line, about her one crooked toenail, and her grandpa Shobu who went crazy in the internment camps.

Janey was talking, her mind rolling with emotion and texture, images from her life clear as water. No one had ever asked her questions like these before, not her girlfriends, not the boys she went out with, not anyone. It was as if he were reaching into her memories and dreams and lifting them onto the tablecloth like colored tiles. She talked until her mouth dried up. He sat back, watching her, smiling, swirling the last puddle of wine in his glass.

"Janey Nomura," he whispered, his eyes glittering over the candle, "I knew when I woke up this morning that I was going to meet you."

Her heart shifted position and she could feel a layer of sweat burst through her skin underneath her hair. *He's reading my mind.* "What do you mean?" she asked.

"I don't know how to explain it. It might sound crazy." A shock of hair fell down in front of his eyes, and he looked like a child.

She leaned forward until she could feel the heat from the flame on her nose and chin. "I want to hear about it," she said.

"Twenty years ago," he said, his voice dropping into a whisper, "I was in Asia. I knew a woman there, a beautiful woman. She had long black hair, almost down to the backs of her knees."

Janey's hand reached up involuntarily and wound a strand of her own hair around her finger.

He hadn't taken his eyes off her since he started speaking. "She looked a lot like you, Janey-chan." He blinked his eyes, as if trying to make her disappear, or perhaps come into focus in front of him. "The last time I saw her, she gave me a little green stone. For remembrance."

She was holding her breath.

"Well, anyway," he coughed, and pinched the space between his eyes. "I live in this cabin way out in the woods, on Miller's Pond. I built it myself, me and my brother Steve, seven years ago."

She followed his voice, listening. She could see it, as he spoke. The cabin flickered, in miniature, in the candle flame. The rough wooden walls, the stained-glass window in shades of blue, ocean and fish, above the wide cedar bed. She could see the immense bookshelves, sanded smooth like stone, filled with books of poetry and art. Janey loved the forest, stories about Little Red Riding Hood and her grandmother's tales of the Japanese Moon Princess. She looked at him expectantly.

"When I went to bed last night, I bolted the door. This morning, I woke up, and there was a marble on the floor, a clear green one." He exhaled, watching her face.

"A marble?"

"I didn't put it there. I had never seen this object in my life, and when I opened my eyes in the morning, it was sitting *exactly in the center* of the woven Indian rug."

She felt hope and wonder rising inside her like smoke, but she waved it away. "Maybe it fell out of your pocket."

"No, Janey. It was never in my pocket. It just appeared . . . while I was sleeping. Dreaming." He raised his eyebrows slightly. He slid his hand into the side of his jacket, then opened his palm on the table. The marble rolled across the wood and hit the Perrier bottle with a soft click.

Janey picked it up. It was warm. *Like some sort of fairy tale.*

"It was a stone to mark my way," he murmured. "The trail of destiny, leading me to you."

The restaurant was almost empty. Darkness pressed heavily on the huge glass windows. Janey stood up, her head swimming. *So what is it, he thinks I'm his girlfriend from twenty years ago?* "That's, um, really interesting."

"It's more than interesting, Janey girl." He pressed his palm against her back with a gesture that was at once calming, and too intimate. It made her shiver, but she didn't pull away. She liked the soft, steady pressure of his hand.

They walked to his car, a blue VW van. The inside of it smelled faintly sweet, like pine incense. She climbed into the front seat and saw a constellation of delicate white bones, she couldn't tell from what kind of animal, suspended from the rearview mirror by a nylon string. She looked at the long slide of his nose, the escaping pieces of hair around the back of his neck, and thought, *Even if he's kind of weird, he's really handsome.*

"Janey," he said, "Come with me for just a few minutes. I want to show you the birds. I know they'll really like you."

She leaned back to look at him, resting the back of her head on the cold glass of the window. Her heart thrashed around, struggling with her. *Only for a few minutes.* "All right," she said. "But I have to get back soon."

As they walked down the darkened hallway of the old brick school building, he turned and put his hand on the side of her neck, underneath her hair. She inhaled quickly and stepped back, fear and arousal spreading through her like sparks.

"Didn't mean to startle you, sweetheart," he said. "Are you all right?"

She didn't answer. Her footsteps echoed on the concrete stairs and she was suddenly aware of the way that Gordon walked, each step controlled, almost noiseless. He stopped to pause at the door that read in white letters across the window, BIOLOGY.

"Welcome," he said, "to the palace of the doves." He opened the door and ushered her in. The room was filled with soft throaty noises and the sharp smell of excrement. It was too dark to see clearly but Janey could feel the presence of the birds, huddled together in one large, fluttering shadow.

Gordon took her elbow and led her to the ceiling-high cage. The doves shifted, separating, as they came closer, making escalating cries of alarm. Gordon made purring noises under his breath, rolling his tongue into bird sounds, and slowly they quieted. Janey stood statue-still as he put his face against her neck, breathing warm air across her skin.

"They're beautiful, aren't they?" he whispered. She felt his mouth making wet marks underneath her ear. "*Kirei, neh?* Just like you."

"Gordon," she trembled, shaking her head.

"Please come home with me, Janey-chan."

She leaned against a metal laboratory table, feeling the breath pressed out of her chest. She imagined the cabin in the forest, lovemaking with Gordon, the full moon shining through the stained glass. He would touch her like some kind of magician. A wizard. He was stroking her hair softly, hypnotically, letting it fall through his fingers. She looked through half-closed lids at the dark mass of the doves as they quivered together, all on a single branch. She reached out to touch the fine mesh of the cage, and the feeling of the wire against her fingertips woke her up.

Cool your jets, girl, she thought. *You don't know this guy from Adam.* A shudder of nerves ran through her and she giggled involuntarily. She shook her head again, hugging herself with her arms. "I can't, not tonight," she said. "I'm sorry, Gordon. Could you just bring me back to campus?"

He shrugged as if it didn't matter, but something behind his eyes darkened and she saw the muscles in his neck bunch together. Janey bit her lip. "Maybe some other time."

His mouth twisted into a small, bitter smile. "I don't give out invitations a second time, sweetheart." He drove her to her dormitory and let her out at the door, and then pulled out of the parking lot without looking back.

The gifts started appearing the next day; always left when she wasn't around, always propped against her door. Janey bent down to pick up the cluster of yellow daisies, dirt still clinging to them. Between the stems lay a blue envelope with her name in swirling brushed calligraphy. She opened it and read, her heart pounding, *Your name falls through my dreams like snow.* . . .

She let out an exhalation of relief. *He's not mad at me.* She wondered if he would call her, if they would go out to dinner again. She thought about the way he had leaned forward to ask her questions, and she found herself trying to think of interesting things to say, stories that she could offer him.

That night she sat at her window, looking down at the town spread out like a sparkling necklace below. It formed the shape of an apron, with a dark scoop at the top that Janey knew was Miller's Pond, with the woods surrounding it. Like a little girl, she plucked the petals off the daisy, dropping them onto her pillowcase. She thought about what it would be like to live in the forest. She wondered what the Asian woman's name had been.

The next morning it was a feather, gray with soft white fringe at the quill. She had woken early, before six, when she could see the mist rising off the pond like a ghost. When she opened her door to go to the bathroom across the hall, the feather was lying in the door frame as if it had blown there by accident. She carried it in her pocket all day.

The gifts materialized as if they had been conjured there, sometimes during the five minutes it took her to brush her teeth in the morning. But she never saw him, never heard footsteps or noises outside her door.

One evening, she looked out the window and recognized the blue van, circling around the parking lot of the student union. *There he is, finally.* She ran to the mirror, brushed her hair rapidly, and then rushed back to the window. She watched the van drive the perimeter of the campus, slowly, then around again, and again. Janey's face was pressed against the glass, creating an anxious cloud where she breathed. The van stopped next to the library, and she saw a little stick figure, someone dressed in a pink ski jacket, approaching the driver's door. The window rolled down and she saw the small dark shape of Gordon's head. She watched, holding her breath, as the pink shape moved around the other side of the vehicle and got in. The van sped up and disappeared through the front gates of campus. Suddenly Janey was stung with anxiety, confusion, jealousy. She hated the girl in the pink coat, whoever she was.

The next offering came in a torn, gritty plastic bag from the Co-op. It was filled with used wooden chopsticks, like the kind the Chinese restaurant gave out, and they were splintered and sticky. She was shaken. *What the hell?*

It continued all week, the objects showing up like strange abandoned children. The packet of miniature pinecones wrapped in velvet was sweet, yet puzzling. Other things were bizarre and disturbing, like the jagged bottom half of a black-and-white photo: skinny bare legs and feet of a child, standing on a dirt road. She turned it over and read the pencil scrawl: "Don't forget Kenji." Her stomach started hurting then. She left a page of notebook paper tacked to her door: *Please do not leave anything here.*

They didn't stop coming. Sometimes there were two or three things a day, left in the middle of a busy afternoon, and nobody on the floor ever saw him. She was starting to feel strange and disconnected, as if her whole life were a nightmare. The only momentary relief was the calm ordinariness of her statistics class.

The bottle of Sapporo beer finally undid her. It had come while Janey was in the shower, wrapped in a satin-lined box, with an envelope of small green stones and a note, "Remember our last drink in Bangkok?" *He's crazy,* she thought. *He's crazy, and I'm the stupidest person on earth.*

I can't take any more of this. In a sudden, violent motion, she tore the daisies out of their glass on her desk, grabbed up the feathers and pinecones and the bottle of beer. She ran into the hallway, panting, and crushed them through the square metal door of the garbage chute. They fell eleven floors, crashing into each other, echoing off the tin walls until she heard the shattering explosion at the bottom.

Two days later, Janey was in the student union buying a package of M & M's when she saw a yellow flyer taped to the side of the vending machine. The little candies spilled out onto the floor as she read the large print: DO YOU KNOW THE BIRD MAN? There was a pencil drawing of a bearded man. His head was turned slightly and she recognized the sculpted nose, the small ponytail. She grabbed the paper, stuffed it into her pocket and ran back to the dorm. Huddled on her bed, shaking, she spread open the flyer and read it, over and over. Under the drawing was printed, "This man may be dangerous. If you have had a bad experience with him or have information to share, please call Katherine at 276-6773." Janey picked up the phone and took a deep breath.

Katherine was a senior living in the campus apartments; an intense economics major with black curly hair. She questioned Janey carefully about the dinner at Millie's, the doves at the high school, the relentless flow of strange gifts to her door. She shook her head, her nostrils flaring out like wings as she listened.

When Janey finished, Katherine said quietly, "He told me I was a dead ringer for his girlfriend from Missouri. His high school sweetheart who wore his varsity jacket when he went to Vietnam."

She lifted her hair up and showed Janey a dangling pearl earring. "He told me that this old girlfriend *had the exact same earrings*. Of course I was too dumb to realize that half the girls in America have them too. I thought it was some kind of *sign*. That's what he said, anyway."

She continued, "Everything he says is a lie. He says he's a biology teacher, but it's not true. I was at his house, and while he was making tea I went in the bathroom. There's this pile of dirty clothes, and on top I see these blue coveralls, and embroidered on the pocket there's his name, and it says *Custodian*. I confronted him, and he admitted it. He's a janitor at the high school, Janey, that's why he has the keys to the building."

Katherine had seen the birds too, had been kissed in that room where pinfeathers floated in the air around them. She had let Gordon lead her by the hand up the stone walkway to the cabin on Miller's Pond. "I felt like Rose Red," she whispered, "and he was the Woodsman." She took in her breath suddenly. "But it wasn't anything like the way he described it."

It was ugly, the way that many fairy tales suddenly become gruesome. "It was like he wanted to get back at her, that old girlfriend, for dumping him or something. Even though I was crying, even though I kept telling him to stop pawing at me, he didn't stop. He kept calling me Laurie Jean." Katherine looked up at the ceiling. "Legally, it was a half inch short of rape. But it didn't feel any different."

Janey closed her eyes, and shook her head. So much for magic. So much for being a sucker for fairy tales and cottages in the woods, and enchantment.

Katherine said, "Did he tell you he's best friends with Kominsky?"

Janey nodded, not wanting to hear what was coming next.

"This guy is a complete weasel. He *knows* that everyone up here worships the guy, that it would be hard to find someone who *hasn't* taken one of Kominsky's classes. But I asked Kominsky, and he's never even met him."

Janey picked up a paper clip from the table and untwisted it with her fingers. "So we're not the only ones?" *I bet one of them had a pink jacket. . . .*

"I've talked with four other women in the same situation. He never does anything illegal, but he knows how to screw with your head. I already called the cops, and they blew me off."

Janey swallowed hard. "You know, Katherine, he's not the only one allowed to pull magic tricks."

Janey and Katherine drove downtown to Woolworth's. They stopped in the pet food section, then the toy section, and sat at the counter to drink lemonade while they talked calmly, their eyes bright with anger.

It was easy to find the cabin. Katherine remembered every turn, pointing the way with little shudders. The Toyota bumped along the dirt road until they came to the mailbox shaped like a log. OAKS was carved into its side. The cabin sat back from the road, the blue van in front.

Darkness was beginning to close in between the trees, and the light from the cabin window was bright, like the screen at a drive-in movie. Janey held her breath and walked closer. Gordon Oaks was lying supine on an old sofa with his eyes closed, mouth open. There was a remote control in his hand, and Janey could see flickers of blue light from the television. She saw the stained-glass oval with the fish design, but it was hanging from a crooked chain, and it was grimy from dust and grease. The bookshelves against the wall were stacked with yellowed newspapers and towers of *National Geographics*. A dark green wine bottle lay on the tattered Indian rug.

She watched him for a minute, then stepped back quietly, motioning to Katherine. *He's passed out*. They pulled the sack of birdseed out of the back seat of the Toyota. Janey put the fishnet bag of marbles under her arm.

"Sayonara, bird man," she whispered towards the house. The birdseed poured like water into the gas tank of the van. She watched as Katherine moved silently toward the front porch, then knelt and placed the marbles on the front step, one by one. They glowed under the moon like magic stones.

Heart Attack

by Vicki E. Lindner

T he woman in her middle thirties returns from the doctor's office and enters the small apartment where she lives alone. Objectively, her apartment is a cheerful place, but tonight the abrupt shift in her expectations has darkened the white walls and red linoleum, as if the light bulb in the ceiling fixture is about to blink and die. She checks the dial on her telephone answering machine; no messages there. For once she feels not desolate and abandoned, but relieved. She would automatically tell the first caller about her illness, and she wants to formulate her own reaction to it first. In fact, she has no concrete reaction. Although this woman, too often alone, has vividly imagined the reality of death, now that she is sick with a potentially fatal condition, the feared final moment eludes her grasp. She does not feel the panic she ought to be feeling. She examines her form in the full-length mirror on the bathroom door, expecting to confront a stranger or a shadow, and sees only the solid, familiar image of herself.

Her doctor has discovered, through a routine electrocardiogram, a degenerative condition in the valves of her heart. According to the cardiologist, there is no need for surgery, medication, or even excess caution at the present time. For the moment there is nothing she can do, except (she thinks ironically) wait for her diseased valves to collapse. Watching herself in the mirror, she raises her hand to her heart and feels it beating—a steady, reassuring flicker.

Her apartment is unusually quiet. The telephone doesn't ring. Static coats the music on the radio. The noises from the street are muffled by rain and do not penetrate the window. Calmly she prepares a simple, broiled dinner, watching her hands make the appropriate motions, as if they were the hands

293

of someone else. She eats and goes to bed in the now appalling silence. If her parents had not been vacationing abroad, she would have called them to recite the news in dire tones and solicit their concern, sharper and more immediate than any she seems to be able to summon for herself. "Well," she imagines herself telling them in a jolly, macabre voice, "it looks like you're going to outlive me after all!" Instead, she pushes herself to sleep as rapidly as possible, obliterating the oppressive silence and the eerie, wedge-shaped reflection the streetlight casts on the wall.

At an indefinite hour of early morning the telephone ring awakens her. This was the time he always called—in the brief margin between the darkest edge of night and dawn. When she picked up the receiver he would remain silent, as if debating whether he wanted to speak or not, then in his flat, toneless accent, say, "I am coming, all right?" Cornered by her own weariness, by the confused labyrinth of retreating dreams, she would answer, "Yes, come on over," no matter how many times that day or week she had battled her desire to see him and told herself she would never let him visit in the middle of the night again—unless he changed, unless he changed, unless everything changed between them.

Sometimes she got up before he arrived and unlocked her apartment door for him, so she wouldn't have to greet him, so she could receive him in a semi-conscious state from which she had no energy or will to reproach herself. Then she would lie, nervously awake, more alert than she wanted to be, until she heard the soft thud of his bicycle tire hit the top landing, and the click-click of its spokes turning down the hall.

Before undressing he always sat morosely on the couch, immersed in a fierce, inaccessible silence which challenged interruptions. The tension between them magnified in this taciturn gulf. Then he slowly stripped away his layers of damp, musty clothes and, forcibly recalling himself to the present moment, would ask, "How are you?"

"Pretty good," she would reply, and discover that all the sentences she had planned to say, carefully composed for their intriguing, humorous or ironic effect, had vanished. His forbidding detachment silenced her. Forced to a wall of nervous cliché, she would ask, "What have you been up to?"

"Working," he'd answer, noncommittal. This brief exchange was always the same, a dull liturgy, which drew her into the exasperating possibilities of what was left unsaid. Then he would climb naked into her bed, lie rigidly on his back without touching her, his skin hot, his breath stiff with an emotion she could never define—anger, fear, passion, perhaps no feeling at all—and completely ashamed, she would run her hand over the planes of his body which shuddered beneath it. His eyes squeezed shut and his breathing deepened until it rasped in his throat; but he never embraced her or said a word. She imagined his rough-textured skin absorbing her lips, her fingertips, the edges of her hair. Afterwards he jerked his body away, almost angrily, and slept with total concentration. Sometimes he stood up, dressed abruptly, and left without a word, returning weeks later, with no explanation. At first she demanded to know why he'd disappeared, what he took her for, the predictably irate questions. He never really answered, and the fact was, he lay in her bed again at an humiliating hour, and she was eager and resigned.

She hadn't seen him now for a month. She thought about him constantly. He was a monolithic presence in her imagination. She told herself that her unhealthy involvement with him kept her away from other men. She dreamed about him, and about symbols she knew stood for him in her mind.

Now, as she groggily reaches for the receiver, she is conscious of an uncomfortable new awareness, and remembers that something is wrong with her heart. Before she fell asleep she had rehearsed the dialogue in which she announced her heart condition to him, constructing his imaginary reply, unable, for once, to conceal his feelings. No, too childish and melodramatic, she tells herself now. She couldn't mention her heart, the repugnant clinical details, to him at all. She wouldn't actually tell him, but give him hints, let him guess. The voice in the telephone speaks in a whisper. "Who is this?" she asks, her own tone automatically sinking to match the caller's.

"You know," whispers the voice on the line. "I love you, Ida. I love you. I've always loved you. I want to make love to you."

"Who is this?" Her suddenly loud voice trembles.

"You know," replies the husky whisper. "You know. I want to make love to you." The voice sounds sincere. There is no salacious tone, or heavy, erotic breath.

"Who is this?" she asks again. She is positive that the whisper represents his voice, though she is reluctant to expose him or call him by name. He must have reasons for whispering.

"Don't you know?" the voice asks, then declares, almost angrily, "You know!"

Bewildered, the woman falls silent, then hangs up. She lies awake until dawn, too agitated by the call to sleep. At first she is sure the phone will ring again, and anxiously awaits its startling peal. She asks herself the obvious questions: How does the caller know her first name, not listed in the telephone book, unless he knows her? Why would he disguise his voice, unless he was afraid she would recognize it? If he was a crank caller, wouldn't he call back, again and again? These questions, however, are formalities, designed to support her conviction with logic. It was the passionate urgency of the disguised voice, the current of underlying anger, more than the circumstances, the trace of accent, or even the words he spoke, that convinced her the man was him.

The few overt gestures of commitment he had made, like this call, were strange and astonishing. Sex always afflicted him with a misery she sensed but could not understand. When she touched even an innocent part of his body, his arm, his foot, he grimaced, shut his eyes tightly, breathed painfully. Once, without warning, he had sat straight up and said very loudly, "Whenever we make love I always give myself to you, Ida. Completely!" She'd stared, shocked, and then he'd continued in a furious voice, "Don't you know that?" He had leaped to his feet, struggled into his clothes, and repeated, "Don't you know that?" before he rushed into the kitchen and wheeled his bicycle out the door. When he'd returned, two weeks later, he had not acknowledged this outburst, and with the increase in his tense, melancholy silence, forbade her to mention it.

This telephone call had the same character: The whispered words, the secret identity, would let him bridge the long separation, commit himself in his ambivalent manner, and simultaneously abandon what he'd said. It was his way of skirting the borders of open passion, of tantalizing her with the possibility of love, that kept her starved for him and obsessed. No matter how oddly he behaved, no matter how deeply he humiliated her, she never doubted that he really cared and that one day she would win his trust. Why else did he keep coming back?

The telephone call afflicts the woman with a nervous excitement. She formulates the words she will say when he reappears and envisions their first, crucial encounter. How will she use his admissions of love to her own advantage? The indirect approach is the most successful with him. If she were to place too much importance on the mysterious call, even to mention it, he would feel trapped by his own declaration and escape, whether he realized he loved her or not. She is no longer worrying about her heart, though her excitement seems to be centered in her chest. She is newly aware of this invisible organ, its speed, its digressions, and when she doesn't feel it, she registers its silence. Every night she lies in bed, half asleep, expecting the telephone to ring again and his voice to say, after a pause, "I am coming, all right?" When he entered her bedroom they would meet each other's eyes for an intense moment; then he would laugh, extended, joyless laughter, as if the whole business was an unhappy joke; but they would both know that everything had changed. The ordinary noises on the street or in the hallway of her building start her heart jumping spasmodically.

Three days after the telephone call the woman comes home from work and finds a conical white florist's package outside her apartment door—a pink-and-green caladium in a straw basket, small chocolate Easter eggs, wrapped in colored foil, strewn beneath the leaves. She looks for a note from the sender, but there is none. She is certain that the plant is from him; it bears unmistakable evidence of his touch. Its leaves are battered and brown around the edges; several are marred by tiny holes, as if an insect had eaten them. It looks like a castaway, a plant found on the street, instead of in a florist's shop. The chocolate eggs under their silvery wrappers are white with age. His infrequent gifts had all had the same dilapidated aura: the paperback book, which he hadn't actually given her, but left behind, its front cover half burned away; a pocketknife that wouldn't open; a cheap, gold-plated locket with an artificial stone that popped out of its setting the first time she'd worn it. He had made a rare daytime visit, shortly after Christmas, to deliver that.

He himself appeared to have been thrown out into the elements. He was seldom really clean, and his body, bearing a number of small, raised scars, smelled dense and wild, like the fur of an animal. Yet his upright posture, the majestic angle at which he held his large head, indicated a vague nobility, achieved through a relentless struggle with deteriorating forces. Once he'd come to her the night after he'd punched out the window of a taxicab that cut off his bicycle at an intersection. The hand was wrapped in blood-soaked white gauze. It was difficult to imagine him emerging from his constant detachment to create such a violent scene. She had fussed over the wound, but her pity only annoyed him. He had stopped her clucking with one firm sentence, "It doesn't matter," and jerked his hand away from her sympathetic fingers.

The next day Ida calls the florist where the plant was purchased and explains that she received a caladium from an unidentified sender. The florist remembers the man who bought the plant, or thinks she does. "Tall and dark-skinned," he says. Though he is tall and dark-skinned the inadequate description confirms nothing. She is too embarrassed to ask the florist more elaborate questions: Exactly how tall? Did he have a beard? How did he walk? No stranger, she realizes, could supply the details that would identify him to her beyond a doubt. He walked as though invisible eddies of air, not muscles, propelled him.

The woman tells the story of the whispered call and the caladium to her closest friend, the only one who knows about her nocturnal lover. She hopes her friend will be at least amused by this tale. Her friend receives her confidence, however, with a judgmental attitude, as if she considers it a duty to separate delusion from reality in Ida's mind. Ida says she thinks he is sending her secret messages, acknowledging, in his ambivalent way, the profundity of their relationship, what it means to him. The friend does not believe the caller is him. "Sending flowers, saying 'I love you'—it's just not his style," she declares. "It's too normal, too romantic." Ida tries to explain why he would do these things. He is keeping his identity secret, she tells her friend, so he can commit so-called normal, romantic acts under the cover of anonymity, which makes them not so normal after all. "It's a game," she says. "He loves games; he loves to trick me." As they discuss the situation further, Ida's friend becomes almost alarmed. She thinks the mysterious caller might be a dangerous character. "If he calls again, you'd better notify the police," she advises.

Ida is annoyed. Her friend is unable to comprehend any truth beyond the boundaries of stodgy, middle-class logic. "If he was a stranger, how could he know my name?" she asks.

"Lots of ways," her friend retorts. "He might be some nut that works for the post office or the telephone company. Don't you ever sign petitions on the street? It could be the Con Ed man, the super—anyone!"

"Why would he whisper then?" Ida asks.

"To make you think you know him, of course," answers her friend. "He doesn't have to be stupid to be crazy."

"You're paranoid!" Ida snorts. She reminds her friend that she is afraid to walk at night, even on a well-lighted street, without her German shepherd to protect her.

The friend replies that her dog is irrelevant. She says that because Ida wants the caller to be him doesn't mean that it is him. "Wishful thinking," she summarizes. Their conversation approaches a quarrel. After she hangs up, Ida realizes that she has completely forgotten to tell her friend the news about her heart condition. She considers calling back, but to reveal her poor health now seems inappropriate. Her friend would only think her illness was warping her judgment.

Two days later Ida returns from her appointment with the cardiologist, checks her mail, and finds an anonymous note in the box. The message is sloppily printed; the letters climb upward to a thirty-degree angle and almost every word is misspelled. The letter says:

> My Dear and Dearest Ida:
>
> The black angels of the intergalactic spaces have sent you to answer my needs. Thirsty, hungry, cold and cruel, I was forced into the night to do their bidding. I did not always know that I loved you, but now the streets will run with blood in your honor. I seek you where the stars are cold. I live in a hole.

The letter is signed with a crude drawing of a man, strangely self-absorbed for a stick figure, carrying a flower.

It all fits in. He always carried a brown notebook with him, which she examined while he slept, hoping to learn the secret details of his everyday life. The notebook contained many names and telephone numbers; some were women's names, but most were of restaurants and other business establishments. The names were hurriedly scrawled in a barely legible script, or half-printed, like the words in the note. Most were misspelled or had letters missing. Some of the pages were waterstained and the ink had run and collected in opaque pools. An occasional muddled drawing graced the margin of a page. Once a sort of poem had been added to the notebook, a neatly printed but formless thought, something about loneliness and, she was almost sure, *angels*. When he delivered his occasional rambling monologues, they were often on a quasi-spiritual subject. She suspected these half-coherent diatribes were designed to ward off questions about his life and to limit, rather than increase, communication. Usually she was far too tense about what was happening, or not happening, between them to focus clearly on their meaning; but his language and the imagery in this letter are in the same vein.

As Ida climbs the stairs to her apartment, the letter in hand, she feels a twinge circulate slowly around her heart. This familiar pain, which she had before ignored, now has a medical name. "Too much excitement," she rationalizes, frightened. Strapped to the intimidating machine in the doctor's office, she had felt distracted, unconnected to her reason for being there. Her mind had dwelled obstinately on the night she had met him, long ago. He had pulled her to him in the back of a dark room, and his embrace had been so gentle it was practically ineffable. Pressed to the shadows of his rich smell, his contained grace, she had known, with an amazing finality, that she loved him. The purity of that moment had all come to this, this maze of hints and confusing speculations, she thought sadly. When the doctor had asked her if she had further questions she forgot the list she had mentally compiled. "No," she answered.

That night Ida dreams she is being chauffeured down the side of a mountain in a foreign country by a tall, dark man. The road is lined with filthy slums; naked children stare at the passing car. Because she is seated in the back seat, she cannot see the driver's face. She strains to catch a glimpse of him in the mirror over the dashboard, but the mirror reflects nothing at all. The car crosses a deep ravine on a wooden bridge; suddenly, the bridge cracks and the car plunges, in slow motion, to the ravine blow. As the bottom of the ravine rises slowly to meet her, she fixes her eyes on the exact configurations of the landscape of her death—the formless, odorless, empty cavern at the end of it all. She wakes up, sweating, her heart hitting her bones. At that moment, the telephone rings.

Though she has been expecting this call for days, the ring still shocks her. It sends her half-staggering, half-crawling toward the receiver across the room. The sound extends and wails, like a siren. She picks up the phone, but her constricted throat cannot squeeze out a greeting. In the space of her silence the familiar whisper asserts itself again, intimate, deafening. "Ida, I love you," it says. "The plant and the letter—they were from me. Ida, can I see you now? Please, Ida!" She has detected his accent; this time she is sure. She wants to say his name, to break the fearful lure of this secret call, but feels forbidden.

"Yes, come!" she says passionately, then drops her own voice to a whisper. "I love you, too. Since that first night. You know that. You've always known that. I need you now. More than you know!" She feels the other receiver dropping toward its extinguishing click. Quickly, she says, "I'll leave the door open for you." She unlocks the door and falls back into bed, feeling the darkness press tightly around her body—her limbs, head and heart—like a squeezing hand. She fights to stay awake; but the images of her nightmare draw her back into them, despite the moment's intense expectancy. Time moves perceptibly. She listens for the sound of his arrival. Perhaps he wouldn't come. No, he always did, once he said he would. She tries to predict the expression in his eyes, prepare herself for the strange, positive shift of his mood. But even this immediate future seems beyond the grasp of her imagination. Oddly, she can barely remember his face. Drifting back into sleep, she foggily tries to calculate the right words to say, but only *Help me!* enters her mind.

The sound of the door opening is the first notification that something is wrong. The knob turns abruptly, the door slams, and the lock clangs shut. No bicycle wheels are turning. He always opened and shut the door so stealthily she could barely hear him enter. Her stomach drops queasily. Half a second later, a heavy, rubber-soled footstep creaks on the kitchen floor and then, after a hesitant pause, the steps tramp definitively toward her bedroom door. The woman is terror-stricken before she realizes the reason why. Her heart cramps painfully and she can scarcely catch her breath. Then, horrified, she remembers: He said *"Can I see you now?"* not *"I am coming, all right?"* Even before she looks up and sees the peculiar dark face, which appears disembodied in the window's wedge-shaped shaft of light, she knows the man who has entered her apartment is a stranger.

The Woman with a Secret

by Mary Morris

I'd lived in the building for years, but I hardly knew Madeline. She'd moved in after I had, into the apartment where the old woman had lived. The old woman was there for forty years. Her children had been raised in that apartment. Her husband died there. One night as I was coming home from work, the old woman stood in the hall. She was all dressed up in a flowered print dress. "Please," she said. She had long chicken-like fingers and they beckoned to me. "Come in. You've never been inside."

That night in her apartment, painted a dull shade of green and white, the old woman fed me an oily soup. She tiptoed across the faded oriental rugs and dragged out the albums containing her past. Her cloudy grey eyes scanned the pictures of her husband in a business suit, her children in the park, and she showed me each with the intensity of a realtor trying to sell me a house. It took hours to pull myself away. I was young then and I had phone calls to return, a television program I wanted to watch, and I was annoyed with this woman who held me captive for an evening.

I never saw her again. The next thing I knew the old woman was gone. The landlord said her son had taken her to a nursing home where later I learned she died. Soon a work crew arrived; four or five men who spoke a strange dialect began stripping paint and redoing floors.

Then Madeline moved in. She was twenty-five, but she looked eighteen. She had thick hair and deep, black eyes, a tiny, compact body, and fluttery hands that reminded me of a bird trapped in a cathedral. She came with her brass bed, her throw rugs, bags of sundresses and colored shoes, with her glass prisms, unicorn dolls, and gigantic hanging plants. She was my only neighbor on the first floor.

301

I wandered by as she dragged giant pillows up the stairs. Her door was open and I looked in. The work crew had the mantel and moldings down to their original wood. They had removed the green from the walls and painted them a fresh white. Above the kitchen they'd built a loft with a window overlooking the garden where she could sit and read, and I thought how much I wanted to live there instead of in my apartment which faced the noisy street.

We introduced ourselves and she poured me a glass of seltzer. "I am an actress," she told me as we sat on her stuffed sofa, a languid white cat between us, "and this is Katmandu." With her aqua skirt hiked above her knees she sipped the seltzer. "I work on a soap, but my heart is in the theater." Presently she said she was playing the part of a woman who had gone with her husband on a honeymoon in Venezuela. There, they had crossed a rope bridge and she had fallen off, tumbling into a river of white water that swept her away. For weeks her husband had searched for her. They had hired helicopters and natives and scanned the banks and the inner depths of the jungle, to no avail.

Then, Madeline told me, her eyes widening, "The woman suddenly returns. She told the authorities that for two years she had been living in the jungle with a tribe who had nursed her back to health. Her husband, who had never given up hope, felt the deep scars on her back, but she would tell him nothing of the time in which she was missing."

Madeline told me, that first evening when we met, this much about herself. "I am a woman," she said, tossing her head back, "with a secret."

I was more aware of the city that summer than I had ever been before. It was my thirtieth year and the first I could remember being alone. Earlier that spring, Zachary, my husband of three years, had moved out. He worked in TV news; everything he did was by the clock. It was a trial separation, by mutual consent, but it left me oddly adrift. Then my sister, Beverly, who'd lived a few blocks away and with whom I had dinner at least once a week, married a cabinetmaker who swept her into the depths of Staten Island to renovate an abandoned building where they lived like squatters. Going to see her became an expedition—a train, the ferry, two buses and a ten-minute walk along a dark and threatening side street—and my visits dwindled to once a month. Then my mother, who'd been recently widowed, left the Bronx where she'd lived all her life and went to a retirement community in Arizona from which she wrote crazed letters about the vast expanse of the desert, the prairie dogs she befriended, the odd-shaped saguaro cactus with arms reaching, "just like men," whose shadows on the hills in the late afternoon reminded her of Calvary.

I was working then as a fact checker for an upscale photographic magazine. My days were spent in the musty reference rooms of libraries or else calling interesting people who lived in far-off places with facts I needed to verify. How do you spell the name of your monkey that speaks? Is it true you began your corporate career as the messenger boy? What is the river you glide down to reach the cannibal tribe?

When I wasn't at work, the sounds of other people's lives that summer disturbed me. The slamming doors of hopeful departures and weary returns. The late night ringing telephones, answered on the second ring or else left reverberating over and over into the night. Often I stayed up, listening to the sirens which I learned to identify—police, ambulance, fire department—and felt oddly soothed by the sounds of people's lives in disarray. And then there were the parties. The opening of bottles, the salsa playing. I imagined myself an invited and welcomed guest. At night, as I tried to sleep, lazy conversations held on front steps floated to my room. I listened to the plaintive tune of the lone black saxophonist, echoing up the avenue. The voices of children and yelping dogs. And the boys who lived across the street.

Most of the boys lived in the old prewar building where the drug dealers were. I knew the drug dealers because they were the ones who'd had their buzzers disconnected. They hung out of windows, clutching bathrobes shut, gold chains dangling from their hairy chests and a sultry woman on their arm, as they dropped keys down to prospective customers after taking a good look at them from above.

The boys who lived in that building or in others up and down the street came from mostly poor or Hispanic families that had been there before the neighborhood changed. They always congregated on the steps of the old red brick building across the street. They'd been in grammar school when I moved in and I'd learned their names because they were always being shouted in the street.

There was Thaddeus and Norm, two very blond boys whose mother often sat on the front stoop, drinking beer and telling them to "Shut the fuck up." And then there was a kid the boys called Zebra because his father was the black saxophonist and his mother was white and probably a junkie. Zebra had a baby sister named Samantha—an almost white child with her father's kinky black hair and dark sad eyes—and Zebra spent his nights sitting on the front stoop, bouncing Samantha on his knee, while his parents battled or made love inside, either of which could be heard from the street. There was Fatso who had a ponytail and a dirt bike but who wasn't so fat since he'd begun to grow. And there was Alex. He was of Eastern European descent and more worldly, it seemed, than the others. Already there was a swagger to his walk, a dourness in his face. He seemed assured of his good looks, his strong build, and the power he exerted over the others.

This was the summer when the boys shifted from their skateboards and dirt bikes to cigarettes and bottles clutched in paper bags and when every other word was an unspeakable curse from their mouths, rising to my window. It was the first summer of my life when I came home with an ache to my bones. I'd rub my temples and put up my feet. I was often too tired to cook and so I'd order in or go to the corner for a sandwich and a beer and then turn on the news to drown out the impinging sound of the city.

I don't know when it was, but sometime during the heat of July the boys made the shift from the front of their building to the front of mine. I'd come home and find them already beginning to gather there, like starlings at dusk. I didn't think much about it at first, but it wasn't long before the boys were there every night.

Madeline came and went at odd hours and this disturbed me. Because it was hot, I had moved to summer quarters—the sofa bed in the living room which was near the air conditioner—and I could hear her opening and slamming her door. She always let it bang too hard as if she were having a fight with someone. Sometimes I thought I smelled her perfume, wafting down the hall. I heard the click of her heels and imagined her, dining in all-night restaurants, with complex actors and influential producers, while I sat home.

Late one evening, just after her door slammed, Zachary phoned. He had been drinking in a bar, watching Monday Night Football. "Hi, A, this is Z." It was what he always said and I used to think it was rather sweet, but that evening it sounded foolish and I felt annoyed with him.

"My name is Angela," I said.

"I just wanted to see how you are doing. I miss you."

"Where are you? What do you want?"

"I want to come over."

In the background I heard the sound of men, applauding some play that had just taken place on the field. I used to dread Monday nights during football season because Zachary would for once forget about time and wander off into the void of maleness—of sports bars and phones unanswered, of beer and shouts. I used to think, "If I die on a Monday night, how will he know?" Or when we were thinking about having a child, "If I go into labor on a Monday night, would he wait until halftime to get me to the hospital?"

"What d'ya think?" his voice warm and somewhat breathless. "I miss you."

"You're drunk," I said. "Tonight you miss me."

"The Bears are winning."

"Don't call unless you've got something concrete to say," and I hung up.

Then I turned off all the lights in my apartment and rested my head in my hands. I'm not sure how long I sat before I heard a sound. It was like a hooting, or a cry. Slowly I lifted my blind and peered into the street.

They were in front of the building, a half-dozen or more. They had cigarettes in their mouths and beer cans, stripped of their brown paper bags and brazenly naked to the world. Thaddeus and Zebra were tossing a football and Fatso was on his bike. But Alex just leaned back, arms resting on the railing. Their hooting grew louder, but I couldn't distinguish their cry. Then Alex looked up and saw me, peering through my blinds. He winked, I thought, as if to taunt me, and motioned two of the boys inside.

The buzzers were right below my bed and I could hear the ringing. Madeline's disembodied voice came shouting through my floor. "Who is it?" she called. "Who's there?" I watched the boys scattering, racing into the night.

The man who lived with the cannibal tribe was back from an expedition and returned my calls. He told me how the women put spikes into their faces to look like jaguars, how they crawled into his hammock at night, their bony spikes sticking out of their faces. "One night," he said, "they sent me an eight-year-old girl. I had to go to the chief and explain that in my culture we don't do this with eight-year-old girls. I went back to sleep and they sent me her grandmother. I mean, this woman was an ancient jungle woman built like a ton of bricks. Her hair looked like a doormat and she smelled like she bathed in a sewer."

I listened to all this, amazed, and couldn't get it out of my mind that night as I sat, watching a movie, when the buzzer rang. "Hello," I shouted. "Hello. Hello," I heard a man call back. "Is that you?" I said. "Yes, it's me." It was Zachary, I thought, and unsure of why I was doing this, I buzzed him in. It took a moment to realize that the tall, swarthy young man who stood in the hall was not Zachary. "What do you want?" I asked.

It was Alex from across the way and he looked at me oddly. "I think I made a mistake," he said.

He was perhaps sixteen, but he had a look in his eye, a sharp, piercing look, the way Superman used to look through steel, that startled me. I opened the door wide. "It's all right," I said, leaning against the molding. "Can I help you?"

"No," he said, peering down the hall at Madeline's apartment, "I'm looking for her."

I closed the door and settled back into an evening of television. But an hour later Madeline knocked. She was dressed up in a pink angora sweater and pink heels. She smelled of French perfume and hairspray. "You look nice," I said, never having seen her dressed up before.

"Have you seen my cat?" she asked.

I shook my head, then looked at her more closely; she seemed weary to me. "Are you all right?" I said.

She sighed, gazing up the stairs for Katmandu. "The writers are having trouble with my character. They want me to reveal my secret."

"So, why don't you?"

"No one knows what it is. The writer who originally wrote my part has gone to another soap and won't tell anyone what he had in mind and no one can come up with anything they like. I may have to run away again which means I'll be out of work. . . ." Her voice trailed off.

"I'll help you find your cat," I said.

Together we ran up and down the stairs, until we located Katmandu on the ledge in Mr. Nicolysen's single room on the top floor. Mr. Nicolysen, a drunk and a bookie, was asleep on his bed and Katmandu sat complacently on his ledge, catching the breeze.

We dropped the cat off and I invited Madeline in for a drink. She lit up a cigarette. "Do you mind?" she asked. In truth I did, but I liked the way the smoke encircled her in her pink angora, like a halo, I thought, though there was nothing about her that struck me as being angelic. She stood by the window, smoking, and it was not long before the boys assembled. I don't know where they came from or how they got there, but there they were below my window. In the dim light of the apartment Madeline looked down and I thought I saw her smile.

The man who lived with the cannibal tribe asked me out to dinner. I didn't really want to go, but he called at six o'clock on a Friday night and said, "I don't know if you've got plans and I know this is kind of last minute, but if you're free, I'd love to take you to this little African place I know down in the Village."

It was my mother's idea for me to circulate. "You can't just sit home, waiting for Zachary to decide what he wants to do."

"I'm not waiting for Zachary, Mom."

"Yes, you are. I'm your mother. You can't hide anything from me."

Of course, I'd hidden many things from my mother. I'd hidden the time when my father crawled into bed with me. He didn't touch me or seem to want anything, except company. He cried softly into the pillow, then fell asleep. I stayed awake for hours, watching him, then kicked him hard as the sun was coming up. I'd hidden from her how once I was old enough I snuck out of the house at night, and how when I was fifteen I'd lost my virginity to the local gas station attendant in the back of his car, his fingernails black with monkey grease. All this I'd hidden from her and more.

In the African restaurant, we sat on the floor and scooped the food up with our hands. His name was Arthur. He was Jewish like me, from Brooklyn, and I found it difficult to believe that a Jewish man from Brooklyn could live with a savage tribe. After dinner Arthur swept me into his arms as we walked down Varick Street. When he kissed me, I smelled meat on his lips. His mouth had an oily taste and I struggled to push him away.

When I got home, Madeline's door was open and I knew she was waiting for me. "My husband is getting impatient for me to reveal my secret." The corners of her mouth shaking as she spoke. It took me a moment to realize she was talking about the part she played and not her real life.

"Why don't you just make something up?" I sat down on the couch beside her. "You know, it could be something dumb like you're the kept woman of a chieftain. Or maybe you've fallen in love with a white man who was passing through. . . ," thinking how Arthur would be perfect for that role.

"They're going to write me out." She shook her head forlornly. "Have me disappear. Then I'll need a new job."

That night was amateur night at P&G's and I went alone, something I haven't done since before I was married. I sat at the bar, drinking vodka, smiling back at men who smiled at me while would-be comedians and singers vied for applause. I didn't want to be alone and for the first time in months I longed for Zachary, longed to have him in bed, not because I really wanted him, but because no one had been in my bed in so long. But soon I began to feel tired, so I headed home.

The redolent smell of incense came from Madeline's apartment and I heard Tibetan bells. When I knocked, she came out, looking misty-eyed.

"Maybe it should be something less obvious," I said.

"What?" she asked, bewildered.

"Your secret. Maybe the jungle is calling you back. Like it's gotten into your skin and now you're a wild thing."

She gazed at me intently, then seemed to dismiss what I was saying. "Interesting," she said, wandering back inside, "but how do you play that out on an afternoon soap?"

In August a terrible heat wave came upon us—the kind that makes the city slow down and the streets stink—and Madeline was written out of the script. The day she collected her first unemployment check, a tired-looking man who carried sheet music in one hand and a small electric piano in the other began to appear. He played scales or Broadway songs like "Hello, Young Lovers" or "Oh What a Beautiful Morning" as Madeline tried to carry a tune. Her raspy voice strained for the high notes and I'd put on background music to drown her out.

One weekend I went to see my sister on Staten Island in order to escape the heat which I only managed to do slightly on the ferry across. It took two hours to get home. On the subway I thought I'd faint. When I reached my building, the street was cordoned off and the bomb squad was there.

It had happened before when threats were made on the drug dealers and the bomb squad was called. But this time the neighbors told me there was a paper bag in the place where the phone tip said it would be. The bomb squad detectors hadn't given definitive word and now they were awaiting the arrival of the bomb squad dog.

The boys were all out on my side of the rope and Madeline was on the other side. They were laughing and waving at her and she kept waving back at them. She wore a thin, red halter top. Her body seemed to glisten with sweat and she twirled like a gypsy as they whistled, calling her name.

I was distracted by the arrival of the brown-and-white dog which the police led into the building with much fanfare and by the applause that accompanied him. But when I turned back, I saw the boys were now on Madeline's side of the rope. They were playing a kind of adolescent blindman's bluff, each one passing her to the other, hands around her waist. In some arms such as Alex's she lingered. Some held her for a long time. Others tried to move their hands up around her ribs, but with a playful laugh she pushed them away. I found myself disgusted, yet intrigued at the same time, for there was something about Madeline that made me think of a doll, the kind I liked to dress and undress when I was a girl.

Eventually the dog emerged and the policemen declared the bag to contain a sandwich. The cordon was removed and I could make my way home, dodging past Madeline as she taunted the boys.

Later that evening when I went out for the paper, I saw eight pairs of shoes lined up in the hall. I put my ear to her door. Music was playing loudly, but other than that, I couldn't hear a sound.

My mother called from Arizona. "This is a great place to grow old. You should come out here," she said.

"Not yet, Ma," I told her. "I'm too young to die."

"It's beautiful here," my mother said. "These giant cactus with flowers you can gaze into for days."

"Not yet, Mom. Not now."

I woke that night to the sound of shattering glass. Pulling open the blinds, I saw a naked man, blood flowing from his wrists, standing in the frame of the fifth-floor window he had just knocked out. This dejected lover, arms outstretched, shouted "Bruce, Bruce" in mournful cries. I was struck by his nakedness, by his elegant, taut lines. Though I prayed he would not jump, I could not take my eyes away. I watched as the police arrived with a straightjacket, forcing him into their car, but his cries stayed with me into the night, well after the sound of the siren which drove him off was gone. I found myself hugging my own body, staring at the window where the naked man had stood.

I don't know how long I'd been sitting there when I saw Alex walk out of his building. He lit a cigarette, took a few drags, then crossed the street. He paused in front of our building. Next I saw him glance up at my window, then head inside. When my buzzer rang, I sat still, thinking how he couldn't have made the same mistake twice. How surely this time he'd come for me. I waited until the buzzer rang again. Then I pulled on blue jeans and a T-shirt, and went downstairs.

Alex stood, cigarette in hand, leaning against the glass door, buzzing my buzzer. When he saw me coming, he looked surprised.

"What do you want?" I said, the glass between us. "Tell me. What do you want?"

He looked at me, then at the buzzer, then shook his head foolishly, as if he himself couldn't believe he'd done this again. "Not you," he said, bringing the cigarette to his lips, "I don't want you."

"Are you sure you don't want me?" I asked, resting my body against my side of the glass.

"I'm sure," he said with a smirk.

"Then don't buzz me," I said. "If you don't want me, don't buzz me." Shouting now, I saw my face, staring back at me in the reflection, and I thought how I hardly recognized myself anymore.

I turned and slowly began to make my way up the stairs. There on the wall I saw, flickering, the shadow of the old woman who lived for forty years in the apartment with the green wall. Her long fingers beckoned. She wants to feed me more soup, I said to myself.

Instead Madeline appeared, robe around her, hair pulled off her face. "What's going on?"

"They want you," I said. "Go to them." I offered her as if she were a goat to be sacrificed.

"It's not my fault," she said.

"Tell them that," I replied.

I went inside my rooms and looked around. The ceiling paint was chipping and there was a shabbiness to the furniture. Already I'd been there longer than I ever thought I would.

It was not long afterwards that Zachary and I reconciled and moved to Prospect Park. I knew it was a mistake from the start, because nothing was any different than it had been before. After a decade of futile efforts, two children, and finally divorce, I got a good deal on a two-bedroom in the old neighborhood where I'd lived when I was first married. Zachary provided somewhat for the children, but I had to return to work full-time for a magazine I didn't like that specialized in fitness and health.

It was odd going back because I'd moved away so long ago, but not much had changed. The drug dealers still seemed to live in the building across the street and I could still shop at Fairway and D'Agostino's, which I usually did early in the morning so I could come straight home from work. But one day I got a late start and had to do my shopping in the evening. I went to International because the other stores were too crowded and stood in line, exhausted, with my cart of veal chops, frozen green beans, and Spaghetti-Os.

I didn't notice the checkout boy as he packed my things and then gazed into my eyes. "Delivery?" he asked.

"No, I can carry it," I said.

He looked at the groceries as if he doubted this, then straight at me. His wavy hair was thin now, his boyish looks gone. He was a bit on the heavy side and I saw that he had not aged well. That piercing look in his dark eyes was dulled. "Don't I know you?" he said, pulling himself up to his full height. "Haven't I seen you somewhere before?"

"I don't think so."

But even as he packed Fruit Loops and Cheez Doodles into a brown paper bag, he couldn't take his eyes off of me. Then it came to him and he leaned his face close against mine. "Madeline," he whispered, his breath blowing hot against my cheeks. "You're Madeline."

I looked at him as he tried to grow bigger, like a tire being pumped with air. "That's right," I said, breathing back into his face, taking the bag from his hands. "I am."

The Fantasy

by Nancy Butcher

From across the street Stella watches his window, the way the streetlights shimmer on the vertical blinds. The blinds are swaying a little—gently, sporadically, like the motion of wind chimes in a breeze. She can see his living room: the dusky glow thrown by a single table lamp, the shadowy walls, the edge of a couch. And then, she sees him. He is walking into the room, approaching the window. He opens it and leans out, then lights a cigarette. Its tip burns orange in the darkness.

Stella watches a moment longer, then gets her keys and coat and goes outside. In front of his apartment building, she waits; when she spots an old man coming out of the elevator in the lobby and hurrying toward the exit, she rushes in, smiles at him without meeting his eyes, lets him hold the security door open for her. Then she gets in the elevator and presses 5.

Once on the fifth floor Stella turns right and follows the wine-colored corridor to the last apartment. A sign on the door reads 5B, McCALL. She knocks, and listens. A record is turned down; the door is opened.

"Yes?" His hair is tousled, his dark eyes express irritation. He is taller than she imagined him.

Stella raises a hand to her mouth. "Oh, I must have the wrong apartment."

He looks at her curiously. "Who are you looking for?"

"Someone in 5B."

"This *is* 5B. Have you got the right building? Four twenty-five?"

She fumbles in her coat pocket, produces a piece of paper, and stares at it. "I think I'm supposed to be at four twenty-six. Listen, I'm terribly sorry." She turns to go.

"Wait."

She pauses, and glances at him, her blue eyes wide.

He shrugs. "Nothing. It's just that you look familiar."

"Oh." Stella smiles slightly, waiting to see if he will go on. He doesn't. "Well, good night. I'm sorry to have bothered you."

"It's okay."

The door closes softly behind her. The record is turned up again: a Billie Holiday song.

When she gets home, her boyfriend Jamie is there, sitting on the couch and watching television. He looks up and smiles at her, and asks her how her day was.

"Fine," she says, and as she leans over to kiss him, she notices out of the corner of her eye that he has shut the blinds.

In her fantasy, McCall is an artist. He is intensely solitary; his days consist of work and occasional walks along the river, and his nights, more work, then restless sleep. He has a few friends whom he sees, rarely, between projects. There are no women in his life—he claims that love affairs are distracting, bad for his art—but the truth is rather that he cannot stand the thought of being touched too deeply, of being too fascinated, too obsessed. Which is why she knows he is feeling slightly unsettled right now, thinking about the woman who showed up at his door. He is lying in bed, smoking in the dark, imagining her—her tall, reed-thin body, her red hair—with great curiosity, and, to his displeasure, the beginnings of a familiar, fatal ache. He is also feeling foolish, because he realizes he will probably never see her again. Of course, Stella knows better.

Like him, she is lying in bed, smoking in the dark—quietly, so as not to wake Jamie. She watches the smoke rings drift up, and dissipate, somewhere above their heads. She knows Jamie has no idea what she is up to lately, and it is just as well. As far as he is concerned, he is the only man she ever thinks about.

Ironically, it was Jamie who first brought McCall to her attention. It happened one Sunday, several months ago, when he and Stella were in the living room reading the paper.

"See that guy?" he said suddenly.

"What guy?"

Jamie pointed to a window across the street, and the man leaning out of it, smoking.

"Him. He does that every day, about four or five times a day. He must be a gigolo or something, being home all the time like that, always hanging out of the window as if he's waiting for someone."

Stella laughed. "You're home almost all the time, and you're not a gigolo. Unless there's something you haven't told me." Putting the paper aside, she craned her neck to see the man better. Even from a distance, she could tell that he was handsome: disheveled dark hair, no shirt, brooding face.

"I really think he is. You know, rich old women and all that," Jamie persisted.

"You have an overactive imagination," she told him, and turned back to the paper. A few seconds later, when she looked up again, the man was gone.

Jamie never brought him up again. Neither did Stella. In fact, she forgot about him for several weeks, until one evening when she was at home alone and happened to see him. His blinds were half-open, and his apartment was dimly lit; she could see him moving around, agitatedly, as if he were looking for something. She watched him get on the phone and talk for several minutes, gesturing furiously with his cigarette, then hang up and begin to move around again.

She continued to watch him for the next hour or so. It occurred to her that what she was doing—observing him as she was—was not quite right, but the thought only seemed to lend the entire matter an aura of excitement, of mystery, and to make it all the more interesting. In fact, everything seemed more interesting suddenly: the evening, the sounds from the street—even the thought of Jamie coming home. It was not just the man's attractiveness; it was the whole idea of watching him, imagining things about him, imagining that there was somehow a connection between him and her.

That was when the fantasy began to grow in her mind.

At first, it was just the cigarette breaks.

Stella figured out quickly that there was a schedule of sorts: short ones at ten A.M. and three, then longer ones at night, at around six and eleven. They were always the same—McCall would come to the window without a shirt and stand there, staring at nothing in particular, a cigarette between his lips. Stella liked to catch him at these times whenever she was at home. The view was perfect; there were no blinds to get in the way.

But the cigarette breaks offered her more than the chance to watch him unobstructed. They told her—in their very regularity, in the way he leaned so broodingly out the window—that he was lonely, full of unspoken desires. In this, she felt a powerful kinship with him, a bond stronger than anything she had with Jamie. She, too, was lonely; she, too, had unspoken desires.

For what was her life? A part-time job at a bank, working as a secretary to a fat, surly man who smelled of onions, and then home to Jamie. There was nothing wrong with Jamie, of course, but it seemed to her that the romance had gone out of their relationship a long time ago. McCall was different—not simply because he was new and unfamiliar, but because of the way their lives, his life and hers, were merging. It was destiny: their two windows directly across from each other on a busy street.

As the weeks went on she found herself watching him more and more, not just during his cigarette breaks but the times in between, whenever she wasn't at work or otherwise occupied. She would sit on the living room couch—with a magazine in her lap, for Jamie's sake—and follow McCall's movements around his apartment. She would note when he turned a light on or off, or opened or closed his blinds, and attempt to imagine what he was doing, immerse herself in the rhythm of his day.

For a while, she was content with this routine. She liked to imagine that at some point, McCall would notice her presence and begin staring back—very surreptitiously at first, then more openly, then for longer periods—until finally, neither one of them would be able to deny that something was happening.

She even had a scenario for how they would meet. After staring at her for a few weeks, McCall would get the idea to hold his cordless phone out the window and gesture to her to give him her number. She would laugh—they would laugh together, silently, across the great expanse of street between their two buildings—and then she would oblige him, tracing figures in the air with her fingers.

But then last night, while she was sitting on the living room couch watching him, she was seized by another, even better scenario: to go to his apartment. She knew that he was on the fifth floor, on the northwest corner; she could simply show up and pretend to be at the wrong place. It seemed far more interesting than just sitting around waiting for him to notice her; and at the very least, it would be a harmless adventure.

It proved to be the turning point in Stella's fantasy.

"What are you looking at?"

"What?" Stella turns, abruptly, from the window. Jamie is standing in the doorway with his hands in his pockets. "Nothing, really. Some man almost got in an accident in the intersection."

"Oh."

Stella goes to the couch and sits down, picks up a magazine. "I thought you were working."

"I was, but I got stuck. I thought I might go out for a walk." Jamie glances at the window. "So how is he?"

Her eyes widen. "Who?"

"The man. The man who was almost in the accident."

"Oh. Fine, I suppose. I mean, there wasn't any accident, after all." Stella pauses, then looks expectantly at Jamie. "Do you want company?"

"No, I think I'd rather go alone. I need to mull over this piece I'm writing."

"Oh, sure." She smiles at him, but he is already on his way out the door. It closes softly behind him.

Stella gets up immediately and begins pacing anxiously. She has not seen McCall since her visit to his apartment last night; he skipped his ten and three o'clock cigarette breaks. She sits down on the couch, stands up, then sits down again. She picks up a magazine and stares at it.

Then, around four o'clock, she notices a shadow across the street. It is McCall, moving around.

Stella gets up and rushes to the window. McCall has turned on a tiny light; he is searching for something. Then he puts on a coat and turns off the light, and his apartment is still and dark once more.

The same impulse that made Stella go to his apartment drives her now to follow him, and in a matter of seconds, she is out the door. Once in the street, she spots him immediately; he is coming out of his building wearing a black coat. He begins to walk briskly down the street, toward the river.

He does not turn around, so he never notices her. Once at the river, he pauses at the railing, looks over, and lights a cigarette.

Stella steps behind a nearby tree and regards his profile, his dark eyes. The scenario seems nearly complete to her, but at the same time she is filled with the terrible temptation to do more—to go forward, perhaps, and speak to him. Up until lately, she has tried to avoid letting her fantasy become too real—she knows that fantasy has a way of turning mundane, or ugly, when it encounters reality—and yet, standing so close to him, having come this far, she feels excited by the possibilities of the situation. She feels powerful, too, because with every thought or action she is pushing the fantasy further and further to its limit.

But before she has a chance to do anything, she sees a figure coming from the opposite direction, walking along the river. It is Jamie. Stella realizes in horror that he will notice her at any minute, and break the spell—or he will recognize McCall, and somehow put two and two together or jump to some wild conclusion, and make a scene. She searches furiously for a way out of her dilemma; in the meantime, Jamie is coming closer and closer in her direction.

But he doesn't notice her at all. Instead, he stops when he reaches McCall. He leans against the railing next to him, and they begin to speak.

Stella feels as if she has stepped into a bad dream. She watches, pale and trembling, as the two men talk to each other in hushed, familiar voices. She cannot hear much, but once or twice she hears what sounds like her name. Then she watches Jamie reach out and caress McCall's face, very gently.

As if in a trance, Stella comes out from behind the tree. McCall is the first to see her, but she does not see him at all. In fact, when Jamie finally notices her, her gaze fixes on his, and for a moment he is the only clear thing in her field of vision. Everything else—McCall, the river, the trees, the street—seems to recede, blurry and fantastic, into the background, until the only reality left is the shock in Jamie's eyes.

Jealousy

by Iris Litt

I try not to think
of what they are doing now
and, whatever it is, of why
he is doing it with her
instead of me
and I try not to remember
what it was like
when he did do it with me

but the mind insists
on remembering
what was delicious
and, after the memory,
begging for another taste.
I tell my mind every time
that it is all grown up now
and when it asks for him
the answer is No
and when it asks Why
I say, Because I said so.

Survival in the Wilderness

by Molly Giles

T he minute Henry left the house, Sherry began to go through his things. She knew it was wrong. She knew if Henry walked back in and found her naked on her hands and knees peering under his mattress she'd die. What could she say? Oh hi, honey, I just lost an earring? That wouldn't work. Henry was too observant for that. He'd see at once that both her earrings were firmly affixed to both burning ears. He'd see she was lying. He'd see she was spying. He'd see that the girl he thought he'd left sweetly asleep in his bed— the girl he thought was so "nice" and "bright" and "funny"—was not the real girl at all, but a fake.

And then he'd break off with her. Because Henry believed in trust. Without trust, Henry often said, there is nothing. And Sherry agreed. She had no trust and she often felt nothing. She slid down on her belly and groped under the bed. Oh hi, hon, she would say, if he burst back through the door. Just looking for something to read. Like your diary.

If Henry kept a diary, though, he didn't keep it under his bed. Sherry struggled up, rocked back on her heels, and studied the stash she'd retrieved: a hiking boot, a compass, a vitamin-C pill and a handful of grey flattened popcorn. She frowned at the popcorn. Would a man, by himself, eat popcorn in bed? Henry had never eaten popcorn in bed with her; did this mean (as she feared) he was seeing someone else? She only knew what he told her. He'd told her he was a simple man with simple tastes who had "strong feelings" for her but liked "doing things"—camping, hiking, sailing—on his own, and that sounded fine, on the surface, but they had been together eight months and it seemed to Sherry that the list of "things" had grown, while the "feelings" had not.

It was time to take stock. Sherry tucked her hair behind her ears, shoved

316

the popcorn back under the bed, and stood up. She didn't have much time—Henry had gone to the city to pick up his son and he'd be back in an hour. She had never been alone in his house before; she'd have to move fast. There were backpacks to go through, address books to read, that lavender letter she'd seen lying on top of his desk last night. She pulled on a pair of jeans, plucked one of Henry's plaid flannel shirts off the back of a chair, and buttoned it quickly over her bare skin. It smelled good, like Henry. It felt like Henry hugging her, not that Henry would be hugging her, if he knew what she was doing.

And what was she doing? Nothing, really. Exploring a bit. The same thing Henry told her he was doing when he took off alone with his skis or his kayak. Scouting the territory. Getting a feel for the lay of the land. The old show tune "Getting to Know You" began to whistle softly through Sherry's teeth. She rolled up her sleeves, put on a pair of thick glasses she kept hidden in a pocket of her purse, and set to work.

Henry's house was like Henry himself, dark and rough and riddled with secrets. It was an old hunting lodge in the hills outside the city, high-beamed, small-windowed, built with deep wooden cupboards and window seats that opened. There was a trapdoor leading down to the basement, and a false brick in the fireplace. Henry had made a great show of opening it up for her once. "See," he had said, "I've got nothing to hide." The grimy little crypt had been empty that time but when Sherry reached in this morning the first thing she felt was a knife. A Swiss army knife, a bullet case, a GI Joe doll, a silver dollar, and a cigarette. She sniffed the cigarette: straight tobacco, stale. It must have been put there by Henry's son Sam, who was eight. There was much Sherry didn't know about Henry but one thing she was sure of: he didn't smoke. Nor would he approve if he knew she did. Not that she did that often. Just when she was alone. Cigarettes helped when she was alone. Vodka helped too, as did Valium, romance novels, chocolate cherry ice cream, crying jags, shopping sprees, and her ancient, trusty, battery-operated vibrator.

Dog, Henry's dove, cooed from the rafters and flapped his dirty white wings and Sherry glanced up and shivered. What if Dog tried to land on her shoulder? He did that sometimes when Henry was home, and she always pretended it didn't scare her, pretended even to like the sharp strong beak an inch from her eyes, the claws tangled in the ends of her hair. "Nature Girl," Henry called her fondly, as she stood there, stricken. "It's just amazing to me the way Dog's taken to you. He doesn't usually like my friends."

What "friends"? Sherry thought. If only Dog were a useful bird, like a mynah, or a parrot, maybe he could tell her the things she needed to know. Who was her rival? What was she like? Was she better than Sherry? Of course she was! She would not be divorced, as Sherry was, and going to law school, as Sherry was; she would not be in debt, distracted, dieting, or despondent, as Sherry so often was. This new girl would be one of those calm, clear-eyed goddesses who baked bread and looked sexy even in Birkenstocks. She would truly enjoy the things Henry enjoyed—the white-water rafting which scared

Sherry speechless, the cross-country skiing which left her limping for days, the long motorcycle rides which she endured with her eyes closed.

She stared hard at the bird. "Don't come near or I'll kill you," she warned. Her voice wavered but Dog seemed to obey her; he flexed his snaky neck and flew to a rafter on the opposite side of the room. Sherry waited until she saw him settle, then quickly reviewed the contents of the mantel: the framed photo of Sam, fishing, the photo of Henry, fishing, the set of deer antlers, the Indian basket filled with matchbooks. Most of the matchbooks came from Thai restaurants and sushi bars Sherry had been to herself, with Henry, but some—Club ChiChi? what was Club ChiChi? a strip joint?—made her heart stop. She didn't want Henry at a strip joint. She didn't want Henry anywhere but right here, with her, where he belonged. When he was with her she felt solid and sturdy and unafraid; it was only when he was gone that she panicked. Henry was so handsome, so good, so sweet and so trusting—any woman would want him. Half the time he didn't even notice how women lit up when they saw him. But Sherry did, Sherry saw it happen all the time. "Why would I want someone else," Henry had soothed her, "when I can scarcely handle you?" He'd laughed his big laugh then and added, "The fact is, most women sort of scare me. They're too needy. Too dependent. Not you. You're . . . I don't know . . . well balanced."

The phone rang and Sherry jumped, almost screamed, then reached for it, pressing it first to her heart as she took a deep breath. "MacKay residence," she said, forcing a loud and languorous yawn. The voice on the other end was young, too young to scare anyone. "This is Jasmine," it said. "From Sporting Life. Would you tell Henry that the collapsible fly rod he ordered just came in?" Sherry nodded, mute with relief, and then thought: *Just* came in? On a Sunday morning at ten-fifteen? The girl hung up before she could question her, and Sherry, frowning, reached for the memo pad. There was already one name on the pad. Rochelle. Who the hell was Rochelle? A dancer at the ChiChi Club? Sherry scrawled "collapsible fly rod," drew a quick, unsuccessful sketch of a fishing pole protruding from a man's fly, wadded the sketch up, and threw it into the wastepaper basket. Then she knelt by the basket and went through it. Used tissues, bottle caps, an empty box of cold tablets. No lipsticks, no tampons, no sign of Rochelle or what's-her-name. Jasmine.

She rocked back on bare heels, reached up, switched the answering machine to play-back, and stared across the room at the rolltop desk. Two drawers, two cubbyholes, and, somewhere in the mess of mail on top, that lavender letter she'd seen last night while she was pouring a brandy for Henry's sore throat. It had been a hard letter to miss: big, splashy, richly perfumed, addressed in loopy purple ink with a drawing of a rose where the return address should be.

She started to walk toward the desk on her knees, but froze as the answering machine began. First there was Henry's voice, deep and slow. Just listening to him calmed her. "Gone fishin'," his voice said. "But I'll catch you later." Sherry nodded, wiped her sweaty palms on her thighs, reached for the stack of mail, then paused. It's wrong to read someone's mail, she told herself; I'll wait and hear his messages first. Henry's voice beeped off and a woman's voice came on. Sherry grimaced, lifting her face to listen as the light lisping prattle filled the room. Her grimace deepened as she recognized the words. It was her. Her own awful voice. "I hope your big bad cold is all better, hon," she was saying—imagine a grown woman talking like that!—"but if it's not it will be soon, 'cause I'm making you a pot of my grandma's special magic chicken soup, guaranteed to cure what ails you."

What crap, Sherry thought. Her grandmother had never made a pot of soup in her life. But that deli downtown did a pretty decent job; all you had to add was a handful of parsley and a few tiny bones to make the stuff look authentic. Henry had eaten three bowls and his cold had cleared up. Sort of. Not enough to permit him to kiss her good-bye when he left this morning. She narrowed her eyes, trying to remember the last time Henry had actually kissed her, one of those long soul kisses that used to make her gulp and shiver with thanks. It must have been about the same time she had had an actual unfaked orgasm. How many had she faked the last time they'd made love? Four? Five? She couldn't remember. She bowed her head and waited for the tape to end, relieved when her baby voice finally babbled its bye-byes. There were, suspiciously, no more messages on the tape; Henry must have erased them.

She craned her neck and looked up at the desk. I'll do the drawers first, she decided. She tugged at the bottom drawer—it was crammed with receipts, credit card carbons, tax records and bank statements, all shoved in together. The thought of looking through all these frail, dimly printed papers for evidence of infidelity dismayed her. She reached for the top drawer—it was full of rocks. Big grey dirty rocks.

She rubbed her neck and stood up. Coffee, she thought. Coffee first, to give me strength for that lavender letter.

She turned the lights on in Henry's small kitchen, filled his coffeemaker, and plugged it in. While she was waiting she leafed through the entries on his Endangered Species calendar on the wall: nothing there but clinic appointments for his cold at the local health center. She checked the drain board—one cup, one plate, one fork—and poked through the plastic bucket Henry kept under the sink for compost: carrot scrapings, eggshells, apple cores. Suddenly she froze. Am I crazy? she thought.

She stood up and pushed her hair back with her arm. Henry had given her no reason to doubt him. He was attentive and affectionate when he was with her, and if he wasn't with her all the time—well, what of it? "You ruin everything," her ex-husband had said, "with your sick suspicions." "You can't hold on to people," her best friend had said, "against their will." "You need to trust more," lover after lover had told her. But lover after lover had left, and her ex-husband had just married her best friend, and if she "sabotaged relationships"—one of her roommates had said that once—well, weren't they ripe for sabotage? "You've had some bad breaks," her last therapist had agreed,

Molly Giles · 319

just before he killed himself, "but that's no reason to think everyone is going to abandon you. Learn to open up."

I will, Sherry thought. She pushed the garbage back under the sink and wiped her hands on her jeans. I'll just open up that lavender letter and then I'll open up myself.

She poured a cup of coffee and carried it back toward the rolltop desk. "Scat," she said shakily to Dog, who was perched on the top. "Scat, scat," she repeated, flapping one hand. Dog rose to the rafters, preened, and chuckled eerily as Sherry stared down at the mail. There was a huge stack of letters. Sierra Club. Greenpeace. Wilderness Society. Jacques Cousteau. Elizabeth Spumoni. Elizabeth who? Sherry plucked that one out and set it aside. Save the Mountain Lion. Save the Condor. Save the Spotted Owl. Nona White. Nona what? Sherry pulled Nona and set her next to Elizabeth. Friends of the Redwoods. Friends of the River. Friends of the Rainforest. Fredrica F. Hamsun.

She pushed her coffee cup back, pressed her palms together, bent her head, and opened Elizabeth's letter first. Not bad. A request for funds for the new natural history museum. Nona next. A thank-you for the canoe paddle Henry had loaned her and her husband for their trip to Oregon. Fredrica last: an invitation to a party two weeks ago, with a map, and a "Hope you can come," which Henry must have ignored, because she'd been with him that weekend, they'd gone camping with Sam.

Sherry took a deep breath and looked up from the letters. Henry hung prisms in his windows and they caught the morning sun, throwing pretty bursts of rainbows here and there over the dark disordered rooms. She exhaled, relieved. There's no one else, she thought. He's just had a cold. He's needed to be alone. He hasn't felt like making love. That's normal. That happens. It doesn't mean he's going to leave me. She stacked the letters and pushed them back. Then she realized that something was missing. Something important: the lavender letter. Her heart began to race and she could hear her own breathing, light and quick. Where was that letter?

Could Henry have taken it with him this morning? On the way out the door could he have skimmed it off the top of the desk? Why? Did he think she might read it? What sort of person did he think she was?

She put her face in her hands. A rank tangy odor rose from her palms, an odor of house dust and garbage. Looking for dirt makes you dirty—who'd told her that? Her ex-husband? One of her ex-lovers? She pressed her hands even closer to her lids, pressed so hard that a dark boggy murk seeped into her skull. Sometimes she thought that if she were ever to do what they all told her to do— if she were ever to "let go" and "open up"—she would reveal in herself a landscape so barren, so bleak, that no one, nothing, in the world could love her. A cold marsh with salt pools and weeds and wolves roaming through it—that was her, the real her. Maybe it was the real everyone. How would she know? All she knew was that she lived there, afraid, most of the time, and no one lived with her.

She shook her head, to clear it, and brushed her fingers against the front of Henry's plaid shirt, to clean them. She felt a lump in one pocket. Curious, she plunged her hand in and fished out four packets. They were plastic-coated, for honey, or mustard, or catsup—Henry was always picking up free things from restaurants—only these were flesh-colored and had the word PRIME written on the outside. Medicine? For his cold? Some sort of salve? A lubri . . . ? Oh, Sherry thought. She sat very still. Condoms, she thought. She'd seen plenty of condoms; she had some herself, in her purse at this moment. It was just that she'd never expected to use them with Henry. She and Henry had an understanding. She understood that he'd always been "careful" and he understood that she had been celibate since her divorce—a lie, but that was what he believed; that was what she had told him.

So the condoms were for someone else.

She waited for the rush of satisfaction to break over her—I was right! I was right!—but all she felt was a slight gassy headache and a numb tangled pain behind her right eye. Stoic, she reached in the other pocket and pulled out a small spiral notebook. She stared at the cover. There, in Henry's big block print, were the words "Survival in the Wilderness." She opened the book. "When lost in snow," she read, "outline your position with bits of bark." She reread the words. They didn't make sense. She turned to the next page. "Never rub frostbite." Was this what Henry thought about when Henry was alone? Hypothermia and snow trench shelters?

She heard the motorcycle outside, jumped up, shoved the notebook back in the pocket, unbuttoned the top buttons of the shirt to get some cleavage, ran her hands through her hair to fluff it out. Bacon! she thought. She dashed into the kitchen, pulled some bacon out of the refrigerator, threw it into a pan, and turned the heat high to get the smell going fast. She took her eyeglasses off, stuck them in an empty knife drawer and checked her face in the toaster for mascara smudge. There was a pot of basil on the windowsill; she tore off a leaf and chewed it quickly to sweeten her breath. Then the front door opened and Sam banged in. He grinned through the kitchen door, a tall, husky, red-lipped boy, already as good-looking as his father.

"We must have driven a hundred miles an hour," he told her. "I think Dad was nervous about leaving you here alone."

"Really?" Sherry handed him a glass of orange juice and patted the top of his head. "I just woke up."

Sam dropped his eyes to her bare feet, which were flecked, she saw, with bits of garbage, and she crossed one over the other while she briskly mixed pancake batter. She heard Henry sneeze as he came through the front room and he sneezed again as he came into the kitchen. How handsome he was! With his hair ruffled from the wind and his cheeks flushed and that big warm smile, how handsome—and how wary! For the first time she noticed that Henry always walked on the balls of his feet, and that he held his elbows high, as if ready to turn and bolt any minute. His quick eyes moved from side to side behind his tinted goggles—surely he could take those off inside the house? She tipped her face up and dimpled.

"Kiss?" she lisped, in that pram-prattle voice. She nestled against him and after a second Henry put his arms around her; she waited until Sam was out of the room and then she laughed and said, "Oops, just a second, there's something in this shirt that's poking me, it hurts, here," and she reached in the pocket and pulled the condoms out, one by one, her expression so perplexed that Henry took off his goggles and started to laugh.

"Oh, sweetie," he said, "do you even know what these are?"

Sherry shook her head.

"They're prophylactics!" Henry said. "I got them at the clinic when I went in for my cold; they were passing them out like toothpicks, free." He dropped his voice. "I thought I'd stick a few in that secret brick for Sam; he can use them for water balloons."

"Just so long as you're not planning to use them yourself," Sherry said, her voice sweet and stern and just a trifle sad.

"Believe me," he said.

"I do," she said, surprised. She did. His arms felt good about her and his heartbeat was solid and steady. In the other room she could see Sam playing with Dog. What a picture they made, the white bird perched on the open hand of the happy child. What a nice world it was, really, or could be. It didn't have to be swamp weeds and wasteland, it could be blue skies and sunlight. She watched as Dog rose from Sam's hand to land on an old arrow quiver Henry had nailed to the wall; she smiled as the bird gave his strange whirring chuckle and pecked at something stuck in the quiver, but her smile tightened and tensed as the bird's beak tore off a long scrap of lavender paper. So that's where he'd put it.

"Something wrong, sweetie?" Henry asked, patting her.

"Not a thing, hon."

"You staggered. You don't feel faint or anything, do you?"

"No. Yes. Just a little. I must be getting your cold. I better lie down. Can you and Sam finish up in the kitchen?"

Henry nodded, led her to the couch, and covered her tenderly with a Navajo blanket. Sherry lay limp and did not open her eyes until she was sure the room was empty. Then she sat up. Darkness deepened within her, the old drumbeat of the hunt. Save me, she thought, as she reached for the letter. Save me, she thought, as she hid it close to her heart.

Ownership

by Jean Marie Ruiz

I've kept men
whose mothers
couldn't afford them,
whose fathers pled guilty
to neglect.
Men who were in love
with their sisters.
Men who never ate fresh fruit
who shaved their chest hair
pierced their eyebrows
and would not explain their scars.
Men who were not paid,
who could only love women
named Yvonne.
Men who could not return
to their homeland.
Men with a terminal illness.

I've given men
false documents and aliases
clean sheets and dark rooms.
I've cut off my hair,
my limbs, my tongue
and had them gift wrapped
for men who never said
thank you.

I've praised their sins
sabotaged their forgiveness
terrorized their art.
I've eaten their genius
like flesh.

I've allowed men
to predict my future
shoot smack in my living room
wear my clothes
and my eyeliner
give me blisters
and bad medicine
serve wine with breakfast
call me by the names of snakes
and abandon me
in the wilderness
without water or air.

Men have written
my autobiography.
I have not told them
this child is yours.
Save her.

The Curse of the Appropriate Man

by Lynn Freed

Half a lifetime of appropriate men can leave a woman parched for adventure. Like someone who has never seen the sea, or heard a foreign language spoken on its native soil. Let other women scan the personals for a DWM, 50s, professional, nondrinker, nonsmoker—this woman wants anything but. She's had it with men who excuse themselves to go to "the little boys' room," "the unmentionable," "where you can't go for me." She's reached the time in her life when she wants a man with a few bad habits. Something unexpected. A wrangler, a wrestler, even a racketeer will do. As for her future, she's got it on hold. For the moment, she wants to be surprised.

And then, one night, at an academic potluck party, she meets a bearded Bavarian in the seventeenth year of his doctoral dissertation. His subject, he tells her, involves the dual fields of ecology and Chinese. For money, he plays the cello on a street corner—tourist stuff—and teaches archery at the local community college. His style of living, he says, is rather unusual. And would she like to come for dinner one night?

She finds her way, as instructed, to a rambling, fake Tudor tenement near the university. It is, she has been told, the victim of a rent control standoff. The garden is overgrown and the doorbells don't work. She must tap out a particular rhythm of knocks to alert the Bavarian of her arrival.

Sure enough, he is at the front door in seconds and leading her into a large hall that is dim and damp and chill. It smells of must and old frying oil. Three or four bicycles are propped and chained to the bannisters. The Bavarian himself is neatly tied and pinned into a waiter's apron. In one hand, he holds a large upholstery needle. "Permit me," he says, "to lead ze vay."

She follows him up two flights of stairs to what must once have been the

325

servants' floor, and then to a door numbered "11"—neither here nor there in her bad luck category.

The room is small and oblong, no larger than a doctor's waiting room. But, with a ceiling almost as high as the room is wide, and a strange arrangement of furniture, it takes time for her to take it all in.

Along one wall is a single bed, disguised into a couch by a good Persian rug and kilim cushions. Above it hangs an enormous wooden bow and a quiver of arrows, a sepia photograph of a bearded soldier in a spiked helmet, and a few strangely shaped knives with ornate handles. A small desk takes up the corner opposite. It holds a gleaming antique typewriter, a few leather-bound books, and a bottle of ink. And, in the center of the room, a card table has been set for two—tablecloth, candles, wine glasses, the lot.

She accepts a glass of wine and is about to sit on the bed when she sees—suspended like a swing by two looped chains—a large piece of driftwood.

"Do you use this for exercise?" she asks, noticing, for the first time, how enormous he is—head and hands and feet, and all that hair.

He shakes his head soberly and lays down the needle, which he has threaded with a thin strip of glistening lard. He comes over, unhooks the swing, and lets it drop. It hangs now just above the outer edge of the bed. In fact, it is more like a ladder than a swing. There are two more struts of driftwood at equal intervals, up to the ceiling.

"Ven I let it down," he explains, "zis is ze bedroom, ja? Ven I hook it back up, like so, it is ze liwing room, ha?" He fixes her with a teacherly smile. "P-sychologically, you see, it is important to delineate."

Suddenly, she is lonely for the old life, for someone who would wonder where she is and come to look for her. But she settles herself onto the couch or bed, hoping that the dinner won't take long.

Bluebeard, however, doesn't even seem to have a kitchen. There's no cooktop, no oven, no spoons or spatulas. Only a tiny nautical fridge under a fold-out ledge on the wall opposite, a copy of The Joy of Cooking propped open to a page she doesn't recognize, and a chopping block on which are laid out two pale and skinless carcasses, the size and shape of miniature rabbits.

"Where do you cook?" she asks.

Without a word, he lifts his face and raises his palms to the ceiling. There, slung up by ropes and pulleys, are a toaster oven, a hot plate, a cello, a music stand, and a wooden chair. He reaches for a winch and winds down the toaster oven, which makes a neat four-point landing on the ledge.

"See?" he says. "My kitchen!"

And then he picks up one tiny carcass and plunges the needle through its flesh, in and out, in and out.

"Are we having rabbit?" she asks.

He smiles. "You can keep a secret?"

"Yes," she says, wondering whether there are laws against killing baby rabbits, and how she could be implicated were she to eat one.

"Sqvuirrel," he says softly.

"What?"

"Zey ver eating my persimmons, so I shot zem. But ze landlord, he vould be werry mad if he found out. He doesn't comprehend ze vay ze ozer half lives."

A few weeks later, dropping off a box of old clothes at the symphony's secondhand shop, she notices a man trying on a pale yellow suit with bell-bottom trousers that stop above the ankles. "Brioni," he announces to her. "Imagine my luck! A thirty-eight long just died and went to heaven. What do you think?"

She thinks that he has lovely hands, cold eyes, a lovely Irish brogue. At the café next door, he tells her that he is writing his sixth novel, none of them published. The cunths in New York, he says, won't consider anything from California. They're into McInerney and Bret Ellis someone. If Dostoyevsky were living now, he'd be selling shoes in Macy's. Forget about writing anything in the past tense. Forget about story.

When he gets to know her better, he calls her a cunth too. "Hello, cunth," he says, or, if he's feeling particularly affectionate, "Hello, you silly old cunth." His two-room apartment is a jumble of books and papers and clothes and bills. Dust and hair and the flimsy skeletons of insects waft here and there around the floor and furniture. Spiders have taken over the corners of everything. Mushrooms grow through cracks in the bathroom floor.

And yet, he will dine off nothing but china, which he also buys at the secondhand store. He will tolerate no stainless steel. He sends her a Valentine's Day card with bows and cherubs. And flowers for every occasion. Holidays make him sentimental. He counts up the months that they have known each other, takes her out for anniversary dinners. She wonders how he can afford such dinners. His means of support are almost invisible. The cunths at the IRS, he has told her, have bled him dry. They have no honor, no decency, no class.

Class, she discovers, is an obsession with him. So is being taken seriously as a suitor. When she comes over, he sweeps the dust under the furniture, puts out a fresh cake of soap, stashes the garbage in the refrigerator to keep the mice away. Some day, he assures her, polishing a wine glass, his ship will come in. She should stick with him, baby, he says, and she'll be farting through silk.

But she doesn't stick. She uses her accumulated mileage to go to Turkey, to Cairo, to Bombay. Far from home she finds that the curse is wearing off. She is tired of tour guides who write her rotten poetry in broken English. Of camel drivers with rotten teeth. Of men with strange smells, no money, and an eye out for a green card. She's running out of money herself. And she is surprised to find herself missing her Irishman. She phones him from Paris to say she is coming back. And buys a black lace garter belt and push-up bra as a joke for the occasion.

At JFK, she runs into an old friend, who has just married a banker and is writing a book on inner sex. Marriage, her friend confides over a drink, allows her to write full-time. It makes her family happy too, and her friends. And, even if the banker won't come to bed without flossing, or putting shoe trees into his shoes—even if he isn't someone to keep in mind when buying one's lingerie—still, he's just a man with a few bad habits. Quite acceptable, once you get over the death of the heart.

Hungry

by Joanna Torrey

When it came to sex, she missed Bill. Sometimes even when it came to mealtimes, although that was rare. Bill liked Greek diners and cuchifritos stands. He would stand on the sidewalk eating rolling dark waves of fried pork skin and pig ears out of a paper bag. Bill didn't know the difference between fine dining and eating to survive. For him, a table was a table, four battered legs and a chipped Formica top. A dish was a dish. He hadn't been interested in food.

Bill built motorcycles. Mostly, he sat at the kitchen table before and after a meal tenderly rubbing small parts of vintage Harleys with a dirty black cloth. He boasted that he would write a cookbook filled with iron-skillet dishes for hungry bachelor men. He ate his grayish layered men's pies with his head down close to his plate, chewing with his mouth a little open, breathing hard, as if he had a cold. She could sometimes see a flat pancake of food inside his mouth. She couldn't imagine him in pink-and-golden restaurants.

She thought she loved Bill, but she saw life stretching before her with no beautiful dinners—bleak, plain. Bill had no ambition. She worried that she had none herself. They would sit forever eating cheap stews out of metal serving bowls along with the kind of white bread that came in loaves so long they filled up the whole bottom of the shopping cart; loaves you could pinch into a wad of chemicals the size of your fingernail. No seven-grain Swiss health bread. No cabernet sauvignons so rich they smelled like the inside of a cathedral. Just brown quarts of beer. Thin, purple-breasted chickens with caved-in gooseflesh. She would turn into the kind of woman who cooked one and a half fish sticks in the toaster oven. She would always be a secretary, worrying about subway tokens and where to buy her morning bagel. They would get strange together. She would start saving tea bags in the fridge to use again, would fold rolls and crackers from restaurants into napkins so that her purse was always filled with crumbs. She, who wanted to grow old sitting on a velvet banquette, her hand developing arthritis around a glass of wine.

When she left Bill, she decided to focus on food. She signed up for courses with international cooking celebrities. Not so much to learn how to cook, but to develop her palate. At a class in Mideastern cooking at an upper East Side town house, the teacher wore a burnt orange caftan with sleeves that trailed occasionally through the flour. They learned to make pigeon pie wrapped in cinnamon-dusted phyllo dough that crumbled like ancient rare manuscripts at the touch of teeth. Reclining on bright red mirrored pillows, holding her plate under her chin and making small sounds of pleasure along with her classmates, she felt for the first time like someone with taste.

On the top floor of Macy's she watched in the overhead viewing mirror as a famous French chef whisked flour and butter into a velvety smooth roux. The black hairs on his magically swiveling wrist were magnified and electrically male. "Beat, beat, you must not stop beating," he said in his charming French accent. When he asked for a volunteer from the audience, she jumped to her feet and hurried down the aisle between folding chairs filled with women, their feet hidden by shopping bags. They looked at her resentfully. Let them go shop, she thought, as she rolled up her sleeves.

Soon she was ready to go to restaurants. Two-star. Three-star. For this she needed certain men. A good meal was not enough, she soon discovered. The food was overrated. Environment was everything. The best dinners stood out in her mind like exquisitely lit paintings at an art gallery. There was the dinner at Café des Artistes with Edward, the financial analyst. He ordered the wine in French, using his hands, making expert bird sounds in his throat. He knew how to cut and eat a fresh fig. So this was what the food reviewer meant by "supernal." The way the fig sat on her tongue and melted around the edges, and the faintest gritty pop as the seeds crunched under her back teeth.

The kind of man who could afford to take her to such restaurants sometimes said disturbing things. "I'm tracking well at Shearson," Edward had said on their first date, leaving in the middle of the terrine to call his broker. This was not the kind of man you could talk to, but she could listen as she ate. She liked expense-account dinners. The way you could order without worrying. The way you felt grateful to the person but not indebted. It was really some large corporation like Smith Barney or First Boston taking you out.

She never wanted to go back to their apartments. After a two-hundred-dollar meal, they sometimes expected it. Even if it was expense account. Things seemed drab after the restaurant. The glow of good eating was gone. She preferred making love first, then eating. Anticipating dinner afterwards made the end of sex less lonely.

She had met Edward on her lunch hour at the stand-up coffee bar at

Bloomingdale's, sipping the daily coffee, Colombia Armenia Supremo with cinnamon.

"It's got a nice nose on it, and it finishes very well," he said. "But I stand by Melitta-drip Vienna roast, myself," he said.

"Actually, I drink instant." She stared right into his small, green eyes.

He laughed appreciatively. "My name's Edward. May I buy you another?"

Edward liked to involve food in their sex. He made his own massage oil by simmering, then steeping, fresh rosemary in extra virgin cold-pressed olive oil for twenty-four hours. He kept another homemade massage cream, a whipped yogurt base with pieces of naturally astringent fresh papaya, in his fridge that was full of condiments with foreign labels. He grew edible flowers in two window boxes on his terrace. Once he placed nasturtiums between each of her toes and ate them, one by one.

One Friday night he took her to a black-tie balsamic vinegar tasting at Palio. All around her men in tuxedos and women in black velvet sipped from paper soufflé cups, each holding a quarter inch of vinegar imported from Modena, Italy. Edward, small and neat inside his tux, swished the vinegars around in his mouth, looking thoughtful. He wrote in tiny secretive handwriting in a miniature leather-bound notebook tucked next to his plate. "Note the balance, the complexity, the viscosity of the must," he said, a sheen of black vinegar on his small, pursed mouth.

Edward showed her how to pull the vinegar back so that it hit the soft palate. She found it unpleasant. Even the most expensive vintage, a hundred dollars for three and a third ounces, stabbed right into the glands behind her ears, making her mouth fill with spit. They ate six courses, each made by a different chef with a different vinegar. In the filet of beef with capers and pomegranate sauce, she tasted hints of the cheap old-fashioned cider vinegar that she had in her kitchen cupboard at home, but she said nothing.

She worried that she had killed off her taste buds. Too much coffee, the five years she'd smoked, harsh toasted bagels scraping the sensitivity out of her palate, scallion cream cheese and butter-pecan cones dulling and clogging her senses. Food people had to be like race horses: alert and keen. Although she'd heard that a well-known restaurateur sometimes ate cold leftover fettucine Alfredo from her own garbage pail in the middle of the night. It scared her the way food could turn on you like that.

Bill had given her the most delicate of orgasms. As his head disappeared under the covers, leaving her staring up at the ceiling in anticipation, her mind played tricks on her. When his big work boots returned to focus near her head, his oily jeans pulled low to show the waistband of his underwear, she blinked, surprised to see him. It always amazed her that such delicacy could come from him.

One evening at supper time, Bill brought their blackened, charred camping saucepan from stove to table, placing it between their plates on a threadbare pot holder.

"Get that dirty thing out of here," she'd screamed, walking into the kitchen. The sight of his faded bandanna frothing from the back pocket of his jeans, filthy and jaunty, enraged her. How foolish of her to be hiding champagne and chocolate truffles in the fridge for dessert.

"What's wrong?" He looked up at her, truly puzzled. This was her problem. If she put out candles and place mats, he made fun of her. Porcini, chanterelles, and morels were "fungus." When she tried describing an article she'd read on risottos, about the careful blending of stock and time and temperature, the watchful eye, the achieving of just the right creamy texture, the history of it, he grunted and said, "Sounds like rice pudding."

On his birthday, as a surprise, she took him to a two-star restaurant. The beautiful, golden-haired waiter in the floor-length white apron with a three-foot pepper mill in his belt stood at their table reciting the specials.

"Tonight we have duck confit and shiitake mushroom egg rolls and gourgons of sea bass with rosemary pasta in zinfandel sauce."

"I'll have a cheeseburger," joked Bill.

The waiter's smile was sweet and pitying. He grated the Parmigiano high above the arugula salads like an altar boy. She knew he was gay, but she wanted to be going home with him. He would serve cognac in large goldfish goblets and warm it in his long-fingered hands and kiss the insides of her wrists and the arches of her feet, sensitive, out-of-the-way places like that.

When she didn't think about Bill, she hardly even remembered that there was sex. Peak sexual experiences seemed like something for the movies, for literature, for self-help books, for certain women who needed to see themselves plugged into an orgasmic life force. The most violent jolting orgasms she'd ever had had come from a vibrator she'd bought through an Eve's Garden catalogue. It came to her mailbox wrapped in brown paper, but she had still blushed violently in her empty hallway. These orgasms were so quick, so intense, they were closer to electrocution. Her body arched and charged and she trembled so much afterwards she could hardly stand.

But it was an addiction. She could squeeze an orgasm out before heading out the door late to work. Once, when Edward was on his way up the stairs to take her to The Sign of the Dove for dinner, she stood in her bedroom in the dark, her dress pulled to her waist. There was a flush in her cheeks when she answered the door, and her hands trembled. "You're looking very well," Edward had said.

When she tried to touch herself, she was filled with impatience. It seemed slow and distant, as though her flesh had been numbed to the delicacy of minute sensation. She wondered if she shared the fate of men whose bellies leaned over jackhammers all day—she was scrambling her insides. One day, after a particularly explosive orgasm, she went to the kitchen drawer and took out a pair of poultry shears and cut the cord near the base. She regretted this impulsive castration the next day, but hadn't yet sent away for another one.

When the fugu shipment came to New York, she immediately called Edward. He'd hired a Japanese exchange student to teach them how to correctly use the sets of inlaid ivory chopsticks he carried in a velvet-lined case at the bottom of his briefcase. She caught him on his car phone, stuck in traffic outside the Lincoln Tunnel.

"Make pretheater reservations at Petrossian and after-theater reservations at Nippon," he instructed. He was eating lunch. She imagined baguette crumbs showering into his lap. He'd have covered his Brooks Brothers slacks with one of the two teal-blue linen napkins he kept in the glove compartment along with a corkscrew, two condoms and *The New Times Gourmet Shopper*.

She went home early from work and took a bath and dressed all in black Lycra and put on layers of dusky gold eye shadow. She'd read that a hundred people a year dropped dead in Japan from eating improperly prepared blowfish, the flesh contaminated by contact with the entrails or ovaries. The risk was part of the dining experience. But she was nervous.

That night at Petrossian, the caviar-and-champagne emporium now favored by Edward for their after work rendezvous, they sat next to an Arab man with two women. "Call girls," said Edward, leaning over to whisper in her ear as he scooped smoked sturgeon from the Caspian Sea onto a thin sliver of toast. A few pearly grey fish roe were stuck in the corner of Edward's mouth. He wasn't the kind of man who would appreciate it if she leaned over and licked them off with her tongue.

When Edward went to the men's room, she looked up at the handsome, dark-skinned young busboy with the beautiful mouth as he refilled her water glass. She was sure she saw him look scornfully at the silvery fish eggs lost on large white plates. She looked at Edward as he crossed the dining room and sat down. Picking up his napkin, he dabbed at his lips, smiling at her. Food made him feel romantic.

When she saw large white linen napkins, she always thought of Bill's huge, strong, black-nailed hands, imagined the napkin tucked into his battered leather belt where he could smear his hands on it like a mechanic's rag. Bill used strange things as napkins. Dish towels. T-shirts. He blew his nose in napkins at restaurants. Once, when she complained, he dipped a twisted corner of the napkin into his water glass, leaned over and gently wiped her mouth, smiling at her. Bill wouldn't know how to delicately bite the head off a quail and suck politely at the skull, like Edward.

She hadn't really enjoyed the fugu, although she'd quite enjoyed the faint numb feeling the fish had left around her lips and tongue. She rubbed a piece of pickled ginger over her lips, relishing the silky, slimy feel, and took a sip of sake. She felt full, but still hungry, the way she often did when they'd eaten two (once even three) meals at different restaurants spaced throughout the evening.

The overhead spotlight at Nippon shone down on the smooth hairless globe of Edward's bald spot. In contrast, the hairs on his fingers as they held lacquered black chopsticks, tweezing at the air, gleamed as though dusted with gold powder. He very deliberately placed his last piece of sushi in the center of his mouth with his chopsticks, having carefully created an edifice of wasabi and pickled ginger around it.

Edward didn't really like sushi. Once, coming back from the ladies' room, approaching their table from behind, she saw him furtively unroll his yellow-tail-and-scallion hand roll and examine the piece of fish as though he was looking inside a diaper. In the same way, she felt the faintest unease from him as he delicately removed her underwear. He did this the way a woman might, inching her panties down over each hip, first one side, then the other. She imagined, as he rooted around in her pubic hair, that he was picking out leaves and twigs and fuzzy bits from a bowl of berries and placing them on the edge of the bowl. She was sure she did not entirely please the refined mysteries of Edward's palate. She was used to Bill's robust, sweeping tug as he stood at her feet, the underwear rolling into a neat, tight figure eight, and tossed into a corner of the room. Edward liked women who were more like birds, or boys. She'd watched his eyes follow thin, flat-chested blondes in pearls and low navy heels as they crossed restaurants and went into the ladies' room. She sometimes felt when he labored over her own breasts that he wished they weren't there.

Edward kissed her in the cab on the way back to his apartment. His tongue was cold and his breath faintly fishy. The fugu had excited him. Upstairs, he asked her to undress, handing her one of the matching kimonos he'd bought at a boutique on the upper West Side, and disappeared into the kitchen. For weeks he'd been talking to her about trying something he'd seen in a Japanese noodle western known for its erotic food scenes. It had to be after they'd had sushi. The fugu night was perfect. Edward enjoyed theme evenings.

He walked slowly into the bedroom balancing a tray holding a blue-and-white sake carafe, two matching porcelain cups, a blue Japanese soup bowl, a large martini glass and a white washcloth. At the bottom of the glass was a large white egg. Placing the tray on the bed, he climbed onto the middle and sat cross-legged facing her. Carefully wiping the outside of the egg with the washcloth, he cracked it sharply against the rim of the martini glass and then began transferring the yolk back and forth between the two half-shells. The egg white streamed thickly down into the soup bowl. Separating the last strands of albumen with his fingers, he plopped the bare yolk into the martini glass and delicately wiped his fingers on the washcloth. Through the side of the glass she could see a faint membrane on the yolk and the tiniest speck of blood. The glass smelled of the dishwasher.

Edward poured sake into their cups, took a sip from his, removed his glasses, then picked up the glass. "Kompai," he said, slowly tipping the egg yolk into his mouth. He made a slight, gagging movement with his chest, then became very still. He moved slowly toward her, his green eyes crossed down, watching the pathway of the yolk between them. He gestured for her to come closer. When their lips were almost touching, he turned his head sideways. She could feel his tongue urging the yolk out of his mouth and into hers. It broke on their lips and the yolk dribbled down their chins onto Edward's fawn-and-maroon Ralph Lauren comforter. She looked down and saw his kimono open to reveal the two white rinds of his heels where his feet crossed, and his small, limp penis. She worried about salmonella for the next twenty-four hours.

She hadn't always been afraid of eating alone. When she was in a good mood, she made up a tray complete with place mat and cloth napkin and sat in front of the TV on her bed, trying to take small bites. Sometimes, if the meal felt elegant, she would enjoy a sense of well-being, of independence, usually when there was wine. But she was afraid of choking. You couldn't help hearing all those stories. Mama Cass Elliot on her turkey sandwich. All those people you actually knew who had to be given the Heimlich maneuver. Once she practiced giving it to herself by pressing against the wall, her fist jammed into her rib cage. What famous writer had choked and died on a bottle cap? All kinds of things could end up in your mouth.

So much was unnatural now. People thought grains and beans were romantic. And the baby vegetables. Miniature squashes and broccoli and brussels sprouts that looked like they belonged in an elf's garden. $8.99, $11.99 a pound. Impossible prices, yet so little and perfect. Not like the grotesque clones they were creating now, chickens with bulbous breasts for extra white meat. And the hormones. Edward had ordered carpaccio of beef one night and she'd hardly been able to eat it. What made the meat so bright red and even-grained? She'd had to spit out a chewed-up piece, all mixed up with capers, into her napkin when Edward wasn't looking, because she felt her throat closing. So many things in this city were unnatural. Like eating outside. People walking right by, models and dancers carrying big battered leather bags, and leaning down into your plate, staring right at your food. All those eating disorders walking by and wanting what was on your plate.

Strange things like this made her miss Bill. The way, when they were sitting on the sofa, he balanced his plate on her head and carefully scraped the fork over the plate so that she could feel the tines on her skull, gently vibrating through the tin plate. He was the only man whose lap she could fall asleep in.

Edward answered the door wearing a white chef's apron. There were faint smears of what looked like blood down the front. Just that morning she'd gotten her period, and all day she'd been feeling angry at Edward, anticipating his distaste. Bill had enjoyed her menstrual blood, had watched it pool and flower in the toilet bowl or on a sheet with the interest of a zoologist studying animal droppings. He had once held her blood on his finger out to her lips, making her taste it.

She knew Edward was making pâté for their first course. She wanted him to be taking her out to dinner. Pâté frightened her, with its mysterious brownish layers of organs, finely ground to velvet, dotted with pieces of dark feral mushroom, and the musty slime it left on her tongue.

Edward's butcher-block table was strewn with small bodies. "I'm using squab, duck and quail livers for my forcemeat," Edward said, picking up a pair of thin latex surgical gloves from a box on the kitchen counter and pulling them over his hands. He smoothed them at the wrists. Underneath she could see the blonde hairs, matted down and swirled into patterns. He picked up the livers and began separating them with the very tips of his fingers. The gloves were instantly stained dark red. The pieces of liver looked tiny and vulnerable, newly pulsing. She felt herself twinge down there, imagining her own blood clots, dark terrifying clumps of herself, detaching.

"This is a squab," said Edward, picking up the small blue headless body and holding it out to her on the palm of his hand. She didn't know what he wanted from her. Reaching out, she stroked the pimply violet skin. With one gloved finger, he pushed the skin back to show her the brownish meat underneath. He still held the bird out. She took it from him as she would a baby, both hands under the frail armpits. The squab hung down between them, small thighs folding in on each other. Instinctively, she sat it on the edge of the butcher-block counter where it was transformed into a tiny deformed child. She jiggled the tips of its wings, so that the elbows seesawed. She giggled.

"Careful! You'll tear the breast," said Edward sharply.

He took the squab from her and laid it down next to the quail and the duck so that the three bodies lined up side by side as though on gurneys.

He pulled another pair of surgical gloves from the box and held them out to her. "Would you like to help prepare the garlic custard?"

"Yes," she said, nodding.

She didn't want to cook. She didn't want to apologize for the blood later. She watched Edward select a small knife and test it against the edge of his thumb. Pulling on a new pair of gloves, he cut a neat slit in the head of a perfectly formed clove of garlic.

Tonight she was hungry, and she didn't want to eat alone. Edward was away on a business trip. Bill was somewhere in the city, too far away to touch. She took a taxi to the Oyster Bar. She felt safe here, the way the long cement ramps led down to it, giving it an air-raid-shelter feel. She only had eight dollars. After studying the blackboard menu for a long time, she ordered two Belon oysters and one Wellfleet. She liked Blue Points, but she'd heard somewhere that oysters from New York coastal waters were the most contaminated.

It was hard to eat oysters slowly. If she chewed them too much, she started thinking about what she was eating and they turned into a slimy mush in her mouth and her gag reflex was activated. She picked up the first Belon and brought the shell to her lips, enjoying the sharp, rough seashore feel, so foreign and special in the middle of the city. She closed her eyes and took the last tiny briny sip that had collected in the bottom of the shell. Placing it carefully back on her plate so it wouldn't clatter, she braced the shell between her thumb and forefinger, and scraped with her cocktail fork at the slight rubbery piece of flesh that was still left. She alternated between the shells with her fork, eating handfuls of oyster crackers with cocktail sauce and horseradish in between, and sipping her water. She wished she could afford a glass of wine.

The Oyster Bar was full for a Thursday evening, and she worried about taking up a seat for too long. But she didn't want to leave. A wide, beef-red face in square gold glasses had started on his second dozen next to her. She tried not to eye them. When you ordered a dozen oysters, they served them in a huge iron shell, the oysters nestled into a mound of shaved ice like separate gifts.

A man buying you oysters wasn't quite the same as a man buying you drinks at the bar, even though he bought her wine, too. First, he asked her executive-from-out-of-town questions. Then he ordered her two of every oyster on the blackboard menu. She stopped worrying about saying no, and thank you, and you shouldn't. She stopped worrying about eating them slowly and scraping the connective tissues from the shells and clacking them together like a poor starving castanet player to make sure they were dry of juice. She gulped and slid them down, not even stopping to savor the differences. The deep-fried soft-shell crabs arrived with two lemon halves tied in red net bags with yellow string, their legs tangled and crispy with batter. Impossible to avoid the intimacy of sharing a tureen of lobster bisque thick with cream and oil beads red as iodine floating on the surface. She tried, by leaning away from him after each spoonful.

"I don't normally do this kind of thing," he said in the elevator on the way up to his room at the Grand Hyatt next door.

"I don't either," she said, giggling. She rubbed at the raised gold fuzz on the wallpaper inside the elevator, noticing that her fingers felt distant, fuzzy, from the three glasses of wine.

A crisp, anonymous raincoat was draped over an armchair near the entrance to the suite. Fruit in an ornate silver bowl sat on a long, low sideboard next to a wide-screen television. The lighting was soft and yellow. She thought of Bill, wondering, with the sudden piercing sentimentality she sometimes felt with wine, what he was doing at just that exact moment. She saw him hunched over in front of the TV, his feet in thin, grayish socks up on the old wooden kitchen chair, eating a bowl of cereal mounded with fruit.

The man ordered champagne, loosening his tie as he stood at the table beside the bed, a gesture so familiar she knew it was from the movies. The champagne arrived on a trolley in a tall cylindrical cooler the murky yellow of dental plastic. There was no ice, just an empty tube of air and space that left the base of the Cliquot dry. He poured the champagne into tall fluted glasses, the stems balanced expertly between different fingers of one hand.

She gulped three glasses. He drank quickly too, his mouth opened wide so she could see, through the bottom of the glass, his teeth wolfish and slightly yellow. Strange, to see a stranger's fillings. They ate fruit from the fruit bowl, standing over it. He unbuttoned her blouse. He tucked bunches of grapes into her bra. He took a banana and unzipped his pants, holding the fruit in front of himself. They started laughing. She felt herself wetting her pants and squeezed the tops of her legs together. She went to lie on the bed, feeling dizzy. He moved toward her, peeling the banana, humming bump-and-grind music, his damp red upper lip puffing out in horn sounds. When the banana first entered her, she could feel the cool soft tip from a great distance. But the banana was too ripe. She felt it give and lose its shape as he pushed slowly. He kept pushing until his palm was flat against her, massaging round and around in circles. The smell of banana rose between them, sweet and rotten.

He sat down next to her on the bed. He carefully twisted two grapes from the bunches tucked in her bra and placed one, then the other, over each nipple so that they stood up straight inside her bra. Looking into her eyes, using both hands, he squeezed the grapes with a single hard pinching motion. She felt the cold trickle of the juice roll down the side of each breast into the underwire of her bra.

"My fruit princess," he said, leaning close enough for her to feel his sharp, winey breath on her face.

She took the fifty-dollar bill from him for the cab ride downtown and gave the driver a big tip, graciously waving it away. Standing in front of her apartment building, she stuffed the rest of the bills into a crisp round ball in her change purse. She couldn't go home.

She walked ten blocks further downtown to Two Brothers' coffee shop. Sliding into one of the back booths, she stared across at the dirty orange bench where she used to rest her feet in Bill's lap. Between bites he would massage her feet with his big hands, digging his fingers between her toes so that by the end of the meal her socks looked like finger puppets.

She ordered a turkey sandwich and french fries. The food arrived too quickly. The plate of french fries was huge. They poked up at her, glistening with fat. She looked up and saw the waiter sitting at a small table smoking a cigarette, watching her. She picked up the sandwich, feeling her meal from the Oyster Bar rise in a rich tide to the base of her throat, then recede.

Under Age

by Martha Clark Cummings

No matter what museum she took herself to on Saturday afternoon, down in SoHo or up on the upper West Side, Chris always ended up on Christopher Street, looking into a particular store window at a particular black leather jacket. Although she was quiet and reserved, she had a secret image of herself that involved this jacket, a motorcycle, and a spray of pebbles when she arrived. Sometimes someone else was on the motorcycle, coming to whisk her away. But in the fantasy Chris was always ready and she was always wearing this jacket.

"I'm like Walter Mitty," she thought, embarrassed, but just about every Saturday evening she went back to look at the jacket anyway. Standing at that window, she met Alice.

When she became aware that someone was standing beside her, she hoped it wasn't a man. The chances of a man walking down Christopher Street looking for women were extremely slim, which was one of the reasons she chose this street to stroll on, but she was still nervous. Men scared her. She was pretty sure she wanted nothing to do with them. She had no evidence, though, that women were what she wanted either. Nothing had really happened yet, between her and anybody.

Earlier that afternoon, Chris had been sitting in her overheated studio apartment on Thompson Street, thinking that her life was very bleak. In her apartment, she had a gray carpet that had once been in her parents' dining room and smelled of dust, and an easy chair with the upholstery worn thin on the arms and a dark stain where her father had rested his head for his Sunday afternoon naps. She had a mahogany secretary that her mother said was just a loan and a single bed with a dust ruffle. She did not regret having left her parents' home in Connecticut, but it was December and since she had started at New York University in the fall, she had not made a single friend.

"Great jackets," a voice beside her said. It was a woman's voice. A girl's really. She turned to find a tall, slender girl slightly older than herself, with long blond hair that fell over her shoulders like silk, bright blue eyes, her hands tucked into the pouch of her hooded sweatshirt, her long canvas coat hanging open. She looked like an angel.

Chris smiled at her. The girl smiled back.

"Which one do you like best?" the girl wanted to know.

Chris had been asking herself this question for weeks, and knew the answer by heart, but now she hesitated. It had been so long since anyone had wanted to know what she thought that her eyes filled with tears as she struggled to answer. Even the professors in her classes at NYU didn't care if she said a word, didn't even know her name.

"The brown one up in the corner," Chris lied, choosing the one she liked second best, a bruised-looking aviator's jacket.

"I like this black one," the blond girl said, choosing Chris's favorite, the one with epaulets and studs and chains.

"I like that one, too," Chris said. "But I wonder if I'd have the nerve to wear it."

The girl laughed.

"I'd have the nerve," she said. "I just don't have the money."

Chris didn't know what she was supposed to do next. More than anything, she did not want this girl to walk away. She looked at her reflection in the store window and couldn't tell if the girl was looking back at her or if she was still looking at the jackets.

"My name is Alice," the blond girl said, extending her hand.

"I'm Chris." She took Alice's hand in hers. It was warm and large. She held it longer than she should have, feeling like she was already in love, imagining herself and Alice, locked in an embrace. "Stay with me," Alice would whisper.

"Don't be ridiculous," she told herself.

"I'm on my way to Bonnie and Clyde's," Alice said. "Do you want to come?"

Chris had no idea what Bonnie and Clyde's was, but she said yes. When they got to the door, Alice turned to her, concerned and a little embarrassed.

"Look," she said. "How do I say this? You look a little young. Like, underage? Do you have any ID?"

Chris shook her head.

"I *am* under age," she whispered, feeling very foolish.

"Come here," Alice said. They went around a corner under some scaffolding. Alice took out her wallet and flipped through it. "Let's see. You have to be over twenty-one. How tall are you?"

"Five-four," Chris said.

"And your eyes are . . ." Alice looked into them. "Green?"

Chris nodded.

"Here we go," Alice said. "This is close enough." She handed Chris a driver's license from Arizona. "Come on," she said, and hooked arms with Chris. A thrill, like an electrical current, ran through her. "This is my girlfriend, Alice," she imagined telling the new friends she was going to make.

They went into a small bar with a large storefront window and sawdust on the floor. There was just enough room for a pool table on one side of the bar. The small wooden tables in the back were occupied, one by two men, the other by two women. They took two stools at the bar. Chris kept her coat on because a cold wind blew on the back of her neck each time someone opened the door. Alice laid her hands out flat on the smooth surface of the bar. The bartender gave them a suspicious look but did not ask for ID. Alice ordered a vodka martini and Chris said she would have the same.

"Olive or onion?" the woman asked. Chris started to laugh, then realized it was a serious question. She said olive. Her drink arrived in a delicate glass with a tall stem. The olive was pierced with a red plastic spear.

"Here's to new friends," Alice said, and touched her glass to Chris's. Before long, Chris thought, they would be toasting each other differently, looking deeply into each other's eyes.

Chris sipped her drink cautiously. The small amount of liquor that she swallowed filled her chest with warmth like the cough medicine her mother had given her when she was a child. It also made her shudder. She hoped Alice didn't notice. She took another sip. The second one was easier.

"Do you live around here?" Alice asked her.

Chris said that she did, then heard herself describing her apartment the way she was planning to tell the kids back home during Christmas vacation. Alice asked her more questions and Chris, grateful for the attention, continued to talk. She described how strange and wonderful the city was for someone who came from a place where everyone looked and acted and thought alike. How wonderful for someone who knew she was different, she wanted to say, but even after she finished her first martini ever she didn't have the nerve.

The bartender appeared in front of them.

"Ready for another round, ladies?" she asked.

"I am," Alice said. "What about you?"

Chris nodded, although her head was already swimming. The light from the street seemed to undulate in the steamy barroom window. She listened to the jukebox, felt the warm glow of the vodka in her chest, and wanted to rest her head on Alice's shoulder, to stay with her in this bar forever.

"I hope we can be friends," she said to Alice.

"Me too," Alice told her. "I could use some normal friends about now." She put her hand over Chris's hand on the bar.

"This is it," Chris thought. "This is how it starts."

"I don't know anything about you," she said. "Tell me about you now."

Alice blushed deeply. She looked down at her wet boots, caked with sawdust from the barroom floor, and began scraping them against the brass rail.

"There isn't that much to tell," she said softly.

"I'll ask you some easy questions, OK?" Chris said, troubled to have upset her with what seemed like such a simple request.

Alice nodded and smiled, then sat back, her hands in her pockets, waiting to be asked.

"Where are you from?" Chris asked.

"Ohio," Alice answered. "Sort of."

"Sort of?"

"It's a little complicated," Alice said. When she spoke, her pale eyelashes fluttered almost shut. "You see, I was born in Ithaca. Do you know where that is?"

Chris shook her head.

"You know how New York State goes like this?" she said, drawing a map in the air.

Chris nodded.

"Well, Ithaca is over . . ."

Alice stopped midsentence, her arm dropping down like the cut branch of a tree.

"What?" Chris said, turning around to see what Alice was looking at.

A skinny girl who couldn't have been more than fifteen had walked into the bar. She had thick curly hair cut short around her ears and large frightened eyes. She was wearing an oversized athletic jacket over a faded denim jacket, and still another jacket under that. She scratched her cheek, rubbed her nose, and glanced nervously around the room. Everyone in the bar was watching her. She was about to turn around and leave. Then she saw Alice.

"Mickey!" Alice said. "How the hell are you?"

When the girl saw Alice, her scared expression fell right off.

"Hola chica," she said, grinning, reaching for Alice's hand, then pulling her into a rough embrace. "How are you, girl?"

Chris noticed that she had a gold ring on each of her fingers. She watched as Alice whispered something into her ear and Mickey nodded solemnly. Alice turned to Chris.

"Don't go away," Alice said. "Mickey and I are just going to step outside for a second, to take care of some business, and I'll be right back, OK?"

"OK," Chris said. But as soon as Alice left, she felt foolish and conspicuous. She turned to face the window, certain that everyone in the bar was staring at her now, that the bartender was going to choose now to come over and ask for her ID.

"Sorry," Alice said, sitting down beside her again. Her cheeks were rosy from the cold. Her pale hair glistened with snow. "I owed her some money. I'd been meaning to pay her back." She sighed deeply and smiled at Chris. "Where were we? Oh yeah. Ithaca."

Chris looked at her, not daring to ask what Alice and Mickey had really been doing outside, afraid that Mickey was one of Alice's girlfriends.

"Tell me about Ithaca," she said.

Alice had gotten to the part where her sister decided she couldn't take care of her after all and was going to send her to another foster home when the bartender came back.

"Ladies?" she said.

"I don't think I'd better drink any more right now," Chris told Alice.

Alice shrugged. "I'm out of money anyway."

The bartender frowned and moved away from them.

"I could make us something to eat," Chris said. Then she covered her face with her hands. "Is that very uncool? People in New York don't offer to cook for each other, do they?"

"Definitely cool," Alice said. "Very cool. Let's go."

As they came out of the bar it started to snow again, a dry mist of sparkling crystals covering the slush. To Chris it seemed like magic. The whole day, in fact, had been magical. Here was this woman, Alice, holding her elbow and negotiating her around a puddle of slushy water, toward her apartment. Alice, who two hours earlier didn't even know she existed, was coming home with her, would maybe even want to spend the night. Chris started thinking about whether or not she should say yes.

They ducked around the corner into the wind. Alice's long canvas coat flapped behind her. Chris wished Alice would put her arm around her shoulders. They walked south on Seventh Avenue to Bleecker Street. When they passed the Catholic church on Carmine Street an old man was standing on the icy sidewalk throwing handfuls of bread crumbs to the pigeons. He watched Chris and Alice, as they walked down the block. "That's a good girl," he said, and it was hard to tell if he was talking to Chris or to Alice or to one of the pigeons on his shoulders. There was a lot of fluttering as they went by. Then one pigeon settled on his chest, gripping his jacket with its claws, gently pecking his face.

"What a nut, huh?" Chris said, smiling up at Alice.

"Yeah," said Alice, but she looked disgusted.

When they got to Chris's apartment, Alice sat down in the easy chair and told Chris she had a real nice place. Chris wasn't sure what she was supposed to do next. She felt nervous and unsteady, and the warm air of the apartment made her feel very drunk again. She asked Alice if she wanted a glass of seltzer, since it was all she had. Alice said, "Yes, please." Chris put a Joan Armatrading album on the stereo and went to the kitchen. When she turned around to get the glasses from the cupboard, Alice was standing in the kitchen doorway and then before she knew it Alice had her arms around her.

"I'm sorry," Alice said, not letting go.

Chris felt their four breasts and pictured them pressing together. It worried her to be having such an odd thought instead of some kind of normal response to Alice's embrace. She could think of nothing to say, either.

"It's just that I haven't felt this comfortable with anyone since Diane,"

Alice said, still holding her around the waist.

"Who's Diane?" Chris asked her, backing away.

"This woman," Alice said. "You know."

She let go of Chris. Her arms dropped to her sides.

"I think I screwed up," she said. "I should go, right?"

Chris looked at her watch, just for something to do. She was scared, but she didn't want Alice to leave. She wanted to ask her if they could talk a little before they did anything else.

"It is a little late," she said instead.

"OK," Alice said.

Chris was immediately sorry and very surprised at her own reaction. She had imagined herself much bolder. "Could you sit down and hold my hand and tell me what you picture happening next?" she wanted to say. Instead she watched Alice walk out of the kitchen.

Alice picked up her bag and went into the bathroom. Chris stood in the kitchen doorway wondering how to keep her from leaving.

"Wait," she said.

Alice didn't hear her.

The bathroom door opened but Alice didn't come out. Then Chris heard her calling. Her voice was weak, as if she were about to fall asleep. Chris walked over slowly. She didn't like barging in on people when they were in the bathroom. Alice was standing by the sink. Chris thought she looked OK. Then she saw that there was a syringe full of blood stuck in her arm and that she was clinging to the basin, her knees slowly collapsing. She was about to fall over.

"What should I do?" Chris asked her. "Tell me what to do."

But Alice's lips were already turning blue and she was slipping through Chris's arms and onto the bathroom floor. Chris stood up and went to the telephone. She would dial 911 for an ambulance. She picked up the receiver with trembling hands. Then it occurred to her that by doing this she could get Alice into terrible trouble with the police. And herself, too. She would be an accomplice or something. She hung up the phone and went back to look at Alice again.

She knelt down on the tiles beside her. Alice was extremely pale. She couldn't tell if she was breathing. She leaned over and put her face very close to Alice's. She still couldn't tell. All she could hear was her own heart pounding. She wanted to run away. She wanted to leave the building and walk over to the Eighth Street Bookshop and browse through the new books, pretending she and Alice had never met.

Chris cast about crazily in her mind for some experience she had had that in any way resembled this one and came up with a story her mother had told her about someone who had taken too much of some prescription drug. It had been important to slap the person back to consciousness, her mother had told her. Since the scuffles of her childhood, Chris had never hit anyone, but now she reared back and prepared to belt Alice in the face. She began, as hard as she dared. Alice's face turned sharply to the right when Chris struck her, but she was still unconscious. She straightened her out and began again, this time hitting her right cheek with the back of her hand, grunting as she made contact. She attempted to raise her shoulders, imagining that she could make her sit up, but Alice was limp and much too heavy. She put her down again. She was going to be sick. She could hardly breathe. She looked wildly around the room, wishing desperately that she were not alone with Alice's unconscious body.

There was no more time. She grabbed a handful of Alice's hair and began striking her, again and again, watching her slack mouth droop from one side to the other, looking for a change in her breathing. There was nothing. It occurred to her that Alice might already be dead. She continued hitting her, over and over, building up momentum and force, all the while shouting into her face, "Wake up! Alice! For God's sake, wake up!"

And then she did. Her pale eyelashes fluttered once, then again. Alice reached over and shot the blood back into her arm, then removed the needle from her skin.

"What time is it?" Alice asked. "How long have I been out?"

"A few minutes," Chris told her. "Are you all right now?"

"Yeah," Alice whispered, closing her eyes again. "Give me just a little more time, would you? It must have been cut with something."

Chris was crying.

"Alice," she said, shaking her softly by the shoulder. Alice's face was an angry red from where Chris had hit her. "Please. How am I supposed to know if you're really all right?"

Alice opened her eyes again, annoyed.

"If I weren't all right," she said slowly, "I'd be dead. I promise." She closed her eyes. "Just leave me here a minute. I'll be right out."

Chris went out to the living room, her body trembling. She wanted to shout at her, "Get out!" She wanted to yell, "I hate you!" and not just because Alice had frightened her so badly but because she was so disappointed. Everything she thought she had found, everything she had been about to discover, was gone now.

"Chris?" Alice called. "Are you there?"

"I'm here. Are you OK?"

Alice was sitting up on the bathroom floor. Chris helped her to her feet. She was heavy and unwieldy, but she was alive.

"I'm sorry," Alice said. Her bright blue eyes seemed veiled. "That was really rude."

"You could have warned me," Chris told her. "You could have told me that's what you do when you feel rejected."

"I was getting around to it," Alice said. "I was getting around to telling you all about this."

They sat down on the bed. Very slowly, Alice leaned over and rested her head on Chris's lap. Chris waited for the next time she would be ready to talk. Outside, the snow was thickening into a severe storm. She could hear the snow-removal equipment slowly grinding its way around Washington Square, the chains on the tires clanking and flopping.

"Don't throw me out," Alice whispered.

Chris looked down at Alice, her soft blond hair spread across the bed just the way she had imagined it.

"OK," she said. "OK. I won't."

Combing

Veronica Patterson

How the chemicals that might heal you singe the hair inside.

How at the wig store you were angry with the clerks
because they had no wig that was your hair.

How when our generation came of age, hair was our exuberant
no, and *Hair* was our musical, and everyone had so much.

How we used hair unthinkingly for our own purposes.

How young girls in shining hair spend hours on a nuance
of curl, and that is youth: hours for a nuance.

How, falling gold into fairy tales, hair reveals the prince
or princess, reflects the kingdom to come.

How heads are shaved as punishment.

How Rapunzel made hair a staircase and a door.

How the woman in the story sold her hair to buy her husband
a gift and then he gave her combs.

How the skull is deeply beautiful, but mortally bare.

How you called yourself vain, but I say the strands of our hair
write our names.

I will bring you a broad-brimmed hat wreathed with fruit—
cherries, frosted purple grapes, peaches so small they
never were, and blossoms—daisies, roses, rue. No one
would dream of bare land beneath such abundance. You would
live in its shade, private and imperturbable.

You would live.

Sadly Ever After

by Karen X. Tulchinsky

I 'll always remember the exact date that we moved into the house on Eighteenth Street. The city was repairing the sidewalk on our block that day and when the workmen left, we all scratched our names and the date into the still-wet cement. We each took a full tile for our name. Katie. Carlos. Michael. Willie. At the last minute I added the date: September 6, 1980. Then Michael ran back inside and brought out a bottle of expensive champagne and four matching blue-stemmed glasses.

"To our house," we all toasted, pleased with ourselves. There was a feeling of optimism in the air. A beginning of something unspoken and wonderful. We were happy to be alive and happy to have found a great house right on the Castro at the beginning of what we felt sure was going to be a fabulous decade for gays and for women.

They say that having déjà vu means your life is on the right track. That you wouldn't have had the sensation of having been there before if you weren't supposed to be there now. As I tasted that first sip of champagne I was struck with a feeling of recognition, a sense of the familiar. The hair on my arms stood on end and I felt a chill run through me.

Everyone's dead now except me and it's only twelve years later. In 1980 I was the youngest at twenty-four. Carlos was twenty-eight. Michael was thirty and I never really knew Willie's age.

"Woman's prerogative," he'd say when I tried to find out. Willie was an African American drag queen, although in those days he was called black. He wanted to be Greta Garbo, although sometimes he came across more like Bette Davis, waving his hands around in the air, smoking endless cigarettes and calling everybody "darling" in a playful yet bitchy sort of way.

I met Carlos first. It would have been the spring of 1980, back in the days when I was still straight. I'd moved to San Francisco from Albany, New York, the year before to get out of the cold winter weather and into the west coast sunshine. I was having lunch in a vegetarian restaurant called Beans and Rice when I looked up from my tabouli salad to see a handsome young man at the next table. He caught my eye and he smiled. There was an innocent sweet boyish quality about him that attracted me right off. Normally I would glare at strange men who smiled at me in restaurants, but I was lonely and Carlos seemed harmless and friendly. When he got up and stood by my table and asked if he could join me I said yes. Conversation between us was easy right away. He was new to San Francisco too, from Mexico City, and so we had in common the disoriented feelings you get when you move somewhere new. When he asked me to have dinner with him later that evening it seemed natural to say yes.

After that we went out all the time. At first I thought he was the last in a dying breed of gentlemen. He'd always see me to my door and would give me a light peck on the cheek, never pressuring me to go inside, or to have sex. After a couple of months, though, things shifted for me and I wanted him to want me. I began to grow worried. Was there something wrong with me? I didn't know how to ask. We went out for burritos one evening and I was so upset I couldn't eat.

"You don't like it?" he asked. "These are practically the best burritos in all of America."

I started to cry.

"Hey," he said taking my hand, "it's not that bad, is it?"

I told him what was bothering me and he sighed deeply. "It's not you, Katie," he said, his dark brown eyes soft with concern.

"It's not?"

"No. It's me."

I waited for him to continue.

"I'm gay."

I stared at him in stunned silence. Then I began to laugh.

"What? What's so funny?"

"Oh Carlos," I managed to say, "I'm so relieved."

"You are?"

"I thought it was me."

Six months later he asked me to marry him.

"Wait a minute, Carlos. We've been through this already. You're gay. That's all there is to it. Marrying me is not going to change anything."

"You don't understand," he said. "I'm not supposed to be here. I'm illegal. If you marry me I can get a green card."

So I did it, of course. I didn't have to think twice. He had become my best friend and I wanted him to stay. We would have to live together to make it look good to the immigration authorities, but we both agreed it would be awkward to bring lovers home if we lived in a small place, just the two of us. That's how we ended up in the big house on Eighteenth Street.

Michael was already living in the house when we found it. He fell in love with the big old Victorian on the hill above the Castro the first time he saw it. Michael was a spontaneous, impulsive person and he signed the rental agreement without even considering how he'd pay for a whole house on his social worker's salary. He put an ad in the classifieds of the *Bay Area Reporter* looking for roommates, which is how Carlos and I found him. It was a great house, with large rooms, bay windows, a big kitchen, a real backyard, hardwood floors and a feeling of peace inside. The outside had been painted robin's-egg blue, and the hand-carved trim around the windows was carefully done in lavender and pink. The front porch was framed by two Roman-style columns which gave the house an old-world look. It was the kind of doorway from which you could make an entrance. It was obvious why Michael loved the house. From the moment I walked inside, I loved it too. We needed one more person to take the front bedroom and Carlos said he had a friend who would be perfect. He had met Willie in a bar a few months before. They'd had a one-night fling and after that became friends.

"We could never be lovers," Willie said to me about Carlos later. "We're both queens. It would be entirely too bitchy, my dear. Now me. I like a big burly leatherman, myself. Someone who will rough me up a little. Um-hmmmm."

For two years life was one big party. It took a little getting used to, living with three gay men like that. I guess you'd have called me a fag hag in those days. When I fell in love with Janet, Carlos took me out for a beer and said, "Well it's about time, muchacha."

"What do you mean?"

"First time I met you, I knew you were gay. I've been waiting all this time for you to figure it out."

I didn't understand. "How did you know?"

He shrugged. "Just a feeling. When I was a little boy in Mexico I spent summers in the country with my Uncle Roberto. He was a deeply religious man, you know, he was always talking to the Saints and all. He said I had something special. Not exactly psychic powers. It's not that I can read your mind or anything like that. It's more like I know people. I know who they are sometimes even before they know it."

It was Carlos who first knew something was wrong with Michael. He came home from work one evening to find Michael at the stove, cooking a big pot of chicken soup.

"Who's sick?" Carlos asked because the only time Michael ever made his famous chicken soup and matzoh balls was when someone was sick. Michael turned around. He was pale and puffy. His eyes were red and he was coughing.

"Me."

The cold seemed to drag on and on. Carlos kept making him drink strange teas made with chili peppers and garlic. Willie swore by his grandmother's homemade cough remedy. I pushed Granddaddy O'Brien's hot rum toddy on him. When he was too sick to get out of bed, I even tried to make chicken soup for him. I guess it wasn't too good. When he put the first spoon in his mouth he made a face.

"This is awful, Katie."

I shrugged. "I make a mean tuna casserole, but chicken soup? Sorry. This is my first try."

It seemed like Michael was getting better until one night he couldn't breathe. It was 1982. We rushed him to emergency where the doctors said he had pneumonia. We all figured he would be okay. Nobody died of pneumonia anymore, other than maybe really old people, and Michael was young and strong and healthy. We all took turns that week visiting him, smuggling in real food, like pizza and Chinese takeout. Michael smiled and told jokes through it all. We waited for his recovery to start, but it seemed like he was just getting worse. The doctors were puzzled. All the usual drugs were not having any effect. Even though he was hooked up with an oxygen mask, his hands and feet were freezing because no oxygen was getting that far. He could only sit up in bed and breathe short shallow breaths, each one slicing through his lungs and chest like a knife. I wanted to call his family in Philadelphia.

"No!" Michael said.

"What? Why not?"

Michael turned his face to the wall.

"Michael?" I said gently.

He was shaking and after a minute I realized he was crying.

"Michael?" I asked again.

He turned to me, his face a picture of anguish.

"What is it?"

"There's no point in calling them. They won't come."

"What? Why not?"

"I haven't spoken to my parents in five years."

I brushed the hair away that had fallen in his eyes and waited for him to go on.

"My father's very religious. Orthodox. I've been disowned." He stopped for a minute and sighed deeply. "Actually it's even worse than that. To them—I'm dead. My father said the mourner's kaddish for me when I told him I was gay. He forbade my mother and my sister to contact me. The last time I saw any of them, I was being kicked out of the house."

"Oh Michael." I felt my own eyes fill with tears. I tried again. "But don't you think if they knew how sick you were, they'd want to see you?"

"No!" His dark eyes were hard with anger. Then he began to cough, deep, dry racking coughs that came from down inside his lungs. I rushed to the bathroom to get him a glass of water.

A few days later, when Michael was having a better day, I tried to bring the idea up again. I thought that, given the circumstances, his mother or sister at least would want to talk to him.

"Tell you what, Katie," Michael said. "Just for you, I'll call my sister, okay? But not yet. I'll call when I'm better. When I'm home."

But he never did come home. Carlos was with him when it happened. It was five in the morning when I heard the front door slam. I rushed out of bed. Carlos was acting crazy, not making any sense. I made him sit down and I poured him a brandy.

He just kept shaking his head like he couldn't believe something. He looked up and I knew from his eyes that Michael had died. Official cause of death: pneumonia.

Our house went into deep mourning. We were in shock. It was all we could do to function in the world, to make it to work, to remember to eat. No one else seemed to understand what we were going through. Unaccustomed at the time to dealing with death, no one knew how to act around us. My relationship with Janet began to sour.

"Men are a part of the problem, Katie. You should be concentrating on women. I don't see why you live with those guys or why you spend so much time with gay men."

"They're my friends, Janet!" I screamed at her, because as my lover, I wanted her to understand me and she didn't.

They weren't just men. They were my family. We'd been through everything together. Heartbreak over love gone bad, lost jobs, problems with our families, my coming out, and Michael dying. Together, Willie and Carlos and I became a fortress against pain. We were the only ones who could comfort each other and at the same time we made each other feel sad just by association. That house was our escape from the rest of the world but it also held so many painful memories that it was hard just to be there sometimes. I think each of us thought about moving out at some time or other, but we never said it out loud. The house was all we had left of Michael. His body had been shipped to his family in Philadelphia immediately after he died for a traditional Jewish funeral. It surprised me that they wanted him back. I didn't understand, but I guess death changes things so that even when you disown your son for being gay, you still want to bury him in the end. I was the one who called his mother in Philadelphia with the news. It was the hardest phone call I ever had to make. I was crying. She was crying. She wanted to know why I hadn't called her sooner, while he was still alive, while she still had a chance to see him.

"He didn't think you'd come," I had to tell her.

The silence on the other end of the phone was worse than the sound of her crying. "It was a big mistake," she said finally and then she thanked me for all I had done.

"Mrs. Rotstein? Uh . . . I think you should know that Michael was loved. He had many friends." I wanted to say something that might comfort her, anything.

"Thank you for telling me." She hung up the phone and I never spoke with her again. A man from the Jewish funeral home in Philadelphia called us to make the arrangements.

As for us, we didn't have a funeral or memorial service for Michael. We didn't know what to do so we did nothing. For a long time, we never properly mourned him or knew how to deal with the deep shock we all felt at having to watch a young man be so sick and then die so fast. We kept Michael with us in other ways. We'd talk about him, almost as if he was still there.

"Oh, not avocados," Willie said once while unpacking the groceries. "Michael hates them."

It was a month after Michael had died. We all looked at each other and said nothing.

We used to sit on the front steps, the three of us, and drink beer, talk about our days and watch the people go by. The Castro was our home, the only safe place on earth for gay people. The only place in America where two men could hold hands in the street and women could walk arm in arm. Even through our grief we still felt lucky to be young and gay and in San Francisco in the '80s. And as we sat there, our time was framed by the sight of our names scratched into the sidewalk. The one square with Michael's name on it became our monument to him, like a tombstone. We took to cleaning it obsessively and one day Willie brought home some flowers. He dug a hole in our small front lawn right behind Michael's tile and he fitted a glass vase inside. When it was just right he placed the flowers in it so that they stood over Michael's name on the sidewalk. It seemed so right that after that, we did it all the time. It became our way of remembering Michael, of being with him, like visiting a grave in a cemetery.

With Michael gone we had a big decision to make. We knew that the three of us couldn't afford the rent now, and there were some outstanding hospital bills that kept coming in. We knew we should put an ad in the paper looking for another roommate but somehow none of us could bring ourselves to do it. We never spoke about it, but I think we were all feeling the same thing. To bring someone new in would be like wiping out Michael's memory and we wanted to stall for as long as we could. Then we got a letter from the insurance company and everything changed. Michael had a life insurance policy from work. He had named the three of us his beneficiaries. It was enough money to pay off the hospital and to cover Michael's share of the rent for years. We put it in a high-interest savings account and celebrated later that day. We pulled out one of Michael's bottles of champagne that he always kept in the basement, brought out his blue-stemmed wine glasses and out on the porch we toasted our friend. People need rituals to mark both happy times and sad, and finally we had found a way to say good-bye formally to our friend.

One morning a couple of years later I came home after spending the night with Donna, my lover at the time. It was only ten o'clock, but Carlos was sitting in the dark living room drinking tequila. I could tell right away that he was drunk and that he had been crying. I sat down on the couch beside him, took his hand and waited for him to tell me what was wrong.

"It's over," he said finally.

"What is, Carlos?"

"Derek. Me and Derek. He says he's in love with someone else now. He wouldn't even tell me who it was. I had to drag it out of him. Turns out it's some little stud muffin he met at a bar. Two years we were together. Doesn't that mean anything?" He looked up at me helplessly.

I didn't know what to say. Certainly I was no expert on the ways of love. Since Janet, I hadn't been with a woman for longer than six months. Donna and I had been seeing each other for two months at that point and already I was feeling trapped. She wanted us to move in together in Oakland. She wanted to be with me every day. She got jealous when I spent time with anyone else but her. She even called me at work two or three times during the day. I couldn't handle it. I knew I was going to break up with her soon.

"Better drink some water with that or you'll get a hangover," I told Carlos. It seemed like the best advice I could give him. A year later we heard that Derek had died. He went to the hospital complaining of a headache. They admitted him and he never came out again. It was 1985 and we knew all about AIDS by then.

"I'm terrified," Carlos said to me the day we heard about Derek.

"What do you mean?" I was scared to hear the answer.

He shrugged. "When I was first with Derek we still didn't know how it was spread." He stopped and looked at me. "We never used condoms."

The sinking feeling started in my belly and spread quickly throughout my body. It had been hard enough losing Michael, but Carlos was my best friend. I couldn't imagine life without him.

"I think you should go to the doctor and get tested for the virus," I told him. "They can do that now, you know. Sometimes it's better that way. There's treatments that they didn't have a few years ago." I was grasping at straws.

"Fuck that shit," he said, waving me off. "I don't like doctors. Don't trust 'em. Forget about it."

"But, Carlos . . ."

"Just forget about it."

We tried to, for as long as we could. When Carlos first got sick we were still in deep denial. It was eerie. He got the same symptoms that Michael had. A lingering cough, shortness of breath, a cold that wouldn't go away. Carlos took some time off work. He'd been cooking in the same restaurant on the Castro since before he got his green card and Jake, his boss, was a friend by then.

"Take as much time as you need," Jake said to him. "Just get better." Which, by 1985 in the gay community, was a euphemism for "I hope it isn't AIDS."

Carlos hated doctors so much, I literally had to drag him to the hospital. He turned out to have PCP just like we suspected. When I came home later that day without Carlos, Willie fell to pieces. That night, the two of us sat out on the stoop. It was a warm June evening. We were drinking Margaritas and we both kept glancing down at the sidewalk tiles with our names on them.

"Remember when we put our names down there?" he said into the night air.

"I sure do, Willie," I said, smiling at the memory.

"A whole lot's changed since then, hasn't it, Katie?"

"Too much," I agreed.

When Carlos died eighteen months later it was from an overdose of morphine. He recovered from that first bout of PCP, came home, and discovered a KS lesion on his knee two days later. He began losing weight and later, during some "routine" tests, the doctors discovered a lesion on his brain.

The night before he left us, we bundled Carlos up in layers of sweaters—he was so skinny by that point he got cold easily—and we each sat in our spot on the front porch.

"You know," Carlos said, "you guys are more my lovers than any lover I've ever had. You know what I mean? You're my family. When I think back on it, what have I ever had? Tricks—that's all. Sex, not love. Hard-ons and blow jobs. But no one's ever cared about me or loved me."

"Come on, Carlos." I hated what he was saying. It was lonely and depressing. "You had some good times. What about Derek? You guys were together for two years."

He waved me off with a violent motion in the air. "Derek! Hah! Right. He broke my heart, Katie. I loved him and what does he do? He dumps me so he can be free to fuck all the young twinkies. He liked 'em young. Did I ever tell you that?"

"Yeah, but you had some good times with him at the beginning. Didn't you?"

"I guess," he admitted.

"Well. It's important to remember that too."

We sat quietly for a while. "I'll be leaving you soon," Carlos said into the quiet night fog.

"Don't talk like that," I begged. "You're scaring me."

"You'll be all right, Katie. You have a heart of gold. You always have. You saved my life when you married me. Without you, I'd have been deported sooner or later. I'd never have had as good a life in Mexico as I had here. It's dangerous to be gay there. People are killed for it."

"I'm glad you stayed too." I grabbed his hand, which was thin and cold.

"Maybe with me out of the way you'll be able to get a lover and keep her. They always get jealous of our friendship, don't they?"

I nodded and smiled even though my eyes were filling with tears. Before we all went to bed that night Carlos grabbed my hand. "I love you, Katie. I do. You've been a sister to me. You know I've never talked to my family since I moved here. If they knew I was a fag they'd want to kill me. That's just how they are."

We hugged in the hallway. He was skin and bones. I could feel his ribs against me. "I love you too, Carlos," I said, wishing I could transfer some of my healthy cells to him, some of my blood and energy. I was not ready to let him go. "Hey," I said before he shut his bedroom door. "Maybe I'll take the day off work tomorrow. If you feel up to it, we could take a drive to the Napa Valley or something. You know, get out of the city for a few hours."

He smiled and blew me a kiss. It was the last time I saw him alive. We found a note on his dresser. It said: "Sorry Katie. I couldn't stand it any longer. You know how scared I am of pain. I wanted to go while I still had my dignity. You know what to do with me now. Just like we talked about. Willie, take care you old queen. See you in another lifetime. Buenas Noches my sweet friends. xxoo Love Carlos."

By then Willie and I were practiced at grieving. We had Carlos cremated and we split his ashes into three bags just like he wanted. The first bunch we scattered into the San Francisco Bay at Fisherman's Wharf. Carlos loved sitting on the docks watching the boats, the waves coming in and the men fishing.

"Most straight men are not so straight when it comes down to it," he used to say. "All men are tramps. All you have to do is look at them the right way and even a straight guy with a wife and fourteen kids'll be down on his knees with your cock in his mouth."

The second batch we sprinkled along Castro Street, especially at the corner of Eighteenth where Carlos liked to stand and watch the cute guys go by.

As for the last bag, we took it home and buried the ashes in the front yard under a lush red bottlebrush tree, where Carlos would have been able to sit and continue watching all the people go by and where we could feel close to him just by sitting out on the steps.

I wasn't too surprised when Willie got sick a while later.

"We're all dropping like flies, girlfriend," he tried to joke with me the first time he landed in the hospital. He had the CMV virus and was starting to go blind. That, along with an intestinal parasite he'd been pretending not to have, tipped him over the edge.

"You know what's always been harder than the thought that I might get sick, Katie?" he asked while we sat together in the visitors' lounge. He had a green silk bathrobe on over his hospital gown and we both sat in wheelchairs smoking cigarettes.

"What?"

"The thought that I might not."

I stared at him and frowned.

"I can't tell you, girl, how many friends and ex's I've already buried. I'm scared of being the last queen alive on the Castro. Can you imagine?"

The image I saw was of Willie in full drag, standing alone in the middle of the deserted street. A wind was swirling litter around his feet. The silence was excruciating.

After Willie died I couldn't bear to stay in that house any longer. I gave it up and moved into a studio suite on Haight Street. The two men who live in the house now have been kind to me. The first time they caught me sitting on their stoop with flowers in my arms and tears in my eyes they invited me inside for a drink. I told them all about me and the guys and they said I could come on over and sit on their porch any time I wanted. David, the older one, is HIV positive and I knew that he understood. They even gave me a key in case I need to use the bathroom or the phone.

I don't know what I'll do if the city replaces those tiles. Move, I guess. Maybe to Oakland, or maybe I'll go north to Seattle. I do have other friends here, but somehow I've never been able to replace the sense of family we created in that house. We filled an empty place for each other and now they've all gone and left me to fend for myself. I know Carlos would be disappointed if he saw me now. He was always hoping I'd meet Ms. Right, fall in love and live happily ever after. It just hasn't happened yet. I've had lovers, more than I care to mention, but they always turn out to be happier than I am and they get upset that I'm not. I guess I need to find someone who has as much grief as I do. We would date for a while, fall in love and live sadly ever after.

Now that I've lost all my best friends I'll never be the same again. I'll be all right, but I'll be different. They say that time heals all wounds. I sure hope it's true. Anyhow, last week on September 6, the anniversary of the day we moved into the house, I had myself a little celebration. I bought a bottle of champagne and I brought over three of Michael's blue-stemmed wine glasses. I drank the first glass alone and when I closed my eyes it was 1980 again and we were all there. Michael, Willie, me and Carlos. It was a happier time, a time when everything seemed right in the world. Then I opened my eyes and realized I had been crying. I wiped my face, got up and knocked on the door to invite David and his lover Matt to join me in a toast.

"L'chaim," David said, holding his glass high and winking at me. "To life."

And I felt just a little bit better.

Wake

by Tess Gallagher

Three nights you lay in our house.
Three nights in the chill of the body.
Did I want to prove how surely
I'd been left behind? In the room's great dark
I climbed up beside you onto our high bed, bed
we'd loved in and slept in, married
and unmarried.

There was a halo of cold around you
as if the body's messages carry farther
in death, my own warmth taking on the silver-white
of a voice sent unbroken across snow just to hear
itself in its clarity of calling. We were dead
a little while together then, serene
and afloat on the strange broad canopy
of the abandoned world.

The Time, the Place, the Loved One

by Susan Welch

I spend a lot of time alone now. It doesn't bother me. The others took up too much time. I am glad that they are gone. But it is January and now and then I think of January in Minnesota, how in late afternoon a rusty stain appears along the rim of the sky and creeps across the ice. The stain seems to stay there forever, spreading beneath the banked tiers of white sky, until it fades suddenly into the snowbanks and is gone. It is bleak then, as if the sun has just slipped off the edge of the world. Then there is only the ice and the freezing wind on the ice as the sky gets blacker and blacker through the long, deep night.

I hardly ever think of Minnesota now that I am content in Florida. There is a garden with a trellis and orange trees. The branches bend to me as I pluck the fruit, then spring back. As I bite into an orange I can taste the juice of the tree still in it, all its green leaves. The thorns on the rose bushes tear my skirt. The house has pillars and a courtyard; it is not far from the sea. Mal has given me all he promised. When Mal comes home he picks up my daughter at her school and she drinks lemonade while we drink scotch, sitting in the gazebo. By the time my head is clear again we have gotten through dinner and put the little girl to bed and are upstairs, lying on the bed.

So I hardly ever think of Minnesota, how dark and still the winters are there. There was an apartment once, but I don't miss it, I just think about it sometimes when I consider how completely I have gotten out of the cold. From the street you could see a pale lamp shining through the window of the apartment, and the reflection of the lamp in the window; it was high up on the second floor above a store. Signs hung beneath the windows: Grimm's Hardware, Shaak Electronics—and together with the streetlights they cast a white glow into the big room all night long. Sometimes, coming home, we would see the snow falling silently in the beam of the streetlight, as if it were all a stage set.

Across the street was an all-night restaurant and sometimes people would leave there late, and yell to each other before they got into their cars. The first night I saw Matthew he was rushing down the stairs of our apartment building to confront some boys on the sidewalk near the restaurant. If I hadn't pressed against the railing he would have collided with me in his descent. I stood watching him through the glass of the door as he told the boys to be quiet, people were trying to sleep. They hooted and snickered as he turned to leave. As he came in the door, almost in tears, the boys were screaming in a mocking, falsetto chorus.

"They laughed at me," he said, bewildered, shutting the door against them, staring out. We started up the stairs together. He was tall and very thin, stooped even, pigeon-breasted in the T-shirt he wore in spite of the cold. His hair was a mass of ringlets and golden curlicues and it seemed full of its own motion like something alive at the bottom of the sea. For a moment, standing in the hallway, he looked very beautiful and strange.

"I live here now," I told him. "In that apartment, there."

His face was haggard, lantern-jawed, but his eyes were gentle as he stared at me. "Come over and visit me tomorrow night," he said. "I'll bake you some brownies."

All day long I thought I wouldn't go. I stood a long time in the hallway looking from Matthew's door to mine, before I turned to knock on his. When he called "Wait a minute," I thought he was a girl, that's how light and high his voice was.

His apartment was immaculate. The wooden floor gleamed. There was a rug made up of swans' heads and necks, dark and light, facing in opposite directions—the neck of a dark swan provided the relief so you could see the neck of a white swan and so on. It was impossible to hold both the white and dark swans together in your mind at the same time. There was a bed at one end of the large room, a table with two chairs, and windows that faced the street all along the wall. There were no pictures up, just plants on a shelf, purple passion, jade plant, wandering jew, and a bulletin board studded with funny clippings, cartoons, a picture of a bald woman in a long smock.

"I see her all the time at school," Matthew said. "She goes to all the rallies and concerts and just walks around the university."

He was wearing a T-shirt that said "Minnesota" and a pair of jeans that hung on him. I saw that he was not handsome at all. He was bony and long and his joints, his elbows and wrists and probably his knees, were huge, like a puppet's.

"How old are you?" I asked.

"Twenty-one," he said, but he looked sixteen or seventeen. "You?"

"Twenty-five."

"I couldn't imagine what your age was," he said. "People are always drawn to you, your looks, aren't they?"

"My mother was beautiful. She's dead," I said.

I looked out the window and saw how the dark was settling in. When I was eighteen I won a beauty prize, Princess Kay of the Milky Way at the Minnesota State Fair. They sculpted my face in a thirty-pound block of butter, put the bust in a refrigerated glass case and it ran round and round on a kind of a merry-go-round so people at the fair could look at it. I liked it and went every day to see it, standing on the dirt floor near the glass, wondering if anyone would recognize me, but they never did. My father told me I looked like my mother in the sculpture, but he thought it was dumb of me to stand around there all day. He made me come home.

"What in the world brought you to this place?" Matthew asked, and then I told him how I had come to be there. I must have been lonely, or starved for someone so nearly my own age, I know that's what made me pour out my feelings to him so. I told him how I had met Mal when I took a job in his publishing company, and how he had left his wife and his children for me, and how he had taken me to live with him five years ago, right after my father died. I told him how Mal called me his suburban Botticelli and how he took care of me and taught me all he knew. Now Mal had sold out his interest in the Minneapolis company and we were moving to Florida, where he had a new business. But I had never been out of Minneapolis, my parents had died here, it was all too sudden. I begged him to let me have a couple of months here, work in the business as it changed hands, get used to the idea of leaving as he got our new life settled. I had found this apartment in a familiar area, near the university, where I, too, had gone to school. Matthew was looking at me so hard his jaw hung.

It was late autumn, just before Halloween, and Matthew and I watched out the window as the sky went down from copper to livery red to mother of pearl. The streetlights blinked on and so did the signs above the stores. The room darkened with the sky but the signs and the streetlights shed pools of incandescent light on the bed, on the floor.

"What kind of person would leave his wife and children?" Matthew asked.

I sat with my head in my hands. "I don't know, he felt so awful about it. They'd been married twenty years. He told me not to think about it. He said it was my face; he loved my face." I pressed my fingers into my cheeks. The flesh gave like wax. But suddenly I was asking myself, what kind of a person was Mal, to leave his wife and children. I had never thought of him in that way before.

Then slowly Matthew began to tell me about himself. It was hard for him to talk, he didn't charm me with what he said or the way he said it, not at all. His voice was a whisper and sometimes it cracked as it came out, no, not a man's voice at all. He had been in love with a girl and she hadn't loved him, but still he kept loving her and loving her and finally he had gone crazy.

He told me what it was like to be crazy. Everything seemed to have a secret meaning, cracks on the sidewalk, a phone that rang once but not again, the world was full of hidden messages.

"It sounds wonderful," I said. "I would love to feel that everything had a secret meaning."

He shook his head and his curls bounced. "You don't know what you're saying. No, it wasn't wonderful at all. It was horrible."

"And the girl?"

"She's gone. Gone a long time ago."

It was hard to talk to him, I had to strain to hear him, his murmurs. It was as if he were used to talking in whispers to himself. His father was a doctor, his mother wanted him to be a doctor, but he couldn't do it, his grades weren't good enough, he couldn't concentrate. So instead he was taking this degree in psychology, maybe something would come of that.

I don't know what it was, I didn't want to leave him. After a while he got up and turned on the lamp by the window, then he put on a record.

"I like that a lot," I said. "Mal and I don't listen to any rock, just classical. Bach. Vivaldi. Telemann. A lot of baroque."

"Don't you know any people your own age?"

I looked at him. "Hardly any. There are a few girls at work but I don't see them much."

It was late when I got up to go. I walked along the shiny dark floor to the door. The lamp shone on the green leaves of the plants and reflected white in the window. I could feel the cold on the street below seeping in around the window frames.

Matthew followed me and stood with me by the door. I thought I had never seen such a delicate-looking man. I could almost see the blood beating in his temples. He took my hands in his huge bony hands. I felt it only for an instant but my hands were throbbing where he had touched them.

A few days later I found a copy of the album we had been listening to wrapped and pushed under my door. When I walked over to Matthew's apartment I could hear the bass pounding in the record he was playing. I stood in the hall for a moment but the door opened.

"I heard your footsteps," he said. But how could he have heard me over the music? We stared at each other. He looked gawky and stupid. I wondered why I had come. "Listen, I've got a coupon for pizza," he said. "Do you want to go?"

As we walked he took my hand in his. I couldn't take it back, my own hand trembled so.

"They removed a rat's memory surgically today," he said. And all through dinner we talked about how the rat experienced everything for the first time, every time.

When he himself had gone crazy, Matthew said, he thought about the same things over and over again. He had thought then that he was refining memories, getting down to their essence and their core. Now he realized that was impossible.

His way of talking was innocent and strange. He thought differently from other people and I had to listen carefully to catch his meaning. Neither of us ate much. We pushed the pizza back and forth between us.

"Do you want to come back over?" he asked as we walked out into the bitter cold. He took my hand again. I just wanted to be with him, I don't know why. Perhaps I admired the sculpted, jutting angle of his cheekbones. He made some coffee and got out a box of fresh pastries from the bakery downstairs. He sat across the table from me, staring down at the coffee, his long legs stretched out until they nearly touched mine. The white light enclosed us in a long oval. He shook his head and ruffled his fingers through his curls.

"Your hair is so unusual," I said.

"I was helping my father give EEGs last summer," he said. "One lady saw me and wouldn't let them put the electrodes on. She thought that was what had happened to me."

We laughed. At that moment, I looked at him and he looked at me. I felt a dizziness, a tightness near my heart. I was snug, safe in his apartment against the cold—I'm sure that's what it was. I have thought about it since.

He put a record on and we were silent, sitting in the pool of light.

After a while he came and knelt beside me and wrapped his arms around my waist. I could see the top of his head, his bobbing curls.

"Matthew, I have a lover."

He ignored me and put his cheek next to mine, holding my head. I could see the fine grain of his gold skin, how tight it was on the bone.

"Do you want to go lie down with me?" he asked and I nodded, yes.

I looked into his face as he undressed me and saw that his eyes were all pupil. For a long time he stroked the place where my hip met my thigh, running his fingers over the pale blue traceries of the veins.

"I love you," I said. Yes, I remember I said it, and I said it many times, I don't know what came over me. And I thought, this is the most wonderful night of my life, nothing will ever be this sweet again. We stared at each other in the light of the streetlamps and Grimm's Hardware sign and we made love. All night long we looked into each other's eyes. He was so young I could see that his eyes were brand new, just budded in their sockets.

Sometimes I fancy I can feel Matthew's tongue, scratchy as a cat's, and the way he wrapped me in his long, long arms. But I scarcely think of him at all now. In fact, I have entirely forgotten him. If it weren't for the little girl, considering her as much as I do, and the way the days are so long for me here, I doubt that I would think of him at all.

Three days later I went to work again. The phone was ringing as I walked into my office and I picked it up, knowing it was Mal. There had been a short circuit in one of the stereos in the electronics store and all night music from a rock station had pounded up to us through the floorboards. Elton John, Matthew told me they were playing. "Love Song." "Come Down in Time."

"What are you telling me?" Mal asked. "You were walking along, just minding your own business, and you got hit by a freight train?"

Light from the apartment flooded into my eyes and behind them as I held the receiver, the pure light on Matthew's face as he twined me with his legs and arms.

"I never should have left you alone, I knew it was a mistake," Mal said. And when I didn't answer he said: "I'm coming up there."

He was waiting for me in the office the next morning. For a long time he wouldn't believe that I was serious, that I wasn't coming down to Florida.

"I suppose his teeth are all white, not stained like mine," Mal said. "And I suppose he has all his hair and a flat belly, that's what you're thinking when you look at me, isn't it?"

"No, it's not," I said, but now that he'd said it it became true. All I was worried about was that he would kill me, and then I wouldn't be able to be with Matthew.

I wanted to tell him how fond I felt of him, how grateful I felt, how it hurt me to see his eyes glaze as he slumped against the window. But I stood speechless.

"I gave up everything for you. I can't let you go," he said.

For a moment I thought of the filthy warped floor in the hall of my apartment building, the way the brown paint on the floors bubbled and peeled. "I was a child then," I said. "That was for then."

I turned my face away as he held me.

"There's nothing I can do," he said. "I can't live without you." For an instant I prayed, begging that Mal would not die.

Then, miraculously, he was gone. He had me fired from my job but I found another where I just had to type. I bore no grudges. I was walking on love's good side. I had Matthew.

From our first night together Matthew was always in my thoughts. I suppose you could say I lived for him. He wanted us to be twins.

"One consciousness in two bodies," he said. "That's what we are." He looked at me in a way that made me feel holy. No one had ever paid this kind of attention to me, no, never. He painted our toenails the same color, green with silver dust. When I got a pimple, he would often get one himself, in a similar spot. We wore each other's clothes, bought matching shoes. We copied each other, walked alike, talked alike. How I loved imitating Matthew. It was no longer lonely being me. We could be each other.

We had been together two months when I found out I was pregnant. Matthew had told me not to get another diaphragm, there could be no mistakes between us. Anything that happened was right.

When I told him, he smiled. "That's wonderful," he said. "I can't wait to tell my family. Now we'll get married."

We drove out to the suburbs for dinner so I could meet his parents. He had told them about me but they had resisted meeting me, until now. We drove to a ranch house with a swimming pool behind it, big as a gulch. His father was a tall, silent man who left in the middle of dinner to go to the hospital. His mother had Matthew's jagged features but none of his softness. She hated me on sight.

After dinner she took me aside.

"Do you realize what a sick boy he is?" she asked. "You're a grown woman, you should see these things. He's been institutionalized for long periods."

"I love him," I said calmly. "He loves me. He knows exactly what he's doing. And it's medieval to think of mental illness as a permanent condition. You get over it, like a cold."

"What do you know about it?" She stared until I dropped my gaze. "Have you ruined your life the way I have, eating your heart out over him?"

We left before dessert.

"Cheer up, honey. We have to go out and get some sour cream cherry pie, some cheese cake," Matthew said as we sat in the car in his mother's driveway. He started kissing me, digging his fingers into my thighs. "There's a great place near here. You'll love their hot fudge cake," he said. "I can't take my honey to bed until she's had her dessert."

We went to a delicatessen where cakes and pies dipped up and down on little ferris wheels. "It tastes as good as it looks, too," Matthew said. We held hands and fed each other hot fudge and cherries on heaping spoons. The rich goo dripped like wax. We nudged and stepped on each other's feet the whole time, pressing each other's soles and toes till they hurt.

"Why doesn't she like me?" I asked. "Is it because I'm older?"

"She'll get over it, don't worry about her," Matthew said. "All she knows is her Bible. That time when I got sick—she thought it was God's rebuke to her. She's just going to have to get used to it."

I scraped some hot fudge on my plate with my spoon. It dried fast, a sweet cement. "You're so old for your age, Matthew. I'm surprised she can't see it. I've always known I could depend on you."

He fed me the last bite of hot fudge cake. "How about some more?" he asked. "Come on, honey, you know you want it."

"Let's have the hazelnut torte," I said.

"Great," Matthew said. "Great. My mother would die. She believes in minimal sweets."

"Mal too," I said. "Seaweed and spinach. He made us eat seaweed and spinach every stupid day." We both grimaced, wrinkling our noses.

Matthew stared into my eyes and jammed my feet tight between his. "Hi, baby." I saw his mouth move but no sound escaped his lips. The waitress put the torte before him. Shrugging and rolling his eyes at me he plunged his fork into the crest of hazelnut lace.

We got married and I moved all my things into Matthew's apartment. Our lives went on much as before.

How did those days pass? They went by so quickly I swear I can't remember.

We had everything in the world to find out about each other.

He took pictures of me with an expensive camera his parents had given him for his birthday. He gloated over the prints. "Look how you're smiling," he said. "How happy I must make you." He set the time adjustment so that we could be in the pictures at the same time, hugging or kissing or with our heads together, staring at the camera. "What a beautiful couple," he said.

He played his guitar as we sang duets of rock songs. He was charmed by my flat singing voice. He even admired my upper arms which had started to get pudgy from all our desserts. He flapped the loose flesh with delight. "That's one of the things I love about you most," he said. "Chubby arms just like a little baby."

One freezing night as we walked home after a movie our boots crunched into the moonlight on the snow. Our gloved hands fitted into each other like the pieces of a puzzle.

"What should we name the baby?" he asked.

"I don't know," I said.

"If it's a girl how about Phoebe, after the moon," he said. "The moon is so beautiful, look how we're walking on silver, baby. And it always seems to have so many secrets."

"But we don't like secrets, Matthew," I said. "We don't believe in secrets."

"I bet she'll look like the moon," he said. "You'll get round like the moon and then the baby will come out and look like the moon."

I woke up once during the night. He was sleeping with his arms around my neck. He slept silently, like an infant. How could he be so quiet? The lights outside flooded his bulletin board, the shiny wooden floors, the carefully arranged cabinets. The radiators hissed then fizzled to a stop. Outside the window the full moon shared the secret of the shadows on the dark street, his beating heart. I almost woke him up to tell him. I wanted to say, I could die now. I am so happy I could just die.

For Valentine's Day he wrote me a song. I sat on the bed while he played it for me on his guitar. He didn't need to breathe with my lungs filling his, the song said. He wanted to die from drinking my wonderful poison. I listened, filled with wonder.

As he played, I watched his hands. For the first time I saw tiny scars on his wrists, fine and precise as hairs. When he finished playing I put my fingers to his pulse.

"Your wrists, Matthew," I said. "Look. Where did all those little marks come from?" He had never told me, yet he said he told me everything.

He withdrew his hands, fixing me with his long stare. "Let's stay in the here and now. Why talk about things that happened a long time ago, things you can't remember right anyway. What did my honey get for me?"

I had forgotten Valentine's Day. The next day I bought him a shirt and an expensive sweater. He thanked me but seemed disappointed. His mother could have given him the same. He had been involved in his gifts, mine were clichés.

The next day I got a valentine from Mal, forwarded from the old office. He loved me, he was thinking about me, he wanted me to come back to him. As I put it in the wastebasket I found the valentine I had given Matthew folded at the bottom.

In the dead of winter it was fifty below for days at a time. We would sit on the bed and watch the smoke rise out of the chimneys in timid frozen curls. When we came home late at night, walking across the huge U of M campus, we would have to kiss and hold each other for twenty minutes before our noses and fingers thawed.

On Sunday mornings we would have breakfast at the restaurant across the street. We sat facing each other, our legs locked, talking about what was happening in our lives. I treasured my separate life for it provided me with stories to tell him. Nothing was real until I told Matthew about it.

After breakfast I walked him to his part-time job at the laboratory where he was working on a hearing experiment. Chinchillas were made deaf in one ear and then trained to jump to one side of a large revolving cage or another, on the basis of certain sounds. If the chinchillas didn't perform correctly they got a shock. That was Matthew's job, running them through tests and shocking them if they made mistakes.

I went with him once and saw the little animals in their cages. They were furry and adorable, bunnies without ears: how could Matthew, the gentlest of people, stand to shock them?"

"They have to be shocked when they're not doing their job," he said. "It's horrible, but that's the way life is."

"Since when do you believe life is that way?"

One evening he came home shaking. A chinchilla had died when its eardrum was being punctured for the experiment.

"Matthew, why don't you quit that job?" I asked, looking up at him from where I sat at the table. "Don't you see what it's doing to you?"

"It's not doing anything to me. I'm fine," he said, standing there trembling. "Do you think you're better, that you wouldn't do that job?"

I stood up and rushed to him. "Matthew, are you angry at me? Please don't be angry at me. I just want you to be happy." I hugged him tighter, tighter. "Do I give you everything you want?" I whispered into his shoulder. "What can I give you?"

"You're everything I want," he said.

"But is it enough? You're so much better at being somebody's lover than I am."

"Yes, I am good at that, aren't I," Matthew said, and I could feel him thinking about it, there was a hum in him like currents in fluorescent tubes.

Then he held my shoulders and looked deeply into my eyes. "Come here, baby. Let me tell you about this experiment I've been thinking about all day."

We sat down at the table holding hands. "When they fasten electrodes to the pleasure centers of a rat's brain the rat will do nothing but push the bar that activates the electrode. It won't eat, it won't drink, it won't sleep, it just keeps pushing the bar for the pleasure sensation until it dies of starvation and dehydration."

We sat silent. "That's interesting," I said. I watched his hand as it moved slowly up my arm, to my shoulder, then curled around my neck.

"You," he said. "You."

Late afternoons Matthew would go to the bakery downstairs and come back with boxes of sweets. Then we would sit at the table, listening to the voices on the street, feeling how the winds lightened and the air became less bitter as spring blew in our windows. We watched the sun on the grain of the table. We cut eclairs with knives and fed them to each other. When Matthew ate chocolate he was in such ecstasy he had to close his eyes. I could see him shudder. It was like when we were in bed. Being around all those sweets made me greedier for them, it was strange. The more I ate the more I wanted. It was like being in bed.

I got fatter and fatter from the sweets.

"If you can't get fat when you are pregnant, when can you?" he asked, feeding me another pastry. Yet Matthew never got fat.

I ate cakes, petits fours, upside-down tarts. At the soda fountain around the corner he fed me hot fudge sundaes.

"Eat, baby," he said. "I love to see your little tongue when you lick the syrup."

My breasts became huge. I swelled like an inflatable doll. All night long Matthew would lie in my arms as I lay there puffed with life and the splitting of my own cells. When we woke up he went downstairs and got doughnuts, filled and frosted pastries called honeymooners, pecan rolls.

Before long it was spring verging on summer and we took long walks along the Mississippi, breathing the crisp shocking air that rose from the torrents of icy water that came with the thaw. Sometimes we took sandwiches and stayed out till two in the morning. On one walk a pale, ovoid form approached us. It was the bald woman whose picture was on Matthew's bulletin board.

She stopped Matthew, held onto his arm, mumbled to him. She had been at the zoo, she said, and fed the elephant peanuts. It had lifted them out of her hand with its trunk, she said, holding up her palm, showing it. Its soft trunk had tickled and nudged her hand, gentle, tender. She could feel its hairs.

"Do you know her?" I asked Matthew, watching her as she disappeared. But Matthew wouldn't answer.

One afternoon after a rock concert we followed the path along a cliff near the river; below us the Mississippi glimmered like diamonds. We walked hand in hand but I was waddling fast to keep up with Matthew's long strides.

"Let me catch up," I said, and he stared at me, his eyes hard.

"You know, I've been thinking," he said, walking faster. "We're really not that much alike."

I couldn't catch my breath. The air was freezing my fingertips even where Matthew held them.

Like how so?"

"Like makeup," he said. "Like you wear makeup and I don't."

My eyes watered from the wind. "But I've always worn makeup," I said. "I'll stop wearing it if you don't like it."

"That won't do any good," he said. "And you take up a lot of the bed. It's hard for you to keep up with me when I walk."

"But I'm pregnant, I've got fat," I said, nearly in tears. "If I weren't pregnant and you didn't force all that food on me, this wouldn't happen."

Tears were streaming down my face but Matthew was walking fast, not seeming to notice.

"I don't make enough to support a baby," Matthew said. "It's all going to be different. It seems cruel. Sometimes I think I can't do the job."

"You know I've got savings. And your parents will help." Now I couldn't stop crying. I halted in my tracks, jerking my hand out of his. The Mississippi roared below us. I waited for long moments by a tree, waiting for him to come back. And suddenly I knew that we would never again be as happy as we once were.

Finally he came back, retracing his steps, and looked at me.

"I'm sorry," he said. "I never want to hurt you."

I looked into his eyes and saw how young and frightened he was. I will never leave you, I said to myself. You need me and I will always take care of you.

That night in our room rainy air billowed the curtain inward on our long embrace. There was the smell of skin, warm salt flesh, clean.

"Please, baby, whatever you say, never say you stopped loving me," Matthew said.

"Oh, never. I would never say that."

"You would never start hating me, would you? You would stop long before that."

Stop? He had never said anything about stop. "No. I would stop before that."

"We would stop while we still loved each other. And now . . . are you going to hug me all night long?"

The next day, on impulse, I called up Mal from work.

I couldn't even wait for him to get over his shock. I rushed into it. "You won't believe this, but I've just got to talk to someone. About Matthew. It's just interesting, you won't mind? He's absolutely terrified of getting fat. He is the skinniest man you've ever seen, yet he's worried about fat. Once he went on a fishing trip with his father and he ate a whole pound bag of M & Ms and he was so appalled he didn't eat anything else the whole trip. And by summer he had got so thin he could see the sun shining through his rib cage. Can you imagine anything so stupid?

"He loves sweets, you know, we live near a bakery, and sometimes he'll get so many good things and eat them, then do you know what he does? He sticks his finger down his throat and throws up. Really, I've seen him do it."

Mal listened, silent, until I was done. "Why don't you leave him?" he said.

"Because I'm happy, that's why," I said, suddenly desperate to be off the phone. "Besides, I'm very fat, do you think you could like me fat?" He didn't answer. "I was just kidding about him throwing up. Do you believe me?" Mal was silent. "Well, maybe he did it once or twice when he was drunk."

"Do you know why I'm fat?" My voice grew shriller in the silence. "Because I'm pregnant. I'm going to have a baby in two months."

I pressed down the button, hoping he'd think we'd been disconnected.

I came home from work one afternoon and found Matthew lying naked on the bed, his stereo earphone on, one leg propped straight against the wall. He was so absorbed in the music he didn't see me coming up to him, see how I was staring at the long red marks on the inside of his thigh. As I sat down beside him he took his leg down quickly and removed the headset, smiling.

"It's spring," I said. "It's gorgeous out, Matthew."

"It's pretty," he said. "Have a good day?"

"Did you?" He said he hadn't been out and, leaning back again, he pulled me down with him. I moved away.

"Matthew, let me see your thigh." He watched me docilely as I lifted his leg. It was as if it were a specimen we were both going to examine.

"What are those red marks from?" I asked.

"Me."

"How did you do it?"

"With my own little fingernails," he said.

They weren't scratches, they were deeper than that. The gold hairs on his thighs spoked up innocently around.

"Matthew, why did you do it?" He took his leg down.

"Don't worry about it. It's nothing. It's something I do sometimes. I put iodine on it, it won't get infected."

"But why did you do it?"

"Because I was having evil thoughts."

"About what?"

He shook his head. "Don't worry about it." He eased me back down. "Don't worry your little head," he said. "Baby. Double baby. Baby squared." He started moving his hands up and down my body.

I pulled away. "Wait."

"What's the matter, baby?" he asked, touching me all over. I felt his tongue in my mouth and I closed my eyes.

One night he came in late, very agitated.

"There was this guy following me down the street just now for about a mile.

He was this weird, juiced-up black guy even skinnier than I am. He was muttering, calling me sweet cakes, doodle-bug, boney maroney. Can they tell about me?" he asked, looking into my face. "Can they tell I've been crazy? Do I give out special vibes?"

I thought of the tense air he always had, the speed of his walk on those long legs.

"He followed me all that way. He kept saying, 'Think you're pretty hot stuff, you creep, you creep.'"

And the bald lady, had he seen her? Matthew wouldn't answer.

"People can't tell," I said finally, but he wouldn't stop looking at me.

"Why are you staring?"

"Because you're so nice and fat," he said, still staring.

Behind that gaze there was intensity that had nothing to do with me. I felt something ungiving in him, the tightness of his skin on the bone. "Stop making me eat," I said. "You're turning me into a monster."

"But, honey," he said smiling. "I like you fat." Then his expression changed. It was a dark look he gave me. "You're eating with your own mouth," he said.

I called up Mal again. "Can you imagine?" I said. "He washes his hair every morning because he doesn't want dirt to accumulate too close to his brain. He's afraid it will penetrate and sink in. And he scratches himself with his fingernails when we have a fight. When I told him to stop buying me so many sweets he thought I hated him and you know what he did? He put a long cut down the top of his arm with a knife."

"He's crazy," Mal said. "Don't you know you've got a mental case on your hands? Why don't you get out before he does something to you?"

"He won't do anything to me," I said, but it was a long time before I could hang up the phone.

When I came home that night Matthew was sitting at the table with a stack of pictures. I sat down beside him.

"What are they of?" I asked.

He looked annoyed but said nothing. I slid the pictures over and started going through them. They were all of him. He had taken twenty-four pictures of his own face: laughing, smiling, stern, pensive, in profile, in three-quarter view, from the back.

"These are really good," I said. "When did you take them?"

"I've really changed a lot," he said. "I've suspected it, but I can tell from the pictures how drastic it is."

"How have you changed?"

"In ways." He put his hand over his mouth, staring at me and then staring at nothing.

"Why are you so indifferent to me?" I said.

"I'm not indifferent." He took the stack of pictures and began looking through them again, humming to himself.

"Why don't you take my picture?"

He continued to sort through the pictures, humming.

"Why don't you take my picture, Matthew?"

There was a long silence. "Sure, I'll take your picture some time," he said, and I saw how his hair flared out in the photographs, like a sea fan.

I remember every detail of the next few days. It was the hottest part of the summer in Minnesota. Night after night I went sleepless in the motionless air, hanging over the side of the bed so Matthew would have more room. I was so huge and moist my nightgown clung to me like a membrane. I had to take it off and lie naked on top of the sheet. When I tried to meet Matthew's eyes he looked away.

"It will all be different after the baby comes," I whispered to him, but he pretended to be asleep.

One evening I could hardly walk when I got off the bus after work. With every step my fat thighs rubbed against each other. They had become so sore and chapped they had begun to bleed. As I walked past the bakery the heat rose in waves; behind the window, a sheet of sunlight, I saw wedding cakes, gingerbread men, cookies with faces, shimmering.

I heard music, coming from our apartment. I twisted my key again and again in the lock. Surely Matthew could hear me? I punched my knuckles against the door. I tried the key again and the lock gave suddenly.

The room was filled with smoke. Matthew was sitting on the bed with the bald woman and a short black man who was even skinner than he was.

"We're tripping," Matthew said. "But there's nothing left for you."

"Who is that?" said the bald woman.

"She lives down the hall."

"I do not live down the hall and you know it, Matthew," I said. "I live here and I'm his wife." I stood there a while and nobody looked at me. I put down my purse and sat down next to it on the floor.

"These are my friends. They're like me," Matthew said. He looked at me with the eyes of a little animal, eyes that were all pupil, the color black, absorbing everything and giving nothing back.

"He's a cabdriver," Matthew said. "You wouldn't think of having a cabdriver for a friend, would you? Or a busdriver? I like cabdrivers."

"I would so have a cabdriver for a friend," I said, but I couldn't think of a single friend I did have. Matthew was my only friend.

"You wear makeup and you're fat and you only want to be friends with editors," Matthew said. "Oh, yes, and friends with Uncle Mal." The bald woman edged closer to Matthew on the bed. Her hand brushed my pillow, the pillow I had brought to Matthew from my old bed. She whispered in his ear, moving her hand to his hip, to the front of his pants.

"We're going now," Matthew said, standing up.

"Wait a second, I'll come too," I said.

"Do you want her to come?"

"No way," said the bald woman.

"See? They don't want you to come," Matthew said. "They're my friends and they're like me and they don't want you to come."

I stood still as they passed, stupefied by my pain.

"Matthew, please don't go!" I said. "It's just a tough time now, baby. Isn't it?"

He stopped in the doorway, staring down at me. A vein like a root throbbed in his temple. His face blurred in my gaze and I saw his eyes staring wide at me as we made love on that bed, silver ghosts in the wash of pale neon. I saw the snow falling silently as we hurried home in the cold, looking high up for the glow of the lamp in our apartment.

He put his hands on my shoulders. His palms and fingers cut into me like brackets. "Stay here," he said.

I watched him from the window but he did not turn to look back up at me.

I lay on the bed watching the ceiling change as it got darker and darker. I don't know how long I lay there or when the pains in my back or my stomach started, they blended so imperceptibly with the other things I was feeling, staring at the ceiling, lying on the bed. Then I lay down on the floor, on the rug of swans' heads and necks, hurting so much I imagined I felt them moving under me, nudging me with their bills. I waited and waited there for Matthew to come back, but he didn't come back. It must have been a couple of days later that I called a cab to take me to the hospital.

The baby was tiny. She was born feet first, the wrong way. They gave me a drug that put me in a twilight sleep, that turned everything pink until I saw her after she was born. She came out curled like a snail and stayed calm in her crib sleeping all the time. She fit over my shoulder like a chrysalis, a tight little cocoon.

It was Matthew's father and mother who came to see me at the hospital and who took me home. I wanted to go back to our apartment, but they wouldn't let me, they said Matthew wasn't there and I needed somebody to take care of me. They took me to the house in the suburbs, but Matthew wasn't there, either. He had taken too many drugs and hurt himself, they had to send him away somewhere, they wouldn't say where. His mother gave me the Bible to read.

He came to see me once, I was still lying down most of the time. He came and sat down beside me near the big swimming pool. He had seen the baby. "She wasn't like the moon," he whispered, or did I dream that? He sat down on a chair next to me in the sun for a little while and he cried.

He got up and started walking toward the house, muttering something.

"Matthew, I know you didn't mean to hurt me," I said, but he kept walking, shaking his head.

"He didn't even recognize you," his mother told me later, glaring at my face in the sunlight.

"Then why did he cry?" I asked. "If he didn't recognize me then why did he cry?" Words from her Bible swam in my head, he whom my soul loveth. We could do anything, be anything, with what we had. Hadn't he always told me that?

I rushed into the house, hoping I could still find Matthew, but he was gone. I took the keys to his mother's car off the kitchen table and ran to the garage, before she had a chance to stop me.

Then I went out to look for Matthew. I looked everywhere nearby, up and down the streets, and when I couldn't find him I drove back to our old neighborhood. I parked in front of the old apartment and went upstairs and knocked and knocked on the door but no one answered. I tried my key but it wouldn't fit into the lock. I pushed at the lock until the key had scratched my fingers and made them bleed. Then I sat down by the door on the floor in the hallway and remembered how there had been heaven in that apartment, time had stood still. No matter what he did, Matthew knew. We had made love all night, in the light of the streetlight and the Grimm's Hardware sign. If I put my cheek to the wood I could feel the vibrations of those nights, still singing in the floorboards of the apartment.

Mal came to the house in the suburbs after I called him. He cried when he saw me and I saw how his cheeks were now cross-hatched with tiny red veins. Matthew's mother wanted to keep the baby for herself, but Mal wouldn't let her. He took me, and the baby, and brought us to this beautiful house where we have been so happy. It is not far from the ocean and we go sailing a couple of times a month if the wind is not blowing too hard. I am thin again and Mal has bought me wonderful new clothes. The little girl calls him Daddy and has never known another father.

I thought Mal would ask me to explain a lot of things, but mostly he hasn't.

"I know you've never loved anybody but me," he said. "I knew you'd come back. That's why I waited." That was four years ago. And more and more I think Mal was right.

Once we were sitting under the trellis and Mal asked me what I was thinking about when I looked so preoccupied and far away. I told him an apparition gripped my mind sometimes.

"It's a picture of a man who looked like a boy and a girl at the same time, a man with hair like a sheaf of golden wires, with eyes as black and shiny as lava chips. You remember, it was a man who confused me, a man who studied the memory and even tried to look into his own head. I must be making it up, don't you think? For no real person could be like that."

Mal was annoyed, he said it was certainly something I had made up. I'd made a mistake and had altered the memory to turn it into something more compelling, so I didn't seem like quite such a fool. It was basic psychological theory, he said.

That was a long time ago. I am content with my life and light of heart. I know how evening rises up in the blue noon and I know every moment by the angle and quality of the sunlight spreading on my lawn and on my courtyard. I stand in the courtyard and watch the days and walk through my garden and wait for my daughter and Mal. For surely, as Mal tells me, I am the happiest of women. But it is always summer here and sometimes I remember how the winter was in Minnesota, how dark and drear. And it is just occasionally, as I watch Phoebe's copper hair growing into tighter and tighter curls with each passing year, that my mind strays back to that time.

Candlemas:
late nor'easter

by Jody Aliesan

came quietly snow small light no wind
but no stopping I could tell
from the beginning it was serious
next morning windows over my bed
white canopy icicle fringes
every day longer crystal chamber
clear bars glass daggers to the ground

even ivy leaves blackened brittle
winter wrens leaving solitary
to flock for comfort early robins
hurtling stiffly onto branches
crying out bird tracks either side
of my eyes growing longer my hands
snakeskin my hair broken grass

veined with its own ice I could sleep
forever without dreams smiling
into last drifts but some voice urges me
make soup sit closer to the fire
wear a cap to bed   this is the way
love goes and goes blood's heat
into black night all we have

each of us soul's candle long
as any sword   heart's pulse
steadier more faithful than any
lying promise of mild spring
parable: another day after this one
and maybe yet another after that
to learn what we have to learn to stay alive

Author Biographies

Kim Addonizio writes and teaches in San Francisco. Her first collection of poetry, tentatively titled *The Philosopher's Club*, will be published in 1993 by BOA Editions.

Ai is of African-American, Choctaw, and Japanese descent. Her books of poetry are *Cruelty, Killing Floor, Sin, Fate* and, most recently, *Greed* (W. W. Norton, 1993). She lives in Tempe, Arizona, with a cat, birds, and a cactus garden.

Jody Aliesan is the author of two recent collections of poetry: *Grief Sweat* (Broken Moon Press, 1991) and *States of Grace* (limited edition letterpress from Grey Spider Press, 1992). She lives in Seattle.

Rebecca Baggett has published poetry, fiction and nonfiction in *Ms., Calyx, New England Review* and *Mid-American Review*. Her work is included in *Cries of the Spirit: A Celebration of Women's Spirituality*. She is the mother of two daughters.

Brenda Bankhead was born and raised in Los Angeles. She is working on a collection of stories about poor Black women and children. Her work appears in *The World between Women, Obsidian II: Black Literature in Review* and *The Time of Our Lives: Women Write on Sex after 40*.

Sallie Bingham is a poet, playwright, and fiction and nonfiction writer presently living in Santa Fe. She has published three novels, two collections of short stories, and a memoir. She is the publisher of *The American Voice*, a feminist quarterly.

Melanie Bishop teaches creative writing at Prescott College in Arizona. Her work has appeared in *Puerto del Sol, The Florida Review* and *The Greensboro Review*.

Louise A. Blum teaches creative writing at Mansfield University in Pennsylvania, where she lives with her lover, three cats, and a dog. Her stories have appeared in *The Sonora Review, Columbia, The Cream City Review* and in the anthology *Lovers: Stories by Women*.

Alice K. Boatwright holds degrees in writing from Syracuse and Columbia and teaches for the UC Berkeley Extension. Her stories and articles have appeared in *Penumbra, Maelstrom, New Hampshire Times* and *Cricket*.

Nancy Butcher was born in Tokyo to an American father and a Japanese mother, and spent most of her childhood there. She now lives in upstate New York with her husband and three cats, and writes books for a children's mystery series.

Thea Caplan is an award-winning Canadian writer whose stories have appeared in *Oxford Magazine*, *Emrys Journal*, *Snake Nation Review*, *Other Voices* and *The Time of Our Lives: Women Write on Sex after 40*.

Frances Cherman has published in *Lovers: Stories by Women* and in *Porter Gulch Review*. She currently lives in Santa Cruz, after doing time in Los Angeles and San Francisco, where she owns a copywriting business.

Laura Chester is the editor of *Rising Tides*, *Deep Down*, *Cradle and All* and *The Unmade Bed*. She is the author of several collections of poetry, fiction, and nonfiction, including *In the Zone*, *Bitches Ride Alone* and *Lupus Novice*.

Kathryn Chetkovich lives in Oakland and is completing a collection of short stories, some of which have been published in *The Georgia Review*, *New England Review* and *The Missouri Review*.

Katharine Coles has published in *North American Review*, *The New Republic* and *The Georgia Review*. Her collection of poetry, *The One Right Touch*, was published by Ahsahta Press in 1992. She is a professor of English at Westminster College in Salt Lake City.

Martha Clark Cummings has published stories in *Common Lives/Lesbian Lives*, *Kalliope*, *Hurricane Alice*, *Sojourner* and *North Atlantic Review*. She presently lives in the Monterey Bay area and has completed her first novel, *Bastille Day*.

Silvia Curbelo was born in Matanzas, Cuba. Her award-winning collection of poems, *The Geography of Leaving*, was published in 1991 by Silverfish Review Press. She is poetry and fiction editor of *Organica Quarterly* in Tampa. Her poetry appears in *Lovers: Stories by Women*.

Paola D'Ellesio lives in New York City and is presently working on a novel.

Jo Dereske grew up in Walhalla, Michigan, and now lives in Bellingham, Washington. She has published short stories and young adult novels, and has an adult mystery forthcoming from Avon.

Gail Donovan lives and writes in Portland, Maine. Her story "Honeycomb" appears in The *Time of Our Lives: Women Write on Sex after 40*.

Sandra Dorr is a public-radio commentator living in Portland, Oregon, with her son, husband, and two cats. Her essays and fiction have appeared in *Ms.*, *Omni*, *Taos Review* and *New Delta Review*.

Molly Fisk lives and writes in Stinson Beach, California. She has published in *Sexual Harassment: Women Speak Out*, *Americas Review*, *Haight Ashbury Literary Review* and *Radcliffe Quarterly*. "Veterans" won first prize in the 1992 National Writers Union Local 7 Competition judged by Adrienne Rich.

Lynn Freed was born in South Africa, studied at Columbia University, and now lives in Sonoma, California. She is the author of three novels, *Heart Change*, *Home Ground* and *The Bungalow*, as well as numerous short stories, essays, articles, and reviews.

Gloria Frym is the author of *How I Learned*, a collection of short stories published by Coffee House Press. Other books include *Second Stories: Conversations with Women Artists* (Chronicle Books) and *By Ear* (Sun & Moon Press). She teaches at the New College of California in San Francisco.

Tess Gallagher is the author of several collections of poetry, most recently *Moon Crossing Bridge* and *Portable Kisses*. Her other books include a collection of short stories, *The Lover of Horses*, and *A Concert of Tenses*, essays on poetry. She lives in Port Angeles, Washington.

Molly Giles teaches at San Francisco State University. Her first collection of stories, *Rough Translations* (University of Georgia Press), won the Flannery O'Connor Award, the Bay Area Book Reviewers Award, and the Boston Globe Award.

Pamela Gray is a lesbian poet, playwright, and screenwriter living in Santa Monica. Her work appears in *Dykescapes*, *New Lesbian Writing* and *Cats and Their Dykes*.

Ann Harleman is on the faculty of Brown College and has published stories in *Shenandoah*, *The Virginia Quarterly Review* and *The Southern Review*. Her collection *Happiness* won the 1993 Iowa Short Fiction Award and will be published in March 1994. Her great-grandfather murdered for love.

Enid Harlow has published in *American Fiction*, *The Southern Review*, *The Ontario Review* and *Southwest Review*. Her novella "The Clown" appeared in *Triquarterly*.

Susan Ito teaches an Asian American women writers' workshop in Oakland, where she lives with her husband and daughter. She is an M.F.A. candidate in the Creative Writing Program at Mills College and is completing a collection of stories, *Filling In the Blanks*.

Ellen Terry Kessler lives and works in New York City.

Binnie Kirshenbaum is the author of *Married Life and Other True Adventures* (The Crossing Press, 1990). Her novel *On Mermaid Avenue* was published in 1993, and another novel, *A Disturbance in One Place*, is forthcoming in 1994, both from Fromm International.

Lyn Lifshin is the editor of *Tangled Vines*, *Ariadne's Thread* and *Lips Unsealed*. Her poetry and fiction have appeared in numerous publications, including *Ms.*, *American Poetry Review* and *Rolling Stone*. She has published over eighty books and chapbooks.

Vickie E. Lindner worked as a freelance writer in New York City for twenty years and now teaches writing at the University of Wyoming. Her stories have appeared in *The Paris Review*, *The Kenyon Review* and *Ploughshares*. Her novel *Outlaw Games* was published by The Dial Press.

Iris Litt lives in Greenwich Village in New York, where she has worked in advertising and editing. Her poems have appeared in *Poetry Now*, *Pearl*, *Earth's Daughters* and in the anthology *What's a Nice Girl like You Doing in a Relationship like This?*

Rachel Loden has published in *New American Writing*, *Yellow Silk* and *New York Quarterly*, among other literary magazines. She lives in Palo Alto, California.

Debra Martens is a Canadian writer working in Ottawa and Montreal. Her stories have been published in *Celebrating Canadian Women: Prose and Poetry* and *Baker's Dozen: Stories by Women*. She has recently completed a novel.

Cris Mazza is the author of two novels, *Exposed* and *How to Leave a Country*, and three collections of short stories: *Revelation Countdown*, *Is It Sexual Harassment Yet?* and *Animal Acts*. She is a native and resident of Southern California but hasn't been to the beach in years.

Jeanne McDonald has published fiction in *American Fiction*, *Memphis Magazine* and *Lovers: Stories by Women*. An editor at the University of Tennessee in Knoxville, she has recently completed a novel and a collection of short stories.

Susan McIver lives with her partner, Anne, and their two miniature poodles on Salt Spring Island, British Columbia. Her work appears in *The Time of Our Lives: Women Write on Sex after 40*.

Joan McMillan is a fourth-generation Italian-American. She has been published in numerous literary journals and anthologies, including *Plainswoman*, *New Virginia Review*, *Catholic Girls* and *Out of Season*.

Mary Morris is the author of seven books: three novels, two collections of short stories, and two travel memoirs. Her latest novel, *A Mother's Love*, was published in 1993 by Doubleday. She is the recipient of a Guggenheim and lives with her husband and daughter in Brooklyn.

Lesléa Newman is a full-time writer and teacher of women's writing workshops. Her books include *Eating Our Hearts Out: Women and Food, Saturday Is Payday, In Every Laugh a Tear, Heather Has Two Mommies* and *Sweet Dark Places*. Her book on writing, *Writing from the Heart*, was published by The Crossing Press in 1993.

Veronica Patterson is the author of a collection of poetry, *How to Make a Terrarium*, from Cleveland State University, and of a collection of poetry and photographs, *The Bones Remember*, from Stone Graphics. She teaches creative writing and works as an editor in Colorado.

Nita Penfold is a western New York native who now resides in Massachusetts. Her poetry appears in *Cries of the Spirit: A Celebration of Women's Spirituality, Catholic Girls* and *If I Had My Life to Live Over, I Would Pick More Daisies*. Her fiction has been published in *Earth's Daughters* and *The Womansleuth Anthology*.

Vicky Phillips has published in *Ms., Common Lives/Lesbian Lives, On Our Backs* and *Siblings of Survivors Speak Out*. Trained as a psychologist, she often writes about love gone ragged and the effects of sexual abuse.

Susan Policoff has published numerous poems and stories in literary journals, including *Permafrost, Other Voices, Alaska Quarterly Review* and *Negative Capability*. She was first published in antiwar underground papers in the '70s and in *Rolling Stone*.

Jean Marie Ruiz grew up in Los Angeles, graduated from UC Berkeley, then lived in Spain for six years—an experience from which she has never wanted to recover. She teaches English as a Second Language to adults. Her poetry has appeared in *Seventeen, The Jacaranda Review* and *West/Word*.

Deborah Shouse has spent some time in love's shadows. Now she seeks the light, seeks to write. Her work has appeared in *Tikkun, New Letters, The Sun* and *The Time of Our Lives: Women Write on Sex after 40*. Her story "Diner" won a PEN award.

Linda Smukler is a poet and fiction writer who has published in *The American Voice, Sinister Wisdom, IKON, Gay and Lesbian Poetry of Our Time* and *Women on Women II*. In 1986 she won the Katherine Anne Porter Short Fiction Award from *Nimrod* magazine.

Maura Stanton has published a novel, *Molly Companion* (Avon), and a book of stories, *The Country I Come From* (Milkweed Editions), as well as three books of poetry. She teaches at Indiana University. Recent work appears in *Lovers: Stories by Women* and *Catholic Girls*.

Amber Coverdale Sumrall is a poet, writer, and editor living in Santa Cruz. Her work appears most recently in *IKON: The Nineties, Pearl, Disability Rag, Eating Our Hearts Out* and *Imprinting Our Image*.

Christina Sunley teaches composition and creative writing at San Francisco State University and is working on a collection of short stories, *Bizarro*. She has published in *Common Lives/Lesbian Lives, Word of Mouth II* and *The Time of Our Lives: Women Write on Sex after 40*.

Joanna Torrey has recently completed an M.F.A. in creative writing at Brooklyn College, where she is now teaching. Her story "Arroz" was published in the anthology *Lovers: Stories by Women*.

Karen A. Tschannen lives and writes in Anchorage, though her stories and poems often reveal her San Francisco upbringing. Her work has appeared in *Alaska Quarterly Review, Inklings* and *The Sky's Own Light*, an anthology of northern poetry.

Jennifer Tseng lives and writes in Oakland. She is involved with Bay Area Radical Women. "Desire" is her first published poem.

Karen X. Tulchinsky is a Jewish lesbian political activist writer who lives in Vancouver with her life partner, Suzanne. Her short stories have appeared in *Getting Wet: Tales of Lesbian Seductions* (Women's Press), *Lovers: Stories by Women* (The Crossing Press) and *Sister/Stranger: Lesbians Loving across the Lines* (Sidewalk Revolution Press).

Carol Turner lives in Denver and pays her bills by working as a technical writer. She is working on her third novel, *Chac Mool and Other Mexico Stories*.

Kate Velten is a Boston-area dweller and writer of fiction whose voices come from everywhere. Her stories have appeared in *Other Voices, Bluff City* and *Oak Square*.

Lisa Vice was raised in rural Indiana and now lives in California. Her roots are buried among barbers, soldiers, suicides, survivors, assembly line workers, Avon ladies, teetotalers quoting scripture and alcoholics gluing rhinestones onto dog collars. Her first novel, *Reckless Driver*, won a Ludwig R. Vogelstein Award.

Susan Volchok has published fiction in *The Kenyon Review, Hayden's Ferry Review, Iris* and *Word of Mouth II* (The Crossing Press). Her novella *Sam's Girl* was released on audiotape.

Susan Welch was a Wallace Stegner fellow at Stanford University. Her fiction has appeared in *The Paris Review, The Pushcart Prize* collection and in numerous anthologies. She lives and works in Minneapolis.

Terry Wolverton is the author of *Black Slip*, a collection of poetry (Clothespin Fever Press), and the editor of *Indivisible: New Short Fiction by West Coast Gay and Lesbian Writers* (Plume) and *Blood Whispers: L.A. Writers on AIDS* (Silverton Books). Recent work appears in *Glimmer Train Stories, Zyzzyva* and *Lovers: Stories by Women*.

Lois-Ann Yamanaka lives in Honolulu and writes in the Hawaiian pidgin of contract workers in the sugar plantations. Her poetry has appeared in *Quarry West, Zyzzyva, Seattle Review* and *Dissident Song: A Contemporary Asian American Anthology*. Bamboo Ridge Press published her first collection of poetry, *Saturday Night at the Pahala Theater*.

Ronder Thomas Young lives and works in the Atlanta area with her husband and three sons. Her first novel, *Learning by Heart*, was published by Houghton Mifflin in 1993. Her stories and essays have appeared in *Catalyst, Writer's Digest, Mothering* and *The Greensboro Review*.

"Heart Attack" by Vicki E. Lindner won a PEN/NEA Syndicated Fiction Prize and was originally published in *The Kansas City Star*.

"Desperate Measures" by Rachel Loden originally appeared in *Green Mountains Review*.

"The Cram-It-In Method" by Cris Mazza previously appeared in *Mid-American Review*.

"French Twist" by Susan McIver originally appeared in *Dyke Review*.

"Red Onion Salad" by Joan McMillan previously appeared in *New Virginia Review*.

"The Woman with a Secret" by Mary Morris originally appeared in *Boulevard* and will appear in her forthcoming story collection, *The Moon Garden*.

"When We Fight" by Lesléa Newman is reprinted by permission of the author from *Sweet Dark Places* (HerBooks, 1991).

"Combing" by Veronica Patterson previously appeared in *The Sun*, December 1992.

"Momma Don't Know Love" by Vicky Phillips, a winner in the Bay Area Literary Awards, originally appeared in the *San Francisco Bay Guardian*, June 1992.

"To Give Our Bodies Away" by Amber Coverdale Sumrall previously appeared in *Pearl*, Fall/Winter 1991.

"The Time, the Place, the Loved One" by Susan Welch first appeared in *The Paris Review* and is reprinted by permission of the author from *Stiller's Pond* (New Rivers Press).

"Rites" by Terry Wolverton originally appeared in *Zyzzyva*, Spring 1992.

"Kala: Saturday Night at the Pahala Theater" by Lois-Ann Yamanaka previously appeared in *Parnassus: Poetry in Review*.

"Edge" by Ronder Thomas Young originally appeared in *The Greensboro Review*.